IN TASMANIA

Nicholas Shakespeare

IN TASMANIA

THE HARVILL PRESS

LONDON

Published by The Harvill Press, 2004

4 6 8 10 9 7 5 3

First published in Great Britain in 2004 by
The Harvill Press
Random House
20 Vauxhall Bridge Road
London SW1V 2SA

Random House Australia (Pty) Limited
20 Alfred Street, Milsons Point, Sydney,
New South Wales 2061, Australia

Random House New Zealand Limited
18 Poland Road, Glenfield,
Auckland 10, New Zealand

Random House South Africa (Pty) Limited
Endulini, 5A Jubilee Road, Parktown 2193, South Africa

The Random House Group Limited Reg. No. 954009
www.randomhouse.co.uk

A CIP catalogue record for this book is available from the British Library

ISBN 1 84343 157 2

Papers used by Random House are natural, recyclable products made from wood grown in
sustainable forests; the manufacturing processes conform to the environmental regulations of the
country of origin

Typeset by Palimpsest Book Production Limited
Printed and bound in Great Britain by
Biddles Ltd, Guildford & King's Lynn

To Max and Benedict, two Tasmanian devils

"The same sky covers us, the same sun and all the stars revolve about us, and light us in turn."

Comenius (1592–1671),
quoted by Julian Sorell Huxley in *We Europeans*

"What would you do, Father, if you had to be present at the birth of a monster with two heads?"
"I would baptise it, of course. What an absurd question."

Graham Greene, *Monsignor Quixote*

Contents

Part I: Father of Tasmania

"... like the legendary lost uncle from Australia"
Günter Grass, *The Tin Drum*

I

IN OUR THIRD YEAR ON DOLPHIN SANDS, A FRIEND TELEPHONED from England. "Did you know you had a double in Tasmania?"

He had contacted directory enquiries and been put through to N. Shakespeare in Burnie on the north coast, who told him: "You got the wrong fella." In Argentina I had once met a Reynaldo Shakespeare, a photographer, but in four decades of wandering, I had never come across another Shakespeare with my initial. So I called him.

A young-sounding man answered. He was not put out to hear from me and the idea of meeting up appealed. "I'm pretty poor on the family side," he warned. "Not a family tree man."

A double is an invitation and a dare. I arranged to be in Burnie the following Sunday.

I found my namesake getting off a glittering black motorbike in the drive of a house behind the Old Surrey Road industrial estate. "I'm in trouble," he grinned through his visor. He had gone to Smithton "for a hoon", as he called his ride, and enjoyed himself so much – "no distraction, just concentrating on the road and what the machine's doing" – that he had lost track of time.

"I've only had him a week," he said.

"What is he?" I asked, feeling a stab of envy. I had never ridden on a motorbike, not even as a passenger.

"Suzuki 750 GSXF," he said, with great fondness, enunciating each syllable. His parents had been dead set against him buying it. His father had worked as an apprentice turner and lost four of his friends on motorbikes. Motorbikies were known widely in Tasmania as "temporary Australians".

"It does look fast," I said.

"Nah, good cheap little cruisy bike."

He took off his helmet and we shook hands. I looked into a decent, laid-back face, early thirties, framed by a thick black beard, brown eyes. I had no idea what he saw, but he knew well enough where I lived: he had installed the alarm for a house just down the road from us and had discussed with his wife buying a property there.

I asked, "What does the N stand for?"

"Nevin."

Nevin Shakespeare ran his own one-man electrical business. Blocking the steep drive was a red van with the Chandos portrait stamped on the doors and the logo "Shakespeare Electricals". Among his clients was the founder of the Delta Force, a New Yorker in his seventies who lived in Tasmania for his safety. "He killed two of his own men so as not to leave them wounded and once had Qaddafi in his crosshairs when orders came not to shoot." Nevin had rewired his home. But he was cutting back on residential work. "You're always chasing the money."

His wife came out to tell him that he was late and he introduced me to Laurelle, whom he had met at a hockey match — "while trying to get off with my sister," she said. Then their two sons: Garion, ten, and Martyn, six — both curious to see this interloper from England with a name like their Dad's.

"Does it interest you to know where you're from?" Nevin asked Garion.

"Not really."

Nevin had also invited his parents, Gavin and Gloria. Gavin so resembled my own father that when I introduced them to each other a few months later, my father leaned across the table and said: "I don't know what I look like, but you look like what I think I look like."

Gavin had a stronger grip on family history than his son. His grandfather James Shakespeare came from Staffordshire in the nineteenth century and was a bricklayer in Sydney. In 1959, he left the Australian mainland to work in the paper mill in Burnie, where Nevin was born.

"I'm darn pleased my parents didn't call me Bill," Nevin said.

"Were you teased?" I wanted to know. In the army, my father was addressed as "the effing swan of Avon", and at prep school I had had to endure everything from Shagspot to Shaggers.

"I was Shakey," Gavin said.

"I was Shakers, or Bill," Nevin said. "'Good day, Bill. Do you write many songs?' They say a lot of weird things here, a lot of misinformation. 'No,' I tell them, 'he wrote plays.'"

"Speaking of the plays," Gavin said. "I was the bottom of every class in English. It was my worst subject."

"Mine, too, pretty much," Nevin said. "That's been passed on. Comes from the bricklayer's side. Don't have to write anything. Just get the bricks level."

We discussed other family traits. Gavin's wife Gloria said, apropos of Nevin's youngest son: "*He's* a Shakespeare."

"What do you mean?" I asked.

Gloria said: "You never argue with him."

Gavin said: "My father wasn't interested in arguments."

"Nevin avoids arguments," Laurelle said.

"No, don't like confrontation," Nevin said.

"Something that can be settled in two minutes he lets drag on for two months, that's my pet hate."

"I'm with you," I said to Nevin. "I hate arguments."

Then Gavin remembered another Shakespeare trait. "My father wasn't interested in family history."

Nevin had inherited this characteristic as well. "Once they go, you've got no idea. It's just a heap of old photos. It's just history."

Even so, Nevin had been reading about Tasmania's forthcoming bicentenary in the *Burnie Advocate* and he felt a grub of regret to realise how little he knew about his birthplace. "We were never taught Tasmanian history at Parklands High School. We were told that Truganini was the last and that the Aborigines couldn't light a fire, couldn't swim and all hated each other anyway. We spent more time on English and European history, which at the end of the day means nothing."

"How much do you know about the man they call the Father of Tasmania?"

"Who's that?"

"Did they tell you about the settlement at York Town?"

"What settlement?"

"Do you know York Town?"

"Of course, I know York Town!" Nevin had driven through it heaps of

times. He had camped there and it was also where he had had the motorbike accident that so alarmed his parents. He was overtaking a line of traffic
when a car pulled out. "I hit the brakes and high-sided, and went surfing
on my hands and knees. The car didn't stop, didn't even know he'd caused
an accident. But I ended up in Deloraine Hospital. Luckily, I knew the
blokes because I'd serviced the ambulance station."

"Well, York Town is near where the Europeans landed 200 years ago,"
I told him. "It's the first place they settled on this coast."

He shook his head. "We knew nothing of it. You ask anyone in the
street, they wouldn't have much knowledge."

An idea was forming. I said to Nevin, "Take me on your bike, and I'll
show you."

II

SEPARATED FROM THE AUSTRALIAN MAINLAND BY 140 MILES OF the treacherous pitch and toss of Bass Strait, Tasmania is a byword for remoteness. As with Patagonia, to which in geological prehistory it was attached, it is like outer space on earth and invoked by those at the "centre" to stand for all that is far-flung, strange and unverifiable.

Tasmania is in myth and in history a secret place, a rarely visited place. Those few who did make the journey compared it to Elysium, or sometimes to Hades. For the first 50 years of its settlement, it was, with the notorious Norfolk Island, Britain's most distant penal colony and under the name of Van Diemen's Land was open panopticon to 76,000 convicts gathered from many pockets of the Empire, the majority of them thieves. The average sentence for the transportees was seven years – to a destination that was described by English judges as "beyond the seas" and might take eight months to reach. "They call it the end of the world," was one convict's verdict, "and for vice it is truly so. For here wickedness flourishes unchecked." Reports and fables of depravity and cannibalism sometimes made of Van Diemen's Land a synonym for all kinds of terror and dread, but after 1856, under the new name of Tasmania, the island – which is the size of Ireland, Sri Lanka or West Virginia – became popular as a health resort. Its exceptional natural beauty, fertile soil and temperate climate attracted immigrants who were sick of the English weather and yet wanted to be reminded of "home". The extinction of the original native Aboriginal population by 1876 further bolstered the illusion of a society that Anthony Trollope, dropping in on the way to

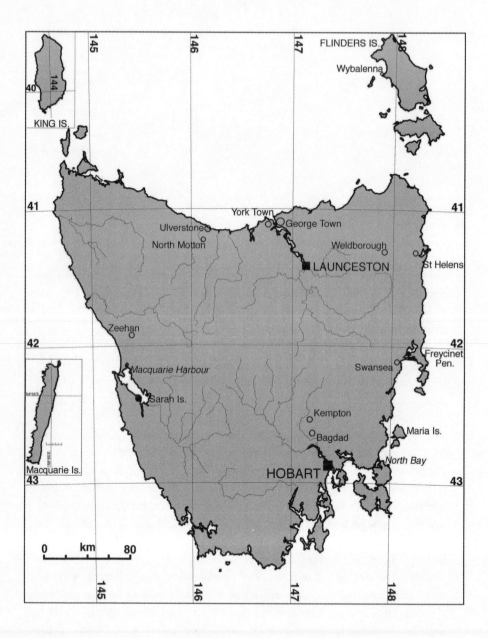

visit his jackaroo son, described as "more English than is England herself". Because it was so far away, it did its best to be very near.

First sighted by a European in 1642, when the Dutch navigator Abel Tasman mistook it for the mainland of Australia, Tasmania was not colonised by the British until the first years of the nineteenth century. It is a place that the Hollywood actress Merle Oberon was persuaded to claim as her birthplace, in which Errol Flynn and Viscount Montgomery of Alamein grew up, and into which all manner of felons and explorers and adventurous sorts disappeared, of whom perhaps the most interesting was a turbulent British officer called Anthony Fenn Kemp and among the most recent perhaps the fugitive Lord Lucan; a place where not even Iran's fundamentalist police would dream of looking for you. In an essay that Salman Rushdie wrote after the fatwa, he quoted a joke that was circulating: "What's blonde, has big tits and lives in Tasmania?" Answer: "Salman Rushdie."

Until 9,000 years ago, Tasmania was connected to the Australian mainland, but at the end of the last Ice Age melt from the glaciers swamped the land bridge, on the other side halting species such as the dingo and koala at the water's edge. Tasmania became an ark, and with one or two exceptions a very extraordinary animal and plant life was left to develop. The world's oldest living organism, King's Holly or *Lamatia tasmanica*, has grown on the south coast without interruption for 40,000 years.

Van Diemen's Land's most notable historian, the Victorian clergyman John West, would by and large still recognise "the park-like lands, the brilliant skies, the pure river and the untainted breath of morning". The roads are superbly deserted, but at night they teem with strange nocturnal creatures: wombats, wallabies, quolls, Tasmanian devils and the ubiquitous possum – plus three varieties of snake that are all lethal. In the fierce light of the Tasmanian day, the emptiness of the landscape can sting with a melancholy that is unbearable. You never forget that the enchanted isle is also a haunted one, the last habitat of the Tasmanian tiger as well as of the Tasmanian Aborigines who knew it as Trowenna. Innumerable lakes throw back the doubles of huge eucalypts with a brilliance that can make their reflections appear more solid even than the trees themselves. The upheld arms of dead white ghost-gums stand in for a vanished population and the shrieks of yellow-tailed black cockatoos are said to be the lament of dead Aboriginal children. "They had gone," writes the Tasmanian author and journalist Martin Flanagan, "in the way that party guests are said to have gone and left a house feeling oddly empty."

What you also notice about the landscape is that, despite the desecration caused by overlogging, it is free from pollution. The Roaring Forties, after blowing unimpeded from Cape Horn, smack at full tilt into the west coast. The result: Tasmania has the purest air in the world as well as some of its cleanest rainwater.

Much of the island's western half remains a protected wilderness of mountains, impenetrable rainforest and torrential rivers. A sailor told a newcomer who arrived a century ago: "In half that wilderness no man has put foot since time began."

The majority of the population of just under half a million live in the southern capital Hobart and in Launceston in the north. Between these rival cities, the central plateaux, which the Tasmanians call tiers, are dotted with Georgian-style houses and churches set amid orchards and open farmland.

The east coast is fringed with bright white beaches and small inlets and has a Caribbean aspect. It is not the ruined coastline of most countries, and it would probably have looked much the same on the blustery November morning in 1804 when Anthony Fenn Kemp floundered out of the water under the bemused eye of the native population.

III

THE MAN WHO CAME ASHORE WAS A 31-YEAR-OLD CAPTAIN IN THE NEW SOUTH
Wales Corps. He was a vigorous entrepreneur with a spot of charisma, and
a great survivor. He became in fits and starts "the Father of Tasmania".

Anthony Fenn Kemp, the son of a prominent wine and tobacco
merchant, was born in London in 1773. After a brief spell working in the
family business in Aldgate, he travelled to France in 1791 during the French
Revolution. What he experienced turned him into a republican. His political sympathies hardened in the following year when he went to Charleston
in South Carolina and met George Washington.

In 1793 he bought a commission, and in 1795 sailed to Port Jackson –
as Sydney – then was probably in the same ship as George Bass and
Matthew Flinders, both of whom also left their mark. Within a very few
years, these two explorers would prove that Van Diemen's Land was an
island.

Kemp served for two years in Norfolk Island, but no record exists of
his time there. By 1797, he was again in Port Jackson where he would
become paymaster of his infantry company and later treasurer of the whole
regiment. Like most of his fellow officers he was engaged in trade and in
1799 he opened a store on the north-east corner of King and George
Street. He was a familiar and tyrannical figure in early Sydney, and had his
finger in most pies. In September 1802, aboard a visiting French corvette,
the *Naturaliste*, he was received into the grade of Antient Masonry: the first
lodge known to have been convened in Australia.

Kemp's dealings with the French put him in a position to alert his commanding officer, Colonel Paterson, of a plan to claim Van Diemen's Land, largely ignored by Europeans since Tasman's original visit of 1642. Startled by the rumour, Governor King of New South Wales directed an expeditionary force of 49 soldiers, free settlers and convicts to forestall the French and set up camp at Risdon, on the east bank of the Derwent River in the south of the island. A few months later, King ordered Paterson to establish a settlement at Port Dalrymple (so named by Matthew Flinders in 1798) in the north.

Four ships sailed from Sydney in June 1804, but gales blew them back. They set out again in October. On board were 181 people: 64 soldiers and marines (and 20 wives), 74 convicts (and two wives), 14 children, and seven officers – including Captain Anthony Fenn Kemp, second-in-command.

IV

ONE HUNDRED AND NINETY-FIVE YEARS LATER, I LOOK OUT OVER A STRIP OF emerald boobyallas onto a deserted nine-mile beach. Through a glass wall of window, I can see a dorsal of pinkish granite jutting into the Tasman Sea. Below the house, there is a fenced-off garden planted with fruit trees, and a tin shed where I work.

One day I open a bag filled with letters which my father had given me at his house in England, and which he had unearthed from the basement of my grandmother's house. Her father had left the letters to her and she had never, as far as my father knew, read them. My grandmother was by now 96.

"I believe we may have a relative who went to Tasmania in the nineteenth century," my father said. "A bit of a black sheep."

That was the first I had heard of a Tasmanian relative and I did not really take it in. The bag remained unopened for several months.

The thick plastic was the colour of old toenail – and the contents smelled of rotten vegetable, not quite fermented but earthy. The first thing I took out was a loose slip of paper, a cheque made out in 1815 against "Kemp & Potter, brandy and tobacco merchants". Potter was my grandmother's name and I remembered that our family had, long ago, been involved in the drinks trade. But the name Kemp meant nothing to me. Nor had my grandmother heard of the Kemps. All she remembered her father telling her was that the papers had belonged to a "black sheep" in the family who had gone to New South Wales.

Also in the bag was a bundle of about 30 letters written on stiff paper in the days before stamps. They were packed in chronological order: the first letter dated 1791, the last 1825. Occasionally they were signed with a woman's name: Amy, Susanna, Elizabeth. But the bulk of the correspondence was between two men: William Potter and Anthony Fenn Kemp.

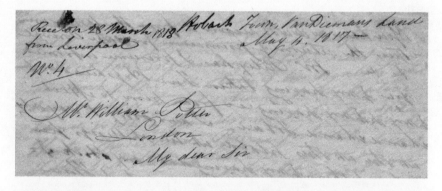

Kemp's letters to Potter were sent from Brazil, Cape Town, Sydney, Hobart. The ink had faded to umber, but the handwriting remained distinctively slanted, the words scratched forcefully onto the page, with exaggerated tails to certain letters. By contrast, Potter's responses – all from an address in Aldgate – were written in a neat, upright hand, and he had made copies of his own replies, so providing both sides of their correspondence.

I opened a red marbled business ledger dated March 25, 1789, the year of the French Revolution. The paper had the scent of nutmeg. On the first page, under the heading *I Anthony Kemp being of Age have this day rec'd of Col John Arnott my guardian*, there was a long list of what Kemp had inherited on his 16th birthday. It included properties in Surrey and central London, stocks and cash. Together it amounted to a fortune today worth several millions of pounds. I wondered what had become of it.

Kemp was a very rich young man, but as I read more of the ledger it became clear that, despite his wealth, he had worked as an apprentice in his father's business at 87 Aldgate, the site today of a branch of Boots the chemist. He appears to have had a pretty free hand in its affairs, though. While the ledger recorded Kemp the father tramping with his samples to Biggleswade and Newport Pagnell, Kemp the son was ordering hogsheads of rum from Antigua, pipes of port from Lisbon and fine shag from plantations in Maryland. Nor did he restrict himself to buying only tobacco and rum. The purchases mounted until they culminated in the outfitting of an entire boat, the *Neptune Galley*, to bring a cargo of cinnamon, cochineal, sugar and silk from Jamaica. Then suddenly the ledger ran out. One of the last entries was in the younger Kemp's handwriting: "June 14, 1789 . . . lost by betting at an horse race £15.10".

It transpired that Kemp had run through his inheritance in two years. By 1791, he could not repay twelve crowns to a man called Page, instead organising for "a very shabby insolent low-bred woman" to march into Page's favourite London coffee house and "utter impertinencies" about him at the top of her voice. Page reported this incident in a letter to Kemp's father, whose reaction was furious. He wrote to his son – who had, it appeared, undoubtedly wisely, absented himself from Aldgate – threatening to sue him unless he reflected upon the situation that "your early vice and infamy has placed you in". Only if Kemp admitted to his "evil conduct" and confessed his faults would he be welcome to return home to his father and mother. "If this overture is rejected, expect that I shall take speedy and effective public measures to prevent further injury."

One week later, a letter was brought to Aldgate by an attorney of Clement's Inn. Its delivery had been delayed by order of Anthony Fenn Kemp until its author was safely across the Channel. Kemp's handwriting shoves aside the centuries. "Hon. Sir and Madam, Behold my reply. At present I am not sensible of what distress is nor pray to God I ever shall and as to returning with compunction I hope when I do come I may."

On the envelope an unknown hand has scribbled "First elopement". Kemp's story was just beginning.

The next letter was written on the day that he arrived in Calais and sent not to his father but to a friend called Frank. Kemp, clearly, was having a whale of a time, parading the streets in "a National Cockade" and finding everything "very Cheap – a Partridge for Fourpence, a Hare for Sixpence, a bottle Burgundy 3/3, Champaigne 4/3". He betrayed no symptom of wanting to return to Aldgate. "I receiv'd a letter from my Father the other day but couch'd in such high terms that I could not accede to them nor do not think I ever shall if I am so well off as I am at present." More attractive even than the low prices were the French women. "Every day

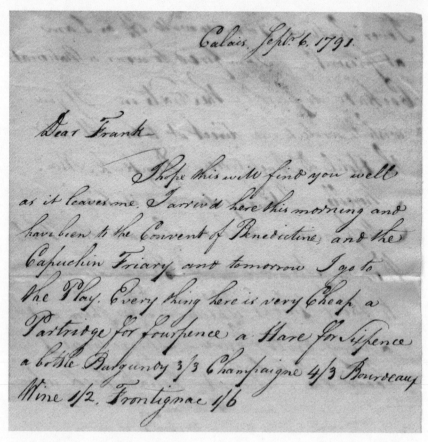

here is high Mass perform'd where all the Fish Women assemble with Pettycoats up their thighs which make them cut a very droll figure. I hope before I leave the continent I shall pick up some Heiress." He asked Frank: "Pray remember me to all inquiring friends."

I riffled through the letters to find out what else Kemp got up to in France, but there was a gap of several years in the correspondence. The next letter I unfolded was dated March 1816 and the address was Hobart Town, Van Diemen's Land.

On our first afternoon, my wife and I had walked 300 yards to the beach. There was a hot equinoctial wind cooling the sea and a clear sky over the hills above Swansea. We threw off our clothes and jumped into the surf and afterwards ran back to the house, startling a young wallaby on the path. It stared at us, then bounded off through the boobyallas, its feet thumping the warm sand with a sound like a heavy fruit dropping.

I would go fishing for flathead at the mouth of the Swan River, where one evening I fell into conversation with an old fisherman who asked my name.

"Shakespeare?" He looked at me, excited, as if he doubted what he had heard. "Not Shakespeare? You couldn't possibly be related to the family who make the fishing tackle?"

I had never been interested in gardening before. For the first time in my life I planted seeds, bought trees, learned about mulching. I was bemused when I found myself, away from the garden, still wanting to dig.

One day, at my desk in my shed with the bag of letters in front of me, I counted out the relationships that I had discovered: Potter, my great-great-great-grandfather; Kemp, my great-great-great-great-uncle. Their letters had revealed that they were more than business partners: they were brothers-in-law. To me, their story was about two ways of being in the world. On the one hand there was Kemp, roistering, opportunistic, peripatetic, corrupt. (The name Kemp, I found out, derived from a Saxon word meaning combat, competitive drinker, "a contemptible, rascally fellow"). On the other was the sedentary, abstemious Potter.

I was still going through their letters. In 1791, the 18-year-old Kemp was being groomed to take over the family firm. But after he left England, his father turned to William Potter, the man who had married Kemp's elder sister Amy. He invited Potter to move into the Aldgate premises and granted him a third share of the business. On the death of Kemp senior, Potter took over the running of the firm. It had become "Kemp & Potter".

There are those who go to New South Wales and there are those who mind the store. Potter inched off the page – in his handwriting and in his character – as the opposite of his brother-in-law: a cautious, fussy, meticulous man, forever advising his family how to behave. The following pieces of advice all appeared in letters to his son: "Never play cards in Grantham *or in any other place with strangers*"; "Remember one above sees and knows all and will reward or punish as we deserve"; "Be careful at Brighton. It's a rotten place." And – oddly (or perhaps not) for a man in the liquor business – there were various admonitions about drink. "Drink no more than you can help," he counselled; on the same theme, in a letter warning his son about which public houses in Ware were "safe": "We must be very careful what we are about . . . the owner of the Little White Lion likes you to spend an hour with him in the evening, which calls for a bottle of wine which you may mix with water."

By contrast, his absentee partner out in Australia was peddling family connections with the rum trade for all they were worth. Or not worth, for Kemp's letters – despite their charm – had revealed that he was a feckless businessman. He borrowed a vast sum from Potter, and never repaid it. He wrote out several cheques in the name of "Kemp & Potter", which he never redeemed. His letters took up to 14 months to reach London and each and every one contained an excuse.

I found it painful to observe Potter's struggles to cope with Kemp's escalating debts. "For 18 months I have had weekly applications from one or another of your creditors for the amount of bills made payable at our house," and yet "not a farthing has arrived [from Kemp], which I am much astonished at." Not even nineteenth-century etiquette can disguise his frustration. "I do not consider 'Kemp & Potter' has anything to do with it. I am now completely sick of shipping goods to you."

Yet Potter could not cut off his brother-in-law. I could imagine him sitting at night at his mahogany double-desk, wearing a calico nightcap. I could feel his sense of responsibility, born of duty, blood, grudging envy and just enough imagination to believe in his brother-in-law's schemes.

I was in my shed one morning when I heard a scratching in the ceiling. The noise ceased the moment I crawled into the attic, but something was rotten in the roof, and a putrid smell and pyramids of chewed cardboard suggested that possums or bush rats had nested in boxes stacked with the previous owner's red and yellow moodscapes. I telephoned Helen, from whom we had bought the house. She did not care what I did with the boxes. At her suggestion I contacted Peter, a builder, who agreed to take them to the tip as well as to get rid of the animals. A month later, Peter had not turned up. The smell had sharpened, and when I telephoned him again he promised to call by soon.

I did wonder if I would ever see him. A hundred years before, a local vicar warned the newly arrived Anglican Bishop, Henry Montgomery, to watch out for "the languor which here soon attacks, as a dry rot, most works of all kinds after they have settled down".

Before Peter could come, my wife woke up with a toothache. It got worse, so I drove her to a dentist in Hobart. The two-hour drive along the coast took us through the county of Glamorgan, to Pembroke, to Buckingham, through countryside eerily similar to that of where we had lived in England: Georgian sandstone houses with deep windows – fingertip to ankle; rose gardens and wicket fences; names like Kelvedon and Lisdillon and Bust-Me-Gall Hill. "The Tasmanians in their loyalty are all English mad," wrote Anthony Trollope, who was tempted to "pitch my staff" here permanently – he liked in particular the mulberry jams. And yet we were most certainly not in England. Though the landscape might resemble an English nobleman's park, beyond the bourgeois topiaries there was sadness. Anyone with ambition, I had been told, followed the example of Errol Flynn, who got out as soon as he could. Young Tasmanians took their leaving as a rite of passage. The old and the very young were left behind.

V

TASMANIA'S CAPITAL IS A TIDY, UNSELFCONSCIOUS PORT WHOSE WATER ROCKS with smooth reflections of white sails, bright façades and a dramatic barn-shaped mountain. ("My predominant recollection is of its apples, its jams, its rose-cheeked girls," wrote Errol Flynn in *My Wicked, Wicked Ways*.) Once the most southerly city in the world and the final port of call for Antarctic explorers, Hobart seems more deserving than Auckland of Kipling's line: "Last, loneliest, loveliest, exquisite, apart . . . " In 1889, Henry Montgomery's first reaction on learning that he had been appointed Bishop to Hobart was to dash to an atlas to see where it was.

I first read of Hobart at my prep school in a novel about the end of the world written by a former pupil, Nevil Shute. In *On the Beach*, a Melbourne scientist evokes the creeping spread of radiation following a nuclear war. "After we're gone, Tasmania may last another fortnight" – although life would still be on earth in the form of rabbits. Faced with impending catastrophe, one character muses: "Say I was to move to Hobart . . . "

Hobart was considered out of reach of nuclear fallout but also of God. In its direst days as a penal colony, the Irish rebel John Mitchel refused to let his daughter be baptised here, not "till she reaches Christendom". A perception lingers even to this day that Tasmania floats in a latitude outside the jurisdiction of normal religious and civic laws.

Tasmania may have been the last place that Iranian bounty-hunters considered looking for him, but until 2001 a Salman Rushdie in drag would have risked arrest under the 1935 Police Offences Act which made it an offence for a man to be seen in a public place dressed up as a woman between sunset and sunrise. Homosexuality was illegal until 1997 and the crime of blasphemy still carried a prison sentence of 21 years. But under the premiership of Jim Bacon (1998–2004) many antiquated laws were scrapped, and the state now boasted legislation that was the most liberal in Australia. "Lesbian Love Bus Triangle" was the *Hobart Mercury*'s headline on the day after the Madrid bombing in March 2004.

Something about Tasmania nonetheless continued to give the impression that it was an outpost, a little like Tangiers, where you went when everything went wrong: when you killed your nanny, when the Ayatollah delivered a death sentence, or when you could not find the right therapist. "I owe a lot to good therapy," said an English celebrity interviewed in *Hello!*. "I probably wouldn't be here without it. I'd weigh about 400 pounds and be living in Tasmania." The island still had a reputation as the kind of place where fugitives of one kind or another, who wanted nothing more than to disappear, washed up. "Marilyn's love child in Tassie" – so began an article about how Marilyn Monroe's 43-year-old daughter – "the result of a brief affair with a musician" – was living as a recluse under the name Nancy Greene. Tasmania was a promise of anonymity. Louisa Meredith, whose family once owned our land, was told by the nineteenth-century naturalist Joseph Jukes that he had decided to omit Tasmania altogether from his travel book because "no one will read what anyone may write about it". Among those who had also bought property on our same beach were the spy catcher Peter Wright, who spent his last years in Tasmania; a woman running away from her husband who used to answer to Sue, but now to Ellen; a solicitor who had defrauded his clients; and a lesbian couple, escapees from the rat race who had started a café already famous for its lemon tarts.

Another local, so it is said, was Lord Lucan, who for ten months rented a two-bedroom cottage on a farm, Glen Gala, five miles from our Swansea home. Pleased to discover that he shared my fondness for fishing at the mouth of the Swan River, I asked his landlady what truth there was in the *Launceston Examiner* story entitled "Did Lord Lucan live in Tassie?"

Patricia Greenhill has a frank, reliable face. She had never heard of Lord Lucan, nor about the murder of his children's nanny, when in July 1992 a figure rode up on an old yellow bicycle saying that he was looking for a quiet place to rent where he could write a book. She recalled a man in his battered late fifties – tallish build, clear face, brown hair going grey and nails that were always clean. "Obviously he'd never had to look after himself much – and yet he didn't have anything in the way of possessions. He wore ordinary clothes and was living on unemployment benefit." He had come to Glen Gala after staying in Swansea at the Oyster Bay Guest House, at the time run by our electrician, Mike Tierney. Mike arrived home after being away awhile to find a hole in his supply of alcohol and "James", as he called himself, smelling of whisky, dear boy, lots of it, dear boy. The next day, James bicycled down the road and rented the cottage at Glen Gala. Patricia said: "It was really hard to get a tenant, and so I was pleased to leave him alone. When he came to pay rent, he'd walk over in the middle of the day, always when no-one else was about. He was very private, but he'd sometimes sit and have a sherry, and talk in a posh voice about trout fishing, and volunteer information about his fishing gear at home in England. So I lent him a rod and he used to go to a creek and catch some small ones."

Mike had intended to employ him as washer-up, but one day in 1993 he left without a word. Patricia found the cottage in a hideous mess. "He'd vacuumed up water with the Hoover and there were carpet burns."

"How do you know it was him?"

The editor of the *Examiner* had sent a photograph of Lord Lucan taken in 1967. Patricia said: "I'm sure it was him. I was later even more convinced when I read somewhere how Lord Lucan behaved in South Africa. It was the same behaviour."

I dropped my wife off at the dentist and went for a walk in Hobart. Opposite the cathedral is the hotel where Roald Amundsen was initially refused entry after returning from his journey to the South Pole. "Treated as a tramp, my peaked cap and blue sweater – given a miserable little room," he wrote in his diary. Residents of Sandy Bay had waved ships off to the icecap for a century. They were not thunderstruck by Amundsen's achievement so much as irritated by the barking of his sledge dogs. Even today, there is something unimpressable about the people of Hobart, as if there is nothing they have not witnessed, no eventuality for which they have not, at some time, prepared themselves – including a Russian invasion. Fortifications, erected in panic after the Crimean War, are to be found up and down the Derwent River, at Sandy Bay, Tinderbox, Rosny Hill, the Cenotaph, Bellerive. But despite the presence of these curious stone battlements, Hobart feels more like an English market town than a nervous outpost on the rim of the world. Mark Twain, on a lecture tour in 1895, thought it "the neatest town that the sun shines on; and I incline to believe that it is also the cleanest." This was still true: I could not stop marvelling at the clarity of the sunlight. Mainlanders put the transparency down to the frazzled ozone layer, but whatever the cause, the light was so clear and over-exposed that there seemed no gauze between it and the first settlers.

If my enthusiasm seemed over-the-top, it was well supported by earlier tourists. In 1830, Elizabeth Fenton, recently arrived from India, stood on her balcony in the Macquarie Hotel and rhapsodised over the stars and clear atmosphere in which, she thought, the planets not only shone with the intensity of moons but appeared to cast a shadow. Some visitors had the eerie impression that they inhabited a painting. "In Van Diemen's Land, almost every landscape is a watercolour," remarked Mrs Roxburgh in Patrick White's novel *A Fringe of Leaves*. On his arrival in 1823, the more often sceptical colonial auditor George Boyes wrote in his diary that "all language . . . must be inadequate to describe the general effect". In a letter to his wife he lost himself in superlatives. The Derwent was "the most magnificent thing I have ever seen", and he went on about its "perfect forms . . . forms that till lately I thought were nowhere to be found but in the imagination of the painter". In 1873, Harry Benjafield, a Baptist medic from the village next to ours in England, was recommended to go to Tasmania by his own doctor, who told him: "Hobart is the most beautiful place in the world. If there is a heaven upon earth it is Hobart." Among those fleetingly tempted to settle was Agatha Christie, who paid a visit with her husband in 1922. "Incredibly beautiful Hobart, with its deep blue sea and harbour, and its flowers, trees, and shrubs. I planned to come back and live there one day."

A century earlier, the 26-year-old naturalist Charles Darwin was likewise affected. His survey ship *Beagle* docked here on its way from Sydney. "If I was obliged to emigrate I certainly should prefer this place: the climate & aspect of the country almost alone would determine me." Eighteen years on, unable to get Hobart out of his head, he wrote to his friend, the botanist William Hooker: "I am always building veritable castles in the air about emigrating & Tasmania has been my headquarters of late, so that I feel very proud of my adopted country."

During eleven days in Hobart in February 1836, Darwin found 63 new species of insect, including a gall-forming wasp. He also made the obligatory five-hour climb of Mount Wellington, as I did on my first visit.

Hobart's omnipresent mountain – in stern command of every street – is a volcano that has not yet erupted, created from a massive dolerite injection up through and into the older rocks. I had been too busy gaping at the view of the Derwent to register the layers of Ferntree Mudstone at my feet, or the brachiopod fossils that transported Darwin 260 million years to a period when Tasmania was not an island. Now that I was living here I had become more curious, but Tasmania's age was a vast thing to absorb, and I had to perform a schoolboy's crude algebra to put the presence simply of *Homo sapiens* into context. Suppose a human life to span 70 years, 30 lifetimes took me to the time of Jesus. The oldest human habitation in Tasmania is estimated at 40,000 years, or 572 lifetimes. I thought back half a lifetime to an afternoon in Oxford and a timid man lining up this number of boys for the school photograph.

It was Professor Pat Quilty, a geologist at the University of Tasmania with a base in Antarctica, who gave me a perspective on the geological record. "I try to get students to think about time, 4,500 million years of it, about 30% of the age of the universe by the latest estimates. The oldest rocks of Tasmania didn't form until about 80% of earth's history had passed." Right up until 160 million years ago, Tasmania was part of a supercontinent, now referred to as Gondwana, and situated much further north. Quilty drew a chart that indicated Tasmania's position as it nuzzled between Australia and Patagonia. Tasmania had then waltzed south at seven centimetres a year and gradually fragmented from the supercontinent. Ice formed in the space that opened up to the south, creating Antarctica.

But what sprang off the page was the situation of Hobart 600 million years ago. It was more than eight degrees north of the Equator. "The farther we go back in time, the farther north it is," Quilty said. "Australia was near the North Pole at 1.6 billion years."

It heartened me to think that Tasmania at one time existed where Africa now is, since I frequently had to correct people who believed this still to be the case. An early Lieutenant Governor, George Arthur, was so enthusiastic about its location – midway between India and South America – that he was confident "it must become the Alexandria of these seas". Its present position confused the *National Geographic*: commissioned by the magazine to write an article on Tasmania, I received an email to thank me for my piece on Tanzania.

Darwin compared in his diary "the older strata at Hobart Town and the bottom of the sea near T. del Fuego". I knew Tierra del Fuego from when I lived in Argentina. The similarities I had observed on a trek along the Overland Trail had a geological explanation. Near Cradle Mountain botanists had dug up fossils of conifer, *Fitzroya tasmanensis*, of which the only living examples were in Chile. Quilty told me that some of the flora

I may have noticed in the Andes were to be found elsewhere only in Tasmania – notably southern beech and leatherwood – and that insects like the Tasmanian cave spider were the sole family known outside Chile. "And they recently found a platypus tooth in Patagonia that's 100 million years old."

Tierra del Fuego broke away from the South American continent at the time that Tasmania moved south of the Australian mainland, becoming a sanctuary for flora and fauna. This is what had excited Darwin. But what no-one knew until the *Beagle* docked in Hobart was that for the first three decades following British settlement Tasmania also existed in its own time zone.

A chance remark by the poet Andrew Sant led me to look up a Hobart periodical, the issue of *Bent's Notes* for March 5, 1836 – and there I read a little-known story that, to me, shed light on an aspect of Tasmania's character. While Darwin was chiselling out 260-million-year-old fossils on Mount Wellington, two officers from the *Beagle* with less to do politely offered to check the town clocks using their chronometers. Heckscher, the "first-rate machinist" in charge of the city's three clocks, had worked for the Emperor of Russia, and was delighted to show off his trusted machines to Captain Fitzroy and Lieutenant Stokes. What they discovered astonished them. The town was faster than the *Beagle* by one minute 45 seconds. For its first 33 years, the established position of Hobart, given as 43 degrees by six south, 147 by 38 east, was incorrect by 27 miles.

Fitzroy was swift to advise Heckscher that it was seriously important for ships to be made aware of this fact "as the consequences may be most fatal". Captains setting their clocks for longitude as they left harbour risked being out by four nautical miles – and so adding to the thousand or more shipwrecks along Tasmania's coast, the positions of the huge majority of which remain unknown.

In the months ahead, I came to believe that George Fitzroy had discovered a unique local phenomenon, a crack in time and space that accounted for so many things that I observed about Tasmania. Into it disappeared ships, novelists, cities, UFOs, archives, promises. "Yes, I'll be there tomorrow. To service your car, build your house, clean the possums out of your roof . . . " Returning 40 years on to his childhood home at the foot of Mount Wellington, Viscount Montgomery of Alamein grumbled that the railway station "looked just the same . . . in spite of repeated representations for it to be modernised". Fitzroy's missing 105 seconds was a paradigm of Tasmania's idiosyncratic relationship to the clock, and reflected the findings of a Tourism Tasmania survey which reported an overwhelming impression among visitors that Tasmania was "caught up in a bit of a time warp". The mindset was understandable, given that the state for most of its history was a rural economy. At the trial for the murder of a North Motton girl in 1921, Chief Justice Sir Herbert Nicholls explained to the jury the attitude of the Tasmanian farmer towards time: "Without saying it in a derogatory sense or attempting to be humorous, it is a plain, sensible fact that a farmer often takes his time from his stomach. In the course of his work he gets no signal as to his meals, but goes home to his dinner, goes back to his work until dark, and then goes to bed. He has no occasion to look at his watch, no occasion to think about the time. It is no slander, possibly, to say that when he looks at the family clock and his watch they don't agree, and probably they are both likely to be wrong."

Tasmania's rural economy and its geographic position ensured that it was a blip that could disappear from the rest of Australia's radar. Tasmanians were long accustomed to being patronised by Sydneysiders for living in "a sometimes forgotten teardrop at the bottom of Australia"; or to being ignored completely, as happened in 1982 when Tasmania was left out of the Australian reckoning for the Commonwealth Games. Andrew Sant captured something of the local fury in his poem "Off the Map":

> Identity deleted,
> Close to the Continent,
> Who wouldn't make a fuss?
> There have been wars for less . . .

About its profile on the map, the Tasmanian-born writer Peter Conrad was taught at school that Tasmania looked like a human heart, or an apple with a bite taken out of it. I prefer to think that it resembled the pawmark that Tasman's sailors came across in the sand at Marion Bay, left there by a wombat or a thylacine. But mainlanders were not so indulgent. Their jokes about the island's shape had entered the *Cassell Dictionary of Slang*: "mapatasi – from 'map of Tasmania', supposed shape of female pubic region. Came into use in 1990s".

To an outsider, these jokes disguised an unease, as if Tasmania was a dumping ground for a nation's bad conscience about itself. Bernard Lloyd put it bluntly in *Beer, Blood and Water*: "Australians project all the things they despise and loathe about themselves – their racism, their homophobia, their parochialism – onto their 'other' Tasmania, the 'Albania of the Antipodes'. They think 'we're not like that – Tasmania is.'" Certainly, in Sydney and Melbourne they appeared to know all about "the Apple Isle", even if they had never set foot there. In Tasmania were committed the worst atrocities against Aborigines; in Tasmania there ended up "the most felonious of felons"; in Tasmania the population – sometimes referred to as Tasmaniacs – was so backward and inbred that visitors were advised, as I was, "to grow an extra head" (in Salamanca Place I could even buy a T-shirt with a spare hole). No-one was terribly interested to hear about the findings of the Menzies Institute, which showed that Tasmaniacs have a lower rate of congenital malformation than the Australian average.

But Tasmania's very remoteness had also protected it. After living here for three years, I could not help noticing that the absence of "progress", which had made Tasmania the butt of so many jokes, was turning into its strongest attraction. Bypassed and undeveloped, this arrestingly beautiful island was enjoying a rediscovery as an Arcadia rather than an Alcatraz. The "hated stain" was being cleaned up on several levels, and, encouraged by terrorism, SARS, and improved transport and communications, not to mention cheap property, visitors were crossing Bass Strait in record numbers.

"Fitzroy's crack" could also suck you down into the human equivalent of Mount Wellington's dolerite core.

In a place as obsessed with history as Tasmania the present quickly leads back to the past. Talking to Bill Penfold, a telephone engineer who had written a book on Hobart's New Town district, I had to ask him to repeat himself when he mentioned that his grandfather had been a convict at Port Arthur, a prison of secondary punishment on the tip of the Tasman peninsula.

"Your great-grandfather, surely?" I said.

But no. His grandfather William Pinfold was a convict from Northamptonshire who had stolen jewellery from a post office – "and probably a thousand other things". He was sent to Norfolk Island in 1847 and then to Port Arthur, where he was one of 12,000 male convicts who reoffended between 1832 and 1853. "He was released and wound up hop-picking, and was listed as a butcher in New Norfolk, a place called Plenty where he stole a sheep and was sent back to Port Arthur for four years." In 1850 he married an Irish milkmaid. William's father was born in 1872, and in 1930 the family changed their name to Penfold. "It was because of the winery," he said, "but also something to do with convicts. People were very reluctant to admit they were descended from convicts, and then in the last 20 years convicts have become the in thing."

When he was incarcerated at Port Arthur, Penfold's grandfather would have known the commandant of the "Silent Prison" [or Model Prison]. A friend of my mother's sent me from Wiltshire this bleak paragraph that she had transcribed from her grandmother's diary: "At Hobarton [Hobart] among other duties my father had military control of the Silent Prison on the convict station, a terrible institution which has long since been given up on account of the number of convicts who went out of their minds. My mother often described to us how sad a sight it was to see the convicts taking exercise in perfect silence and knowing that except to their jailers some of them had not been allowed to speak to anyone for years. Once as she passed she stuck a piece of sweet scented verbena into the hands of one of these silent prisoners & heard that afterwards the poor fellow was on his knees weeping over it in his cell."

As the state prepared to mark the 200th anniversary of its settlement by Europeans, there were signs that Tasmania itself was beginning to emerge from a long, traumatic period of silence in which certain topics could not be discussed.

Until very recently the past was regarded as discreditable, to be put "out of sight and out of mind" according to Lloyd Robson in the first part of his two-volume history of Tasmania. Many growing up here in the 1950s felt, like Conrad, that "Tasmania possesses too much history". Pete Hay is another writer who believes that Tasmania has never made an authentic accommodation with its past: "That past has the stature of a dark family secret."

The name-change to Tasmania a century before had been a deliberate attempt to wipe clean that slate. Van Diemen's Land, wrote Trollope in 1873, had "a sound which had become connected all over the world with rascaldom"; it seemed "to carry a taunt in men's ears" and was "harsh with the crack of the jailer's whip". And yet pages scissored from records in the Hobart archives suggested that shame about the past had endured. The state archivist Ian Pearce says that his relatives glossed over a convict ancestor who was spoken of many times as "a sea-captain". "I discovered when I was working here that he was a fairly boring London convict who had pinched lead from church roofs." Pearce considers that up until the 1970s people were unable to talk about their history, and became quite distressed to learn in the Public Search Room that they were descended from convict stock. He credits the television drama series *Roots* for planting the genealogy bug, a process that has continued with a younger generation of Tasmanian writers, among them the novelist Richard Flanagan, whose *Gould's Book of Fish* takes for its subject a convict artist sentenced to Sarah Island. Pearce says: "There's been a massive sea change in people's attitude to their convict past that's moved into an obsession, a pride almost – from 'don't talk about it' into 'this is our heritage'."

VI

WAITING FOR GILLIAN TO BE FINISHED WITH THE DENTIST, I FOUND MYSELF thinking about Anthony Fenn Kemp. Had he come here as a convict, and was that why my grandmother referred to him as "a black sheep"? Passing Kemp Street, I wondered if the name was connected in some way with this cousin. I dismissed the thought as ridiculous, but then, in Murray Street, realising that my route was taking me past the Hobart archives, I went in. Habit, I suppose: a writer's reflex action. I told myself, as I climbed the stairs, that I was being led less by an investigating spirit than an extinguishing one. I'll just quickly check him out and then I can be done with him, I thought.

The archivist was a friendly woman. I told her what I knew about Kemp and asked her whether she had heard of him, and where she thought I should start my researches. At this she smiled and told me that Anthony Fenn Kemp was known as "the Father of Tasmania".

The Father of Tasmania. The man who up till now I had been thinking of as some low-life in the rum and tobacco trade. Nothing in the letters I had read so far had prefigured this distinction.

"He also wished to be known as the George Washington of Van Diemen's Land and the Father of the People," she told me, adding, however, that there was some debate over whether this last sobriquet recognised Kemp's role in Tasmania's history, his sublime egoism or his 18 children.

Kemp had in fact been one of the first colonists to set foot in the territory. He had helped to establish the first permanent settlement in the north and for seven months was in command of half the island. Nor was his influence limited to Van Diemen's Land. He was witness to many crises in the early history of Australia itself and personally responsible for several more. He fomented one mutiny, saw off two Governors of New South Wales and three Lieutenant Governors of Tasmania and risked armed conflict with the French. He was also the great-grandfather of the Victorian novelist Mrs Humphrey Ward and the great-great-grandfather of Aldous and Julian Huxley.

I felt rather pleased. I told the archivist with unconcealed pride that he was a distant relative.

"If I was you, I would not go round divulging that information." She pressed her yellow pencil to her chin. "He's a man of whom I've heard not one word of good."

VII

SO I BEGAN TO SIFT IN EARNEST THROUGH THE VAST, MESSY JUNK DRAWER OF
Anthony Fenn Kemp's life.

I hoped to fill the gaps quickly. The so-called Father of Tasmania would
surely have inspired a biography. But no. Despite his credentials, it seemed
that little had been published about Kemp; and although he began to pop
up everywhere, he resisted any move to fix him.

I might have stopped there, left Kemp alone, but I had trained a muscle
too well – and I felt singled out, as if the bag had chosen me. Stories, like
small children, as I was shortly to discover, have a life which demands to
be expressed: "I want to be told and you're going to be the person to do
it." Just when my doubts were strongest, the Tasmanian historian Henry
Reynolds sent me back to my shed. Kemp, he told me, was indeed a true
pioneer of Tasmania who had lived through its most formative years to
become a crucial political figure. "Kemp was important because he lived
for a long time; he was in both colonies; he was present at important
moments. There wouldn't be many figures who are as interesting."

I began to seek out his tracks: in libraries in Sydney, London and Hobart;
in leather-backed books and bow-tied files that the archivist brought to
my desk; in interviews with his descendants. The person who emerged was
not the indigent remittance man I had expected, but a significant and
extraordinary figure – one of the founding sires of Australia, who led like
a lightning rod back to the island's past, giving me a portrait of the whole
bizarre and brutal early history of Tasmania and New South Wales.

And as I followed Kemp to Australia, I felt myself to be Potter's accidental auditor, crossing the world, as Potter never did, to bring Kemp to account. It was the opposite of everything I intended. I had come here, as had Kemp, to begin afresh. But you cannot just shed yourself like that, not even if you go and live on the rim of the world. Too often the Potter and rarely the Kemp, I was back at my desk, a clerk once more.

VIII

SATED IN DUE COURSE WITH FISHWIVES AND BURGUNDY, ANTHONY FENN KEMP
headed south from Calais on foot. He walked through a country in turmoil,
a penniless outcast driven by a need to escape his family's censure.

In Aldgate concern about his safety had confined his mother to her
bed. Susannah Kemp was a highly strung woman who rode for her health
and was addicted to a tincture of valerian and castor known as "Bevan's
nervous drops". When she died, six months after her son left, the
young man was in Liège, dancing the "Marseillaise" around the cap
of Liberty.

His resentment of his father had worked itself up into contempt for
all authority. He sympathised with the revolutionaries, who egged him
on – he was able to communicate his feelings expansively in their
language. He had learned his French at Dr Knox's school in Greenwich
(where, according to an obituary which I looked up in the *Tasmanian
Times*, he also acquired a fondness for quoting Latin "which afforded
frequent amusement to his intimate friends"). He was never happy "unless
talking".

In fact, he talked himself out of most friendships, being prone when
piqued to address his listeners in rather an abrupt manner. One of very
few to take him at face value was James Erskine Calder, retired surveyor-
general and author of Kemp's obituary in the *Tasmanian Times*. Perhaps
Calder's profession made him receptive to the island's "time warp" into
which, he observed, men like Kemp tended to vanish. "I have often thought
there must be something either very Lethean in the atmosphere of Tasmania

or defective in the mental power of her people which causes such rapid obliviousness of those which having deserved well out of the country ought not to pass out of recollection." Calder considered it his duty to rescue Kemp from this oblivion.

In his late eighties, Kemp spoke at length to Calder from his wheel-chair in his manorial estate outside Hobart, Mount Vernon. He talked about his anarchic experiences in Liège, the wild excesses he had witnessed, and revealed how, after gaining a taste for republicanism, he spent the next year in America "as a pleasure-seeking traveller". It was there, at a farm in South Carolina, that he had a brief, if unlikely meeting with the only man he ever professed to admire. He loved George Washington, he told Calder – with a power for self-deception that remained undimmed at 95 – for strengthening his "inherent aversion to despotism".

But not even America was far enough from Aldgate.

Why else did Kemp go to Australia? From the books in Hobart library, I got the impression that people who went to Australia were either felons who did not want to go; those sent to guard them, who also did not want to go; and a handful of free settlers who were making a huge gamble, comparable, at that time, to settling on the moon. No-one came with the high ideals of the Founding Fathers. It was, in fact, a very odd place for someone like Kemp to choose. It must have suited him to be some 14,000 miles away from home. Distance is a great aid to a rascal. And Kemp was a rascal: on his return from America in May 1793 he was immediately arrested for debt.

He cannot have known it, but he was pioneering a tradition. "An odd person, absolutely English," Tolstoy later wrote in his diaries of a character like Kemp. "He has *evasive* jokes and words ready for every occasion: 'I love to squander money, and afterwards *I will rough it* in Australia.'"

At 20, and possibly with the assistance of his father, Kemp bought a commission in the 102nd Regiment of Foot (later called the New South Wales Corps), raised to manage convicts in a new penal colony at Port Jackson, a wild, empty, desperate place at the other end of the world. He was one of only 18 officers, but his red and white sash was never a coveted uniform. Kemp himself calculated that 200 of the 460 soldiers under him were former convicts, recruited from the ranks of those they had to garrison. In the opinion of John Hunter, second Governor of New South Wales, the behaviour of Kemp's Corps was "the most violent and out-rageous that was ever heard of by any British regiment whatever". In 1795, two years after joining the Corps, Kemp and the newly appointed Hunter

sailed together to Australia, along with the town clock, a windmill and a
returning Aborigine suffering from flu.

The decrepit *Reliance* left Plymouth on February 15, travelling at an
average speed of five knots and calling at Tenerife and Rio. The long
journey had few distractions. George Boyes followed in Kemp's wake 30
years later: "I just begin to perceive that the voyage is more in the imagination than anywhere else. The time slips on almost insensibly." From the
poop deck, Kemp watched sperm whales and green turtles and hundreds
of gulls and petrels – known as "Mother Carey's chickens" – that flew
around the ship with piercing screams. There were also albatrosses that
criss-crossed the sky with a slow, infuriating wingflap. Some men killed
time fishing for these birds and reeling them in through the water on
hooks baited with red cloth. Then there were strange sails that appeared
on the horizon. England was at war with France and the *Reliance* had
only ten guns.

   The French were not the only danger. Kemp had to guard against scurvy,
seasickness and drunkenness. In Hobart's Tasmaniana Library I found a tiny
book, *Medical Hints for Emigrants*, that was full of the kind of advice that
Potter might have offered.

   – "To preserve health during voyage: Be on deck as much as possible.
     Be very clean in your person; use your hair-brush and a comb night
     and morning."
   – "Drunkenness: Men who have been drinking hard for two or three
     days together are apt to fall into a miserable kind of illness known
     by the name of delirium tremens."
   – "Snakes: Best advice I can give you about snakes is, do not get bitten."

Scurvy was to be defeated by a diet to prevent the gums from becoming
spongy – raw potatoes in vinegar. The best cure for seasickness was to lie
down, wrap up warmly, "and tempt the stomach with a bit of toasted fat
bacon".

   Kemp, as an ensign, shared responsibility for the convicts on the *Reliance*.
They slept in a reeking hold in 18 inches of space, four to a berth, in
bedding drenched with water that cascaded continually through the
hatches. Kemp took them up on deck for two hours a day to fill their
lungs and to exercise. But the deck was treacherous: the tar melted in the
sun and the swell made walking on it slippery. The *Reliance* was slow and
leaky so that if a man fell overboard she was unable to tack in order to

lower a boat without danger of keeling over. "I never sailed in so compleat a tub," wrote her captain after the voyage.

The ugliest on board were chosen to play the part of Neptune and his family when the *Reliance* crossed the Equator. Their faces painted and glued with false hair, they were hauled on an old cask along the quarterdeck to a tub of water. There Neptune shaved Kemp, who had not previously made the crossing. Kemp was ordered onto a plank. His eyes were bandaged and his chin smeared with a lather compounded of "all sorts of filth" which was scraped off with a foot-long razor. Neptune then hoiked out the plank from under him.

Cooped up for so long in close quarters, Kemp could not hide his character from his fellow passengers – a situation, one traveller wrote, that "may produce contempt, aversion, hatred, jealousy or scandal, to the great annoyance for the time of the parties concerned".

Who were Kemp's passengers? The most conspicuous was the sick Aborigine Bennelong, one of two Eora tribesmen kidnapped from Port Jackson and presented to George III as the "Cannibal King". (The King was not very curious to meet him at the levée at St James's: "Being thin of company it was closed in an hour.") Days later, a reporter observed Bennelong with his young companion Yemmerrawanyee staring through a shop window in St James's Street. "What their ideas were, we will not attempt to guess." During his two years in London, the stout Bennelong – he was named, he claimed, after a large fish – listened to debates in Parliament, and learned to box, to skate and to dress in ruffled lace shirts. He was an accomplished flirt and mimic, but the English weather broke him. His companion died of a lung complaint and lay buried in a Baptist cemetery in Eltham, and now Bennelong was shivering with influenza and homesickness. "I do all I can to keep him up," wrote Hunter, who had forked out £159 for Bennelong's expenses in London, "but still am doubtful of his living."

The man who restored Bennelong to health was the *Reliance*'s surgeon, a six-foot Lincolnshire man named George Bass. Bennelong reciprocated by teaching the young surgeon his language – so that Bass was able to communicate with the Aborigines near Sydney. From remarks that he made about Tasmania's Aborigines, it is possible that Kemp, never willingly excluded from a conversation, also may have gossiped on the poop with Bennelong.

Kaia is a young woman who worked for six months as a sailor on a ship the same size as the *Reliance*. Her journey on the brigantine *Windeward*

Bound celebrated the bicentenary of Matthew Flinders's circumnavigation of Australia. She says: "Alliances are formed. You find the people you connect with and you stick with them through thick and thin."

Kemp had met negroes in South Carolina, and his republican sympathies naturally allied him to an underdog. Crammed together for 206 days, Kemp may have felt drawn to play bridge or cards with Bennelong, or to sit beside him carving buttons from a shark's skeleton. It is not inconceivable that in conversations with the Aborigine he learned details of his tribal customs; of the previous Governor's French cook – whose walk and voice Bennelong could imitate to perfection; of the Englishwoman he once had kissed.

He is also likely to have learned of Bass's project to explore the south-east coast of New South Wales. To this end, Bass had lashed to the *Reliance*'s deck a small rowing boat that he named the *Tom Thumb*. Bass discussed his plans with Governor Hunter and another determined Lincolnshireman, the 21-year-old master's mate Matthew Flinders. Hunter knew the coast well, and confessed his doubts about Cook's chart that showed an unbroken coastline between the mainland and Van Diemen's Land.

Kemp's fellow passengers, in other words, are counted among the most significant figures in Australia's early colonial history. Bennelong would give his name to the point where the Sydney Opera House now stands; Bass to the strait that he discovered with Flinders three years later, and which proved that Van Diemen's Land was an island; and Flinders to the island off Van Diemen's Land that became home to the last Tasmanian Aborigines.*

On the evening of September 7, 1795, Kemp sailed between the Sydney Heads into slack water. For seven months and one week, he had ricocheted between the walls of a cabin with no headspace and poor ventilation, breathing in the stench of sanitary buckets and subsisting on a diet of powdered beef soup and "insipissated juice of wort". It was late spring, the air hot and scented. A crew of bluejackets rowed him ashore. He saw a town settled on spurs of sandstone that were covered with immense grey trees. Flights of strange birds jabbered at him and the sinking sun gave to everything a ghost-like quality. It was a mesmerising setting, though not altogether foreign. One settler called it, in a magnificently dotty description, "a Wapping or St Giles in the beauties of a Richmond". It was also a microcosm of all that was riotous in Georgian society.

---

* Flinders was also the first to give the name Australia to what had previously been New Holland.

The town was seven years old and spread back from the harbour in a shabby crescent. The population of 3,000 lived in tents and bush-timber huts plastered with rammed earth. Rationing was in force and there was not much to eat "except rats". Few people knew about agriculture or how to grow food. In this strange, banished society they took their relief in alcohol. On his way to Barrack Square, Kemp passed men and women slumped beside buckets of pure spirit which they drank from quart mugs until they passed out. Historians unite in describing colonial Sydney as a drunken society from top to bottom. Thanks to Kemp, it soon became even drunker.

In Port Jackson, the 22-year-old Kemp proved adept at swindling his way to the top. It was his good fortune to find himself at large in a society that thrived on the commodities he knew about: tobacco, which the convicts prized above food and sex, and rum (a term used to describe any spirit), which they prized even more. Kemp exploited their craving with an unexpected ace up his sleeve: the good name and credit of "Kemp & Potter".

Born into the trade, Kemp knew the shippers and agents in Mauritius, the Caribbean, India. (By far the most profitable liquor, he told a government commission, was Bengal rum: "There is a particular flavour in it which the lower orders prefer.") His contacts and his education quickly secured him the post of the Corps's acting paymaster. He knew Latin, and his father, he assured everyone in one of his rare honest statements, was "one of the most respectable men in the City of London". First up the ropes when a ship entered harbour, he purchased the cargo using a combination of promissory notes to "Kemp & Potter" and the treasury bills with which he was supposed to pay the regiment. He then sold the cargo to his captive clientele, through his store the "Golden Corner", at grossly inflated prices.

In November 1799, Kemp paid half a crown to lease a plot opposite the George Street barracks. Here, surrounded by paddocks and bush and tree stumps, he erected an antipodean version of 87 Aldgate. But his business methods were not learned from Potter. An Irish rebel, Joseph Holt, described how Kemp threatened to flog those men who came to request their monthly wages. Kemp, instead of paying the soldiers, would point to his shelves of striped shirts, muskets, snuff. "I have very good tobacco, ten shillings the pound, and good tea at 20 shillings the pound . . . "

"Sir, I do not want any of your goods."

"You don't! . . . Begone, you damn mutinous scoundrel, or I'll send you to the guardhouse."

Kemp's entry in the regiment's official history reads: "Renowned bully".

He was not alone in his racketeering. (Beet-faced Judge Atkins, whom Kemp would one day succeed, wrote in a lucid interval: "Almost every article was monopolised by the officers for profit in a most scandalous manner.") But by most accounts, he was the most energetic and unscrupulous of the officer-traders. His special racket was rum. He and a ring of army cronies bought every incoming barrel for as little as seven shillings and six pence a gallon and resold it for up to £8, a mark-up of more than 2,000%. Soon rum was the currency of the colony. For half a pint of "Bengal", a desperate settler gave three bushels of wheat, a convict would chop 100 feet of timber, a woman offered her body. Not even the proud and stubborn Bennelong was immune. Two years after his return home, he had become, in the words of one witness, "so fond of drinking that he lost no opportunity of being intoxicated, and in that state was so savage and violent as to be capable of any mischief". Kemp was chief supplier. His commerce earned the regiment its nickname: the Rum Corps.

In the same month that Kemp opened his emporium, Judith Simpson, a 25-year-old convict woman, became pregnant with his child.

Judith had worked as kitchen maid for a Mrs Silk in Westminster, in one week filching a moth-eaten bombazine gown and a linen apron. Missing these articles, Mrs Silk stormed round to her lodgings and was furious when Judith opened the door dressed in her employer's clothes. Mrs Silk recognised a red wine stain on the apron and some moth holes she herself had sewn up. Charged with the theft of objects worth 16 shillings and sixpence, Judith was transported for seven years to Port Jackson, where in due course she was employed at Kemp's store.

She had 18 months of her sentence left to serve when she gave birth to a daughter. Emily's arrival on June 4, 1800 stirred in Kemp unusual emotions. He put pressure on his friend the Governor who, the same day, granted Emily's mother an absolute pardon.

Five months later, Kemp sailed home on leave with his "concubine" – as Judith is called in the Female Muster – and their daughter. As a family unit they merited a rare berth. On board the *Buffalo*, Judith conceived again.

The return journey took eight months and for one man on board it was too much. On Christmas Eve, Kemp and Judith were warming themselves by a fire, when they heard a loud swearing coming from the main deck. A midshipman stood stripped to his trousers, his face flushed from drinking, his mouth foaming, threatening to destroy anyone who came one inch nearer.

Kemp shut the man in his cabin, but five minutes later he escaped, appearing stark naked on the gangway. As Kemp ran to stop him, he shouted: "Make haste, messmates, I'm going to drown myself" – and plunged overboard. Night had fallen and there was a swell. The *Buffalo* – another leaky, heavy ship – had no alternative but to plough on.

Once in London, Kemp moved to patch things up with his father, but his homecoming was less impressive than he might have hoped. Only one communication survives an eleven-year silence between them, a letter describing how Kemp has decided to marry the woman he decorously calls Miss Crawford. Perhaps ashamed to introduce his pregnant "moll" to Aldgate, he took lodgings at 15 Baker Street, from where he wrote to his father: "I feel my Happiness entirely depending on your acquiescence to accomplish my union with her, having Mr & Mrs Crawford's consent." He was confident that his marriage to Miss Crawford would "add much to my prosperity in New South Wales".

But Kemp's father sent a cousin around with a blunt message: his son was free to do what he liked.* Three weeks later Kemp did exactly that – abandoned Judith in London, dumped his 18-month-old illegitimate daughter Emily on the Potters and scarpered for a second time to the antipodes.

Tasmania – alone of Britain's former penal colonies – has a tendency to sit on its family secrets and be nervous about them. We had been settled in our new house for some weeks before I discovered that Emily's descendants owned a vineyard just ten miles from where I lived.

The farmhouse was at Coombend, in the middle of a small valley. It had once served as the district post office and belonged to a family from what I later learned was Tasmania's landed gentry. ("You've really scored," said Helen. "I lived there ten years and haven't been invited for coffee.") I fell into conversation with the proprietor, an agile man of 60 with blue stubborn eyes. Twenty minutes later I was sitting in his drawing room and examining what he claimed to be Anthony Fenn Kemp's christening mug – a pint-sized silver tankard which his wife had been using as a vase. They were clearly interested in my research, although their curiosity was hedged with anxiety about what discoveries I might have made in this new haul of letters. With a markedly casual air, the winemaker said: "It's very fashionable to be descended from convicts."

---

* The response of Kemp's father may have inspired these lines in William Moncrieff's 1830 play, *Van Diemen's Land*: "Hence from my doors! I do renounce – disclaim you! The husband of a convict shall be no son of mine!"

I picked the flowers out of the tankard – it was more drinking bucket than christening mug and smelled of rancid stems. Stamped onto the side was the crest of a long-necked vulture standing on a wheatsheaf, and the words: *Sic copia campis*.

"'Let there be plenty in the fields'," said the winemaker's wife.

Her husband started to laugh. "The only thing I know, he was a bastard. It's stressful being a philanderer, but they live to a great age." He shot me a look: "The genes, they come down."

A fortnight later, I was buying some sausages in a Hobart delicatessen when a woman who introduced herself as the winemaker's sister darted round the counter and gripped my shoulder: "Welcome to the family." She had red hair and direct eyes and gave me a discount. She glanced at my wife, conspiratorial: "Are you going to call him Fenn?"

We knew it was a boy thanks to a young nurse in Launceston. I had asked in a general way if it was possible to tell a child's sex at 14 weeks, whereupon she pointed at the ultrasound image: "Oh yes." The fact of a son had overwhelmed me. Like his gender, which was already formed, his character was presumably out of my hands. I had started thinking that it was a good thing that there was no technology to tell you whether you were going to get a Potter or a Kemp; whether this child would lean towards the ledger or the rum.

While in London with Judith in 1801, Kemp had his portrait painted in enamel by the court painter to the Duke of York. I learned of a man in the north of Tasmania, a descendant of Kemp, who had a copy.

When I arrived at the weatherboard cottage in Hawley Beach where Paul Edwards lived, he showed me the picture straight away, with few preliminaries: Kemp in the scarlet tunic of a Rum

Anthony Fenn Kemp

Corps Lieutenant. He had the strong profile of a determined sensualist: large brown eyes, powdered white hair, a prominent nose.

"He's a very devious, interesting gentleman with a cruel mouth," Paul said. "My children wonder how I can sit here with him looking at me."

Paul, an amateur genealogist and retired papermaker, was a descendant of Kemp via his marriage to a 16-year-old girl called Elizabeth Riley. Kemp met her in Sydney soon after he sailed back from London; they had known each other, at most, for a month before they were married, but they remained so for 63 years and she gave birth to 16 of his children.

A miniature of Elizabeth showed a pale round face framed by telephone coils of chestnut hair. Kemp introduced her as the daughter of a prosperous London bookseller. Others believed that her father was a forger hanged for defrauding the East India Company. She never inspired much affection in Kemp's two sisters. Susanna describes her as "cool", writing tartly to Amy Potter: "so much childbearing must weaken the constitution".

Paul Edwards said, gruffly, "Fancy siring 16 children on a woman. I reckon that's disgusting."

And Judith? According to Edwards, she ran a series of pubs and boarding houses, was jailed for debt and died in Sydney in 1836 aged 61. I assumed that Kemp never gave her another thought, but then later I came across a poem he had published in a Hobart newspaper 22 years after abandoning her with their second child. Titled "The Contrast", it is a shockingly sentimental tribute to a distraught young woman who had relied on a man's promise:

> *Floated upon her forehead in dark waves*
> *Unbraided and upon her pale thin hand*
> *Her head was bent, as if in pain . . .*
> *There was one whom she loved undoubtingly*
> *. . . She had given*
> *Life's hope to a most fragile bark – to love!*
> *'Twas wrecked – wreck'd by love's treachery.*

IX

AS KEMP EXPANDED, THE POTTER IN ME CONTRACTED. A MONSTER AND A ROGUE he may have been, and yet there was something satisfying about the repeated pattern of his life – one minute facing catastrophe, the next getting off scot free. And the next chapter in Kemp's story turned out to begin in the same way as the last: with him striking out at a father figure.

On his return to Sydney, Kemp found himself at loggerheads with the new Governor. Philip King was a pious, gout-afflicted anti-Republican, with a mission to tidy up Kemp's cartel of army racketeers who controlled the colony. He cut both the price and consumption of spirits and when the supply ship *Atlas* sailed into port with a cargo of rum, he refused permission to unload. Kemp hated King "abominably". While the *Atlas* lay uselessly at anchor, he began to plot against him.

In June 1802, a French corvette appeared off the Heads with only four men visible on deck. British "tars" who climbed aboard the *Géographe* found a crew sick with scurvy; even the animals were affected. The ship was part of a French scientific force which had been mapping Van Diemen's Land during a lull in the Napoleonic wars, and in the days ahead it alarmed King to discover that the affable French commander, Nicolas Baudin, had baptised the coast after members of his expedition. On the south tip of Maria Island at the far end of our bay, Cape Péron commemorated a one-eyed zoologist who used a contraption known as Régnier's Dynamometer to measure the handclasp of Tasmanian Aborigines (he concluded they had a weak one); while the Freycinet Peninsula opposite our home was named after Baudin's cartographer.

At the time relations between Britain and France were delicate. The thought of Lieutenant Freycinet unrolling charts and possibly marking regions of Australia "Terre Napoléon" unsurprisingly panicked King. Nonetheless, he gave the sailors safe passage ashore to treat their blackened gums. And he allowed them to buy 800 gallons of rum from the *Atlas* – on Baudin's strict word that the spirits would be consumed on his ship.

King's kindness outraged Kemp. Smarting over the loss of his potential profits, he fanned a rumour that Freycinet and one other officer had secretly rowed the rum ashore and sold it. King summoned the accused in order to investigate this "inflaming report". They swore that the charge was false. French officers demanded a duel. Baudin pointed his finger at the man responsible – "Monsieur Kemp" – and added that he had never experienced such dishonesty from an English officer.

The crisis was eventually averted – anticlimactically – after Kemp sent a written apology to both men. But the strangest part of the affair was the identity of the second French officer, Jacques St Cricq. Kemp had accused a fellow mason.

Freemasonry is a guarantee of clannishness, but in 1802 it had seditious connotations as well. It was particularly strong among French revolutionaries. The latest treaty between Britain and the French Republic was not expected to last and many of Baudin's crewmen were enthusiastic to see the British colony in Republican hands. On the voyage out, Baudin had told his men that their expedition had "a political purpose . . . a more thoroughly utilitarian aim than the mere gathering of objects of curiosity or passing fancy", and the one-eyed Péron would later write a report entitled: "The conquest of New Holland [Australia] as indispensable for our political relations".

On the evening of September 17, 1802 – a fortnight before he made his apology – Kemp boarded Baudin's sister ship the *Naturaliste* to participate in what was the first Masonic meeting in Australia. His certificate, written in French on almost transparent paper, elevated "le chère frère AFK" to the position of Master Mason and was signed J. St Cricq.

What was going on? Was Kemp preparing the spadework for an insurrection of his own? One contemporary said of Kemp: "He is anybody's body." Or did his Masonic loyalty prove as flimsy as the certificate once his monopoly was threatened?

At any rate, the French were so outraged by his behaviour that an artist on the *Géographe* drew a caricature of Kemp that ridiculed his courage, his boastfulness and the rampaging sexual appetite of his young wife. Kemp was shown with a padlock on his sword, a pair of stag's horns sprouting from his head and two bubbles containing remarks that he had made about the size of his house. The caricature is lost, but it was passed around town. Kemp saw it – and said nothing. But it gave him an idea.

In November, Baudin's expedition left port. No one knew his destination, but that did not prevent Kemp from starting another rumour just hours after the topsails vanished over the horizon. He implied that French officers had been overheard speaking of their intention to establish a settlement on Van Diemen's Land. Indeed, he had heard that one of them had even marked the proposed site on a map. Kemp's understanding was shared by a young Danish sailor on the *Lady Nelson*, an armed brigantine which had recently surveyed Bass Strait. A decade later, Jorgen Jorgenson claimed in a letter to the Colonial Office that Baudin had sailed "under a pretence of making Discoveries, but in reality to espy the Situation of the English Colonies in New South Wales".

Governor King had learned to trust the wayward, sympathetic Baudin. But what if the Frenchman's ambition extended beyond measuring handclasps? Van Diemen's Land offered vital access to southern waters, and yet it dawned on the puzzled administrator that the island had not been claimed by anyone. Alarmed by the spectre of a hostile French colony, and without waiting for London's reaction, King seized the initiative. He fitted out a schooner with three marines and launched them after Baudin "to make the French commander acquainted with my intention of settling Van Diemen's Land". His party found the French scientists peacefully netting insects on an island in Bass Strait. The marines hastily tied a Union Jack to a tree, fired a volley over the tents and gave three aggressive hurrahs. Insulted once again, Baudin complained to Governor King about this "childish ceremony". (The flag, he noted acidly, was hoisted upside down and resembled a dish-rag hung out to dry, and he had had to lend the English dry gunpowder to make their salute.) He assured King he had no intention of claiming a territory that had in any case been discovered in 1642 by a Dutchman and was, in his opinion, already inhabited by Aborigines. Once again he identified the culprit. "The story you have heard, of which I suspect Mr Kemp, captain in the NSW Corps, to be the author, is without foundation."

By now, King's illness had advanced into his chest, and he had been forced to take to his bed. But Kemp's vendetta continued. Somehow a tightly rolled piece of paper found its way to the bed-bound Governor. On it were "seditious drawings" of King and two short poems: "Extempore Allegro", a brisk assault on the Governor's character ("for infamous acts from my birth I'd an itch"), and "Epitaph", which cheerfully anticipated his demise ("A wretch to whom all pity is bereft").

This anonymous doggerel enraged King. He arrested Kemp – who had been appointed the Corps's paymaster – and prosecuted him. The trial was a farce. King, a naval man, had to draw the members of the court martial from Kemp's army cronies such as the Rum Corps commander, Lieutenant Colonel "Phlegmatic" Paterson, an inebriate botanist with failing eyesight who had been witness at Kemp's marriage; and Major Johnston, Paterson's no less alcoholic second-in-command, who had been the first officer to step ashore at Port Jackson. This was a tribunal that protected its interests.

On February 25, 1803, the trial was suspended and Kemp acquitted. A startling dispatch from the Colonial Office advised King to forget the whole business and "consign to oblivion" all that had passed. He was urged to proceed with his plan to colonise the virgin territory of Van Diemen's Land.

The idea of founding a colony had been pretty vague until Kemp started circulating rumours about the French. King now blundered in to fill the empty vortex. In August 1803, he chartered two ships – the *Lady Nelson* and the *Albion*, captained by the whaler Ebor Bunker – to unload a party on the Derwent estuary. The 49 passengers included a surgeon, a store-keeper, 21 male and three female convicts, seven free settlers, and a lance corporal and seven privates from the New South Wales Corps. A few months later, King assembled a second and larger force to take control of Bass Strait. He asked Colonel Paterson to lead it. Paterson, as commander-in-chief of the New South Wales Corps, wanted to be in full charge of his own area and refused to answer to a junior officer in the settlement on the Derwent. King agreed to divide the island in two, with Paterson in charge of the northern half. In London, knowledge of the island's geography was so hazy that Paterson was given the go-ahead to establish a settlement at Port Dalrymple with its "advantageous position . . . upon the Southern Coast of Van Diemen's Land". King had to point out that Port Dalrymple lay on the north coast.

In October 1804, King left his sick bed to wave off Colonel Paterson on board the *Buffalo*, with Kemp as second-in-command. The four vessels carried 181 soldiers, convicts and settlers, including Kemp's brother-in-law Alexander Riley, who was to act as storekeeper. The Governor's relief at seeing the back of Kemp – his "concealed assassin" – must have cheered him at least a little; at any rate, he provided an eleven-gun salute for the expedition's departure.

At 7 a.m. on Sunday, October 14, the *Buffalo* edged away from Government Wharf to the tune of "Rule, Britannia!" and the hearty cheers of a "delirious" population – and sailed smack into a tempest.

X

ON A CLOUDLESS MORNING I DROVE TO GEORGE TOWN AND PARKED ABOVE THE beach where Kemp eventually landed. The river mouth was sprinkled with caravan parks and bungalows sporting names like "Ups-n-downs", but the shoreline was pristine, the sand empty and the sea an outlandish ultramarine.

Emerging from the tempest, Kemp's ship had slammed into an unexpected sandbank off Lagoon Beach. I doubted the future "Father of Tasmania" was happy to be on board. He would have been separated from his grog store. He would not have shared my love of the sea: for him it would have been something for convicts to wash in. He would have avoided the sun so as to preserve his complexion and distinguish himself from the Aborigines who watched the bungled landing of the *Buffalo* in puzzled silence.

Kemp and the crew hurried to unload the stores on the east shore of the river. The wind blew in heavy squalls and was still blowing four days later when Colonel Paterson took formal possession of the colony and swore in Kemp and Riley as its magistrates.

Riley owed his presence on the beach to a conviction that this latitude was the most productive possible for plants and fruit, with a climate that shed "fruitfulness on the earth and happiness on mankind in general". He believed that the further away people were from this latitude, the less happy they were. Impatient to test his theory – which, he assured Kemp, "never fails" – he had come out from England with hopes of making a fortune from growing silk, opium, hemp and rhubarb.

A quick walk along the east shore revealed brackish water and stony soil. Paterson left Kemp to oversee the erection of a church and jail, and crossed the Tamar River. He decided to establish a permanent residence on the edge of a shallow rivulet. Riley's optimism had infected him. "It is my opinion," he wrote in his diary, "that the Country will turn out to be Superior to any yet discovered."

The settlement of York Town is recollected today by a bronze map in a deserted picnic spot beside a garden supplier. The pyramids of wood-chips and "chook-poo" are, at first glance, all that remain of the first permanent settlement in the north.

I was poring over the map when a man drove past and parked in front of a shack. He tracked me with a sheepish expression as I walked towards him, and looked even more apprehensive when I explained that a relative of mine had founded a town that was possibly buried under his property. Had he, I asked, come upon any evidence of the settlement?

He nodded. Only ten weeks ago he was clearing the bush out the back when his spade struck something. Now, he called over to his son, who had come onto the porch. "Michael, remember those convict bricks?"

"Yeah."

"Can you show them to him?"

Michael led me through the scrappy back yard – a dog in a cage watched on hind legs – and into the bracken and thistles. He darted his glance here and there, unable to find what he was looking for, and then I saw a clearing. In the clearing, a floor of pale red bricks.

He let me take one. "We hit those when we were pulling up scrub and then we broomed it."

I could see the ironstone in the brick. The iron ore that Paterson dug from here in December 1804 was the first mineral deposit found in Tasmania. "If I had carts," he wrote, "I could load in time the whole Navy of Great Britain."

Kemp's cottage, possibly one of two prefabricated wooden houses brought out in the *Lady Nelson*, was on a high piece of land among the black wattle and gums. It looked down on the quarters housing 42 convicts and a flat area of five acres, known inaccurately on the bronze map as "Major Kemp's garden". Kemp was a captain and the original garden was, in fact, Paterson's creation.

His horizons reduced by ophthalmia, Paterson concentrated on his plants and apple orchard and soon was able to treat Kemp to a corned beef dinner served with eight different vegetables and an impressive cucumber. But his optimism had started to ebb.

In York Town, Kemp watched his commander go steadily barmy. The site had been a disastrous choice. The closest a ship could anchor was six miles away. After rain, the place became "a complete swamp". The climate was windy and the temperature colder than in Sydney. As winter set in the animals started to die. Soon half of the settlement's 622 Bengal cattle had perished and Kemp and Riley were having to hoist the surviving animals into slings and daily massage their legs. And there was trouble in the garden. Nettles had grown with a sting so violent that it killed four dogs and gave several officers a terrible fever. In February, Kemp discovered that a small white insect, "the most destructive in the world of its size", had devoured his coat and hat and was advancing through the vegetables. Paterson surrounded his garden with soapsuds in a forlorn attempt at defence, but his potatoes and French beans were eaten anyway, by rats. Then one morning, Paterson woke to find that unidentified predators had devoured his ducks and chickens: only their feathers were left.

By June, the community was on half rations. Desperate and homesick, the colonists were hanging on by their fingernails when they received a further blow – the pirating of a supply ship by a convict crew. Bringing much-needed pork and flour, the brig *Venus* was also carrying letters from Kemp's brother-in-law, which the captain had stored in a small deal box. Not even Kemp could have choreographed the fate of William Potter's correspondence. In his embarrassed deposition, the captain described how, just before his ship was seized, he saw an object hurtle overboard: the box of papers belonging to Kemp, thrown into the sea by a drunken female convict ("very corpulent with full face, thick lips and light hair") who would help navigate the ship to New Zealand, where she took up with a Maori chieftain.

In August, a sick and fatigued Paterson sailed for Sydney. He had left behind Kemp as acting Lieutenant Governor and enough rations to last five months. Unable to withstand another "Breeze of Wind", Paterson reported to the new Governor that he had put his government "in tranquillity with Captain Kemp".

Years later, as a bankrupt in London, Kemp argued in a petition to the government to restore his land grant that he had spared neither trouble nor expense "converting a howling wilderness into a cultivated plain". But he was not a natural leader and under his command the settlement almost starved to death. His barn burned down and floods destroyed the crops that the injured Riley had managed to grow in spite of his "painful circumstances" (he had been speared in the loins by Aborigines). The settlers survived on seaweed and pigs which they had fed on whale scraps and that tasted of lamp oil. In

February, Kemp sent five men in the longboat to row and sail 600 miles to seek help on the Australian mainland. They were never heard from again.

Kemp's most important point in his petition was that he had been responsible for the first crossing of the island by a European. In the same month as he dispatched the longboat, he ordered Lieutenant Laycock, the tallest man in the Rum Corps, to walk to the settlement in Hobart and seek help. Laycock and four men, relying only on a compass, trekked for nine days until they reached the Derwent. They walked through plains of silver tussock and kangaroo grass and pines 100 feet high, and discovered a pair of lakes that Laycock named "Kemp's Lakes" (now Lakes Sorell and Crescent). But having penetrated the interior, Laycock found that the southern settlers were starving too. Stricken with scurvy, catarrh and diarrhoea, they told him: "We can afford no relief."

In April, Paterson sailed back up the Tamar to a settlement in a state of anarchy. He had been away two months longer than anticipated. Stepping ashore, he was greeted by naked, shoeless men who needed "every species of provision". Paterson sought out Kemp who admitted that in order to ward off famine and mutiny he had been obliged to distribute guns to the convicts to hunt kangaroo, and at least ten of these prisoners had stayed out in the bush, harassing the settlers. Paterson wrote prophetically: "It is much to be dreaded that they will become a desperate and dangerous banditti." Nor had Kemp succeeded in cultivating crops. Rather, he seemed to have added to his fortune by selling kangaroo flesh to the government store at three times the official rate. In charge for seven months and eleven days, he told Paterson that he now wanted to leave. Complaining of "extreme ill health", he requested permission to take his wife and nine-month-old son George to Sydney. The placid Paterson agreed, but warned Kemp that the new Governor, William Bligh, was a different kind of man from the Governor who had preceded him.

This was Bligh of the *Bounty*, the man who 17 years earlier had been set adrift in a boat by Mr Christian and his fellow mutineers. Now he had arrived in Sydney with the express intention of stamping out the rum trade. He was not favourably disposed towards Kemp's return – he considered Rum Corps officers to be "tremendous buggers" – and was suspicious of his reasons. As it turned out, he had excellent cause. On a scorching evening five months later, on what is now ironically Australia Day, the Rum Corps mutinied and it no longer surprised me to discover who marched up the drive at their head, sword drawn, into Government House.

I wondered briefly whether this was Kemp finally exercising his republican ardour; but it transpired – of course – that his rebellion had been prompted by liquor and corruption. Major Johnston, acting Rum Corps Commander in Paterson's absence, conceived a desire to unseat Bligh, a plan that was largely formulated when Johnston and Kemp were drunk. "What do you think he told me?" Kemp railed. "Yes! Told the oldest merchant in the colony – *that he came here to protect the poor.* That is not the Governor WE want!!!" And so it was that the mutineers barged into the Governor's residence around supper time and after a couple of hours stumbling around the house, frightening Bligh's recently widowed daughter and an Irish parson who was there to comfort her, discovered Bligh hiding in a room upstairs. One of Kemp's soldiers noticed a bedcover twitching, prodded it with his musket, and struck a boot. There was the Governor, covered in spiderwebs and with his shirt hanging out.

By 8.30 p.m. the mutiny was successful, the only casualty being Kemp's friend Laycock, who fell through a manhole, landing on his "principal joint". As a reward for his part in unseating Bligh, Johnston gave Kemp 24 cows, 4,000 acres of land, and appointed him Judge Advocate. A lampoon described him as "a grinning tobacco boy" whose prolific learning was praised to the skies. For the next seven months he ruled as the supreme legal officer in an area the size of Western Europe, a position of extraordinary power. For seven months there was no court of appeal after Kemp – except to God. With tremendous relish, he transported former adversaries like William Gore, chief of the constabulary, to seven years on the Coal River. "Take him away, take him off; take him away, take him away."

Kemp's duties also expanded to performing all the marriages in the colony. I discovered from a copy of the *Tasmanian Times* dated November 4, 1868, a terrible story. One morning, with eleven services to conduct, through a combination of impatience and drink he married the wrong couples. "The Parson–Captain, when subsequently applied to, bade them 'settle it amongst them, for he could interfere no further!'"

XI

ONE DAY IN 1810 THERE WAS A KNOCK AT POTTER'S DOOR IN ALDGATE: KEMP
had come home from New South Wales to give evidence at Major
Johnston's court martial. Bligh had singled out Kemp as the person he
particularly wished to see prosecuted for the mutiny, but – of course –
Kemp managed to avoid punishment. Commended for his candour in the
witness box, he forfeited only his 4,000 acres and his 24 cows, rather than
his freedom.*

Nevertheless, his return home was hardly triumphant. A letter from his
sister Susanna calls him "a strange man", often silent, very proud – and a
bankrupt, just as he had left England 20 years before. From the letters I
gathered that he was briefly a shipping agent, a pawnbroker, and a wine-
merchant, but "lost much on Bordeaux wine speculation". At one point
he lost a bet of £150 against the capture or death of Napoleon.

By 1815, he had exhausted his options. The world regarded him, he
complained, as "an uncertificated bankrupt, alias an outlaw". There was
nowhere to go but back to the antipodes. He prepared to flee the country
for a third time. Pursued by "clamorous" creditors, he went cap in hand to
see Potter in the house where he grew up and, with staggering optimism,

---

* In an unlikley story passed on by his daughter, Kemp instantly announced to his wife:
"My dear, the Colonel is sending in his papers and I am buying his commission."

"Very well, my dear, if you want to be Colonel of the Regiment do so, but you will
have to choose between the regiment and me. Much as I love you, I will not face three
months more of seasickness on the way home for any man on earth."

"Very well, dear, then I will give up the regiment."

requested his biggest loan to date: an amount equivalent to the entire annual turnover of "Kemp & Potter".

Kemp asked Potter to guarantee two shiploads of goods worth "upwards of five thousand pounds". He assured Potter that he would be able to sell the goods at considerable profit in Van Diemen's Land, thanks to the exceptional contacts of his other brother-in-law, Alexander Riley, who had recently built Sydney's new hospital and made £30,000 from the contract ("some say Fifty, but he is a *close man* and no person could tell exactly how much"). A similar "most splendid fortune", he promised Potter, would be realised by "Kemp & Potter" from the cargoes of tobacco, brandy and seedlings. Kemp required the money only for nine months and would pay full interest.

Unbelievably, Potter agreed.

But Kemp did not stop there. Since 1801, the Potters had looked after his illegitimate daughter Emily. Before he boarded the *Dawson*, Kemp also unloaded on them his legitimate children George and Elizabeth.

The first sign of trouble came in a letter dated several months later from Paraiba (now João Pessoa) in Brazil. Kemp's ship was detained after losing her anchor. Her captain "appears to me to be a little deranged". And Kemp has run out of money. "I have been under the necessity of drawing on you for sixty pounds."

Potter hears nothing else for the next two years. He wrote letter after letter appealing to "our agreement with your good self", but they remained unanswered. By now Kemp's father had died and Potter was having to steer the firm from the rocks on which Kemp's negligence threatened to pitch it. At Aldgate, his desk piled up with demands for Kemp's £5,000 (more than £400,000 today). Kemp's sisters wrung their hands uselessly. Susanna wrote to Amy: "It's complete swindling to fly one's country for speculation."

At last, in August 1817, a letter arrived from Hobart. It begins breezily: "I arrived here about six weeks ago and have commenced my mercantile pursuits." But due to "the severe trials" lately experienced, combined with "unprecedented mercantile circumstance", Kemp fears he will not be able to make his remittances "so punctual as I would wish". He details his sales to date.

Tobacco: "I am sorry to say there is no market for that now" – although he did sell some sacks of Prince's Mixture in Cape Town ("You was either rob'd or cheated," Potter replies).

Brandy: "The market is completely glutted with spirits and all other goods – such that to force sales would be ruinous."

The seedlings: "They are unsaleable and good for nothing."

But Kemp was encouraging. "What is possible for man to do shall be done. You may rely on it, there is no cause for alarm."

The family's distress is summarised in one of Susanna's letters: "There are characters in life who care very little for each other, self-consideration their first and justice their last." Complaining about his "false excuses", she united with the Potters in wishing never to see her brother again.

XII

KEMP WAS ONLY TOO DELIGHTED TO BE SEPARATED FROM ALDGATE "BY THE circumference of the globe". On January 12, 1816, he was rowed ashore in Hobart. The town consisted of 1,000 people living in wattle and daub huts, and resembled more a campsite than a capital. That night, he dined in Government House (actually a barn) as a guest of the volatile Lieutenant Governor, Thomas Davey. He brought the "great news" of Napoleon's defeat at Waterloo and informed Davey of his "valuable cargo" and of his wish to become a free settler. He was now 43.

Davey, who liked to entertain in shirtsleeves, was a jovial incompetent known as "Mad Tom". He had the habit of screwing up his forehead if anyone put him on the spot, and yelling out "Pondicherry!" An ex-Marine who received his letter of appointment in a debtor's prison, he was also the most alcoholic of Kemp's superiors.

Davey's favourite tipple was "Blow my skull", a cocktail he served in half-pint glasses consisting of rum, brandy, gin, port, Madeira, sherry and claret.

He and Kemp had plenty to discuss over dinner.

Kemp's first discovery was that the island was no longer divided in two. The reason was an improbable episode involving Major George Alexander Gordon, the third northern commandant at Port Dalrymple, as the area around York Town was known. Kemp was fascinated to learn the details: Gordon, besides being his successor at Port Dalrymple, was "an old school friend of mine" and a fellow regular at the Old Slaughterer's Coffee House in London. Furthermore, Kemp recently had used Gordon's name as a reference in his appeal to have his confiscated land grants returned. When Davey explained that Gordon had been relieved of his duties after suffering sunstroke, Kemp understood why the authorities in London had remained unimpressed.

Sunstroke was not all that unusual – one of Matthew Flinders's sailors died of it "in a state of frenzy" – but its effects on two men at Port Dalrymple in February 1812 were possibly exceptional. In the week that Gordon was carried off to recover in the barracks in George Street, an Irish entrepreneur, Jonathan Burke McHugo, was passing through Bass Strait from Calcutta to Sydney where he hoped to sell a cargo of rum, tea and trousers. Davey told Kemp that McHugo's illness demented him into believing that he was a member of the British Royal Family.

It was a story that Kemp would remember as an old man in his wheel-chair. The harbourmaster who boarded the 100-ton brig *Active* was led into the presence of a man seated on a sumptuous settee who introduced himself as General Count McHugo. He was, he said, travelling under cover on behalf of the Government of India. He had heard that the population of Port Dalrymple were living in a deplorable state, and had come to inves-tigate any grievances and to punish those responsible. On landing, General McHugo went to meet the sick Gordon and revealed to the commandant that McHugo was an assumed name. McHugo told Gordon what he later wrote to the Colonial Office: "Every intelligent man who knows me must be aware that although the Son of an Irish snuff and Tobacco seller, I am the lineal descendant of Earl Bothwell and Mary Stuart, Queen of Scotland . . . Consequently the rightful Heir to the Crown of England." In his fever, Gordon believed this nonsense and surrendered his command. He explained that he fully thought that McHugo was "one of the Royal Family Incognito and possessed of Authority at pleasure to supersede All Governors".

The mad Irishman sentenced Gordon to hang. Gordon was only saved by the reappearance of a subaltern on leave in the highlands, who arrested McHugo and sent him under guard to Sydney, where, examined by the Governor's doctor, he was pronounced to be in "a state of Outrageous Insanity". Davey's latest information was that he had discharged himself from an asylum in Calcutta and was now in London seeking compensa-tion from "those time serving satellites of that unfeeling illustrious usurper the Prince of Wales".

Meanwhile, Gordon had been recalled and the whole island was now under Davey's precarious control in Hobart.

Dinner wore on and the neurotic Davey explained his difficulties.

He was engaged in a desperate struggle with bushrangers, convicts who remained out in the bush as kangaroo hunters and terrorised the island – to the extent that Davey had had to declare martial law, ordering a curfew after 8 p.m. and putting a price on their heads. Kemp was familiar with the problem. The bushrangers were, after all, a direct legacy of his administration eight years before.

The bushranger who posed the biggest threat was Michael Howe, a sailor from Yorkshire transported to Van Diemen's Land for highway robbery. In 1813, Howe absconded and set himself up as a counter authority to Davey, styling himself the Governor of the Rangers and warning Davey that any soldiers he sent after him "he would hang them up by the heels to a tree, let out their entrails, and leave them hanging as he would a kangaroo". Howe saw himself as a "shepherd" in the tradition of Robin Hood, but a line from a contemporary play described him better: "He carries off bullocks as if they were kids, and values life as little as a turnip."

One midnight on the Coal River, where Davey owned a property, Howe had kicked awake a detachment of soldiers with the words: "Lay still, you buggers." He stole their muskets and said that he wished Davey had been there because he would have sent some buckshot "through his old paunch". Armed with these muskets and with their faces blackened with charcoal and water, Howe's group then burst into a house in New Norfolk, terrifying the owner's wife, Mrs McCarthy, who scuttled under the table after one of them swore that they had not come to hurt anyone "except that damned whore Mrs M and she they would f—". She was coaxed out of her hiding place to make tea.

The band answered to a thickset, black-bearded man dressed in kangaroo skins with a cap pulled tight over his eyes whom they called "Captain". This was Howe. He had an Aboriginal girl with him, "Black Mary", and spoke of escaping to India.

Howe later returned to the same farm and this time soldiers from the 46th Regiment were waiting. They opened fire in the dark, fatally injuring one of Howe's men who staggered towards him crying "Take my watch!" – a prearranged code for Howe to cut off his head so that no one would claim the reward. (Howe carried the head around for a time in a bloodied handkerchief, the decapitation taking place, according to one account, "before life was extinct". It was found in the bush two years later.)

Because of Howe, the island was now in a "Most Wretched State of Disorganisation, Anarchy and Confusion". A letter written to Davey in what appeared to be blood claimed that Howe had an informer in Davey's camp who told him everything. Howe taunted that he "could set the whole country on fire with one stick", and Davey's fear was that convicts could be tempted to join the bushrangers and create a challenge to his rule, forcing the settlers to give in.

It could not have been a more opportune time for Kemp to arrive in Hobart. Anxious to encourage the right sort of settler who would bring security to the interior and make it "more safe and commodious for travellers", Davey greeted the earlier northern commandant with open arms. Tucked inside a letter to Potter, I find a faded copy of the grant which gives the bankrupt Kemp 800 acres and four convict workers and appoints him a magistrate.

Kemp acted swiftly to exercise the authority that, as a bankrupt, he had fraudulently received. He agreed with Davey: lenity towards villains like Howe was "ill-applied", and he urged the Lieutenant Governor to increase the bounty on their heads. A sum of 520 guineas was raised from "prominent citizens", but this only provoked the bushrangers to further attacks. In July, Davey was alarmed enough to show Kemp another letter, written on a page torn from a stock-book and signed by the "Lieutenant Governor of the Woods", warning that if Davey's "Blood Hunters" came into his territory, Howe would force "meatballs" down their throats. To make his point, Howe led two raids on Davey's farm on the Coal River. In the first he "borrowed" the Lieutenant Governor's dictionary, as well as filling a knapsack with wine, sugar and green tea (he was sick, he said, of drinking black tea); in the second, Davey's convict servants were ordered to join in a Yuletide drink "or they would be shot for Christmas". These threats were not idle: Howe once shot a man for speaking Irish.

In the summer of 1817 there was a breakthrough when soldiers disguised in civilian clothing surprised Howe and Black Mary in the bush north of Kemp's grant. Howe ran off and Mary tried to keep up, but fell back – rumour had it she was pregnant. When Howe turned round, he saw the soldiers closing in and fired, wounding Mary in the arm. He afterwards claimed to Kemp that he was aiming at her pursuers. Mary, however, was persuaded that Howe had tried to kill her, and agreed to help the soldiers track down her lover. A month later, Howe gave himself up and for the next few days Kemp interrogated him.

Howe's story, published in 1818 in a limited edition of 100 copies, is considered the first work of literature to be printed in Australia. Sadly, records of Kemp's interrogation of Howe and Black Mary were lost when Davey sent his papers to England. All I could learn was that Howe's depositions were "voluminous and tedious". Also lost was the "dream journal" – a small notebook with a crude wrapping of kangaroo hide that was discovered in Howe's knapsack, and which Kemp may have read. The entries were written in kangaroo and possum blood with the assistance of Davey's dictionary, and recorded Howe's nightmares: of being murdered by Aborigines, of meeting the man whose head he had cut off, of his sister in England. The diary also contained lists of flowers, seeds and plants, copied down from a gardening book he had stolen. They persuaded the playwright William Moncrieff that Howe had intended to turn his mountain retreat into a rustic Yorkshire garden. "Aye, I like flowers," dreams an unlikely Howe in Moncrieff's *Van Diemen's Land*. "I'll set some round our cave . . . give me those roses, those violets too, they smell so sweet and fresh; they mind me of my home, when our cottage had a jessamine."

Howe's most startling revelations concerned Kemp's fellow magistrate, the Reverend Robert Knopwood, a conspicuous figure who rode about town on a white horse. Howe insinuated that the clergyman, one of the first settlers in Hobart, had been a prominent member of his gang, and that Knopwood had often received Howe at his house in Hobart – and had even tried to seduce the wife of one of Howe's confederates.

The allegations were so serious that Davey ordered Kemp to investigate. Kemp summarised his ruling principle of justice as "decide first and try afterwards". He recognised a kindred spirit in the priest, a zealous flogger and a man fond of drink and swearing, who had squandered his £90,000 inheritance at the gambling table. Unable to reach any other verdict owing to the fact that vital papers relating to the case had mysteriously disappeared, Kemp concluded that Howe's allegations were "wholly unfounded". Knopwood, on his part, understood that he owed Kemp a favour.

In the same week, Kemp had the "high satisfaction" of announcing "the nearly total destruction" of the bushrangers – convincing evidence that "the displeasure of a Supreme Being" had been at work, and an outcome, he added, that afforded "a striking instance of retributive justice".

XIII

HOBART TOWN, WHERE KEMP DECIDED TO MAKE HIS HOME, WAS THEN THE
southernmost settlement in the world and yet it resembled in the opinion
of practically every early visitor "a country village in England". In the after-
math of the decades-long French wars there were plenty of English looking
to emigrate and to take advantage of the government's offer of free land.
Would-be settlers could apply for land in proportion to their "means to
bring the same into cultivation". A free man who brought with him £500
received a grant of 640 acres. Settlers – many of them, like Kemp, claiming
fictitious capital – soon outnumbered bushrangers. When Kemp had left
Port Dalrymple in 1807, the population of Europeans on the island was
3,240. The figure had doubled by the time of his return eight years later.

Within 18 months of Kemp's arrival, the town had grown one mile
long and half a mile wide with a population of 1,200. It contained 300
houses, most of them single-storeyed and situated at some distance apart.
The land between them was planted with briar hedges, rose bushes, gera-
niums and vines. Hobart's vegetables were "remarkably fine", observed
Lieutenant Jeffreys, "comprising all those reared in an English kitchen
garden". The air was fragrant with local wattle and eucalyptus, and a stream
of fresh water ran down through the centre, right past Kemp's red brick
cottage on Collins Street. For all the tranquil village life veneer, Kemp's
wife and four youngest children looked out over their garden fence at a
fairly violent frontier society. The policemen went about barefoot and
public hangings took place in full view of the wharf – on one occasion
in a single morning 10 men were executed. The gibbeted bodies, according

to the *Hobart Town Gazette*, "became Objects of Disgust especially to the Female sex", and in June 1816 the place of execution was moved two miles away to Queenborough (now the site of the Wrest Point Casino in Sandy Bay).

Kemp's grant lay 30 miles north of Hobart. Despite his bravado, bushrangers made it "too dangerous" for him to inhabit his property, and so he decided to use Potter's wealth to create, in effect, a parody of Potter's world. He mortgaged the land against a building in Macquarie Street where, three months after stepping ashore, he opened a ramshackle store in collaboration with a former convict transported for stealing an eyeglass. In a letter he assured Potter: "I have given a person a share in the concern who is a complete man of business." In July 1817, the *Gazette* carried adverts for Potter's hogsheads of tobacco, Potter's brandy, Potter's Souchong teas – "to be sold on a liberal Credit". Potter never saw a penny.

Kemp's store in Macquarie Street was not quite Aldgate but he endeavoured to make it so. By 1820, Kemp controlled 80% of the spirits landed in Hobart and, according to one pained official, "nearly all the Rum in the colony". There was an unflagging appetite for his merchandise. Van Diemen's Land had been linked with alcohol from the moment the First Fleet came in sight of its south coast: "As soon as we saw the land we drank each 2 bumpers of claret," wrote a sailor on January 7, 1788. The first European to be buried near our future home at Swansea was Thomas Hooley, a convict servant who drank the best part of a gallon of rum and then fell to the ground quite dead, having suffered, according to the inquest, "a visitation of God". A tradition of unusually heavy drinking entrenched itself under Lieutenant Governor Davey. "He did not mind who the Devil governed," a contemporary said, "so long as he got his Bottle & Glass." Davey's formidable consumption left a bequest. It was the "greatest regret" of Lieutenant Governor George Arthur that duty on Kemp's spirits accounted for more than half the state's income, and remained the main source of revenue until well into the nineteenth century. "The place is quite unsuited to sober people," believed Edward Braddon, a settler from India. Hobart was a town of pubs. Minutes after coming ashore in 1847, the evolutionist Thomas Huxley found himself "stuck" at the Ship Inn, "imbibing considerable quantities of toddy". Perhaps unsurprisingly, he married the daughter of a local brewer.*

* In Tasmania, it remains a badge of honour to drink like a fish. Stocky batsman David Boon is still believed to hold the record for consuming 52 cans of beer on a flight to London in 1989.

As he had in Sydney, Kemp kept the colony supplied with: "Port wine in pipes", "Jamaica rum in puncheons", "cognac brandy in hogsheads", "French liqueurs in cases", "sweet wine in quartercasks". He guarded his monopoly with a mixture of greed and flammability. He overcharged customers and lent money at 42% interest. He boarded ships without permission, saying he would do so "when and where he pleased". He demanded that the Governor put an immediate end to the very practice that he himself pioneered in Sydney – paying for labour with spirits. The only magistrate to own a pub, he invoked the law to protect his interests. When a rival merchant accused him of acting "like a peddlar", he sent him to prison.

Truculent, intolerant, inconsistent, Kemp exemplified the transition from rollicking empire-founding to the humbug of empire-ruling. In August 1817, sitting as magistrate, he rounded on his creditors with the same spleen that he had gone after bushrangers. While in Aldgate, Potter wrote yet another despairing letter (referring his brother-in-law "to my letters No 1, 2 & 3"), Kemp placed announcements in the *Hobart Town Gazette* warning he would sue his debtors unless they settled instantly. Astonishingly, Kemp brought one action to recover twelve crowns. He would not have noticed the symmetry: it was the same sum for which he had fled England as an 18-year-old.

His father had died while Kemp was sailing to Hobart, but Kemp's antagonism to anyone who reminded him of his upright parent never diminished. He treated all in authority with "Wicked and Foul abuse", beginning with Davey who had to evict him from Government House because of his "extreme rudeness". When the next Governor rode past him in the street, Kemp refused to take off his hat and laughed at him. His attitude to successive Governors was that they were all "equally bad".

On December 4, 1819, Potter wrote his last letter to Kemp. "In every letter I have requested to know if you receiv'd a Copy of your Father's will, mourning ring, etc etc . . . to these repeated questions I have not as yet got an answer."

He directed his son up a ladder to remove all evidence of Kemp. Up went: "William Potter & Son".

I can see him hesitate as he begins to clear Kemp's papers from his desk. Endings are always difficult. The end of a failed business is like the end of a failed love affair, charged with the same nostalgia and sadness. Perhaps unrequited love is not so far from the unrequited loan.

He stores the letters away.

Potter without Kemp eventually peters out. As Potter muses to his son:

"An Englishman fails because he fears he shall and is continually stumbling over the shadow his fancy raises." Potter's son lives faithfully by his maxims and rises to become Master of the Vintners Company, where I find an entry in the minutes book commending him for "his able and zealous discharge of the duties of his office and for his kindness and courtesy on all occasions". But these qualities, on their own, are not enough to save the business and the family moves to Birmingham, where my grandmother – the last of the Potters – was born.

And Kemp without Potter?

XIV

"GARNET IS AS GOOD AS DEAD. WHAT USE IS A BOY TO HIS MOTHER, OR ANYONE else, living down there in Van Diemen's Land?"

Kemp's family in London could not forget him soon enough. He was more than a black sheep: he was a dead ringer for the dissolute Garnet Roxburgh in Patrick White's novel, *A Fringe of Leaves*, headstrong and unwise, who had fallen among bad company and come to a place where people who defected "to sensuality and worse" were packed off as quickly and quietly as possible. As Garnet says: "Most of us on this island are infected."

Kemp, too, had run the gamut. He had already been in charge of the colony's finances, religious affairs and judiciary – as well as spearheading the tradition, still vibrant in Australian politics, of jobs-for-the-boys. But I had underestimated my uncle. Almost the last virgin territory to explore was to be Kemp the Puritan. His penultimate incarnation was a caricature of all that he had fled: the God-fearing, respectable and abstemious family man of Aldgate, William Potter.

The tender shoots of Kemp's moral awakening can be credited to Davey's successor. Colonel William Sorell was a rare example of someone prepared to stand up to Kemp and, unusual in this cast of characters, teetotal. During his six-year rule, Sorell became the benevolent patriarch of the colony: a fatherly, much-loved administrator, known because of his snowy shock of hair as the "Old Man". Friendly with the citizens of Hobart – he stood at his gate to hear their complaints – Sorell was wise, honest, grave and firm. But he had an Achilles heel that Kemp went for.

The 44-year-old Sorell arrived at Government House in April 1817, accompanied by a beautiful wife pregnant with their fourth child. Kemp detested Sorell from the start, but he seemed – for once – to have come up against an authority who was unassailable.

The roots of their dispute were petty: a quarrel over a wall and a refusal by Sorell to assign Kemp two more convict servants (because he already had 17). Menacingly, Kemp reminded Sorell's secretary of what had happened to Governor Bligh. Sorell's reaction was to strip Kemp of his magistracy and to describe him as a sordid and mischievous man with a slanderous tongue and a black heart. A month later, Sorell fined Kemp £1 after he had refused to supply a list of the people in his house – and sent him to prison for an hour.

Kemp's 60 minutes in Hobart jail unleashed in him a hysterical desire for "retributive justice". He was unused to being detained, let alone crossed. On another occasion when a Governor contradicted him his response was equally intemperate. "I am piqued, Sir," he told a journalist whom he buttonholed in the street, "and will be piqued, Sir, and mean to be piqued, Sir – 'tis a most unwarrantable liberty, Sir, with a man of my bearing, Sir, and I was never so piqued in all my life, Sir." Lloyd Robson observed in *A History of Tasmania*: "No prima donna was more sensitive of her reputation than the upstart settlers of Van Diemen's Land." Soon Kemp was slandering Sorell in his shop and in the streets, "wherever he could find a listener".

To begin with, no-one did listen. Sorell's popularity was, in the words of his obituary, "as unbounded as it was merited". Then a package arrived from Potter containing a bundle of English newspapers.

This, I realised, was the bundle stuffed at the bottom of my grandmother's bag of letters, but it was only when I opened a copy of *The Times* of London and read about a court case against Sorell, who was charged with "criminal conversation" after eloping with another officer's wife, that I understood Kemp's excitement.

Kemp raced about Hobart showing the article to everyone. The elegant "Mrs Sorell" was none other than Mrs Louisa Kent, the wife of an aggrieved lieutenant in the 21st Dragoons who had successfully sued Sorell for substantial damages. Oblivious to any parallels between Sorell's mistress and his own former "concubine" Judith Simpson, Kemp launched a vindictive attack on Sorell for his "immoral Habits and pernicious example".

Conceiving it a duty that he owed his family, Kemp sent off letters to Lord Bathurst, Lord Liverpool and the Bishop of London. He asked Bathurst to peruse *The Times* of July 7, 1817 for the trial of Kent v Sorell, "and after you have perused it, I am persuaded to hope it will occur to your honourable Mind that Mr Sorell is not a fit and proper person to administer the Government of this Island."

It was Kemp's "painful task" to write on behalf of "all the married men of Respectability". He had watched Sorell's mistress ride through town in an open carriage at government expense, and considered it "lamentable to see the highest authority in the island living in a public state of concubinage". Even more distressing to Kemp than Sorell's habit of introducing Mrs Kent as his wife was the woman's presence at church. "On seeing Mrs Sorell in the Government House when Divine service was performed under the veranda I determined to decline all further intercourse." Kemp subsequently read prayers to his family at home. Confident that this insult to public decency could not be forgiven, he bluntly requested that Lord Bathurst remove the Governor from office.

In Kemp's words I wondered if there were not the residue of his father's indignation towards his 18-year-old self. He appeared to savour his new role as the safeguard of Vandemonian rectitude, as if in felling the paternal and honest Sorell, he could take the stand against not only his father but all those who had sat in judgment.

"What hypocrisy and falsehood!" Sorell replied. He told a commission of enquiry that Kemp's accusations were "a malignant tissue of lies". Kemp could not have seen Mrs Kent in church at Government House for one simple reason: the house had been pulled down. "He was never there, nor has ever attended divine service." He complained that Kemp had vilified him non-stop – ever since Sorell's arrival in 1817. He was "the most seditious, mischievous and the Man least meriting favour or indulgence of any kind in this whole Settlement". It was a damning portrait, but Sorell was not finished. He was able to assert "without fear of contradiction from anyone with whom Mr Kemp has come into contact, that his conceit and credulity, envy and malice, turbulence and arrogance, have been at all times equal, to which may now be added a total disregard of truth . . . "

But the same habits, Sorell reminded the commission, had characterised Kemp throughout his life – "from the moment that emerging from behind his father's counter, he became an ensign in the New South Wales Corps".

Unfortunately for Sorell, Kemp's mud stuck. Kemp had exposed what Sorell admitted was "the one great error" of his life. In October 1823, Sorell was recalled.

Days after the news leaked out, an extraordinary public meeting was held in Hobart. The motion was passed unanimously. An urgent petition was to be sent to George IV entreating him to extend Sorell's tenure as

Governor. It must have astonished Sorell to discover the identity of the committee's chairman. Starting with an admission that they had had some difficulties in the past, the speaker, Anthony Fenn Kemp, went on to lavish praise on Sorell as a leader who showed "steady, calm, decided and experienced Judgment, uniform impartiality and disinterestedness".

Too late. In June 1824, Sorell, Mrs Kent and their six children left Van Diemen's Land on the *Guildford*. The citizens of Hobart had followed them en masse to the shore. In the words of Sorell's obituary, "each colonist seemed as if he were losing a cherished personal friend."

XV

WHENEVER I PEERED INTO TASMANIA'S EARLY HISTORY, EACH TIME I RUBBED away the dust I found Kemp staring out. The next episode involving him was one of the goriest ever to take place in Van Diemen's Land, and it began – innocently enough – with an attempt to pirate his boat.

Anchored alongside the departing *Guildford* was a cargo of merino fleeces. Thanks to Potter's loan, Kemp had bought some of John Macarthur's merino rams to upgrade his wool as well as a schooner to ferry the wool to his warehouse on the wharf. Two years before, on the evening of March 30, 1822, five convicts were arrested on board as they grappled with the anchor. Their trespass had consequences that have since riveted historians from John West to Robert Hughes, and the story was well-known in Tasmania, though I had never heard of it.

The attempted pirating of his boat infuriated Kemp, who was never lenient towards those who tried to rob him. A thief caught escaping from his cottage in Collins Street with a gold watch and "trinkets" received 200 lashes and was shackled in leg-irons for a year. In his attitude towards anyone who crossed him Kemp reminded me of the officer in Kafka's story "In the Penal Colony", who is keen to show off his chosen instrument of punishment, the harrow, and who decides every sentence arbitrarily, without a trial. "My guiding principle is this: guilt is never to be doubted."

Unfortunately for Kemp, he was no longer on the Bench since Sorell had suspended him. "It broke down under me some years ago," he complained to a journalist, "and has never been since repaired." Nonetheless, he was owed a favour by the adjudicating magistrate in the case, his friend the Reverend Robert Knopwood, who had baptised two of his children and shared Kemp's notion of justice. The punishment that Knopwood handed down on the gang's leader, Robert Greenhill, and his rumoured lover Matthew Travers, would traumatise them.

Greenhill, the wiliest of the group, was a 32-year-old sailor from Middlesex transported for stealing his wife's coat. In Van Diemen's Land he had worked as a stockman in the bush north of Hobart, and there formed a close friendship with Travers, an Irishman convicted of theft. Shortly before Greenhill ate him, Travers confessed that the two of them had always communicated on every subject, "and had entrusted each other with the most guarded secrets".

The attempted hijack of a valuable schooner belonging to Hobart's "most respectable merchant" was a serious crime. Mindful of the role that Kemp had played in clearing his name four years before, Knopwood ordered the men to receive 150 lashes.

I had read umpteen accounts of floggings, but it was not until I untied a grey folder in Hobart's Tasmaniana library that I had a notion of what Greenhill and Travers suffered. The folder had belonged to Kemp's obituarist, James Erskine Calder, and inside was a letter written to Calder by a man suffering from vertigo – possibly brought on by his memory of the event. In horrified tones the letter described a flogging by the government executioner, Mark Jeffries, "one of the most horrible and inhuman monsters in the shape of man".

The lashes fell every 30 seconds, watched by other prisoners who formed a circle. No word was spoken except "NOW" and not a word was spoken by the victim until his release – all blood and raw opened flesh, from his neck to his loins.

"Jeffries threw off his coat, bared his herculean arm and with evident and demoniacal pleasure in his horrible countenance gave the first lash with all his strength, cutting into the flesh and so placed that the wound was one straight and continued line till it ended round by the wretched sufferer's ribs where the knots of the newly made cat made a deeper and more sanguinary end of that line.

"Can you imagine what must have been the state of that poor wretch's back after receiving 50 such lashes from such a monster, can you imagine, can you picture to your mind the awful scene? Those 25 minutes appeared to me like so many hours."

Knopwood sentenced Greenhill and Travers to a lashing three times longer. But the clergyman was not done. He ordered the men to be shipped to Sarah Island, a place of secondary punishment that had opened three months before on Tasmania's remote west coast.

XVI

BEHIND KNOPWOOD'S SENTENCE ROSE THE SPECTRE OF THE FRENCH REVOLUTION.
The Tasmanian historian Peter Chapman told me: "Knopwood represented
a society where crime and social order were a burning concern. 'Look
what happened in France,' went the thinking of his political masters in
London. 'They stormed the Bastille and killed everyone. Who's next?'" It
would not be Knopwood.

It is hard to resist the conclusion that Van Diemen's Land – occupied
specifically to prevent French occupation – had stumbled into becoming
a penal colony, and that it drifted for several years in the wake of New
South Wales without a clear strategy and with its government left chiefly
in the hands of a rabble of cashiered officers. Until Kemp's reappearance
in Hobart, the occasional boat of convicts had sailed from Sydney, but not
until 1818 did regular shipments from England begin. By 1833, an average
of 1,700 male and 300 female convicts were sent each year to Van Diemen's
Land and Sorell's stern successor, Lieutenant Governor Arthur, wrote: "The
whole territory is [now] one large penitentiary."

Nonetheless, as Arthur complained, the colony's distance from England
meant that it was difficult to obtain "accurate statements of facts" about
Van Diemen's Land. Horror in a small place touches everyone and it also
travels. Trollope became aware on his 1872 visit that "no tidings that are
told through the world exaggerate themselves with so much ease as the
tidings of horror. Those who are most shocked by them, women who
grow pale at the hearing and almost shriek as the stories are told to them,
delight to have the stories so told that they may be justified in shrieking."

Writing to his sister, the exiled Irish MP William Smith O'Brien must have shocked a reader or two with his description of Port Arthur: "as near a realisation of a Hell upon earth as can be found in any part of the British dominions except Norfolk Island". But Lloyd Robson cautions against accepting every description as gospel. "The artist who painted the society of Van Diemen's Land employed a palette well-equipped with blood-red to execute scenes of brutishness, bawdiness and hair-raising and grisly death."

The misapprehension survives that those sent as convicts to Hobart were all locked up from the moment they landed in lurid institutions like Port Arthur and Sarah Island. The fact is that these two prisons were designed for men and women who reoffended once they arrived in the colony. The majority of the 76,000 convicts who came to Van Diemen's Land between 1804 and 1853, when transportation ceased, were sent in gangs to build public bridges, roads, houses and boats, fell timber and make bricks; or "assigned" to settlers like Kemp to work as farm labourers and domestic servants. After a year or so of good conduct, they might be given a ticket-of-leave, and freedom to live and work within the island – so long as they reported to the police once a month and attended church every Sunday. To the majority of convicts, this is what happened. It was a penal system that was open to appalling abuse – and it deteriorated further in the 1840s when assignment was scrapped in favour of probation – but the philosophy that drove it was more humane than one might gather from *The Fatal Shore* or from Marcus Clarke's 1874 novel, *For the Term of His Natural Life*. The potter Edward Carr Shaw writes in his memoirs that people from his district in Ireland were known to steal "a loaf o' bread or some heggs" in order to be given free passage to this new country full of opportunities. "Jus' make sure you gets caught . . ." The truth lies somewhere in the middle, namely that transportation was successful in providing a better life to thousands of men and women who were sentenced to it. "Thus it is," Arthur explained to the Archbishop of Dublin in 1833, "that every man has afforded him an opportunity of in a great measure retrieving his character and becoming useful in society, while the resolutely and irrecoverably depraved are doomed to live apart from it for the remainder of their lives."

In Knopwood's judgment, the men who had attempted to pirate Kemp's schooner were "irrecoverably depraved". Until 1821, he would have sent Greenhill and Travers to the town jail on the corner of Murray and Macquarie Street, but in that year Sorell established a penitentiary on an

island in the middle of Macquarie Harbour, 200 miles north-west of
Hobart.

I drove to Strahan and took a boat through Hell's Gates into the large
inlet of Macquarie Harbour. Sharp rocks weathered to the profile of frozen
surf guarded the narrow entrance and an eight-knot tide was running in
from the sea. A couple held on to each other until the *Lady Franklin* had
passed safely through.

The island where Greenhill and Travers were imprisoned is a tree-covered,
15-acre hump that lies at the far end of an immense sheet of water and four
miles from the entrance to the Gordon River. It is hemmed in on one side
by a battering ocean that runs, without interruption, to Patagonia, and on
the other side by a damp sclerophyll forest more impenetrable than the
Amazon.

In 1822, the nearest settlement – Hobart – took up to 77 days to reach
from here by sea. Escape was scarcely an option, although in the first five
years of its existence 116 convicts tried it, of whom 75 "perished in the
woods". Christened "Devil's Island" by the convicts, Sarah Island became
the most dreaded penal station in the southern hemisphere: associated,
wrote John West, with "inexpressible depravity, degradation and woe".

I stood on the deck of the *Lady Franklin*, waiting for the island to come
into sight. Button-grass plains grew in peaty soil to the water's edge.
Beyond, there spread a line of ti-trees and, further back, the darker foliage
of sassafras, laurel and myrtle. The sun had burned off the mist and in the
clear morning sky I could make out, to the east, the familiar quartzite peak
of Frenchman's Cap, one of the mountains from which Greenhill took his
bearings.

I had first seen Frenchman's Cap – so called after its resemblance to
Kemp's republican cockade – on a trek with my wife-to-be. Early in 1999
we had flown from London to Sydney and then, on Valentine's Day, to
Tasmania. Our idea was to walk for a week through the Central Highlands
before returning to Sydney, but the landscape cast such a spell on us that
we delayed our departure.

The Cradle Mountain National Park, where we camped for eight days,
was founded by an Austrian, Gustav Weindorfer. In 1910, he climbed Cradle
Mountain, about 40 miles to the north of Frenchman's Cap, and the view
from the summit – the layered ranges, the glass-clear lakes, the haze raised
by the blue gums – prompted him to fling out his arms. He turned to his
wife: "Kate, this is magnificent. People must know about it and enjoy it.
This must be a National Park for the people for all time." He named his

hut Waldheim from his native Tyrol, and welcomed visitors with a garlic-based wombat stew and the energetic greeting: "This is Waldheim, where there is no time and nothing matters."

We trod out across fragile alpine heath between poa tussocks and something that smelled of lemon thyme. The landscape was virgin and kept this way by strict rules governing our passage. Simon, our guide, was a modern disciple of Weindorfer. He made sure that we buried our toilet paper, did not wash our dishes or teeth in the creeks, and that we kept in rigid file on duckboard tracks lest our footsteps damage the plants. There must be no evidence of our passing through. We were weightless, freightless creatures and with each step the twentieth century receded behind us.

Simon's sermons on environmental friendliness irritated at first, but once he explained the reasons – it takes 40 years, for example, for an indented cushion-plant to grow back – I stuck to the path, until early one dawn I looked up at a berry pink sky and thought that this was how the world must have appeared before *Homo sapiens* put it to his filthy purposes. The perfect trekker, Simon said, decomposes en route. In this landscape I recomposed myself.

Where once were sent the most hardened recidivists was now marketed as a paradise of unpolluted skies, turquoise seas and glacier-made landscapes that can induce a sensation of pure well-being in those lucky enough to behold them. "A lover of nature would come upon this spell-binding scene and exclaim with the traveller Thomas Moore: if there be an Elysium on earth, it is this!" So reacted a visitor in 1887. But not every traveller was so minded. It was, wrote the historian James Bonwick, "a country forsaken even by birds".

In the same year that I hiked through those mountains, a grandmother from Queensland made a pilgrimage to Sarah Island to find out about her convict ancestor. She was upset to discover that he had been eaten.

"What am I going to tell my grandchildren?" she asked.

"Lady," Richard Davey consoled her, "they're going to love it. It's their story too."

Davey is a 64-year-old playwright whose vocation is to resurrect and dramatise a history of Tasmania that his father and forefathers suppressed. On Sarah Island, he points out the ruined penitentiary, home to a population of 170 convicts when Greenhill and Travers arrived. "In 1926, an engineer from Queenstown came down here with dynamite and blew it up because of the shame that it carried." Davey's approach is to restore the past, not to destroy it. "The stories can't escape from here. We have to face up to them in the end."

He stands on a wall above the brick jail and bewitches a group of Melbourne tourists, converting them for the duration of an hour into felons of "bad character and incorrigible conduct" – they might be Greenhill and Travers. "The cell is the exact size of your grave. Escape is impossible. You'll be worked incessantly, no rum, no tobacco, no tea – plus you're out of mobile phone range. Contemplate your mortality in silence and darkness."

Before going on, he pauses to indicate a sign beside the path, Sorell's instructions to his first commandant: "You must find work and labour, even if it consists in opening cavities and filling them up again." Many bloodcurdling tales survive to describe the impact that such work could have on the convicts, including the gagging and drowning of a penal station constable who had the misfortune on the one hand to have been valet to the Duke of Devonshire and on the other to be called George Rex.

Davey's performance lasts until a hoot from the *Lady Franklin* summons the group reluctantly to the jetty. It is a drama that he has recited for ten years, an incantation against forgetting.

A former Dominican priest and a descendant of Lieutenant Governor "Mad Tom" Davey, he believes that Macquarie Harbour is "an heroic landscape, a battleground for good and evil, demanding Herculean labours, Homeric challenges". He points to the mountains that surround it. They ring, he says, with the names of the epic debates of the nineteenth century. Owen, Huxley, Jukes, Darwin . . . "The raw material for epic narratives."

The convicts dressed in yellow flaxen sailcloth dipped in celery-pine tan that discoloured their uniform to a dusky pink. Against the rain they wore kangaroo-skin boots and jackets, and their tunics were stencilled with arrowheads.

The most troublesome were sent in felling gangs to saw Huon pine logs for what Davey calls "the largest boat-building industry in the Empire". At Sarah Island, he says, 130 ships were launched in twelve years. Greenhill and Travers worked for one of these gangs. Five months after their arrival, Greenhill was sawing pine on Kelly's Basin when he led Travers off in a second attempt at escape. On September 22, 1822, they turned on their overseer, bound him to a tree and with six others rowed across the harbour. After smashing holes in the hull of their stolen boat, they vanished into the forest.

Greenhill plunged ahead, hacking a path with an axe. He was a skilled navigator. He had no compass, but he had the stars, the sun and Frenchman's

Cap, and for the next 40 days – until his death – succeeded in maintaining an easterly course.

Travers stumbled close behind. Their hope lay in movement, but they were ill-equipped and progress was excruciatingly slow, 500 yards an hour through a tangled labyrinth of southern beech and Huon pine. The undergrowth formed a barrier compared to which, one later traveller wrote, "the famous Gordian knot was simplicity itself." Every breath was snatched with difficulty. Every step stirred up clouds of new insects. The surveyor Henry Hellyer came through this way five years after Greenhill. "The air in these dense forests is putrid and oppressive and swarms with mosquitoes and large stinging flies, the size of English bees."

On the second night they stopped to bake damper on rocks, but the guards at Sarah Island had spiked the dough with ergot to prevent foodhoarding. The poisoned bread induced hallucinations.

Within a week, they had finished their rations. A constant rain drenched their clothes and tinder, and the nights were "excessively cold". They had walked less than twelve miles, crawling and stumbling over rotten, moss-covered trunks. The cutting-grass tore at their shirts and faces, draining their energy and patience. Nor could they see where they were going. Above them spread a horizontal scrub in a canopy so thick and strong that a century later it could support a bulldozer. There was little chance of catching animals to eat. Eyes stared at them between the leaves, flicking away at the least movement.

In the hissing flames, Greenhill and Travers boiled the bark from peppermint gums and roasted their kangaroo-skin jackets.

On the sixth night one of the men, William Kennelly, lit a fire and, according to a pockmarked Irish shoe-thief, Alexander Pearce, he cracked a tired joke. "He was so hungry that he could eat a piece of man."

The remark lay on the damp earth between them. Fresh in their minds were Franklin's passage through the Canadian tundra and rumours of cannibalism. There was also the story of a Nantucket whaleboat rescued off the Chilean coast. In the boat, two emaciated men sucked marrow from the bones of their dead comrades – survivors who had drawn lots to determine which one was to be killed.

Kennelly's remark set Greenhill, a sailor, thinking. Next morning he brought up the subject of eating one of their companions. "He had seen the like done before and that it eat much like a little pork." It was the "custom of the sea".

Someone started to object. Greenhill stifled his protest by saying that he was happy to eat the first mouthful himself, "but you must all lend a hand that we all may be guilty of the crime." In a whisper, he nominated Dalton, an Irish ex-soldier, who, he claimed, had volunteered as a flogger.

At three in the morning, Greenhill crept over to the snoring Dalton and crashed down the axe on his neck. He signalled for Travers to apply the skills that he had learned as a shepherd in New Norfolk. "Travers took a knife, cut his throat with it and bled him," according to Pearce in his testimony. "We then dragged the body to a distance, cut off his clothes, tore his insides out and cut off his head. Then Matthew Travers and Greenhill put his heart and liver on the fire to broil, but took them off and cut them before they were right hot. They asked the rest would they have any, but we would not eat any that night. Next morning the body was cut up and divided into equal parts, which we took and proceeded on our journey a little after sun rise."

Revolted by the violence that his remark had triggered, Kennelly and another convict offered to carry the tin-pots and go ahead. They had walked 300 yards when they melted into the bush. Greenhill stopped and "coo-eed", but no answer. The two men made it back to Sarah Island, and died in the prison hospital without revealing that the dry pieces of meat in their pockets were human.

Dalton's flesh had given Mather, a baker from Dumfries, an upset stomach. (More so than its female counterpart, male flesh is deficient in carbohydrates.) Constantly having to stop to drop his trousers, Mather was appalled to discover that he had lost the tinder that Greenhill had given him with orders to keep it dry, and which he had stuck inside his shirt. Travers raised the axe and said he would kill him if he did not find it. Mather discovered it down his trouser leg, and a fire was made.

Lots were cast. This time it was the turn of an English labourer, Thomas Bodenham. He requested a few minutes to pray for his "past offences" and was left alone, looking into the fire, when Greenhill attacked him. He split Bodenham's skull and after removing his shoes – they were more comfortable than Greenhill's – he rolled the body over for Travers to butcher.

Eighteen years later, James Erskine Calder was trekking through Wombat Glen when he discovered several articles "in the last stages of decay" in the hollow of an old gum tree: an old yellow pea-jacket, boots, a broken pot and a large gimlet. Possibly they had belonged to Mather, next to die.

Refusing to eat more of Bodenham, Mather boiled up a tea of fern roots in the hope of quelling his stomach, but the brew made him vomit, and as he retched, Greenhill, "still showing his spontaneous habit of bloodshed", struck him on the head. The blow was not strong enough. Mather leaped up, shouting "You won't see me killed!" and grabbed his axe. They walked on in an uneasy file, Mather nursing his bruised skull, his bowels rumbling and his ergot-fed paranoia fanned by the close relationship of Travers and Greenhill. "They had a respect for each other," Pearce said, "which they often showed to each other." As Mather sat warming himself by the fire, the pair came forward to throw more wood on it, and jumped on him.

After wolfing down Mather, the three survivors – Greenhill, Travers and Pearce – stretched out beside the fire and slept off the "sumptuous feast".

On they went, crawling and tottering across the dolerite mountains of the Central Highlands and scattering kangaroos and wombats that looked back at them from between the snow gums. Then Travers was bitten by a tiger-snake. His foot swelled up and he lolled in and out of consciousness, bleeding from the ears. In lucid moments he begged Greenhill to leave him behind. His pleas took on a hysterical tone after he overheard Greenhill mutter that it would be ridiculous to abandon him, "for his flesh would answer as well for Subsistance as the others". Greenhill refused, and with Pearce's help dragged the man – who had become, in effect, their larder – to the Nive River. A non-swimmer, like many convicts, Travers clung to a log and was pulled across. But his foot had turned black. Unable to walk another step, he was killed by his mentor who "was much affected by this horrid scene and stood quite motionless to see one who had been his companion". His contemplation over, Greenhill dissected and ate him. He advised Pearce that the thick part of the arms tasted best.

Two men remained. His stomach filled with his lover, Greenhill did not dare let go his axe or fall asleep. He watched Pearce over the fire and Pearce through hazel-blue eyes watched him, "never trusting myself near him, particularly at night". In the end, Greenhill's eyes drooped first. Pearce inched closer, slid the axe from under his head, "and struck him with it".

The consumption of Greenhill's thigh and arm induced in Pearce a nightmare worthy of inclusion in Michael Howe's "dream journal". He felt Greenhill staring at him and screamed: "Come out, you bastard, and face me." Staggering into a pasture of sheep, he grabbed a lamb by its throat and was devouring it raw when he felt a ring of cold steel pressing into his head. The musket belonged to a convict stockman. Pearce had been walking for 49 days.

Brought up again before Knopwood, Pearce damned Greenhill and Travers for having introduced him to an appetite that had grown with the eating. Knopwood didn't believe a word: Pearce's "depraved" confession was manifestly a cover story to protect his mates – presumably still at large. Accusing him of "being in possession of stolen sheep", Knopwood ordered Pearce back to Sarah Island, where he escaped a year later, and in a fit of rage at a companion who could not swim, ate another convict. His sixth.

Pearce was hanged in Hobart in July 1824, one month after Sorell departed on the *Guildford*. But the story of his cannibalism haunted the island, and embedded itself into the Tasmanian psyche. No name-change could erase the power of it, any more than changing its name to Carnarvon would exorcise Port Arthur, or drowning a lake would obliterate the memory of Lake Pedder. In the image of Pearce and Greenhill eyeing each other over the coals was hatched a sense of Van Diemen's Land stalking Tasmania, ready to gobble it up. Until well into the twentieth century, down even the most innocent-looking country lane, there was the feeling that a dark shadow was ready to step out from the hedge and wrap its arm around you.

XVII

JUST WHEN I HAD DECIDED THAT I WOULD HAVE TO FIND ANOTHER BUILDER, Peter turned up. He was a broad, handsome man with blue, twinkling eyes, thick wavy grey hair, and the trace of a Scottish accent. He reckoned the animals pissing over my head were possums, and was confident that their smell would disappear once he had fitted wire over the gutters and cleared Helen's paintings from the roof.

I left him to his work and drove to Hobart. I was still threading my way through Kemp's life.

Arriving at dusk, I parked on the waterfront and went and had a fish and chips in The Drunken Admiral, where Kemp's warehouse had once stood. The trevalla was fresh off the boats, and eating it I could not help feeling a twinge on Potter's behalf to think how, a decade after his return to the island as a bankrupt, Kemp was riding about this wharf on a small pony and being greeted as "the principal merchant of Hobart". All because of Potter's loan – which he never repaid – Kemp owned not only a schooner and this stone warehouse on the wharf, but a country estate of 2,000 acres, a house on Collins Street (built of "valuable stone and brick walls"), and a store in Macquarie Street that provided the colony with a range of English and European goods, as well as most of the wine and spirits consumed in Van Diemen's Land.

By the mid-1820s Kemp had reached the apogee of his power. His advertisements in the *Hobart Town Gazette* signalled his return to prosperity. He sold gentlemen's superfine hats, ladies' gloves, boxes of eau de cologne, chintz bed laces, mottled soap, butter in jars, Westphalia hams, Berlin chairs, cut wine glasses, cream jugs, "ornamental china of all descriptions" and "Jamaica rum of the strongest proof and finest quality". He arranged tickets and freight on boats to England, and packed the holds with his sealskins, whale oil and wool. Kemp and his partner enriched themselves, but "they were none the less invaluable to the colonists," wrote a local historian. "Through them came the ploughs and axletrees, window glass and tools, among the thousand and one articles needed in a new country."

Who were Kemp's clients? The population had quadrupled since his arrival. In 1824, there were 12,556 Europeans, of whom 6,261 were convicts (5,790 male and 471 female). It continued to grow under Sorell's successor, the Evangelical bureaucrat George Arthur. His project was to organise Van Diemen's Land into a penal settlement so strict and efficient that it would function as a deterrent to criminals in Britain; at the same time, he worked tirelessly – using the bait of free land and free convict labour – to bring in a "more respectable class of Settlers than the early emigrants to Van Diemen's Land" – i.e. than Kemp. For twelve years, Arthur strived to maintain what the historian Peter Chapman calls this "dynamic balance". Kemp did not take to him at all. On Arthur's recall, he would write a memorial to the Secretary of State thanking him for freeing the colony from the "tyrannical Lieutenant Governor Arthur".

Among those whom Arthur tempted into settling were several respectable Protestant families from Northern Ireland, a group of retired army officers from India, a shipload of 150 mechanics and, rather less useful, 76 paupers sent by the Bristol Guardians of the Poor. Convict families were given a free passage as were a number of single young women, who were lured by the opportunities of becoming farm servants, milliners and wives. Early Van Diemen's Land was a colonial society so top-heavy with men that at a ball in Hobart in 1821, 150 bachelors were compelled to dance the polka – with each other. Selected by Mrs Elizabeth Fry and a committee of ladies working for the London Female Penitentiary and Refuge for the Destitute, 1,280 women arrived over three years to balance the ratio, although contemporary moralists declared that the free-immigrant women were often more depraved than the convicts. Practically all of these people beat a path to Kemp's shop.

Kemp's prickly character meant that he ran through several business partners. His first partner complained: "He was always an obstinate fellow; thought no person knew any thing but himself." Kemp saw no reason why the colony should not be governed like his store.

The success of his various mercantile activities put Kemp in a strong position to interfere in the state's affairs. His wealth had bought him social and political prominence. "In no part of the world were riches more honoured than in Van Diemen's Land," wrote Lloyd Robson, "no matter how they had been secured." By 1825, Kemp the former bankrupt was President of the Bank of Van Diemen's Land, Vice-President of the Agricultural Society, and, most significantly, chairman of the movement to procure separation from New South Wales.

During Arthur's "tyrannical" rule, Kemp became ringleader of a group of radicals, such as George Meredith, a cantankerous landowner on the east coast, who opposed the smallest interference in their affairs. These men did not want to recreate a colony that was simply like "home": they chafed to make it "home" as it ought to have been, a society where the settler oligarchy was in the saddle. They championed political liberalism and representative politics just so long as it was their interests that were being represented. One man who got in their way remarked that they "concentrated in themselves such an assemblage of talent and seditious spite that their very breath seemed to threaten poor me, an individual and a convict to boot, with destruction". How many of the group were fellow masons it is hard to tell, but all had something in common with Kemp's friend Robert Lathrop Murray, who was described in 1826 by the *Hobart Town Gazette* as "self first, self last, self middle, without end". Their ultimate ambition was to transfer power from Britain – and its "evil genius" on the spot, George Arthur – to themselves.

To this end, Kemp chaired public meetings at the Hobart Court House arguing for an elected Legislative Council. On behalf of "the Free Inhabitants of this Colony", he petitioned Arthur for a system of trial by jury; also, on behalf of all merchants and traders, for a reduction in taxes on tea and wines. He wrote letters to the press in Hobart and in London under the pseudonym "Scrutator" or "A correspondent". Most took their tone from the journalist on the *True Colonist* who announced in May 1836: "Governor Arthur is ordered home!!! . . . We now have a prospect of breathing."

Kemp and his group caused such ructions that Arthur warned the Colonial Office: "There are some busy characters in this Colony whose whole happiness appears to consist of making trouble; there is, for instance, a Mr Kemp who is continually writing, as he says himself, to his friends . . . and to 20 other persons, misrepresenting every circumstance, and framing statements, either for the purpose of being communicated to your Department, through different channels, or, of appearing in some of the London Papers as the effusion of 'a Correspondent'."

Kemp's "despicable manoeuvring" may have had some effect – at least in Kemp's eyes – and on December 3, 1825, Van Diemen's Land was proclaimed constitutionally independent from New South Wales. This was a start, but it was not enough. Three weeks later, the man who had blackened the names of Governor King, Governor Bligh, Lieutenant Governor Davey and Lieutenant Governor Sorell, led a petition in favour of a free press, in which he expressed "the natural abhorrence which Englishmen invariably feel against personal vituperation and slander". He declared: "Where the Laws of England extend, there also are the Rights of Englishmen enjoyed." His petition was successful. Arthur was ordered by London to relax his censorship law.

Inch by inch, Flashman was becoming Prince Albert.

In the same year, Kemp chaired a banquet in Stodart's Hotel to celebrate George IV's birthday. "We are bound to say that a more numerous, respectable or social party never assembled in Van Diemen's Land," wrote the *Hobart Town Gazette*. The Lieutenant Governor could not attend, but Arthur's place was "admirably occupied" by A.F. Kemp Esq. "And but one spirit prevailed at the banquet – the spirit of patriotic happiness." After dinner, Kemp rose under a salute of 21 guns fired from the *Governor Phillip*, and proposed the first bumper toast: "The King lives in our hearts by the Constitutional liberty which under his beneficent sway we all enjoy." He proposed a further toast to "the Ladies of Van Diemen's Land" and to "Van Diemen's Land", after which the band struck up "This Tight Little Island".

Then in 1826 he almost went under.

XVIII

NEXT MORNING, I DROVE NORTH TO ROSS AND LEANED OVER THE MAJESTIC sandstone bridge that spanned the Macquarie River. I was searching for the face of the Anglo–Danish convict who rescued Kemp's empire. I found it carved into the third arch. His visionary gaze fixed on a family of ducks, he did not have the pose of an informer. He had a thick moustache and a crown on his head. Kemp had looked on him in a fraternal light, and not simply because the man had saved him.

I first heard Jorgen Jorgenson's name on our trek through the Central Highlands. As we emerged after eight days in the bush onto the shore of Lake St Clair, our guide mumbled through his patriarchal beard that one of the earliest Europeans to trek through this landscape – four years after the cannibals Greenhill, Travers and Pearce – had been the ex-King of Iceland.

All eight of my wife's great-grandparents came from the

north-west coast of Iceland. She pricked up her ears. She had never heard of a King of Iceland.

"He was the only monarch," our guide said sombrely, "to have left London for the antipodes in a convict ship."

Jorgenson's connection to Kemp began one evening in January 1827 when he was drinking in a pub in New Town Road and overheard a man boast that he was about to make his fortune from £5,000 of forged treasury bills. The Dane reported him, the bills were found, and the man – the son of a Bristol solicitor – was hanged, his last words on the scaffold being: "I am sure I shall go to heaven, I can see heaven." Kemp admitted that had the forgeries been presented at his warehouse or store they would have "ruined" him.

Kemp demanded to meet the man responsible for saving his business. He shook hands with a younger version of himself, a bow-legged 46-year-old with an oval face, thick lips and a weak chin. Kemp recognised him immediately: the previous August, Jorgenson had come to ask Kemp a favour. Jorgenson then had been setting off on an exploration of the north-west on behalf of the Van Diemen's Land Company. Since he would be passing through Kemp's land, might Kemp give him a letter of recommendation? Kemp had done so. As a result, Jorgenson went on to meet "with the most hospitable reception, particularly on the estate of Mr Kemp", and on his return to Hobart he moved swiftly when he learned that Kemp's interests might be threatened. He told Kemp that "his motives for coming forward were to have a valuable property restored to its rightful owner".

Overcome by a deviant spirit of gratitude, Kemp asked Jorgenson about himself. Jorgenson threw out his arms and began talking, which he had a habit of doing non-stop. The story that Kemp heard would move him to his first recorded act of generosity.

Kemp's saviour was a pedantic and boastful fantasist, transported to Van Diemen's Land for pawning his landlady's bed-blankets. He had arrived in Hobart with a guinea in his pocket nine months before, one of 144 prisoners on board the *Woodman*. He watched the broad sweep of the Derwent come into sight, the farms with their pleasant looking cottages, and was strangely affected. He had been here, as a British sailor, 23 years before, before even Kemp – "when no white inhabitant occupied a single spot in Van Diemen's Land, and when all around was a wilderness".

He told Kemp his life story. He was born in Denmark, the son of the royal watchmaker, but from the age of 14 had served on British ships. In

1803, he sailed with Flinders up the east coast of Australia and helped the
first settlers to disembark at Hobart. The spot occupied by the Bank of
Van Diemen's Land (founder and President: A.F. Kemp) "was then an imper-
vious grove of the thickest brushwood, surmounted with some of the
largest gum trees that this island can produce". Jorgenson had axed some
of them down.

The two men shared further connections. In January 1804, as First Mate,
Jorgenson had assisted in a marine survey of the coast around Port
Dalrymple. It was owing to the *Lady Nelson's* exploration of the Tamar
that Governor King had decided to dispatch Paterson to form a settlement at the river mouth. Quite possibly, Kemp and Jorgenson had sailed
together, Jorgenson in charge of the sloop that attempted to convey
Paterson's expedition from Sydney in June 1804, before a gale drove them
back.

And something else they had in common. Like Kemp during his seven-
month reign in Port Dalrymple, and afterwards in Sydney, Jorgenson
knew what it was to govern. He had spent the intervening years "at the
opposite extremity of the globe" where, before his slide into gambling
and drink, he had become ruler of Iceland.

On honeymoon in Reykjavik, I visited a two-storey white building in
Austurstræti, not far from the centre, that now houses a bar called Pravda.
The rain slanted in from the bay, drenching a pair of greylag geese, and
in the bar the mutter was of how to overturn the whaling ban. The building
was 200 years old, with a tin roof. It was here on a rainy day in 1809 that
the 29-year-old Jorgenson installed himself as "Protector of the whole of
Iceland, and Commander in Chief by Land and Sea".

Jorgenson wrote three versions of the coup. The further away in time
and geography from the event, the more important his role in it.

From Van Diemen's Land, where he claimed to have been the first man
to harpoon a whale in the Derwent, Jorgenson had sailed to Europe. His
arrival coincided with Denmark's declaration of war on England. He
captained a Danish privateer, but was captured off Filey following a battle
with HMS *Sappho* that lasted 44 minutes. In his defence, he said that most
of his crew were drunk.

While on parole, he met Samuel Phelps, a soap-maker impatient for
tallow. Jorgenson had learned of a consignment of 150 tons waiting in
Iceland for a market. He convinced Phelps that the population were
starving under their Danish rulers – so hungry that they had stripped the
moss off the mountains – and would seize the chance to exchange their

tallow for food. He did not reveal that he was a POW who should properly be in Reading.

Inspired by Jorgenson's assurance of rich pickings, Phelps chartered a boat with a cargo of barley, rum and hats, and hired Jorgenson to come along as interpreter.

They arrived in Iceland on a black December day to discover that the absent Danish governor had forbidden all trade with the English. Local merchants would have nothing to do with Phelps. His cargo was unloaded unsold and he and Jorgenson sailed back to England to fit out another ship. Instead of the hoped-for tallow, they carried stones. The expedition had been a disaster.

In London, Jorgenson introduced Phelps to Sir Joseph Banks, an ardent Icelandophile who favoured Britain's annexation of the island. The botanist was well disposed to Jorgenson – he had already lent him money and Jorgenson had presented him with a pair of Tahitian men (the son of a Tahitian chief and his young servant) – and Banks, at least to begin with, had been fascinated to learn about Jorgenson's experiences of mapping the Tamar, from where Colonel Paterson had sent him the heads of a male Aborigine and a female thylacine.

Jorgenson exaggerated to Banks the warmth of their reception in Reykjavik ("The joy of the natives was great"). It would be easy to capture Iceland. Phelps offered to do the job with a privateer. Bank's over-enthusiastic response paved the way for a dramatic invasion.

In June 1809, one year after Kemp unseated Bligh, Jorgenson and Phelps sailed into Reykjavik, a town of 60 wooden houses coated with red clay and tar. This time the Danish Governor, Count Tramp, was *in situ*. Inventing a rumour that a company of 100 armed Icelanders were about to storm his ship, Phelps ordered his arrest.

On the morning of Sunday 25 June, Phelps, Jorgenson and 12 British sailors marched through Reykjavik and deposed Tramp as he sat in his house after church. According to the third and final account that Jorgenson wrote, in an alcoholic stew, for the *Hobart Town Almanac*: "I went straight to the Governor's house, and dividing my little troop into two bodies, I stationed six before and six behind the building, with orders to fire upon anybody that should attempt to interrupt me. I then opened the door and walked in with a brace of pistols. His lordship, Count Tramp, was reposing upon a sofa, all unsuspicious of what was in progress, and was completely surprised by my abrupt appearance." And that was that. Jorgenson was not aware of any revolution "more adroitly, more harmlessly or more decisively effected than this".

In Count Tramp's account, written in sober fury in Brown's Hotel in London, Jorgenson was the last man into the room. Jeering at Tramp from behind everyone else's shoulders, he had insinuated that the Governor was a spy, at which Tramp threw him a look of such contempt that Jorgenson shot out of the door. From now on, Tramp fixed his sights on Jorgenson as the main object of his revenge.

Tramp was led away without a shot fired and locked up in a dirty cabin on Phelps's chartered boat, where a tearful secretary brought him his bedclothes. Otherwise, his capture was regarded by one or two churchgoers "with perfect indifference".

Phelps was in Iceland to trade, but someone had to run the country. He was happy to leave the day-to-day task to Jorgenson, who spoke the language. Jorgenson leaped at the role with the quixoticism of a "petit Napoléon".

Jorgenson had come to Iceland imbued, like Kemp, with the principles of the French Revolution. He now had the opportunity of a lifetime to put them into practice. The island of 50,000 people was under the "tyranny of Danes", and although himself a Dane, he had lived since the age of 14 on English ships, imbibing "the maxims, the principles and the prejudices of Englishmen".

Determined to do his best for these downtrodden people, he formed a militia – six vagabonds released from prison, sneered Tramp – and rounded up all weapons: about 20 muskets and some metal-tipped pikes for walking on the ice, or to fend off polar bears that occasionally floated over from Greenland on icebergs. He next issued a series of fantastic proclamations, stamped with his seal and using the royal address: "We, Jorgen Jorgenson". His package of laws included independence from Denmark, suffrage for all males, the recall of parliament, proper new bedsheets for the boys' school at Bessastadir and a systematic training of midwives. Jorgenson also designed a new flag – a shoal of three white cod floating on a marine blue background. But there was no adequate dye available, and the strip of bleached canvas that he hoisted above Phelps's warehouse to the salute of eleven guns was a dirty purple.

Jorgenson's "reign" was more benign than Kemp's junta in Sydney. He did not seek to enrich himself and he never pretended to be King of Iceland. The Danish press liked to call him this in order to show the Icelanders as stupid. But the name caught on and so he became "King of the Dog-Days", his rule of eight weeks and one day coinciding with the rising of the Dogstar Sirius and the long clear days of the Icelandic summer, "when the grass is so tender that even the dogs can eat it". His adventure spawned a musical, a pantomime and a television comedy show, in all of which he is cast as a buffoon. But in the Hotel Holt in Reykjavik, I met Anna Agnarsdottir who had written a thesis on Jorgenson and who regretted that he had not stayed longer in power. "We now have a new view of him in Iceland as someone who really wanted to help us," said Anna, who was Dean of the Faculty of Humanities. "I feel it's just a pity no-one took more note of him. The extraordinary thing is that he didn't fire the people with enthusiasm. It's as if he never arrived. That's what I find so tremendously sad. He left nothing. We had to wait for another 135 years for independence."

The only reminder of his rule is a strip of wallpaper that he donated to a house where he stayed in Hafnarfjör while on a tour of the country-side. To consolidate his hold on the island, he rode north for ten days, over the heaths of Mosfells and past the abrupt volcanic rockface of Thingvellir, sitting on a small Icelandic pony so that his legs brushed the turf. He had his militia with him, but nobody attacked. The population were more bewildered than overjoyed to be greeted by their new Protector. One woman refused to let him graze his pony in her field. Another Icelander wrote him a letter posing the question that many would want to know: "But who are you? Everywhere you will be cast away, hated, banished, cursed . . . You have only eternity left to you. I urge you immediately to embark on a new and better life."

A rare enthusiastic note was sounded by Gudrun Johnsen, a good-time girl, who earned the nickname of "the Dog Day Queen". She swiftly over-turned Jorgenson's initial prejudice against Icelandic women as "stout and lusty but excessively filthy". In the closing days of his rule, he danced with her through the night at a ball in the Danish merchants' club.

Jorgenson's nemesis was a correct and aristocratic British naval officer who sailed into Reykjavik in August and was perplexed to see a dirty purple flag "unknown to any nation" fluttering in the sky. The Hon. Alexander Jones's concern mounted as he read a proclamation declaring the island free, neutral, independent, "and at peace with all nations"; and converted into horror when he encountered Jorgenson incorrectly dressed in the uniform of a post captain. Jones interviewed Count Tramp, who let out a geyser of scalding complaints against Jorgenson that had been accu-mulating in his "filthy" cabin. Jones decided that the best course was to escort Tramp, Phelps and Jorgenson back to England.

On the last night of our honeymoon, we stayed in Reykjavik with a friend of my wife's who was the government epidemiologist. When I mentioned

Jorgenson's name, Haraldur took from his shelf a 1,000-page book that his uncle, Dr Helgi Briem, had written on Jorgenson's eight weeks in Iceland.

"After he left Iceland," Haraldur said, "we don't know what became of him."

The book did not look as if it had been read.

Jorgenson's two months as Protector of Iceland was the high point of his life. Arrested on his return to England at the hysterical urging of Count Tramp, he was charged with violating his parole and imprisoned with 800 men on the hulk *Bahama*. Confined beneath deck from 4 p.m. to 8 a.m., he lived in daily terror of being mutilated by Danish POWs after someone spread the rumour that Jorgenson had attacked Tramp with his sword. The fate of one victim, who lay dreadfully scarred in the hold of the hospital ship, preyed on his mind – "his face burned with gunpowder with Buonaparte in letters".

Jorgenson blamed the hulk as the place where he picked up the "vicious habits" of drunkenness and compulsive gambling that led, ultimately, to his transportation. He spent his next 15 years in and out of jail. One September day in 1813 he looked through the bars of his cell in the Fleet Prison for debtors and recognised the high cheekbones of his Dog Day Queen. He had intended to marry Gudrun had he stayed on in Iceland, but she had shifted her affections to another bankrupt and now shared a cell in the Fleet with Phelps's irascible supercargo, James Savignac, sleeping with him beneath an Icelandic eiderdown. Jorgenson joined them for a time in a curious *ménage à trois*. One evening, he wrote, "18 pots of porter and 2 bottles of gin were drank immediately after dinner and much more during the course of the evening".

From now on, Jorgenson put his faith in drink and gambling – "my besetting sin" – plus petitions to the famous. He had a shopping list of influential personalities whom he pestered for money and sympathy. Cold-shouldered by former patrons like Banks (whose hardened opinion was that Jorgenson "deserved to be hanged"), he turned his attention to Mrs Fry, the brewer Samuel Whitbread and the Duke of Wellington. Not even the Regent was spared, Jorgenson looking forward to the moment "when you and I, when King and beggars shall one day stand trembling indiscriminately before the Throne of ineffable resplendousness to receive judgment."

Imprisonment had one further unfortunate effect on Jorgenson: he became an author. From 1810 until his death 31 years later in a Vandemonian ditch, he produced a series of directionless, prolix works across an ambitious range of subjects and in a variety of forms. Simultaneously with his first narrative of the Icelandic revolution, he wrote a play, *Duke d'Angiens*, a tragedy in Five Acts, dedicated to Lady Baroness de Banks and based on a royal would-be assassin of Napoleon. He also wrote a four-act comedy, *Robertus Montanus or the Oxford Scholar*, an account of his travels through Germany and Italy; plus a 429-page religious tract, the outline for a new economic system, and a narrative of his travels with the Tasmanian Aborigines.

The most patient of his patrons – and most regular of his dedicatees ("I was in prison, and ye came unto me") – was Banks's friend, the botanist William Hooker, whose life Jorgenson had saved in Iceland when their boat caught fire. Jorgenson never allowed Hooker to forget what he owed him. On two occasions Hooker had to plead for Jorgenson's life and not a month went by when he did not receive a request to pay off a gambling debt or a printer's bill. Once, after treating him to a Christmas dinner at the Crown Inn in Reading, Hooker was asked to buy up copies of Jorgenson's latest work, *The Copenhagen Expedition traced to other causes than the Treaty of Tilsit*. "You know yourself at any other time, I would not say a word about such matters, but every little helps said the old woman, when she p—d into the sea."

After such a life, Jorgenson's undoing was prosaic. On May 25, 1820, he was indicted at the Old Bailey for stealing a bed, two blankets and a quilt from his landlady in the Tottenham Court Road. In court, Jorgenson insisted that he was going to pay her back. "Did I not show you a £50 bill?" The judge asked if this was true. "He showed me a two-penny stamp," said the landlady, contemptuously, "and said it was a £50 bill and that it came from Lord Castlereagh." The prisoner then made "an exceedingly long and unconnected defence".

He was sent to Newgate prison, but Hooker managed to get him a conditional pardon provided that he left England within a month. This he fully intended to do, but on the way to board his ship, "I had the misfortune to meet an old acquaintance on Tower Hill." A few months later, Jorgenson was detained again in one of his "wretched haunts" and sentenced to hang.

Once more, Hooker rallied to his rescue. This time, instead of to the grave, Jorgenson was transported to Van Diemen's Land.

Jorgenson's adventures made a vigorous impression on Kemp. "He began to laugh, and continued laughing until the tears absolutely ran down his cheeks," was how one contemporary described Kemp's reaction to a story that he had particularly liked.

How much they had in common! Jorgenson, like Kemp, had known Van Diemen's Land as a free man at a period when it was an uninhabited paradise. He had returned when it was a penal colony, as a convict. In between, he had ruled over an island half as large again. It is not too fanciful to see in Kemp's generosity towards him the response of a brother in spirit. Kemp had unseated an unpopular Governor. Kemp had known the gambling table, the bar, the bankruptcy court. And had he not, like Jorgenson, been "wonderfully industrious in raising enemies"? They were a pair of long-winded, conceited romantics; twins in everything, and above all in their self-belief. These words that Jorgenson wrote to Hooker could have been addressed as easily to Kemp. "There are some curious peculiarities attached to my character which baffle the penetration and judgement of my best friends and well wishers, and which indeed puzzle my own mind to such a degree at times that even in my most solitary hours and in the midst of the deepest meditation I cannot understand myself . . . Yet after taking a careful and repeated survey of my own mind, I think Genius may often be mistaken for madness. My good-natured friend do not smile at my presumption, I talk to myself when I talk to you . . . "

In a gesture Kemp was never to repeat, he offered Jorgenson £50 for his part in uncovering the forged treasury bills. Then, on January 15, 1827, he pushed the boat out further than he had done for anyone. He wrote a petition to Lieutenant Governor Arthur urging that Jorgenson be freed, and had the letter signed by 16 other merchants. A few months later Jorgenson received his ticket-of-leave.

It was not a free pardon – that would not come until 1835. He had to be in his lodging by curfew, attend church on Sunday and report once a month to the district muster. But the pass allowed Jorgenson to work for money and to hold a government position. So he became a policeman.

Jorgenson's last 15 years in Van Diemen's Land did nothing to curb his boastfulness. As a district constable, he was in charge of one of the roving parties sent out in search of Aborigines. His failure to find any members of the Oyster Bay tribe was no impediment to his becoming a self-proclaimed expert on their culture, habits and languages ("I am the only one who possesses the vocabularies complete"). As an employee of the Van Diemen's Land Company, he made three expeditions in the unrealistic hope of finding grazing routes – in the last of which the Company's surveyor Clement Lorymer drowned before his eyes. ("I have now explored the whole of that part of Van Diemen's Land which is marked 'unknown' . . . there are few who are better acquainted with this island, its mountains, gulleys and rivers than myself.") As a writer, he lost none of his prolixity. His *Observations on the Funded System* appeared with a preface of 44 pages, and in 1834, grossly influenced by Kemp, he published in pamphlet form *An Address to the free colonists of Van Diemen's Land on Trial by Jury, and our other constitutional rights.* "I have," he wrote, "at various periods exercised great influence over the colonial press." Not enough, however, to recover seven pounds and five shillings owed to him as a sub-editor on *The Colonist* – his action against the paper being rejected on the grounds that he was employed to write addresses on envelopes.

A stone or two below him staring out at the ducks were the chiselled sandstone features of Jorgenson's "queen".

Only in his role as a husband did his relentless optimism falter. He might have married Gudrun or the god-daughter of the Grand Duke of Hesse, to whom he was engaged when on a mysterious spying mission for the British government. Instead he married Norah Corbett, an abusive and illiterate ex-dairymaid from Limerick of "extremely drunken habits".

That evening I drove north to Campbell Town and walked up Tragedy Hill to a pale orange house with a tin roof. A flowering hedge of heather and protea spilled over a wooden fence, and along the Western Tiers a forest fire was competing with the sunset. The house was once the Campbell Town Inn where Jorgenson was lodging when he met the 23-year-old Norah.

He had arrived in Campbell Town to track down some sheep-rustlers. Norah was living with them in the bush. One day she walked into the Inn: five foot four, dark brown hair, brown eyes. An instant attraction was formed. She moved into Jorgenson's room and agreed to testify against her former companions.

Norah's evidence resulted in three convictions, but her betrayal unbalanced her. Her reputation as a police spy made her the target of whispered remarks, according to Jorgenson, such as "there goes the woman who hanged so many men". Two members of her gang waited for days by the road with the declared intention of shooting both her and Jorgenson. Norah took to leaving the Inn disguised as a man. All this, combined with her addiction to ginger beer and gin, resulted in "a visible derangement of intellect". After she tried to commit suicide a fourth time, by swallowing a mouthful of copper sulphate, Jorgenson paid a man to watch her.

Jorgenson's employer in the district, Thomas Anstey, knew nothing about Norah, save for "her propensity to beat and scratch Jorgenson when she is intoxicated". There were frequent complaints of the two of them fighting in the street. Increasingly, it was Jorgenson who came off worst. In Anstey's opinion, Norah wasn't the only one suffering from mental delusions, and he did his best to argue Jorgenson out of his "infatuated attachment". But the policeman's passion could not be subverted "by reason or reflection". Anstey concluded – correctly: "His ruin is inevitable if he marries this woman."

In his obstinate choice of wife Jorgenson most deserved his description of himself as "a veteran of misfortune". They married in New Norfolk, far from where anyone would recognise them, but within a year she had been removed from her husband and placed for three months in the Female Factory in Hobart, where she spent a further two sessions. Her crimes included theft and assaulting other women, but the most common charge was drunkenness.

In the end, Jorgenson could not cope. A year before his death he presented his last petition, begging for the police to lock up his wife for a further six weeks. She was, he wrote, past redemption. "She lugs me continually down hill with her. I do not like to appear myself for fear of future violence." He did not care if he never saw her face again.

Jorgenson's last link with the life he had left behind came in the shape of a visit from the son of his old friend, William Hooker.

Joseph Hooker was on a voyage to Antarctica on the *Erebus*. Calling in at Hobart on the way south, he went ashore at his father's request to look up Jorgenson. He was "an extraordinary man", his father wrote. "I stood him friend for as long as I could, but he proved too bad for me . . . The man's life would form a perfect Romance if written with the *Strictest Attention* to truth . . . His talents are of the *highest* order, but for his character, moral and religious, it was always of the lowest order."

The figure that Joseph Hooker tracked down was lachrymose, half-tipsy, dressed in rags. After their final meeting, at which Jorgenson called on him and begged for half a crown, looking miserable, Hooker wrote to his father: "His drunken wife has died and left a more drunken widower; he was always in this state when I saw him and used to *cry* about you. I have consulted several persons, who have shown him kindness, about him, and have offered money and everything; but he is irreclaimable; telling the truth with him is quite an effort."

On the way back from Antarctica, the *Erebus* docked again in Hobart, where Hooker learned that Jorgenson's body had been picked up in a ditch a few weeks before. He had died of pneumonia in January 1841 and his body had lain in the open for a day before it was discovered. But then Jorgenson had always known that the joys of human life were fleeting.

"They may be likened to two friends meeting each other on a hasty journey, who ask a few questions, and then part perhaps forever, leaving nothing behind but a tender regret."

I could not deny that a reason his story interested me was my wife's ancestry. Although raised in Canada, she was Icelandic. This meant that our son would be half-Icelandic. Like Jorgenson, he would have a stake in two islands literally poles apart – and I wondered if one day, like W.H. Auden, he would travel through Iceland on a bus and spot the familiar shape of Australia in a patch of snow.

Back home, Peter had finished cleaning out the possum shit. "Ah, you won't get them in now."

I explained what I had been doing, and it stirred him to tell me in the casual, understated way so typical of Tasmanians how his niece in Hobart was involved romantically with the Crown Prince of Jorgenson's native land. At first, I was wary. This was the kind of thing that Jorgenson used to boast about – how he "figured in courtly scenes and made much stir on the literary and political world of Europe". But a few months later I opened the *Mercury* and there was the news of their engagement. One day Mary Donaldson, my possum-catcher's niece, stood to be Queen of Denmark.

XIX

RESCUED BY JORGENSON, KEMP THRIVED FOR A WHILE. APPROACHING 60 AND wearing spectacles, he looked out on a busy port, macadamised streets and shingled roofs that reminded Mrs Prinsep, a visitor to his store, of no place other than "old England". She wrote in a letter in 1829: "I dare say you have never dreamt of Van Diemen's Land as of any thing else than a kind of wilderness; an appropriate insular prison for the vagabonds who are sent to it yearly from England. You have never supposed that it has a beautiful harbour, a fine metropolis, with towns, streets, shops, and pretty shop-keepers, like some of the larger towns of Devonshire . . . " As she walked up Macquarie Street towards Kemp's emporium, "I enjoyed a thousand English associations . . . cats and cottages, ships and shops, girls in their pattens, boys playing at marbles; above all the rosy countenances, and chubby cheeks, and the English voices." The only discordant note was the extraordinary number of spirit shops – about 50.

"While I am now writing it is snowing on the mountain opposite my cottage." So Kemp described the Hobart winter of 1816 in a letter to Potter. During the long dark evenings of June and July, he sat by his fire with books and tracts borrowed from the library. A growing number of them warned against the dissipation caused by drinking the gin he sold: *Satan's Snares*, *Don't Go to the Gin Shop* and *The Bottle* (drawings by Cruikshank). "I don't think much of them," he once said in disgust, returning some Puseyite tracts. "The writers were paid for saying what they did." At this, a look of pious horror crossed the face of the neigh-bour who had lent them. "What, Mr Kemp? Do you think that a minister of the Gospel would sell himself in that way?" Kemp answered: "Well, Sir, as to that I have my own opinion. I am all for the right of private judgment, Sir." While Kemp's wife studied manuals like *Kind Words for the Kitchen* and *Female Excellence or Hints for Daughters*, Kemp liked to "peruse" the London *Times* that arrived six months late, along with the Christmas editions of *Punch*, the *Illustrated London News*, the *Quarterly Review.* In later life, he admired Arthur Stanley's *Life of Thomas Arnold* and Charles Dickens's novels which he read in serial form. Kemp recognised Vandemonian connections in at least two of Dickens's most striking creations: the pickpocket Fagin in *Oliver Twist* and the convict Magwitch in *Great Expectations*. The character of Fagin is said to have been inspired by "Ikey" Solomon, who in 1831 was transported to Hobart for 14 years for receiving stolen goods; Magwitch was a fugitive from the same hulks in which Kemp's friend Jorgenson had been incarcerated.

On Jorgenson's death, Kemp was one of but a handful of settlers who had known the colony since its foundation. He identified its fate chiefly with his own. In Kemp's opinion, it was owing to his persistent lobbying that Van Diemen's Land had become separated administratively from New South Wales in 1825. But Kemp would not rest until the colony won the right to govern itself, independent of London and its meddling Lieutenant Governors.

In 1829, he cornered the author of the first Australian novel, the locally printed *Quintus Servinton*, in Hobart's Commercial Rooms. He told Henry Savery that "until we have a House of Assembly and trial by Jury, we shall do no good, Sir."

Kemp's House of Assembly was a castle that would remain in the sky for a quarter century more, but he was preparing for it, he told Savery, by "practising talking".

"Whose style of eloquence do you most admire, Sir?"

"Whose style, Sir? Few equal to my own . . . "

His laws, he said, would include an Act to annul all former Laws and Acts ("nothing like a clear stage, and plenty of elbow-room") and an Act to compel everyone to eat a daily hot lunch, with two pounds of meat per head, "so as to encourage the consumption and raise the price of livestock".

Savery wrote of Kemp as having "a considerable degree of eagerness in his manner". But on the next occasion they met he considered that Kemp was less animated, and that his "hasty impetuosity" which had at first startled him had declined into "a look of moody, disappointed ambition". Over a drink at the Waterloo Hotel, Kemp complained to a visitor from

England: "Good God Almighty, Sir, the colony is ruined. All going to the Devil."

Another bee in Kemp's intransigent bonnet was transportation. Transportation ceased to New South Wales in 1840, but not for another 13 years to Van Diemen's Land. Until 1853, convicts came into the island at the rate of 5,000 per year and from all quarters of the Empire: South Africa, Ireland, India, China, Canada, New South Wales. At the same time, assignment was replaced by the probation system. The convicts worked in gangs and lived together in a network of remote stations, including one established on Maria Island and another on a spectacular cliff outside Swansea. It was during this period that Van Diemen's Land consolidated its reputation, as the *Gippsland Guardian* put it, as "that pandemonium of the most wicked and debased of England's children".

Kemp had been only too pleased to build up his business using free convict labour, but now that he was a God-fearing and respectable family citizen he resented the stigma that "convictism" had lent to his adopted colony, not least in the eyes of Potter and Kemp's sisters back home.

In 1837, Potter read a letter in *The Times* that confirmed any lingering doubt as to the character of the society in which his brother-in-law had settled. The letter, written by Alexander Maconochie, private secretary to Lieutenant Governor Franklin, was part of a blistering attack on the effect of transportation to Van Diemen's Land. "It seems to me too severe for any offence whatever" – and in every case involved "further deterioration of character". Maconochie warned that distress, vice and dissipation were common "among the free as among the bond", and he had no hesitation in characterising the established settlers like Kemp as slave-drivers. "The evil, then, is crying and I almost hesitate as I thus sum it up; for it seems at first incredible that, being so great, it should not sooner have attracted notice." Once detected and publicised, Vandemonian evil was impossible to sweep under the carpet. Committees looked into it, Lieutenant Governors reported back on it and the Colonial Office worried what to do about it.

Until 1853, when it decided to end transportation, the Colonial Office had to field a flow of reports of unnatural practices indulged in, wrote Lloyd Robson, "on a scale not dreamt of by readers of Catullus". In 1843, the newly arrived Lieutenant Governor John Eardley-Wilmot brought to Lord Stanley's attention "the prevalence of a nameless crime among the male and female prisoners". The previous year, Elizabeth Ainsworth had been convicted of this nameless crime "with a *woman*". A trawl through court records unearthed yet more dramatic cases. In 1843, John Demer,

Stewart Jenett and William Chiffet were convicted "with a *mare*" and in 1846 four men with a goat. ("Acquitted Edward Spackman and Robt Earl, one with a cow, the other with a bull.")

"The capital charge is seldom sustained," complained one superintendent, but in 1845 Job Harries and William Cottier were executed for the rape of a boy at a coal mine. The medical officer could not say "who has diseased him because the act had occurred on his being lowered one day into the Mines to work when five or six of the men seized and dragged him to one of the dark passages and there forced him to submit to their will." In 1845, a former prison warder at Pentonville, James Boyd, made a private report into the probation station on Maria Island after visiting the dormitories. The following text was omitted from the account that reached the House of Commons: "I have every reason to believe that crime in these wards was, prior to my arrival, by no means infrequent . . . In one night I found that eight men had removed the separation boards, and were sleeping together . . . They were tried and sentenced to nine months' hard labour in chains . . . Two of the eight had the bold and disgusting effrontery to tell the visiting magistrate that they had never heard [of] sleeping together prohibited at other stations where they had been." Nor did the probation stations have a monopoly on vice. The Irish convict Patrick O'Donohue wrote to his wife about Hobart: "I suppose the earth could not produce so vicious a population as inhabits this town; vice of all kinds, in its most hideous and exaggerated form, openly practised by all classes and sexes."

The official most shocked was William Gladstone, Secretary of State for the Colonies. His attention had been drawn to "this great moral evil" by his Permanent Under Secretary, James Stephen, who passed on a conversation he had had with an old friend from Van Diemen's Land, George Dougan. "My informant told me that the state of vice and moral debasement at the gangs which he visited was something so shocking that (I believe I quote him exactly) it made his blood curdle to think of it. He told me that he had no doubt that more than two-thirds of the members of these gangs were living in the systematic and habitual practice of unnatural crimes, that people were actually paired together, and understood as having that revolting relationship to each other; that his own host, the physician, came to a knowledge of these things by the loathsome diseases resulting from them . . . and that the whole scene was such as not to be fitly described in words."

Stephen's words galvanised Gladstone. He believed that the convicts of Van Diemen's Land had "fallen into habits of life so revolting and depraved as to make it nothing less than the most sacred and imperious duty to adopt, without the necessary loss of a single day, such measures as may best be adapted to arrest the progress of pollution."

Almost as important a factor in Kemp's growing antipathy to transportation was the cost to his own pocket. The implementation of the probation system withdrew convicts from the free labour market. New regulations meant that those who wanted to use convict workers had to pay for them: four shillings and eight pence per day for a mechanic, and two shillings and tuppence for a labourer. In addition, free settlers were required to foot the bills for policing and imprisoning convicts, as well as to finance their own passage to the colony. And on top of everything there was the influx of 5,000 convicts a year. On October 3, 1850, Thomas Arnold, who had recently married into Kemp's family, wrote to his mother: "The hateful red flag is flying at the signal staff, showing that another ship with male convicts is coming in. A thousand more of the *worst* among men are expected before the end of the year. Conceive what you would think, if every year 20 men, embellished with every hue and shade of villainy, murderers, burglars, forgers, thieves, etc., etc., were sent to your valley and permanently established there, and you will be able to realise in some degree the horror and disgust which those feel, who are bound to this unhappy country by ties which they cannot break, who see free emigration entirely stopped and its place supplied by the deportation of the felonry of England to their shores."

In 1842, New South Wales was granted a measure of self-government, the Legislative Council henceforth being two-thirds elective. From then on, the abolition of transportation and the introduction of self-government became Kemp's chief ambitions. Here is an extract from the Hobart newspaper *Britannia* of July 6, 1848: "A.F. Kemp, Esq. – We are gratified in being able to announce that the father of the people, the Washington of Van Diemen's Land, has recovered from his recent severe indisposition, and that, in his mental energies, he is as strong as ever. We wish him to live long enough to take his place, even if it be only for a day, in an elected Legislative Assembly, and then having consistently and successfully fought for the freedom of his adopted country, he may retire to *Mount Vernon* until the colony, in the usual course of events, is called upon to mourn his loss. Every man has his peculiarity, and Mr Kemp's peculiar peculiarity has been the expression, on all occasions, of his hope to see Van Diemen's Land with her *irons* off, enjoying liberty, not in mere theory, but in *reality*. We write this brief notice of Mr Kemp, on the 4th of July, the anniversary of the day on which the United States of America declared their independence, after having been for years ridden rough-shod over by a tyrannical British ministry with whom, as with those who deal in the most vital interests of this Colony, 'might is right'. Will it last for ever? No – the hand-writing is on the wall."

No hand had been busier than Anthony Fenn Kemp's. Although less in evidence at political gatherings, Kemp remained an influential figure locally. He was the first person that the landscape painter John Glover, "the English Claude", turned to as a referee for his land grant application at Mills' Plains. He was one of the founders of the Theatre Royal; he was reappointed a JP; and in 1845, he staged a Punch and Judy show outside the Legislative Chamber, helping to defeat a bill that threatened to raise taxes. But from 1830 until his death in 1868 his energies were focused increasingly on his estate outside Green Ponds.

At "Dulcet", surrounded by his fat pastures, Patrick White's Garnet Roxburgh had "paraded the assured insolence of the lapsed gentleman". At Mount Vernon, surrounded by his numerous family, Kemp was ready to develop his final incarnation: Father of the People.

XX

HE WAS BORN EARLY ONE OCTOBER MORNING AND WEIGHED ALMOST TWELVE pounds. "That's not a baby, that's a giant," the midwife said. We christened him Max George Tasman Shakespeare.

Genealogy may generally be the preoccupation of the elderly, but the impulse to look back at the tracks in the sand can be triggered by having a child of your own, especially when that event occurs, as in my case, somewhat late in life.

In the uproar of my son's ancestry were some pretty disappointed expectations, but like any incipient parent I was prone to self-deception and wishful thinking. I wanted his life to be perfect.

The genes, they come down. If I had a say, whose genes did I wish to dominate my son: the sensible Potter's or the adventurous Kemp's?

Kemp was a baby once, some mother's darling. So would have been Potter, for that matter. Their letters made me think that what held both men back was that each was not more like the other. If Kemp had hurried a little more slowly, if Potter had left his desk and lived a little more . . .

Perhaps every affair of business, of love, of writing itself, calls for a necessary balance between the Potter and the Kemp, between the Apollonian and the Dionysiac, between the ledger and the rum. And I wished this balance for my son.

XXI

THE FATHER OF TASMANIA HAD BEEN QUICK TO ABANDON HIS OLDEST TWO legitimate children in London with the Potters: the nine-year-old George, who was born in York Town, and his seven-year-old sister Elizabeth. Kemp wrote in a letter to Aldgate that his children were "ever uppermost" in his mind. "I am sure that you and my sister's goodness of heart will not let them want for anything until I have it in my power to make remittances."

Whatever scepticism I had about Kemp's paternal feelings, I found it heart-rending to read of his wife's anguish over their daughter Elizabeth's illness that is 14 months old by the time Mrs Kemp learns of it from Potter. "Does Betsy grow tall? Her ninth birthday is just past. I hope as she grows abler she will mend in every respect. Oh! that I could but for five minutes behold her, but I fear it will be many a long day first."

Since 1801, the Potters had also been taking care of Emily, Kemp's daughter by Judith Simpson. Emily remained in England. But once they had come of age Elizabeth and George returned to Van Diemen's Land, where Elizabeth asserted her independence by getting married to the son of Kemp's bitterest enemy.

Kemp had not become so Puritan that he could not forgive and forget. In 1825, a year after Lieutenant Governor Sorell's departure, he gave away his 17-year-old daughter to a thin, sallow man with bristly hair reckoned to be "a bit of a sis".

William Sorell had not seen his father since he was seven, when Colonel Sorell eloped with Mrs Kent, but at the urging of his mother – since reduced to selling fruit in Covent Garden – he had sailed out "to assert his claims on his father's attention in person". He arrived in Hobart only to discover that Kemp's vendetta had caused his father's recall. William briefly considered returning home. What decided him to stay on was the ravishing Elizabeth Kemp.

A reserved bureaucrat, William did not impress anyone with his intelligence. In Kemp's daughter, he believed that he was marrying a woman "who hates and abominates discord and strife". He could not have been more wrong.

On her return to Hobart, Elizabeth had flowered into a headstrong, beautiful woman – "perhaps the most beautiful woman you ever saw", in the eyes of the diarist George Boyes, although he added that she was also "a very devil incarnate". She had her father's impulse of bolting from any situation that failed to agree with her, and five years after marriage to the dull Sorell – who managed to get a job as Registrar in the Supreme Court – she was restless. Mrs Fenton, on a visit from Calcutta, met Elizabeth at this time, and wrote in her diary that the young woman was rather too eager to know all about her sea journey. "She affected a becoming sort of wonderment at my 'astonishing courage' to undertake a 'voyage' alone. I was much amused. I assured her the days of Pamela-like adventures were fairly gone and away, and every one but the very young girls, or very simple old ones, might travel where they list as fearlessly." A seed had been planted.

In 1838, after 13 years of marriage, Elizabeth kissed her husband goodbye on the wharf in Hobart and boarded a ship for Europe. William Sorell understood that she was taking their five children to visit their paternal grandfather in Brussels – where "Old Man" Sorell had gone to live. In fact, she was sailing to meet her lover, Lieutenant Colonel George Deare, an officer in the 21st Regiment with whom she had had an intense affair in Hobart. Leaving her children with Sorell, she and Deare eloped to India. Kemp never saw Elizabeth again, nor did her own daughters.

Her great-grandson would draw on Elizabeth for the alluring and destructive Lucy Tantamount in his novel *Point Counter Point*: "A perfumed imitation of a savage or an animal." Aldous Huxley was responding to the family's precosity for havoc. He and his brother Julian were raised on tales of "the wild and forcible Kemps" and their dominating characteristic: "an ungovernable temper". No one incarnated this wildness with more allure than Elizabeth's daughter Julia.

It took two years for Colonel Sorell to arrange for his humiliated grand-daughter to return to her father in Hobart. In 1847, Julia had her portrait painted by the convicted forger and poisoner, Thomas Wainewright. She is pictured with her head on one side and pitch dark, seductive eyes. The watercolour does not show that she has lost some of her teeth; nor that she is driven by the "intemperate passion" that guided her maternal grandfather – a passion that she directed at a gentle 26-year-old inspector of schools with a slight stammer who arrived in Van Diemen's Land in 1850.

XXII

THOMAS ARNOLD WAS THE YOUNGER BROTHER OF THE POET MATTHEW, AND favourite son of Dr Arnold of Rugby. "Never was a child dearer to a parent than you were to him," wrote his mother after he landed in Hobart. Less well known are his connections with Anthony Fenn Kemp.

Arnold had departed England with a reputation as the handsomest undergraduate at Oxford. A rabid democrat – the model for the hero of Arthur Hugh Clough's poem "The Bothie of Tober-na-Vuolich" – he was consumed by the idea of finding an answer to the conundrum "what, namely, is the ideal of human life". He was also a hopeless admirer of George Sand's fiction, and had sailed to New Zealand in a spasm of "young and democratic despair" after a girl rejected him. But his notion of founding a classless Pantisocratic society in a five-acre block on Porirua Road, near Wellington, had

Tom Arnold

petered out, and in 1849 he accepted the offer of a salaried post in Van Diemen's Land.

He had been in Hobart only a month when a lawyer invited him to a party in Davey Street. He arrived late. A regimental band dressed in blue jackets was playing the polka. A woman sat on a sofa in excited conversation with a red-coated officer. Arnold described the next hour in a private memoir that he wrote for his children: "Looking around the room on entering, I saw a lady in black, wearing a single white camellia in her black hair, with a singularly refined and animated face." She stood up to be introduced. They examined each other, he wrote, *à la dérobée*. "I remember how strong the feeling was upon me I *must* have met her before; a sense of moral likeness, an overpowering attraction and affinity, drew me to her. For me it was certainly 'love at first sight'!" Soon afterwards, he wrote to Miss Sorell. "I could not help looking at you every instant and envying everyone on whom you vouchsafed a word or smile; so much so that some young lady, Miss Swan I think, declared that she would never dance opposite Mr Arnold again . . . for his eyes were always turned towards – you can guess whom."

Forty years on, the memory of Kemp's granddaughter – her dark eyes with an expression "full of meaning", a short upper lip "shaped like a cupid's bow", her firm figure – still had the power to make Arnold catch

Julia Sorell

his breath: "O my own Julia, I shall never forget how beautiful and capturing you were that night; nor what a rage I was in, at finding you had gone home without me." On her leaving the party, Arnold agreed to dance an insufferable quadrille with a Mrs Chapman, and it may have been she who filled him in on the "alarming" reputation of the young woman with whom he had been conversing.

The 24-year-old Julia had days earlier broken off her engagement with a Lieutenant Elliott of the 99th ("he had been ordered away, & I do not think she either expected or wished to see him again"). She had been engaged to at least two other men, including Chester Eardley-Wilmot, the son of the last Governor, who lent her novels and went riding with her on a white pony. Not only that, but there were rumours concerning Julia and the late Governor himself – rumours, later proven false, that had contributed to the latter's premature death from "complete exhaustion of the frame".

Arnold admitted to his children: "Your mother was no unknown person at the time . . . among women she had her detractors." According to her enemies, Julia was alleged to have seduced Sir John Eardley-Wilmot one night at Government House, where she sometimes played scenes from Shakespeare. (In one scene, reported by her daughter, she stood on a pedestal and gave an indelibly inert performance of Hermione in *The Winter's Tale* – "till at the words, 'Music! Awake her! Strike!' she kindled into life.") The affable, courteous Eardley-Wilmot had come to Hobart without his wife and was well known to the diarist George Boyes for his "fondness for the younger part of the fair sex". When young girls visited Government House, he occasionally put his arm around their necks. "They seemed to enjoy these little familiarities amazingly."

One evening Julia Sorell was overheard to say that if she were a man she would have as many women as she liked without marrying.

Eardley-Wilmot answered: "Why, you are a perfect devil."

"And if I am, Sir John, you are another."

What on earth had passed between them to justify this exchange became the subject of hot debate, especially among a group of local clergy opposed to the Lieutenant Governor, who, in the kind of language used by Kemp against Sorell 30 years before, put it about that Eardley-Wilmot was living "in scarcely concealed concubinage" with Kemp's granddaughter – a very young woman whose mother's conduct had been "only too notorious".

By April 1845, the story circulated to the ears even of Julia's dim-witted father, who called on the Lieutenant Governor and told him that he had heard that Eardley-Wilmot had taken Julia up to New Norfolk, where they had spent the night. Eardley-Wilmot denied the rumours – they were "the grossest falsehoods that ever oppressed an English gentleman" and had been "invented and circulated by my opponents" – but he could not prevent their spreading to the Melbourne correspondent of the *Naval and Military Gazette*, who commented: "No people of any standing will now enter Government House except on business; no ladies can."

This was too much for William Gladstone, Secretary of State for the

Colonies. In a letter marked "secret", he wrote to the Lieutenant Governor, suspending him without recommendation for another government post until these rumours about his private life were disposed of. The letter broke Eardley-Wilmot. He collapsed and died in the house of his private secretary in Hobart.

The discovery of Julia's "undisciplined" past did nothing to dampen the ardour of Thomas Arnold, whose favourite Sand novel was *Jacques* – about a man of democratic ideals who embarks on a fantastically ill-advised marriage with a vain, vituperative and air-headed young woman not unlike Julia. He wrote to her of the only rumour in Hobart that mattered to him – which was that "I neither look at, nor speak to, or think of, any other person than Julia Sorell."

From that night she was continually in his thoughts. "I schemed to get invited to the same houses to which she was asked; and she put no obstacles in my way." Among his papers at Balliol College, I read letter after letter that he wrote to Julia from Launceston and Swansea and Campbell Town – wherever he had to ride on his bay Harry to inspect a school. "Dearest darling love I wish I could give you this very minute as many kisses as there are days in the year and 365 times that." One night in March 1850, he slept on the edge of Kemp's property at Green Ponds. There was a problem at the school – the local clergyman had driven away all Roman Catholic children, and he wrote to Julia: "The parson's foot has been in the broth and spoiled it." She read nothing extraordinary in the observation. Dazzled by his father's reputation, she perceived Arnold as her ticket-of-leave from the military and settler society, "which was all the colonies could give her". But buried in Arnold's innocent line about Catholicism was a sympathy that would grow to give her untold "grief and indignation". One man who nurtured it was Kemp.

Arnold's host at Green Ponds was a pious friend of Kemp's who talked about how Kemp ribbed him unmercifully. Arnold flirted with the idea of introducing himself to Julia's grandfather: "This morning I felt strongly tempted to call at Mount Vernon as I passed, but I remembered that if I did so it would probably cause a day's delay in my return to you, so I refrained." He wrote: "Oh Julia, you may believe how I thought of you as I passed the house, but indeed I do little else at present, sleeping or waking. You told me, I think, that you used often to stay there when you were a child. I wondered which of the windows was that of the room which used to be the little Julia's? The little creature with her tempers and perversities, how well I can fancy her."

He had been reading "the scene of the night interview in *Romeo and*

Juliet and never felt its beauty so much as now. Oh, that I could speak to thee with the tongue of Shakespeare and the imagination of Milton, yet all would come short of what I feel for thou."

In fact, a poem does survive, written after he had married her:

> *Sometimes after days of hard riding*
> *On my rounds to the schools of the land*
> *As I paused on some hilltop dividing*
> *Two glens sloping down to the strand*
> *Sublime without rivalling brother*
> *The mountain far off I could see*
> *And I thought how the beautiful mother*
> *At its foot there sat waiting for me.*

Thoughts of Julia crammed his mind as he rode south from Perth through the bush. "The fresh bracing air and the sweet smells of the forest were most exhilarating. Smooth lawny glades chequered with light and shade spread themselves between the trees in all directions, and the clumps of the silver wattle relieved sometimes by the darker green of the native cherry were most beautiful. I have felt a growing affection for the land that gave you birth; its hills and plains have been invested to my eyes with a colouring only love can give. The beauty which we think is in nature comes generally from our own hearts; we do not see it when we are unhappy." He was shortly to be so.

In the same month, Arnold asked Julia to marry him. "Seeing how completely in love I was she resolved to accept me, chiefly because I was my father's son."

A "dear military friend" passing through Hobart took one look at his fiancée and tried to persuade Arnold to break off the engagement forthwith, candidly arguing – amongst other things – that she was not "well-adapted" to be the wife of a poor man like Arnold. But it was no good: Arnold loved her, he said, "better than life".

They were married on Dr Arnold's birthday at St David's Cathedral, Hobart, in June 1850. Arnold wrote: "I know that in my eyes a thing so beautiful has rarely been seen." He swiftly discovered that his wife was not simply beautiful, but financially extravagant, prone to passionate outbursts of temper and liked to "nag, nag, nag him till he almost lost his senses". She burst into tears at their wedding reception, and when five years later Arnold converted to Catholicism at St Joseph's, the pioneer Catholic church in Hobart, she arrived with a basket of stones and hurled them one by one through the stained-glass window, saying that "the earth had crumbled under her". She was without any religious convictions, she told her husband. She was one of those unhappy people whom God had abandoned. She had one belief only, and she clung to it with an "imperial will" right to her death: very few families had been "cursed" with an upbringing such as hers.

Arnold well understood what she meant when, on the eve of his unexpected conversion, he and his wife were invited by the head of her family to a New Year's Eve party at Mount Vernon. Anthony Fenn Kemp was ringing in not merely another year, but a momentous moment in the island's history: the granting by Queen Victoria of his long-fought-for new constitution, including a bicameral Parliament comprising a Legislative Council and House of Assembly. The Queen had also agreed to legalise the colony's new name. From January 1, 1856, Van Diemen's Land was set to manage its own affairs under a "more euphonious" title: Tasmania.

XXIII

I DROVE TO MOUNT VERNON ALONG THE SAME ROAD THAT THE ARNOLDS AND their two children rode in their phaeton. The signposts were punishingly familiar – Glenorchy, Chigwell, Brighton – but a reminder, too, of how few Aboriginal place names I had come across since living here. In their project to annihilate distance with sameness, colonists like Kemp ignored native words and replaced them with domesticating ones like Egg and Bacon Bay and Blinking Billy Point. In the north-west I had come across the hamlets of Paradise and Nowhere Else – after the comment of an early settler who, whenever he saw people cross his property, would tell them they had proceeded far enough. "The track," said Charles Ivory gruffly, "leads nowhere else." And yet the landscape had fought back. I found myself making a list of those who had presumed to rename it:

Tasman – d. in disgrace; Baudin – d. in Mauritius of dysentery; Flinders – d. on the day his *Terra Australis* was printed; Schouten – allegedly stoned to death; Hellyer – committed suicide; Lorymer – drowned when surveying the north-west coast with Jorgenson; Jorgenson – d. in ditch.

I could not discover the fate of the Royal Marine private who passed this way in 1804, to hunt kangaroos to feed a starving population in Hobart. Hugh Germain had reportedly packed two books in his knapsack, the Bible and *The Arabian Nights*, and with the insouciance of a seed-sower he flung names at the hills and rivers, some of which I could see through the windscreen: Jerusalem, Jericho, Abyssinia, Jordan, Lake Tiberias, Bagdad.

★ ★ ★

Bagdad lay a few miles north of Brighton. On the car radio the news from Iraq was that American troops from the 3rd Infantry were sweeping through the eastern suburbs. Crowds were throwing flowers at them and 20 American tanks had taken up position in the centre of Baghdad. The day was Wednesday April 9, 2003.

In Bagdad, Tasmania, the morning was overcast. Signs beside the Heritage Highway advertised "canaries for sale" and "clean dirt" and "chook-poo – $3 a bag". Leaving the Hobart Gun Club on my right, I stopped for petrol at the post office, where there was another sign. "WHEN YOU BECOME QUIET IT JUST DAWNS ON YOU".

"I change the message every day," Roland Berry explained, a compact, ex-army man in a Caltex bomber-jacket. "Saturday I was going to put on 'GEORGE W OUR POST CODE IS 7030' – in other words 'Don't mistake us for the other side', but then a bloke came in and wanted something for his wife's birthday."

Berry's wife was the postmistress. She said it was all nonsense.

"What's nonsense?"

"The stories about hate mail and stuff being sent to Saddam Hussein here and we can't cope with it. Not one iota. You'd think people have better things to do," she told a woman who had come in to buy barley sugar.

Roland had just returned from Victoria where he had grown sick of showing people his car licence. Even so, you could not have a madman running around the world. "They should have learned from history. In 1936, they should have stopped Hitler. Compared to the First World War, this is a skirmish."

"What if they don't find Weapons of Mass Destruction?"

"Plant some."

He was descended from an English poacher, and his grandfather was a rabbit-trapper who sired eight children. "Grandad on mum's side won a Military Medal at Gallipoli and was gassed in France. He wouldn't talk about it at all, but the man could drink, I'll give him that."

I ordered a "cappacino" from the chalked menu and sipped it while leafing through the latest issue of the *Bagdad News*: the Bagdad singers were seeking a pianist and a number of items had "gone walking" from the kitchen in the Community Club. "Please check your cupboards and see if they mistakenly made their way into them." And an advertisement for a voluntary position for six months, starting immediately. "Have you got what it takes to be a Vice-President? If so, the Bagdad community needs you."

Further up the road, Neville Gangell, the ex-butcher of Bagdad, shut his door on me, but I spoke to a farmer who remembered Bagdad when every inch of its soil was planted with apples, and you could see blossom all the way to Kempton. Geoff Chalmers was not interested in the goings-on in Iraq. "I've lived in Bagdad all my life. We know there's another one on the other side of the world. But this is Bagdad. It's always been Bagdad."

I left Bagdad and drove up Constitution Hill – so called, the locals joked, because you needed a very strong constitution to climb it. Kempton lay in a shallow valley on the far side.

XXIV

KEMP WAS 57 WHEN HE DECIDED TO WITHDRAW TO HIS ESTATE. HIS 800 ACRES were situated close to Kemp's Lakes, in countryside named after him during Laycock's crossing of the island. Daring attacks by bushrangers, and later by Aborigines, had meant that he had so far only grazed the land – with merinos purchased out of Potter's loan. Their wool brought him sizeable profits, but he complained frequently of sheep-stealing – "a hundred at a time, being driven off their pasture ground and never heard of again". He was afraid of bushrangers, who had long memories of his brutality as a magistrate.

His enthusiasm to develop his grant coincided with the return of his eldest son from Aldgate. With no concern for his safety, Kemp dispatched the 19-year-old George into the interior – where immediately he came up against one of Tasmania's most dangerous outlaws, Matthew Brady.

In March 1825, Brady stole a valuable horse belonging to Kemp. A month later, George found a message nailed to the door of the local inn, the Royal Oak. It was addressed to the Lieutenant Governor, but might as well have been directed at George's father. "It has caused Matthew Brady much concern that such a person as Colonel Arthur is at large. Twenty gallons of rum will be given to any person who will deliver this person to me." Three months later, George was shaken awake in his brick cottage – Brady, holding a pistol to his temple. Brady demanded tobacco, tea and sugar, as well as a copy of the *Hobart Town Gazette*. He stole George's guns, and two weeks later let it be known that his gang would shoot Kemp's horse – "as they would him, if they fell in with him". Back in Hobart,

Kemp gathered 48 signatories and sent a petition to Arthur, writing that he had witnessed "with inexpressible alarm the manner in which the banditti now at large have continued to evade apprehensions and to contrive to carry their Depredations upon the peaceable Inhabitants of the Interior, keeping even the Metropolis in a State of continued agitation & alarm." The bushrangers' threats were not empty. In 1830, George discovered two charred corpses on the farm: one poisoned after corrosive sublimate of lime had been added to the man's rum; another, "Pretty Jack", sewn into a raw hide and burned to death.

But by the early 1830s, Brady was dead, the Black War had driven the Aborigines from the Midlands, and Kemp felt that it was safe to retire here. He commissioned a government architect to add a grand façade to the cottage and to convert the whole into a full-blown Regency building, and in the grounds he planted his signature pear trees and oaks in rows that traced out a Masonic sign, the only known instance of his ever doing anything as a Mason.* Mrs Prinsep described the effect in a letter: "At the back of his estate rise hills, like downs, naturally bare of trees and clothed with excellent pasture for sheep, with which their sides were covered. The Jordan meanders below, on the banks of which the farm

* Among the plumbers and glaziers who worked on the extension at Mount Vernon was possibly James Woodcock Graves, a former composer from Wigton who one evening in 1824 had sat down and written impromptu the first five verses of "D'ye ken John Peel". In 1842, he was detained for apparent insanity at an asylum in New Norfolk.

houses are situated, and between us and them rich fields of corn and grain stood ready for the reaper."

Soon Kemp had expanded his estate to 3,400 acres. He introduced drought-resistant dwarf American corn, and bred horses for his racecourse and Sambhur deer for his pleasure garden. He even had his own football team, Kemp's Tigers, and in 1838 the local township – which used to be called Green Ponds – was named Kempton after him, a punning parody of the royal resort.

It was through Kempton that the Arnolds drove their phaeton on New Year's Eve, 1855.

The house is still there, at the end of a half-mile drive: tall, two-storeyed, with a façade the colour of dried orange peel. And guarded by a pair of Rhodesian ridgebacks. They bounded out as I climbed from the car. One had something bloody in its mouth. Close to, I saw that it was growling through teeth clamped to a fleece.

In the 1930s Mount Vernon was owned by a butcher-cum-builder who razed the handsome sandstone outbuildings and carted off the rubble to create the foundations of Hobart's Wrest Point Hotel and Casino. The house was then occupied for 27 years by Zelda Dick, a Kemp descendant.

I had met Zelda the afternoon before. She sat in her tidy apartment overlooking the Wrest Point Hotel and spoke of the day she moved in to Mount Vernon, and how she stood dumbfounded at the foot of the staircase. "The windows were so filthy you couldn't see through them." On the arms of her chair, her knuckles whitened at the memory. "The last owners had taken the handles off the doors. They'd kept cheeses in the upstairs bedroom and there were circles of grease on the Huon pine floor. They'd skinned rabbits in the sun room. They'd ripped the lead from the bathroom roof and the iron railings from the veranda – and buried them under the Casino." The stairwell to the ceiling was the length of one roll of wallpaper. Zelda had spent her first months stitching 20-foot curtains for the drawing room, and in the evenings she shot possums from the veranda. "The brutes were eating my mulberry trees and roses. I was known as Dead-Eye Dick. It was either them or my roses."

An archivist today owns Mount Vernon. "God, you're a beauty," was Barrie Paterson's response when he saw the advertisement and the "unbelievable" small amount of money attached. He arrived on a sunny morning, "place shining like a jewel". But he had not reckoned on the wildcat frosts that in winter pounced from the hills behind and gripped the house for two or three windless days until the pipes froze.

He walked me through a hallway littered with modern novels and rocking-horses to the two tall front rooms. They were fitted with floor to ceiling windows and red cedar shutters that folded across the old glass to keep away the frost. I looked out, the ridgebacks barging against my legs, and it was an odd feeling to think that this grand crumbling house would not be here today if Kemp had not embezzled my family's money almost 200 years ago.

The shutters were also to black out Mount Vernon against bushrangers. One night there was a hammering at the back door. A maid raced across the flagstones to see who it was.

"Come and have a look," said Paterson.

I followed him into the kitchen, and he showed me a door made of cedar – save for one panel, which, he said, had been replaced by the coffin-maker.

He opened the door, letting in a bolt of cold air. "They shot her through it."

XXV

IN SPIKY, RIGID HANDWRITING LIKE BARBED WIRE, JULIA HAD REPLIED TO HER fiancé: "I almost wish that you had called at Mount Vernon on your day off. I should like you to have seen the place."

Since his marriage to Kemp's granddaughter, Arnold had had plenty of opportunities to stay at Mount Vernon. "Here, on the score of relationship, my wife and I were of course welcome," he wrote with diplomatic restraint in his autobiography. His dreamy poet's face and his stammer, not to mention his famous father – Kemp had read Stanley's *Life of Thomas Arnold* – contributed to make Arnold the most satisfying audience that Kemp had enjoyed in several years. And yet on Arnold's part there was a definite sense that "poor old Kemp", as he had come to call him, was beginning to represent all that his delicate nature was beginning to resist. Six months earlier, on June 26, 1855, Arnold had written to Julia from Tunbridge: "I went to Mount Vernon on Saturday morning and stayed there over Sunday. The old gentleman tried hard to make me stop another day, but it would not do." Though Arnold was reluctant to accept the latest invitation, a refusal was out of the question. Kemp had ordered his vast brood to Mount Vernon to celebrate the new colony, and with one or two glaring exceptions, like Julia's mother, all twelve of his surviving children were expected. Startling comparisons to the Last Supper must have floated into Arnold's mind.

Also in the phaeton was Arnold's four-year-old daughter Mary, "a child more obstinately self-willed I certainly never came across. It is very painful to punish her (which I usually do by locking her up) for the resistance of her will." Mary had very possibly been conceived in Mount Vernon, possibly in the four-poster bed that Kemp had swapped for 30 of Potter's ewes. Fifty years later she tried to understand "the extraordinary transformation" that was going on in her father's head as the phaeton turned up the long drive to Kemp's house. By then she was arguably the most famous living author in the world, ranked by Tolstoy as England's greatest, and her name known to tribesmen in India for novels like *Helbeck of Bannisdale* (in which she had drawn on her mother's anguish for the portrait of Laura Fountain). And yet not even Mrs Humphry Ward was satisfied that she had the answer. "He was never able to explain it afterwards, even to me, who knew him best of all his children. I doubt whether he ever understood it himself."

Arnold was vague about his abrupt defection: "Moved by various influences I resolved to be a Catholic." His daughter's explanation was that his mind for ten years had been in a "welter of uncertainty" on the subject of religious truth, and then, when staying in a pub while inspecting a school, maybe in Swansea, he had read the Life of St Brigid in Alban Butler's *Lives of the Saints*, and had heard a mysterious "voice" as he rode in meditative solitude through the sunny spaces of the Tasmanian bush.

But I found a less anodyne clue among his papers at Balliol: the fragment of a novel that he started at this time, and abandoned. The hero – plainly Arnold – arrives in Van Diemen's Land, where he meets and marries "the fairest of Australia's damsels". However, there is a fly in the ointment. For some unspecified reason, he became "ashamed of his rabid democracy after witnessing the absurd failure of all its most ardent votaries." Strong stuff – but who did Arnold have in mind? Since coming to live in Hobart five years before, Arnold could not have met any democrat more ardent than Anthony Fenn Kemp. He had lost count of the occasions when he had had to sit and listen to Kemp drone on; of the evenings when Kemp had, as Arnold wrote, *"glorified himself on account of his democratic experiences"*. Rereading that line in his autobiography, I began to suspect that the "absurd failure" of Arnold's democratic ideals had something to do with Kemp, and that Arnold's exposure to his cranky, bigoted and irascible father-in-law had led him to doubt that Kemp could be the representative of any political or religious truth whatsoever. The hero of Arnold's unfinished novel "needed but some slight impulse from without to turn the balance irrevocably in favour of belief. In some way or other an impulse was given." Had his host at Mount Vernon provided it? As I walked through the house, I found myself succumbing to the Tasmanian habit, when unable to explain or locate a fact, of permitting a latitude and longitude as exaggerated as the geographic location that I was in.

I stood in the drawing room and pictured the scene.

Dinner is over, but midnight still some way off. Kemp turns from the black marble fireplace: bespectacled, silver hair curling in waves over a high forehead, an expression of fierce joy in his small proud eyes.

He raises his glass. *Sic crescat liberata Tasmania!*

The toast is echoed round the room.

In his other hand, Kemp clutches a copy of the *Mercury*. All day he has marched up to each of his twelve children in turn and pestered them to look at the editorial. Arnold, too, has read it. He agrees: the settler does rather resemble his host.

The editorial hails the New Year and also the new colony from the perspective of an early settler: "One who had come into this land ere it was yet peopled and in his first rude attempts was obliged to content himself with a rough log hut which his own hands helped to rear and sowed his first seed on land from which the stumps and blackened logs were only half removed . . . Now he can look abroad from his elegant portico, glance his eye over hundred of acres of corn and grass land and count his flocks by the thousand."

Kemp has always linked the character of the colony with his own. His contemplation of its new name moves him to do what he loves best: make a speech. He asks his family to recall the previous occasion when he summoned them – to St David's Cathedral, three years ago. Then it was to celebrate the island's jubilee and the arrival of the last convict ship. At the New Wharf they had eaten slices from a massive cake – 14 feet in diameter and carried by eight men – and sung the national anthem to new words:

> *Sing! For the hour is come!*
> *Sing! For your happy home,*
> *Our land, is free!*
> *Broken Tasmania's chain;*
> *Wash'd out the hated stain*
> *Ended the strife and pain*
> *Blest jubilee.*

But the end of transportation is insignificant compared to the event that brings them here tonight.

During the next two hours he takes his family back over his life. His exploits in the French Revolution; his part in overthrowing the tyrant Bligh; and, most imperishable, his life-altering conversation with George Washington, when he was his guest at the original Mount Vernon. As they all know, Washington's example has governed Kemp's almost every action in New South Wales and Van Diemen's Land. From the moment when he landed on the beach at Port Dalrymple, he has battled to secure the liberty of the individual and the independence of the new colony. His veneration of Washington has inspired the name of the house in which they are sitting. Also – his eyes grow smaller, graver – the sobriquet by which he is known throughout Van Diemen's Land.

A number of possibilities flash through Arnold's head. He clears his throat. He will be leaving in six months, taking his family to England, and will never return. I hear him stammer: "And . . . and what is that?"

XXVI

I CLOSED THE DOOR AND WALKED OUT INTO THE COLD AFTERNOON AIR, UNTIL I no longer heard the scratching of paws on wood, and climbed into the car.

I felt strangely dissatisfied as I drove back to Swansea. I had made my dotty pilgrimage to Mount Vernon, but what had I to show for it? A handful of picaresque images: a spry old lady shooting possums from her veranda; a maid blasted to death through a cedar door; a dump-truck filled with sandstone blocks to build a casino. And, elusive as ever, the Father of the People. He sat in my mind in the same ludicrous position that he once occupied when chairing an anti-transportation meeting at a hotel in Kempton: on an elevated seat "festooned with a canopy of laurels and evergreens".

The road home was deserted, just every now and then the flattened pelt of a road-kill. I drove through Sorell, Runnymede, Buckland, Orford, and was passing through Triabunna when the Aboriginal name dislodged something, and the obscenity struck me. The Tasmanians over whom Kemp assumed his paternal role were European colonists like himself. He was no father to the original inhabitants. In fact, Kemp's life in Van Diemen's Land from his arrival to his death pretty well coincided with their extinction.

Part II: Black Lines

"The read and write mob the one bin doing all the killing. They never write down what they did. We don't read and write but we hear about what bin happen before from our mother and father and we still got it in our mind."

Statement of Peggy Patrick, March 27, 2003

I

THE FIRST EUROPEANS WHO CAME TO TASMANIA NEVER SAW ANY ABORIGINES.
One Easter Sunday, I drove south to the Forestier Peninsula to find the monument that marked where they landed in 1642. A sign by the road warned of wombats crossing and over the backs of grazing merinos a black swan chased its hard and distinct shadow. This was pastoral country, and I had to open and close eight gates before reaching the inlet of grey shingle. Across the bay a line of breakers marked a rocky bar. The waves changed from blue to green as they rose over it, and the air had the iodine smell of seaweed.

The monument stood in the shade of a stringy gum, an ugly concrete obelisque ten feet high. Cut into a block of Maria Island granite was a stilted inscription to Abel Tasman that concealed a mountain of controversy.

The new colony took its name from the man who had named the old one, a laconic, pious Dutchman who learned his sailing on a mackerel sloop in the North Sea and died in a lingering cloud of disgrace, in Indonesia, suspected of drunkenly trying to hang two impudent sailors with a halter.

Tasman was 39, a captain in the Dutch East India Company, when he sailed out of a hailstorm on the west coast of Tasmania and saw a row of sharp peaks above the slop. "This land being the first land we have met with in the South Sea, and not known to any European nation, we have conferred on it the name of Anthony van Diemen, our illustrious master who sent us to make this discovery." He had been at sea for 72 days since sailing from Batavia, and as he understood it the peaks marked the tip of a continent.

Pythagoras, Plato, Aristotle, Eratosthenes, Hipparchus – a lot of people believed in Australia for a thousand years before its discovery. There had to be a commensurate weight – somewhere Down Under – to counter the northern land mass. In the second century AD, Claudius Ptolemy, a mathematical geographer from Alexandria, was the latest to write of an "unknown Southland" that was crucial, he believed, to maintaining the balance of the world. The *Geographia*'s republication in 1478 incited European navigators to look for this *Terra Australis incognita*.* To further confuse matters, the continent was dubbed for a while *Austrialia del Espiritu Santo* – in honour of the House of Austria – and *Temperata Antipodum Nobis Incognita*.

The French, especially, believed in Australia's existence. In 1504, an expedition under Gonneville was blown off course and spent six months on a land mass east of the Cape of Good Hope, where the only sailor to survive reported that he had been kindly received by the natives. Another Ptolemy was Louis Antoine de Bougainville, who had been present at the fall of Quebec and sought to restore in the south what France had lost in the north. Galvanised by a desire for alternative trade routes, France sent off seven expeditions in the late 1700s to seek Gonneville Land, of which Nicolas Baudin's "voyage of discovery to the Southern Lands" was the last. None of these expeditions had marvellous outcomes for their commanders. Marion Dufresne was eaten by Maoris, Kerguelen convicted of fraud, D'Entrecasteaux died of scurvy, while the most famous, La Pérouse, vanished without trace. A fleet sent to find him found only rumours of Aborigines who had waved at a passing rescue ship and, when the telescope was trained on them, appeared to be dressed in the tattered remains of French naval uniforms and "making shaving gestures".

Tasman's discovery of Van Diemen's Land had given a shot of hope to all these navigators. They studied his log closely.

The gales continued. Unable to land he was forced south, around what is now Tasman Peninsula, to North Bay. An hour after sunset on December 1,

* In the 1420s, Chinese eunuch admirals accurately mapped south-west and north Australia. The first Briton to reach mainland Australia was William Dampier in January 1688, north of Broome.

1642 he dropped anchor into a bed of light grey sand and fell to his knees thanking God.

His patron, Van Diemen, had been eager for him to find "precious metals" of the kind that the Spanish were mining in Peru. Next day, Tasman lowered two small boats to explore. As they rowed through the narrows and across a calm bay to Boomer Creek, it alarmed the crew to see columns of smoke rising above the trees. The fires were weeks old, left by the Oyster Bay tribe. If the weather was fine, the smoke might smoulder on in stumps for two months. The tribe had migrated after the duck season and were now in the highlands west of Swansea.

Even though Tasman's men saw no one, they had the impression that they were being watched. On landing, they heard what sounded like human voices and the noise of "a small trumpet or gong" – probably a native hen or clinking carrawong, a bird that makes a harsh, resounding note on the in-breath as well as the out. And on the trunks of two large blue-gums they noticed freshly carved notches "fully five feet apart", leading them to speculate whether the natives in these parts were exceptionally big.

The secrecy of the Dutch East India Company ensured that little was known about Tasman's voyage until the eighteenth century when details of the tall mysterious inhabitants sparked the imagination of Jonathan Swift, who, in the fifth paragraph of *Gulliver's Travels* (1726), shipwrecked his hero on an island "to the north-west of Van Diemen's Land". Four years later, Gulliver was marooned again – driven by a violent storm to "a great Island or Continent . . . on the South-side whereof was a small Neck of Land jutting out into the Sea, and a Creek too shallow to hold a Ship of above one hundred Tuns". Like Tasman, the captain dispatched a longboat to look for water. At first the crew found no sign of any inhabitants, but above the tree-tops there suddenly appeared a huge creature, as tall as a church spire and calling out in a voice "many degrees louder than a speaking Trumpet". Running away, Gulliver came up against a stile impossible to climb. "Every Step," wrote Swift, "was six Foot high."

Van Diemen had been overly ambitious in his expectations for the voyage. Tasman told his patron that in the absence of any natives to act as guides, his party of 18 men had spent the rest of that day – December 2 – inspecting the shoreline for signs of silver and gold. They had returned to their boats disappointed, carrying bunches of herbs, some gum from the split bark of a black wattle and "the voided excrement of a quadruped". Presented with specimens of dried herbs and the cube-shaped droppings of a wombat, Van Diemen castigated Tasman for not being inquisitive enough.

Tasman, it turned out, had not even set foot in the place. The closest he came was on the following afternoon. In deteriorating weather, he boarded the ship's boat and rowed for the nearest bay, where he intended to plant a flag "that those who shall come after us may become aware that we have been here, and have taken possession of the said land as our lawful property". A strong north-easterly was blowing, splashing water over the gunwales. Gingerly, Tasman approached the inlet, but the waves threatened to dash his hull against the reef and he fingered the ship's carpenter to swim ashore with the flagpole.

The pole that Pieter Jacobaz clung to may have helped him over the reef. From his pitching boat, Tasman directed Jacobaz to the centre of the bay where four tall eucalypts stood in a crescent, and gestured Jacobaz to plant the pole before the tallest. The trunk had been burned and Tasman was unable to decide whether the topmost branches reminded him of a stag's antlers or a rolling pin. The carpenter unravelled the blue, white and red flag of the Dutch East India Company, and swam back through the surf.

"After its first blunder-born discovery by a Dutchman," wrote Melville in *Moby Dick*, "all other ships long shunned those shores as pestiferously barbarous . . . " But three centuries later, a group of academics decided to work out where, exactly, the carpenter had landed, and to erect a cairn on the spot. In October 1923, an expedition sponsored by the Royal Society of Tasmania, the oldest scientific body in Australia, left Hobart on the SS *Toorah*. Within an hour the party of 17 had divided into two rancorous camps who stood in the mess room yelling at each other. The director of the Tasmania Museum objected to having been brought on a wild-goose chase, while the leader of the expedition railed against "bloody mutineers". If they had been on his ship, he shouted, he would have known what to do with them.

Unknown to some on board, a maverick member of the Royal Society had nine months previously mounted his own expedition and positioned the landing-place a few hundred yards from the chosen site: not at the head of the inner bay, but on the north side of the reef. He claimed even to have found the stump of the tree described in Tasman's log.

On landing, the party divided. The Opposition pitched their tents at a distance from the Official party and refused to have anything to do with the building of the obelisk. The argument raged long after the memorial was unveiled. At a crowded special meeting, the Chairman, a government botanist, said that tree stumps were of no value to mark the position: blue gums only lived 150–200 years. A former hydrographer, who suffered from heavy stuttering, conveyed to a frustrated audience his opinion that the carpenter had not landed in this bay at all, but in another one entirely. A motion was then carried to alter the inscription on the monument from "At this spot" to "Near this spot".

I walked up to the granite plaque to see if anything had been done about it. The obelisk with its little corrugated iron roof had the air of something hastily erected and abandoned. Its builders had not even tidied up the spot where they had mixed the concrete. Nor had they changed the words on the monument: "At this spot the expedition under Abel Janszoon Tasman, being the first white people to set foot on Tasmanian soil, planted the Dutch flag on December 3, 1642."

Tasman wrote that he left his flag and pole as "as a memorial for those who shall come after us, and for the natives of this country, who did not show themselves." In a conscious echo, the Royal Society's inscription informed the rare visitor that their monument was put up "as a memorial to posterity and to the inhabitants of this country." It rang hollow because in 1923 members of the Royal Society were united on one matter. There were no natives to show themselves.

II

THE GRANITE CAME FROM AN ISLAND OPPOSITE NORTH BAY, A COMBINATION OF horseshoe beaches, fossil cliffs and forests of eucalyptus and casuarina. Tasman is thought to have named it after the wife of his patron Van Diemen. Today, Maria Island is a national park, 14 miles long and eight wide. It is almost my favourite place in Tasmania.

Baudin visited Maria Island for nine days in February 1802. During four of those days the French had contact with the Oyster Bay tribe. Much of what little is known about Tasmania's pre-colonial Aborigines comes from material gathered by Baudin and his scientists over the course of these four days.

I take a small boat across to Shoal Bay where the French anchored. A school of dolphins skims alongside us, their fins slicing the water like the tips of a great rotary blade. They converge on a patch of sea where gannets are already diving, the birds mortaring the bay in a line of white explosions. "A ball of mackerel," says the captain.

Up until 1803, Europeans landed in Van Diemen's Land only for fresh water or to repair their ships or to explore. Baudin's prime purpose, as described in the orders he was given, was scientific: "to study the inhabitants, animals and natural products of the countries in which he will land". His expedition was one of the most extraordinary in naval history and yet European historians have neglected it. His three-year odyssey resulted in the first complete map of Australia and the discovery of 2,542 new zoological species, including the emu which came to be painted on the ceiling of the Empress Josephine's bedroom. It also produced a 49-page report that François Péron wrote for Baudin on the behaviour of the Aborigines on Maria Island, which they called Toarra Marra Monah.

Péron was a tailor's son from Cérilly who had lost his right eye when defending the Republic against the Austrians. By some he is considered a manipulative and ambitious bigot, and by others as the world's first anthropologist. He said of himself that he was "irresponsible, scatter-brained, argumentative, indiscreet, too absorbed in my own opinion, incapable of ever giving way for any reason of expediency".

The boat drops me on the beach where Péron came ashore in the dinghy from the *Géographe*. It was here on February 19, 1802, that he encountered the Tyreddeme people of the Oyster Bay tribe. They had crossed from the mainland, five miles away, on canoes made from bundles of reeds.

To begin with, relations were friendly. Péron noticed the regular pattern of sun- and moon-shaped scars that decorated the men's shoulders, arms and buttocks. The scars were raised from the skin, filled in with powdered charcoal, and designed possibly as a badge to signify membership of a particular tribe. The women also had scars and Péron speculated on whether these marks were the result of domestic violence. He noted that the Aborigines bound their sore feet with seaweed and that they wanted bottles, glass beads, and buttons, but not arak, biscuits or bread. They ate birds as soon as the feathers were burned off and were not dextrous at spear-throwing.

The Aborigines in their turn pulled at the gold ring in Péron's ear so hard that it came out. "We were so novel to one another!" he wrote. They were fascinated by the whiteness of his skin and also "they showed an extreme degree of desire to examine our genital organs." Puzzled by his clean-shaven face, they wondered if he and his fellow sailors might be female. "They never failed to feel in the trousers of those of us who had no beards," remarked midshipman François Desiré Breton.

As he had with previous tribes encountered on the voyage, Péron attempted to test their physical strength with his dynamometer. He invited them to squeeze this machine between their hands and to pull it up by the handle while keeping both feet planted on the base. The strongest race on earth were the English, with an average measurement of 71.4 kilos. At the opposite end of the scale, Tasmania's Aborigines, "the most savage people of all . . . *the true children of nature*", registered 50.6 kilos.

Their feebleness was confirmed to Péron by their response to a Frenchman's erection. Among the French sailors, Citizen Michel had a "slight build and lack of beard". To prove his gender, Péron persuaded him to strip. But Michel did more than that. He "suddenly exhibited such striking proof of his virility that they all uttered loud cries of surprise mingled with loud roars of laughter which were repeated again and again. This condition of strength and vigour in the one among us who seemed the least likely surprised them extremely. They had the air of applauding the condition as if they were men in whom it was not very common. Several with a sort of scorn showed soft and flaccid organs and shook them briskly with an expression of regret and desire which seemed to indicate that they did not experience it as often as we did."

Their reaction compelled Péron to make an "important conjecture". The hardships endured by these primitive people had led to a drastic weakening of their desires, "and to quench them promptly in the midst of winter, and sometime also in the anxiety of lean times".

To his critics, Péron's anthropological observations are nowhere more questionable than in this thesis, which was interpreted by one school of thought to suggest that the Aborigines were suffering "a slow strangulation of the mind" as well as of the body. Henry Reynolds, one of these critics, says: "The French assume that this is what they are saying: 'What men are these!' They have no idea whatsoever."

Péron's encounter on Maria Island caused him to throw his scientific principles to the wind and to conclude that the Tasmanian Aborigines were "the most feeble people" he had ever seen. But his leader Baudin viewed their behaviour differently. In some way that they failed to understand, the French had transgressed. And Baudin foresaw what would happen if Monsieur Kemp and the British occupied a land not theirs but "inhabited by men who have not always deserved the title of savages or cannibals which had been given them". He warned: "You will presently remain the peaceful possessors of their heritage, as the small number of those surrounding you will not exist."

III

"THE MOST INTERESTING EVENT IN THE HISTORY OF TASMANIA, AFTER ITS discovery, seems to be the extinction of its ancient inhabitants."

In 1875, Kemp's obituarist James Erskine Calder sat down to write *The Native Tribes of Tasmania*. So far as he knew, one full-blooded Aboriginal remained alive on the island. A year later Truganini was dead. With her passing, it came to be generally accepted what Darwin had written – "Van Diemen's Land enjoys the great advantage of being free of a native population" – and that the Tasmanian Aborigines had shared the fate of the Beothuks of Newfoundland: two distinct races which became extinct in the nineteenth century. But Truganini's death was not the end of the story.

I had been only a few weeks in Tasmania when, on a visit to her house in Hobart, I saw my new-found Kemp cousin produce a faded Edwardian case of the sort used for storing fish knives. She carried it to the table and opened it. Inside on the felt was a halo of green Mariner shells, each the size of a child's tooth.

I had seen shell necklaces before, but nothing like this.

"To get that colour," she said, "they soaked the shells in urine and scratched the outside off."

"Where does this come from?"

"It was Truganini's," her face solemn. And she told how Truganini used to call at the kitchen of her grandmother's three-storey house in Battery Point, and ask for food and grog, usually hot ale and ginger, and in return Truganini gave the daughters of the house necklaces. "Granny kept the

necklace in the china
cabinet and we would
play dressings-up with it.
It was so long that I
would wind it two or
three times around my
neck."

I lifted the frail circle,
and imagined the hands
that had polished and
strung these tiny shells.
James Bonwick had
described Truganini as
"exquisitely formed, with

small and beautifully rounded breasts". An American captain who entertained
her on board his ship towards the end of her life was transfixed by "her
beautiful eyes". Margaret thought that Truganini had started coming to the
house in Hampden Road after the last male Aborigine died and his head
was stolen. She said that Truganini was desperate, upset, miserable.

"It didn't mean anything to us. At school, we were told Truganini was
the Last Tasmanian, but no-one was very interested. I knew it wasn't true."

"What do you mean it wasn't true?"

Margaret said that she had grown up with Aborigines and that now
there were many on the island who called themselves Tasmanian Aborigines.

"How many?"

She smiled. "About 15,000."

This was four or five times the accepted number that had been on the
island when Kemp arrived.

I was excited and pestered her with questions. How had they kept their
culture? What did they look like? Where would I find them?

Margaret warned that it would not be straightforward. The majority
looked "like you and me" and had white faces and blue eyes. She and her
friends never made conversation about Aboriginal people in a public place.
"Because you never know who is an Aborigine."

IV

THE VIEW OF THE "ORTHODOX" SCHOOL, SOMETIMES CALLED BY ITS DETRACTORS the "black armband" school, is that the English colonists – in the space of 73 years – wiped out the Tasmanian Aborigines, if not as a deliberate act of genocide then as an unfortunate but inevitable concomitant of frontier warfare and disease. It was a view expressed as early as 1853 by the traveller F.J. Cockburn: "Here, as in most other places, it has been the old story – aggression on our part, retaliation on theirs, and then persecution on our part for safety's sake."

But since 2000 there had sprung up a newer, more contentious and revisionist version of Tasmanian history: we did not kill very many, they were all dying out anyway, we do not have too much to worry about. Therefore, we do not owe the Aborigines any apology, compensation or land.

I went to a debate in Hobart between these rival factions, hoping to learn more. The invasion of Iraq was eight days old and the news dispiriting. British soldiers had not been greeted, as expected, with "tea and rose petals". A young man from *Jane's Defence Weekly* talked on the radio about the tactical misinformation put about by a Ministry of Defence spokesman. The young man had trained as a journalist. "Where is the second source for the story of a woman in Basra hanged after she waved at British forces?" He complained that we were only getting one side of the story: our side.

The lecture in the Dechaineaux Theatre was billed as "Telling Histories" and took place on the wharf where both Kemp's warehouse and Hobart's original execution site had stood. I spotted the author Keith Windschuttle in a tight green suit and open blue shirt. He glanced round, neon blazing from his sunburned pate. It was a full audience and people were standing against the walls. Like me, they had come to hear Windschuttle debate the fate of the Tasmanian Aborigines, about which he had recently self-published a book that was dividing opinion on the mainland. The historian Geoffrey Blainey had called it "one of the most important and devastating written on Australian history in recent decades". In the judgment of James Boyce, "the book is the most ignorant and offensive publication on Van Diemen's Land in at least a century, arguably ever."

The Chairman introduced the panel. It included Windschuttle, a Sydney academic, former Trotskyist, and author of *The Fabrication of Aboriginal History, Volume I, Van Diemen's Land 1803–1847*; Henry Reynolds, one of Tasmania's foremost historians; and Greg Lehman, a Tasmanian Aboriginal who had successfully lobbied to have Risdon Cove, site of a notorious early "massacre" by British soldiers, handed back to the Aboriginal community.

The chairman allowed them four minutes each on the subject: "How do you collect information and what do you decide to leave out?" All exceeded their brief by a wide margin.

Windschuttle was the second speaker. The gist of what he said was this:

Over the past 30 years, university-based historians like Reynolds had presented a widespread picture of killing of Aborigines that in the words of Lyndall Ryan was "a conscious policy of genocide". Windschuttle had been a true believer of this story for most of his adult life. "I used to tell my students that the record of the British in Australia was worse than the Spanish in South America." Then, in 2000, he began work on his book, expecting to write a single chapter on Tasmania, and for three years had checked the footnotes of historians like Reynolds and Ryan, along the way discovering "some of the most hair-raising breaches of historical research imaginable". After examining all the available evidence he concluded that myth had been piled on myth.

Singling out the man beside him, he gave this example. In 1830, according to Henry Reynolds, Governor Arthur had written of his fear of the "eventual extirpation *of the Colony* [my italics]" – hence his initiation of the Black Line, in which more than 2,000 armed convicts, settlers and soldiers fanned out across the island in a human dragnet to round up all remaining Aborigines. But Reynolds had altered a critical word. What Arthur actually wrote was his fervent hope that by careful measures he could prevent "the eventual extirpation *of the aboriginal race itself* [my italics]." Reynolds, in other words, had radically changed the meaning of one of the most significant documents in early colonial history.

Windschuttle's thesis was that during the first 30 years of settlement the British had killed 120 of the original inhabitants, mostly in self-defence. This was one-tenth of Reynolds' estimation. In fact, Tasmania was probably the site where the least indigenous blood of all was deliberately shed in the British Empire. "My quarrel is not with the Aboriginal people at all, my quarrel is with historians who told lies about them." Those historians who had perpetrated the idea of a genocide had "betrayed their profession and misled their country".

In his response, Reynolds remarked that Windschuttle had been dining out on other people's footnotes. "I'm a little concerned about you, Keith," he said. "I wonder if you had a childhood problem with reading." The fact was that Windschuttle had misread what Reynolds had written and attributed to him ideas and attitudes that did not exist. There had been no fabrication, other than in Windschuttle's book. In claiming, for instance, that the Aborigines had no concept of land possession, Windschuttle had profoundly misunderstood their culture. What he had produced was a pitiless vilification, "the most sustained attack on a native Aboriginal community for a long time, and perhaps ever".

After each of the speakers had had their say, Jim Everett, a Tasmanian Aborigine from Cape Barren Island, stood up at the back. In a steady and dignified voice, he complained that Aboriginality had not been understood in the discussion because it was not part of the discussion. The reason there was no word for land was because "we define land as something that is part of us – not separate." He said: "We continue to be researched and over-researched," and he looked forward to the day when his community would grow their own historian. At this everyone clapped except Windschuttle.

The last and most devastating question was asked by a black man in a wool cap. His name was Douglas Maynard. His people, he said, came from Wilson's Promontory. He had spent six years working in the archives. "I'm going to ask you historians, where's your integrity?" There had been a conspiracy about genealogy. "*You* know, Mr Reynolds, about it. I'm a black man, I sit here listening to you talking about my people. Mr Jim Everett doesn't know about my people." Then he delivered an unexpected remark that caused the theatre to erupt in chaos: "I thank Mr Windschuttle for bringing out the fraud that's going on."

As they filed from the hall, many who had sat through this bunfight asked themselves: What *was* going on?

V

IT DID NOT TAKE LONG TO REALISE THAT ANY ATTEMPT TO UNDERSTAND WHAT had happened to the native population in Tasmania was frustrated by the absence from the written record of the Aborigines themselves. Their descendants had to depend on a body of work produced for the most part by "white" witnesses, colonisers and historians who did not in every instance agree. The debate had the effect of polarising many of the participants, who assumed fundamentalist positions and were exasperated by the others' intransigence. "Something about Tasmanians," says the poet Andrew Sant, "means that they find it very difficult to hold two contradictory opinions. There is a tendency for Tasmanians as a small community to box themselves into one camp or the other and for the debate to become heated and, worse, personal." As with the rivalry between Launceston and Hobart, or between the factions of the Royal Society of Tasmania, there was a lot of rancour, little authentic dialogue and a tendency to take an à la carte attitude to the historical record in order to shore up a settled position. Certainty combined with dismissiveness, and the deepest hostility was generated for anyone caught searching for the middle ground. Beneath the salvoes, the complexity of what took place then, and what was taking place today, risked slipping by unnoticed.

And so I turned back to Kemp. He was not a reliable guide, but he was a devil I knew. He also had a rare, if not unique, knowledge of both Hobart and Launceston.

If my hunch was correct, Kemp's formative contact with Aboriginal culture began on his first voyage to Australia when he was shipmate with Bennelong

on the *Reliance*. Six months together in the same cramped space, perhaps
learning a smattering of Eora, gave Kemp unrivalled exposure to a people
whom *The Times* of London characterised as "exactly on a par" with "the
beasts of the field", and could well explain his initial sympathy. Kemp
reminds Henry Reynolds of Colonel C.J. Napier who rejected the idea
that Aborigines were "a race which forms a link between men and
monkeys", and argued that these "poor people are as good as ourselves".
In their turn, the Aborigines who watched Kemp come ashore in November
1804 saw him as one of their own. They thought he was a dead Aborigine.

They had known no other people for 9,000 years, ever since Van
Diemen's Land was cut off from the mainland. Patsy Cameron is a
Tasmanian Aborigine from Flinders Island. "How would *we* perceive
strangers coming off a spaceship that looked like us – but had skin coloured
purple?" Her ancestors, she thought, understood Kemp to be Num, an
Aborigine who had returned from the home of the departed, a heavenly
island that he called England and they called Teeny Dreeny, to which he
had travelled on the back of a seal. One day they, too, expected to jump
up on an island as white men. "They would have seen him as a spirit, but
they wouldn't have known whether evil or good."

Kemp had returned from a previous life because he knew the country,
and if he behaved in a strange way it was because the trauma of dying
had affected him so that he had forgotten how to behave. To begin with,
the Aborigines treated him as a child. As he began to learn their language,
scattered with whatever words Bennelong had taught him, it was as though
he was recalling it. As he began to recognise them, they thought: "Oh, he's
remembering us, the journey to England has wiped out his memory, and
gradually it's coming back." Meanwhile, they looked at Kemp for some
resemblance, some mark or gesture that gave him his kin place. "They
think in kin terms," Henry Reynolds says. "Everyone is related to everyone.
They would try and decide who Kemp had been in an earlier life and
then assume that position." Only much later, when it was too late, would
they say: "We realise you're nothing but a man."

Kemp watched his men hoist the flag on Lagoon Beach on November 11,
1804. A royal salute was fired from the *Buffalo* plus two volleys from the
soldiers. Perhaps attracted by the noise, the first natives appeared the
following day, a body of about 80, who approached to within 100 yards.
The men were stark naked. The women wore kangaroo skins over their
shoulder. Their black hair was woollier than Bennelong's, resembling, to
one observer, "the wig of a fashionable late eighteenth-century French

lady of quality". It was streaked with marrow grease and red ochre, and the reddish-brown skin on their arms was patterned with scars.

Kemp was all set to make friends. He ordered them to be given a tomahawk and mirrors. They looked into the glass and "put their hand behind to feel if there was any Person there". Tantalised, they stepped closer to the tents – making a grab for tools and clothing. Then disaster. They hauled away a Royal Marine sergeant and were on the verge of throwing him into the sea when he or one of his privates fired a musket, killing one Aborigine and wounding another. The dead man's was the "very perfect native's head" that Paterson sent in a box to Joseph Banks. Although not on the same scale as the episode at Risdon six months earlier, the incident marked, as Paterson predicted, a transgression. "This unfortunate circumstance I am fearful will be the cause of much mischief hereafter, and will prevent our excursions inland, except when well armed."

Almost the next casualty was Kemp's utopian brother-in-law, Alexander Riley, whose belief that he had come to a latitude "conjointly equal to any other spot on earth", and perfect for growing rhubarb, was about to be challenged. Frantic to find a more suitable place for the settlement, Paterson sent Riley off to look for better pastures, but after walking for four hours Riley found his path blocked by 50 Aborigines who made a lunge for his cravat, exclaiming "walla, walla", and then speared him in the back. He managed to crawl 15 miles to his boat, but he remained in a fever for several weeks. "Mr Riley has not been well since," wrote Paterson. "I rather think the Spear has penetrated close to the spine."

Months later, Paterson appointed Kemp acting Lieutenant Governor. These were the instructions that he passed on regarding the Aborigines: "You are to endeavour by every means in your power to open an intercourse with the natives, and to conciliate their goodwill, enjoining all persons under your Government to live in amity and kindness with them; and if any person shall exercise any acts of violence against them, or shall wantonly give them any interruption in the exercise of their several occupations, you are to cause such offender to be brought to punishment according to the degree of their offence."

How much Kemp abided by his orders is hard to tell. But there is evidence to suggest that he continued to take the Aboriginal side, despite their assault on his brother-in-law. The surgeon who dressed Riley's wound was Jacob Mountgarret, who had arrived from Hobart with an Aboriginal boy, three or four years old, with "nice" table manners. Mountgarret had adopted the boy and named him Robert Hobart May. Robert was able to tell Kemp his story without any "fear or apprehension": how his parents

were killed in front of him at Risdon by soldiers with whom Kemp had
served in Sydney.

Risdon Cove on the east bank of the Derwent was the site of the first
settlement in Hobart. What happened there on an autumn day in May
1804 was, wrote Mark Twain, out of all keeping with the place: "a sort of
bringing of heaven and hell together".

Twenty-six years after the event, a former convict Edward White testified that he was hoeing ground near the creek when there suddenly
appeared a circle of 300 Aborigines, including women and children,
hemming in a flock of kangaroos. "They looked at me with all their eyes,"
White remembered, suggesting that the sight of him turning the soil was
the first indication that they had had of any English settlement on the
island. The Aborigines reportedly belonged to the Oyster Bay tribe. White
was positive, he said, "they did not know there was a white man in the
country when they came down to Risdon". The Aborigines did not
threaten him and he claimed not to be afraid of them. Even so, White
reported their presence to some soldiers and resumed his hoeing. Then, at
about 11 a.m., he heard gunfire. The great difficulty is to imagine what
happened in the next three hours until, at about 2 p. m., troops under the
nervous command of Lieutenant Moore apparently fired grapeshot into
the crowd, who had, Moore claimed, turned hostile.

According to White, "there were a great many of the Natives slaughtered
and wounded; I don't know how many". Nor can anyone else know how
many. The truth floats between the written record – which is that three
Aborigines died, including Robert Hobart May's parents – and the oral
record, which is that up to 100 died. But the incident stuck in the historical memory and, likened frequently to Eve's bite of the apple, came to be
understood as the original transgression.

In September 1830, at a time of maximum tension in the colony, Kemp
remembered Robert's composed testimony when chairing an urgent
meeting in the Hobart Court House. The hall was packed with the colony's
most prominent citizens and Kemp was first to address them. What he said,
although prolix, was not quite what anyone expected. "Mr Kemp
commented at some length upon the aggressions committed by the blacks,
which he attributed in a great degree to some officers of his own regiment (the late 102nd) who had, as he considered, most improperly fired a
four-pounder upon a body of them, which having done much mischief,
they had since borne that attack in mind and have retaliated upon the
white people whenever opportunity offered . . . "

Henry Reynolds says: "It's a pretty extraordinary thing to say about your own regiment. A regiment is like a club. Even a cad doesn't badmouth his own regiment." Kemp went further in his condemnation when speaking to the historian James Bonwick. Although referred to only as "a settler of 1804", he is the probable source of Bonwick's story that Robert Hobart May's parents were shot at Risdon during "a half-drunken spree . . . from a brutal desire to see the Niggers run". Kemp repeated his version to a commission of inquiry in 1820 as a way to explain the bitter attitude of the Aborigines: "the spirit of hostility and revenge that they still cherish for an act of unjustifiable violence formerly committed upon them".

And yet what is perhaps remarkable about the first 20 years of European occupation is the absence of clashes. Following Riley's spearing, colonists settled into a relatively amicable relationship with Aborigines. Kemp's protégé Jorgen Jorgenson, for instance, thought them "inoffensive and friendly". The two groups traded with each other, the settlers offering sugar, tea and blankets in exchange for kangaroos, shellfish and women. As late as 1823, *Godwin's Emigrant Guide to Van Diemen's Land* wrote of the Aborigines that "they are so very few in number and so timorous that they need hardly be mentioned; two Englishmen with muskets might traverse the whole country with perfect safety as they are unacquainted with the use of fire-arms." In March 1823, George Meredith, a good friend of Kemp, wrote in appreciative terms to his wife about a group of naked Aboriginal women encountered in a small bay on his way to Swansea. "We were honoured by the visit of six black *ladies* to breakfast next morning who caught us craw fish and Mutton Fish [abalone] in abundance in return for bread we gave them – you would be much amused to see them Swim and Dive. Although I do not think you would easily reconcile yourself to the open display they make of their charms. Poor things, they are innocent and unconscious of any impropriety or indelicacy. They were chiefly young and two or three well proportioned and comparatively well looking. So you see had I fancied a Black wife I had both opportunity and choice."[*]

Plenty of sealers and bushrangers availed themselves of this opportunity – like Michael Howe, whose companion, Black Mary, Kemp had interrogated in 1817. But by the mid-1820s the situation had shifted. Aborigines were no longer prepared to surrender their women and children to

---

[*] Meredith's eldest son, also George, after violently quarrelling with his father, went to live on Kangaroo Island with an Aboriginal girl, Sal. He was killed by a jealous Aborigine.

Europeans without a fight. They observed with mounting alarm how these Num not only raped and beat their "lubras", but infected them with "loathsome diseases", often with the result that they were unable to breed. Twenty-six years after Kemp's arrival there were not enough Aboriginal women on the island to sustain the dwindling population. Of the 70 or so natives who remained in the north-east by 1830, only six were women. None were children.

The Aborigines resented, too, the way that settlers like Kemp and Meredith seized their best hunting grounds, the grasslands and open bush that supported the densest populations of wallaby and kangaroo. Under Governor Sorell grants to new settlers soared to almost one million acres. By 1831, the European population had further doubled (to 26,640), two million acres of native woods and grassland had been ceded, and the numbers of sheep grazing on the land had increased five-fold. Around Swansea, Meredith was able to fence off large tracts of land, including not only the beach where I now lived, but Moulting Lagoon behind our house, a vital gathering place for the Oyster Bay tribe. Deprived of their women and their food supply, the Aborigines retaliated. By 1825, Meredith was warning his wife: "The natives, I fear, must now be *dispersed wherever* they make their *appearance*."

The Oyster Bay people were regarded by the man who subdued them as "the most savage of all the aboriginal tribes". Their chief was Tongerlongetter, derived from the Aboriginal words meaning "heel of the foot" and "great". He was a gigantic figure who measured six feet eleven inches and was capable of drinking a quart of tea at a sitting. He used rust from the bolts of shipwrecks to colour his ringlets, and had scars in the small of his back, tattooed with an oyster shell, that resembled dollar coins. Known in captivity as the old Governor or King William, Tongerlongetter was a robust, intelligent leader, a man of "great tact and judgement" in the opinion of George Robinson, who was responsible for persuading the chief to lay down his arms.

Before allowing himself to go with Robinson to Hobart, Tongerlongetter explained why his people had behaved as they had done: "The chiefs assigned as a reason for their outrages upon the white inhabitants that they and their forefathers had been cruelly abused, that their country had been taken from them, their wives and daughters had been violated and taken away, and that they had experienced a multitude of wrongs from a variety of sources."

In the fens at the back of our house, Tongerlongetter had attacked hayricks and huts with spears of lighted punk, sending panic among the

settlers who believed that they were in danger "of being ultimately exterminated by the Black Natives". Just two months after Meredith expressed his admiration for their women, his neighbour and former employee in Wales, Adam Amos, looked out of the window at Glen Gala to see his house surrounded by Aborigines. "One, a woman came to the door, I made signs for her to go away. She did and in a short time about six made their appearance amongst the bush in the river close to my hut. I fired small shot at about 50 yards distance, they ran off." On December 13, 1823 Adam sent his oldest son "to shoot them again but missed by minutes". Next day, after the same group set fire to the grass near his farm, he again sent out his son, who was joined by two of Meredith's men "who fired at them and wounded one of the mob". A month later, Amos organised another posse. "I had a hunt after the natives on Friday they appeared on my plain." He and his sons followed 30 men for two hours to a marsh about two miles from his farm. "We fired they run away and left their dogs and spears which we destroy and brought some of them home and two dogs." But he was swatting shadows. "The blacks are playing old gooseberry with us," he wrote to a friend. "On one occasion I saw one, and, while in the act of levelling my gun at him, he disappeared as if by magic, and I could see no more of him."

The greatest attacks came during periods of starvation. That winter, one of Meredith's stockmen had been killed on the edge of a sheltered lagoon where sometimes I walked on windy afternoons. Tongerlongetter's men had surprised Thomas Gay as he ate breakfast. He made a dash for Meredith's farmhouse and had run 200 yards when he was speared in the back. A few days later Amos came looking for him. The dogs started running around, smelling something as they approached Gay's hut. The bodies of two unskinned kangaroos and a dead cat lay by the door, and clothes were scattered about the earth floor. Amos found Gay's mangled body in a shallow pool, one hand above the surface. His eyebrows had been cut off, his nails separated from their quicks, his teeth beaten out of his head, and he had nine spear wounds. "The ravens had taken off part of two fingers that had appeared above water."

Gay was the second of Meredith's servants to be killed. "In neither case was provocation given by the whites," Meredith told the Aboriginal Committee that assembled in April 1830, six months before the Black Line. "The present feeling of the natives in our neighbourhood towards the white population is and for a considerable time has been that of *avowed* and *unequivocal* hostility." He went on: "their present object is most determinedly the *death* of every victim which may unhappily fall within their power or premises without respect to either sex or age." The worsening relationship between settlers and Aborigines was, he said, a "truly *momentous subject*", and he recommended "the earliest possible importation of bloodhounds . . . not to hunt and destroy the natives – but to be attached to every field party – to be held in the hand and thus to track unerringly and either ensure their capture or if indeed the alternative must be resorted to – their annihilation."

VI

ANNIHILATION WAS EMPHATICALLY NOT GOVERNMENT POLICY, BUT IN THE backwoods of Swansea settlers made their own vicious law. Anne Rood, one of our neighbours, remembered speaking to Jackson Cotton who grew up at Kelvedon, an estate six miles away. "Jackson's grandfather, a Quaker, had told him with horror of farmers he knew who had given Aborigines bread buttered with arsenic."

Poisoned bread or damper was not the only deterrent. Sarah Mitchell was raised on a farm adjacent to Kelvedon. In her unpublished memoir, handwritten in 1946, she included this abbreviated paragraph: "Twenty yards from the house at Mayfield there was a hut called the Black Hut and store room for the men. One of the Buxton family told me they noticed flour was stolen. They set a steel trap at night. In the morning a blackman had cut off his hand and left it there . . . " The next pages are missing, but the injured Aborigine was most likely Tongerlongetter, who in July 1832 revealed to George Washington Walker that he had lost his forearm when it was caught in a rat-trap set by a white colonist. In the description of the *Colonial Times*: "the trap was found about 100 yards from the hut, and the hand in it . . . The unfortunate creature must have undergone dreadful agony, as we hear that the sinews and tendons of the arm were drawn out by main force, and to use the expression of our informant, resembled those of the tail of a kangaroo." Tongerlongetter later altered his story to say that he had been shot by white men in moonlight, but the conical stump was examined at his post-mortem in June 1837 and the doctor confirmed from the extensive lacerations that the arm had been "violently torn away".

It is impossible to know how widespread was the use of such traps any more than it is possible to verify the number of little fingers cut off to be used as tobacco-stoppers. But on a farm seven miles north of Swansea I was taken to a bluestone barn known as the Cellar.

The farmer led me through a low door. White nails along the lintel were hammered into old possum claws, and inside he had hung the walls with skinned hares, their ribs pressing out through the shiny red flesh.

The door had been built this low to stop intruders from entering in a hurry. "They were under a few pressures," the farmer said. He was small, with a wide nose, and two of his teeth were framed in gold. He gestured at a narrow aperture set in the massive wall, about four feet from the ground and five inches wide. The hole was no bigger than an arrow slit. "But narrow enough to get in the old muzzle-loader."

I stared out between the bars. His two grandsons played on the grass where the first settler had blasted his shot at Tongerlongetter's men. The farmer said: "The Abos got in and pinched stores through the shingle roof. The owners used to have a big man-trap. They reckon the Abos got in here because someone was taking the grain. When they came back a foot was in it. They found a hoppy-legged Abo over in Avoca and reckon it was the same fella. I'd be running too, I reckon."

I stepped back into the cavernous room. The wall at the rear was cut into the bank. Once, the farmer said, it was lined with barrels of cider and there was a press. The farmer remembered his father working the press.

"Where was the coffin?" I asked. I had read that the man who built the Cellar had used his coffin as the coolest place to store alcohol.

"He probably bloody did put it here."

The Cellar was erected as a cider house for a deadly brew made of crab-apples, Sturmers and Early Janers brought out from England. We went outside and the farmer showed me a bedraggled orchard where a creek rippled past. "There used to be beautiful eating ones. 'Lady in the Snow' – red skin and white flesh, real sweet. And cooking apples. Mum would stew 'em or else the green parrots made a mess of 'em. But they now taste pretty woody."

It was not only the Cellar I wanted to see. I had also read that on this property were the remnants of the oldest surviving log cabin in Tasmania. We walked down to the sheep pen and there it was, a sorry sight beside three plum trees and a rusty water tank with a hole in it. All that remained of the cabin was a stack of old blue-gum spars spattered in grey lichen; a pile of sandstone rocks; and a concrete block with a metal plaque to commemorate William Lyne's arrival on Christmas Day, 1826.

★ ★ ★

Lyne had managed a country estate in Gloucestershire. Then the lease ran out. He was a tall, proud man with five children and a wife who hated Tasmania for all the 47 years she lived there. Before he emigrated, he had his men make him a coffin from an old oak on the property. He packed it with lead, pewter, saucepans, five swords, six guns, and five pairs of pistols. He also took with him a church organ, keeping out a flute and violin to play on the voyage. He filled other crates with a cider press, an anvil, a bellows and a copper furnace. Then he shot his lovely saddle horse and sailed to Hobart.

On his arrival, he was told of the problems with bushrangers and Aborigines, and was recommended New South Wales. But he was a stubborn man. He walked four days to Great Oyster Bay and found 1,500 acres east of Adam Amos: a warm valley, lightly timbered, with a tidal marsh. The turf hut that he built with his wife collapsed when someone leaned on it, and so, early in 1827, they put up a log cabin, 20 feet square, made of large gums scooped out at the end.

It would not be his cider that killed him, or a ti-tree spear, but a bone that lodged in his throat while he was eating dinner. By then he was living in a Georgian sandstone house that today the farmer used as a barn. Built by convicts, it closely resembled the stately home that Lyne had looked after in North Cerney.

In the early years, he never left his low door without a gun. He made a small seat on his plough and strapped his six-year-old daughter Susan into it so close to the ground that she could smell the turned earth. One day a man panted up, a stockman who worked for George Meredith. His companion had been murdered by blacks. Abandoning his plough, Lyne ran to the valley that he had called Coombend after the estate in Gloucestershire, and found a dead man with a spear four and half feet long sticking from his back. Another time a movement caught his eye and he turned to see a large band of Aborigines 70 yards away. He raced inside and dressed his wife in a long man's overcoat and handed her a gun. When he led her outside, the Aborigines scattered at the strange spectacle. But he could not always be there to protect his family. In February 1828, Susan and her ten-year-old sister Betsy were guarding a herd of calves near the tidal marsh when they failed to see a group of a dozen Aborigines who had concealed themselves behind a large rock. Betsy ran screaming to the cabin. Susan fell unconscious in the shallow lagoon, struck by an Aboriginal weapon – a spear or the heavy stick known as a waddy.

The farmer leaned against the remains of Lyne's old hut and hesitated. "When I was a kid, this was still a square block. A door here, walls this high" – and he rebuilt them in the air.

"What do you feel," I asked, "standing there?"

He rested his hand on the spars of wood carelessly heaped up. "Probably like to know what went on." He nodded at a slope once covered in white gums, a folk memory returning. "Over that bank, by the large rock, one of the girls got speared in the side."

We walked over. The rock was large – about ten feet high, the size and shape of an obelisk.

He went round the back. "See that ledge, reckon that's where he was sitting when he speared her." He went on gazing at the rock, and on a sudden it was not an Aborigine he was seeing, but himself. "It's a beautiful place to sit. As a kid, I used to sit there playing cowboys and Indians."

VII

IN *Medical Hints for Emigrants,* I FOUND THIS ENTRY FOR SPEAR WOUNDS: "These are more serious than mere cuts. If any vital part is injured, you can do very little except keep the patient quiet and send for the clergyman and surgeon. If a shot or spear has passed through or into one of the limbs, bind it up, and treat it as you would a cut."

Whether Lyne's daughter had been struck by a waddy or a spear, she recovered. So did Edith Stansfield's great-grandmother.

Edith lived two miles from us, in a white weatherboard house off the road into Swansea. She told me that her great-grandmother as a little girl was speared in the back not long after arriving at Plassy, under the Western Tiers north of Ross.

Her mother, she said, was often shown the wound. "My mother was allowed to put her hand on it. It was a deep scar in her back, in the fleshy part below the shoulder, and deep enough to feel through her clothes."

"She felt it through a dress?" I thought of a young girl performing her Braille, mapping the bloody history of this island on her grandmother's back.

"No way would she have shown her flesh to her grandchildren – not like mine, who wander in when I'm having a shower."

VIII

IN THE MIDDLE OF THE BEST HUNTING GROUNDS, MOUNT VERNON WAS A PRIME target. Kemp told Bonwick that in 1821 he saw about 300 Aborigines "poking" after bandicoots. "He immediately guessed that his hour had come and thinking, he said, that he might as well die with a good heart as a bad one, he started his dogs into the mob, and on their flight, took himself heartily off." The attacks escalated after a sawyer was speared to death within half a mile of Kemp's property. In 1826, 60 natives pursued Kemp's servants and tried to plunder Kemp's hut. In one raid, Aborigines surrounded a hut and dared the settler inside to shoot at them, threatening in good English "to put his wife into the bloody river". It was hard to resist the conclusion that the Aborigines were directing towards settlers' wives the frustration they felt over the fate of their own women and children. A few miles from Mount Vernon, Ann Geary was killed by an axe through the skull. Geary's neighbour Esther Gough fell to her knees shortly before her own death. She begged: "Spare the lives of my Piccaninnies." One of her attackers responded: "No, you white bitch, we'll kill you all." In October 1828, 15 Aborigines ambushed Mrs Langford in the heart of Kemp's township. They speared her small son to death in her arms and also his 14-year-old sister. The girl and her mother survived. This last group was rumoured to include two white men. One of those who pursued them, Zacharias Chaffey, recognised a former convict servant of his father named Green, who had blackened his face and wore only a striped shirt. No longer taken by Aborigines for the spirits of their dead, these convict fugitives were welcome allies in the resistance against invaders like Kemp.

The gradual deterioration of Kemp's relationship with Bennelong's people was dramatised in a three-hour play that opened in London on February 10, 1830. In *Van Diemen's Land; or Settlers and Natives*, William Moncrieff transposed Bennelong from Sydney and promoted him chief of the Broken Bay Tribe. Those who watched the play in the Surrey Theatre were given a picture of Bennelong that more accurately resembled a North American Indian than an Aborigine like Tongerlongetter. But if his taste for yams and canoes struck a false note, his fury at Kemp's type was authentic. He called for "just revenge" on the colourless strangers that had "usurped our plains, and would fain extirpate our race". He pointed out: "These white men can speak fair and promise well. But what has the dark chief ever found from them, save this, that they have striding legs and grasping hands – have over-run our isle, and seized our all, because he wore not the same hue with them." And he spoke of his visit to England in 1792. "I went far over sea, to white man's lands, where their King dressed me in his warrior's dress, and gave rich gifts, then smiled on the dark chief, and bade him make his people like to them." But what had Bennelong found on his return with Kemp? "He found the white man chief – he found his lands all seized, and he, their prince, the white man's slave." Before the arrival of the white man, his people had coveted nothing, taken nothing. "They've taught me something; I will profit by it – taught me to plunder and deceive."

His sister Kangaree echoed his distress: "Caffres have black faces but white hearts; but white men's faces white, their hearts black."

Crude though Moncrieff's drama was, it captured a truth about the Aborigines' new attitude. Num were no different to other men. In fact, they were worse.

IX

GEORGE ROBINSON ONCE ASKED AN ABORIGINAL WOMAN WHY SHE CRIED AFTER her sick husband was admitted to hospital. She replied: "Why black man's wife not cry as well as white man's?"

As part of their response, many colonists disagreed that Aborigines and Europeans shared the same humanity. They sided with Kemp's friend, Mrs Prinsep, who dismissed it as a romantic notion that Tasmanian Aborigines could be noble savages. "They are undoubtedly in the lowest possible scale of human nature both in form and intellect," she wrote in 1830. "Jaws elongated like the Ourang Outang and figures scarcely more symmetrical."

In 1829, Arthur alienated the Aborigines further by giving away another 208,000 acres in grants. Between February and July 1829, eleven white people were killed, and eleven more between August and December 1830. They included Mrs Emma Coffin, speared in her right breast. Her child was found weeping. He pointed to a mob of Aborigines: "There is the blacks that killed mama." In the past seven years approximately 187 Europeans had died. Even enlightened colonists like George Boyes understood the need for action. "It has become apparent that unless means were devised for allaying the cruel nature of these wretches, of making them prisoners . . . in some well adapted part of the country, or, otherwise, of exterminating the race, that the country must be abandoned."

To classify Aborigines as "Ourang Outangs" or "wretches" made it easier to sanction the drastic measure that Lieutenant Governor Arthur decided on in October 1830: to mobilise the white population into a human chain. This was the reason for Kemp's appearance at the packed Court House.

★ ★ ★

Once he had got off his chest the cause, as he saw it, for the atrocities, Kemp changed tack. His volte-face was in character and received with "much applause". His honourable spirit of moderation had evaporated. Initially well disposed towards the native population, Kemp now judged them to be "like all other savages, expert in ambush and ferocious in vengeance". A few weeks later, Bennelong's former shipmate tabled the following resolution: "that the atrocious character of the Aborigines of this Island – manifested by their cruel and wanton murders of the white inhabitants, perpetrated without distinction of age or sex, and with increasing barbarity – renders the life of the Settler insecure and operates as a most serious drawback to emigration to this country; and consequently to its commerce and prosperity." The motion would be carried unanimously.

For now, he saluted the Governor in his endeavour, and perhaps for the first time in his career gave a superior his unstinting support. He looked forward to the success of "the great object now about to be undertaken . . . to subdue the Aborigines and put them in a place of security which I sincerely hope may lead to their civilisation".

Without being at liberty himself to join in what became known as the Black Line, he proposed that he and a number of free settlers should form a town guard for as long as the military were occupied in the bush. It was, he said, "the duty of every man cheerfully to contribute to the common cause every assistance in his power". He appointed himself "Field Marshal" of this Home Guard.

The duties that Kemp supervised were tiresome and unnecessary. Visitors to Hobart from early October to late November 1830 were amused by the spectacle of respectable civilians patrolling the streets in ill-fitting military clothing or parading stiffly up and down on horseback. "Gentlemen," was one old soldier's response to Kemp's initiative, "you may call yourselves marshals, generals and colonels, but the duties assigned to you are usually performed by a corporal's guard."

Meanwhile, a line of 2,200 settlers, convicts and soldiers were beating the bush from Moulting Lagoon through Campbell Town to Quamby Bluff in the Western Tiers. Day after day, Colonel Arthur rode up the line in his visored blue cap, his blue frock coat and curved sabre. His purpose: to drive the Aborigines "like deer in the Highlands" into the Tasman peninsula.

Six weeks later, the *Hobart Town Courier* mocked this "Grand Army" and asked what had been gained by the enormous expense of such a gigantic military manoeuvre. "The answer is, unfortunately, a simple dysyllable — *nothing!*"

At a second meeting chaired by Kemp in the Court House, he was forced to lament "that the expedition against the Aborigines had not been attended with the success that we all fondly hoped would have been effected, but what is money compared with the protection of our lives and properties? Away with such mercenary ideas . . . "

Nonetheless, his obituarist was scathing. The Black Line, wrote James Erskine Calder, recently arrived in Hobart, was an absurd passage in the history of the colony: "too chimerical in its conception, too absurd in its progress and too inconsiderable in its results". It had cost £30,000 — that is to say half the annual budget — and resulted in the capture of one Aboriginal man and a 15-year-old boy. The tribal people were still there, had passed like water through the hands of their would-be captors.

But the tradition of scoffing at the Line as altogether ineffectual is astray.

X

I HAD LIVED IN TASMANIA TWO YEARS BEFORE I WAS ABLE TO COME TO TERMS with the Black Line. Powerful though the image was, Arthur's response to the Aborigines seemed too theatrical to have been a real historical event. I felt that had it been presented as such at the Surrey Theatre the audience would have hooted it off the stage. Historians like Calder, Bonwick, Reynolds and Windschuttle evoked it graphically enough on the page: a cordon of beaters in a hunt, men blowing bugles, firing muskets, and shouting their names to keep in touch with those out of sight. There was supposed to be one man to every 100 yards in the first days, with the line stretching 120 miles from Great Oyster Bay to Lake Sorell. But I only had to spend a morning in a clumsy attempt at emulation to understand the impossibility of maintaining a formation. For three hours I scrambled up and down, into hollows, over boulders, through outcrops of rock, dipping into ravines, pushing through dense chest-high grass, blundering over rotten branches. It did not surprise me to learn that many of the beaters ended up walking in single file along the main roads. Nor that they failed to capture more than two Aborigines. It was easy, though, to picture their quarry every 80 yards or so, indistinguishable from the blackened stumps and keeping still in the dead bracken, the fallen logs. Tongerlongetter and his people must have been terrified.

I did not properly grasp the Black Line until I discovered that a local version of it had taken place a year later, in October 1831. The episode, which has seldom been brought to light, happened within sight of my house.

★ ★ ★

The Oyster Bay people had dwindled from about 800 to about 30 since Kemp's arrival on the island. Bonwick put it that the Aborigines, "harassed by continual alarms, worn out by perpetual marches, enfeebled by want and disease, had sunk down one by one to die in the forest". Tongerlongetter was not to know that Arthur's extravagant measure was a one-off and the Black Line knocked the stuffing out of him. "It showed the Aborigines our strength and energy," wrote Jorgenson, and when, in November 1830, George Robinson told a group of natives in the north-east about the operation, "the whole of them was in tears throughout the whole of the day". Tongerlongetter's distress would have been no less intense. He might have escaped the Black Line, but it left him stranded, trying on the one hand to avoid capture – there was a £5 bounty on the head of every adult, £2 on every child – and on the other to adhere to his traditional migratory patterns.

On October 13, Tongerlongetter and the remnants of his tribe appeared at a hut near Amos's farm. In great alarm, George Meredith wrote to Arthur explaining how "with their usual cunning" they had removed a batch of weapons. They plundered one of Amos's huts, and another belonging to Meredith, this time stealing flour and two dirty shirts. Meredith believed that Tongerlongetter was heading for the tip of the Freycinet Peninsula where it dropped into Schouten Passage. Each year the Oyster Bay tribe came looking for shellfish, ochre and swans' eggs in Moulting Lagoon, camping on a flat neck of land beyond the Hazards. Meredith had established a whaling station inland from this narrow isthmus. He planned to trap the Aborigines in "their customary resort".

Meredith sent his son Charles to the whaling station. If Charles saw any natives he was to light two fires. On the following Wednesday morning, Meredith saw the signal through his telescope and reported it to the police station in Swansea, "but extraordinary as it may appear to the whole colony the Police Magistrate *at such a time* had departed to a distant duty". In the magistrate's absence, a constable and four soldiers were dispatched in a leaking vessel to the Fisheries, but they rowed back the following evening, claiming that they had seen no-one.

Meanwhile, Meredith and Amos had each sent a party to the river mouth, "expecting, of course, that the Civil Power would be on the spot, to decide and legalise their proceedings". Meredith advised Arthur that he was busy alerting William Lyne and other settlers on the coast to drum up every available man in order to keep the Aborigines hemmed in.

By Friday evening, a total of 84 soldiers and farm-workers had gathered at Meredith's whaling station, leaving a skeleton force to guard various properties. Fires were lit every 100 yards or so across the isthmus, three men sentried at each, and they sat down to wait. The isthmus "being nearly a mile", they clearly thought the game was in the bag.

Acting in lieu of the police magistrate, Swansea's local doctor had taken upon himself the surprising step of handing out rations from the Commissariat. He gave to each man the same per diem as Arthur had allowed for the Black Line: two pounds of flour or biscuit, one and a half pounds of meat, half an ounce of tea, three ounces of sugar. "The tobacco and soap I have not furnished."

On Sunday, there was a new moon. Dogs were heard howling and there was a rustle in the silver wattle. At sunrise, Meredith discovered fresh footprints on a patch of burned ground and some dogs feeding on the carcass of a whale. He also found 12 spears left behind under a rock. The number of footprints suggested that there were between twelve and 20 people, some of them children. But it was clear that a "slab" of Aborigines were still hiding in the rocks and caves. Two settlers told Meredith that "they observed the blacks on a rock not far distant, endeavouring to escape".

By now, Meredith was concerned that he did not have sufficient men "to form scowering parties as well as to maintain the line". He sent urgent messages to Spring Bay and Little Swanport, which he expected to produce another 40 people. Once these arrived, "more effective measures may be entered upon".

But before Meredith's reinforcements turned up, Tongerlongetter and his people did indeed escape.

They darted through the line at 10.00 on Tuesday evening, between two huts about 80 yards apart. The night was dark – the new moon had only just risen – and the fires were becoming low due to a shortage of wood. The soldiers did not see them coming.

The first to hear the alarm was William Lyne's eldest son John. Fifty-six years later, as Member of Parliament for Glamorgan, John Lyne would introduce the bill that attempted to eradicate the Tasmanian tiger. Towards the end of his life he remembered the pitch-black night when he tried to trap a band of the last Tasmanian Aborigines. "It was my turn to patrol. I was at the time [urging] the men Keep a good watch as the native dogs were seen amongst the fires in front and after passing one of the soldiers on duty about 50 yards I heard him call 'Halt'. He comes there firing off his gun to give the alarm and on my running quick I heard a rustle like as though a mob of wild cattle were passing but could see nothing for it was very dark except near the fires and the low scrub had been previously burnt making the ground of the like colour of the natives. Next morning we tracked their footmarks very plain, the ground being soft from previous rain." Apart from their footprints, the Aborigines had left behind one bloody piece of evidence. Lyne told his niece that "the next day was found a large piece of the scalp of a black on a wattle stake, quite low, the poor thing had raced past and struck the tree."

The wattles were restless with honey-eaters on the afternoon I crossed the isthmus. I walked out along Cook's Beach, pleased to see no-one on it. "All we have in April are our own footprints," a guide had told me on my first visit. On that occasion, she pointed out an ancient hut hidden in the gums. I had not been inside it, but now I could not resist opening the door. Inside, old copies of the *Mercury* insulated the walls, and seeing that one page, dated February 1958, had an advertisement for a horror movie starring Boris Karloff, I read it.

I escaped onto the dazzling white sand. A flight of yellow-tailed black cockatoos moved very fast and high over the tops of the gums, uttering loud harsh cries. The same casuarinas. The same orange-lichened rocks. The same cerulean sea. The Aborigines had been coming here for 40,000 years and yet the only traces of their presence were a few flint tools and a midden of white shells. I watched the tide hiss up past a mud oyster on the sand and come away rolling it over and over, and tried to think of Truganini. She was a member of the Bruny Island tribe, but I had an odd notion that she might have visited this beach, ever since reading Sarah Mitchell's memoir. "My father and I went to see her in Hobart and he asked her if she were of the East Coast tribe and she was. She went down with a basket to gather oysters and said, 'Plenty of shark there.' Father said, 'What did you do with the shells?' She looked at him as if he were stupid and said, 'Why throw them on the bank sometimes.'" But I could not get out of my head the advertisement on the wall of the hut. "Can you take it? Shock! From the dead they come to haunt and terrify you." It was no more melodramatic than the events that occurred here on a Tuesday evening in October 1831. Or the fate that awaited Tongerlongetter and his people.

XI

TWO MONTHS AFTER ESCAPING MEREDITH'S CORDON, THE OYSTER BAY CHIEF was found camped in thick bush a few miles north-west of Lake Echo where he and 13 others had joined up with the Big River tribe. The man who discovered him was George Robinson, a tubby 43-year-old syco-phant with a head of wavy auburn hair, most of it a wig. When Tongerlongetter spied this puzzling Englishman, he advanced towards him crying his war whoop and shaking his spear. But the noise died away as Robinson stood his ground.

Robinson was a Wesleyan and former bricklayer appointed by Governor Arthur to negotiate peace with the Aborigines. A remarkable though vain and flawed man, he shared a passion for the fate of the Aborigines that was equalled only by his ambition to rise in his own society. He some-times used one concern to promote the other. Calder knew him well: "He was more patronising than courteous and somewhat offensively polite rather than civil." His dispatches to Arthur, wrote Calder, were interminable and "in magniloquence of style throw into the shade altogether the official bulletins of such men as Napoleon, Wellington and others".

An Aboriginal woman in Swansea told me 170 years later: "Robinson, as far as I'm concerned, was a weak, egotistical do-gooder who did real bad!"

Mark Twain, however, was impressed. "It may be that his counterpart appears in history somewhere, but I do not know where to look for it . . . Marsyas charming the wild beasts with his music – that is fable; but the miracle wrought by Robinson is fact. It is history – and authentic; and surely there is nothing greater, nothing more reverence-compelling in the history of any country, ancient or modern."

Robinson had his extraordinariness and his journal at least rivals Baudin's report as the richest source of knowledge concerning Aborigines.

As Robinson described it in his journal: "I then went up to the chiefs and shook hands with them. I then explained in the aborigines' dialects the purport of my visit amongst them. I invited them to sit down and gave them some refreshments and selected a few trinkets as presents which they received with much delight. They evinced considerable astonishment on hearing me address them in their own tongue and from henceforward placed themselves entirely under my control." In words that Tongerlongetter's descendants remember to this day, Robinson wrote: "I have promised them a conference with the Lieut. Govr and that the Governor will be sure to redress all their grievances."

MR. ROBINSON ON HIS CONCILIATION MISSION.
(From Mr. DUTERREAU's great picture.

On January 7, 1832, Robinson led Tongerlongetter into Hobart. The two tribes had shrunk to a total of 26: 16 men, nine women and one child. Along with them followed more than 100 dogs. They walked down Elizabeth Street with their dogs, watched by citizens such as Kemp "with the most lively curiosity and delight". At Government House, Governor Arthur greeted their arrival with a military brass band and gave each Aborigine a loaf of bread. A large front door was then hauled onto the lawn so that they could demonstrate their "wonderful dexterity". Among the observers was Jorgenson. "At the distance of about 60 or 70 yards they sent their spears through the door, and all the spears nearly in the same place." Then one Aborigine stuck a crayfish onto a spear, retreated 60 yards and hurled two out of three spears through the bright orange shell. The fact that they were in "the greatest good humour" reflected their understanding that they were celebrating a treaty, not a defeat.[*]

Ten days later Tongerlongetter boarded the *Tamar*. He had agreed to Arthur's complex negotiation to exchange Van Diemen's Land for Flinders Island. Robinson wrote: "They are delighted with the idea of proceeding to Great Island [as Flinders was called], where they will enjoy peace and plenty, uninterrupted."

---

[*] While they were camped in Elizabeth Street, Kemp's friend the artist John Glover took some sketches and used them in various paintings.

XII

I FLEW TO FLINDERS, A 35-MINUTE FLIGHT IN A SMALL PLANE FROM LAUNCESTON with two other passengers. The sky was grey as a beard and Flinders rose into it, a bleak spine of rock springing sheer from the sea. Forty miles long and 23 wide, this was where Tongerlongetter allowed himself to be removed in exchange for his ancestral lands. The airstrip was surrounded by scorched meadows and at the empty terminal building there was a warning: "European wasps are active in this area – please dispose of rubbish with care."

Robinson had promised Tongerlongetter that if he came here his people would be able to keep their way of life. Instead, they were forced into Christianity and trousers, and told by the superintendent to scrub the mud and rust from their hair.

The Aborigines camped at an unsuitable lagoon near Whitemark while convicts built the settlement of Wybalenna for them, and in 1833 they moved there. The name Wybalenna meant "Black Man's Houses". For many, it was their last home.

Flinders is geographically to Tasmania what Tasmania is to the mainland. A young man in the pub at Lady Barron tried to explain it: "Sometimes you think in Tasmania: 'This is the best kept secret.' Then on Flinders you think: '*This* is the best kept secret of that secret.'" Its history lies close to the surface. A woman told me that her father, as he was putting down a cattle-race at Prime Seal Island, found a leg in leg-irons. He said: "I moved it further away." For more than a century, that is how many settlers on Flinders tried to deal with what happened to the Aborigines at Wybalenna.

I found the bricks still scattered in the damp grass: the foundations of eight houses for the military, the sanatorium and dispensary, and, behind a mound, the L-shaped terrace of 20 cottages built for the Aborigines.

The only building standing today was a brick chapel built by George Robinson in a grove of casuarinas. It was here that Greg Lehman had got married in 1985. He told me that not long before my visit two Aboriginal women had tried to enter, but the door refused to open. They pressed their ears to it and what they heard made them walk away, very fast. "Inside, they said, they heard a roaring, blowing wind."

No-one escapes the wind on Flinders. Almost the first thing I noticed on the road from the airfield were the doubled-back trunks of the paper-barks, sculpted by the Roaring Forties to resemble trees from a children's book. The latitude splits the island in half. "You are now passing the 40th parallel," read a white signpost on another deserted road. Below it, someone had scribbled: "Oh, what a feeling." I lodged nearby with an old Scottish woman who complained how the wind transformed all her vegetables into propellers. "I've watched from my bedroom window a cabbage plant being blown round and round and then spin right off out of the ground."

I arrived on Flinders shortly after the wind had fanned a forest fire across the island. The fire blazed for three weeks, driving flames from the hills in every direction and leaving the fields in their wake a dramatic rust colour. Clumps of ti-trees stood out like puffs of solidified smoke, and already in the forks of the burned branches the shoots were coming back in feathery green stems.

At Wybalenna, it had stopped raining and on the mound above the chapel the crickets were shrilling. But it was on a day like today, windy and damp, that Tongerlongetter caught his cold.

He sat in his wet English clothes, no animal fat on his massive body – the superintendent discouraged that too – and shivering.

On the evening of June 19, 1837, he was joking with his wife when he collapsed in "excruciating agony" and started vomiting. Earlier he had complained of a rheumatic pain on the left of his face, but now his chest was so inflamed that he howled when Alexander Austin, the medical atten-dant, touched his skin. Austin immediately bled him, taking 50 ounces from his arm, and administered an enema. "For the first six hours he was perfectly sensible and his cries of 'Minatti' piteous."

Robinson had already that winter watched 14 Aborigines die from pneu-monia. The prospect of losing the chief whom he had renamed King William was too much for him. "Poor creature!" he wrote in his journal.

"I turned from the appalling scene. It was more than my mind could endure . . . " He left the room without saying goodbye. Later, he heard the lamentations and knew.

Not until the wailing died down did Robinson go and see the corpse. "Oh, what a sight," he wrote. The Aborigines stood in silence, tears streaming down their cheeks. He left the room, shaken. "The death of King William has thrown a halo over the settlement."

On a remarkably fine morning two days later Robinson led the mourners at the Christian funeral. Tongerlongetter's body lay in a gum plank coffin on two trestles in the schoolroom. At 11 a.m., the Aborigines in new dresses sang an improbable hymn: "From Egypt lately come/Where death and darkness reign/We seek a new a better home/Where we our rest shall gain."

Then Robinson addressed them: "When I first met him he was in his native wilds, those parts where white men never trod. He was then at the head of a powerful tribe. Their very name spread terror and dismay throughout the peaceful settlements of the colony . . . It was to subjugate this man's tribe and that of his colleague that the famous military operation was entered upon, namely the cordon of the island commonly called the Line." But as the eulogy went on, Robinson faltered. He looked into the faces around him and thought of how Tongerlongetter's people had since been treated after relying "with implicit confidence on my veracity". He battled to console himself that at least they had discovered Jesus. "My sable brethren," he told them, "you now not only have a knowledge of God, but you have a knowledge of the principles of Christianity." But his heart was heavy. He had portrayed himself as a Pied Piper, promising to lead Tongerlongetter to safety and civilisation. In a letter he wrote to the surgeon, he could not contain his bitterness: "He is no more and the white man may now safely revel in luxury on the lands of his primeval existence."

I could see the cemetery through the chapel window. One half contained the graves of Europeans; the other half was an empty field. The 100 or so Aboriginal graves were once indicated by wooden pegs painstakingly laid out on the mowed grass, but one night a farmer ploughed them up.

The crickets added to the sense that Wybalenna was a haunted place. On a clear day, Tongerlongetter's widow would climb up to Flagstaff Hill and peer with longing towards Tasmania's north-east coast, 60 miles away. I thought of another ghost story that Greg Lehman had told me. "In the early 1980s, some Aboriginal kids went and sat on the hillside above the graveyard to watch the sun set. They sat up yarning, but when it got dark they were terrified to see a number of lights rising from the graves."

On June 22, 1837, Tongerlongetter was buried somewhere beneath the undulating strip of grass. His widow followed soon after.

Jetty at Wybalenna

XIII

AT THE TIME OF KEMP'S ARRIVAL ON THE TAMAR IT IS THOUGHT THAT THERE were nine tribes of Aborigines in Tasmania, with between 250 and 700 members each. It is impossible to know accurately their total population, but educated estimates range between 3,000 and 5,000. There were some 400 alive in December 1831, the month that Tongerlongetter submitted to Robinson. When Kemp died in October 1868, there were 103,000 Europeans on the island, but only one full-blooded male Aborigine.

In the museum at Wybalenna there was a photograph of William Lanne. He was dressed in a waistcoat and a canvas shirt with leg-of-mutton sleeves, and wore a colourful neckscarf. But the energy seemed punched out of him. He stared at the ground, unsmiling, his brow furrowed. The face of a man sick of being looked at. Sick of what he had seen.

He was brought to Wybalenna when he was seven, but ended his days in Hobart. At a regatta some years before his death, he was introduced to the Duke of Edinburgh as "the king of Tasmanians". He stood on a podium with Truganini and watched her present a prize for the crew of *Duck Hunt* – and then, "delighted with his share in the proceedings", called for three cheers. His spirit had been crushed several years before. In 1847, the Aborigines were removed once again – from Wybalenna to a settlement south of Hobart. Lanne's impotence shrieked out between the lines of his complaint that the women, including Truganini, were receiving inadequate rations: "I am the last man of my race and I must look after my people."

He died on March 3, 1869. He had come off a whaling ship and taken a room at the Dog and Partridge Hotel in Barrack Street when he fell ill

WILLIAM LANNÉ, THE LAST MAN.
Photographed by Mr. C. A. Woolley, 1866.)

with choleraic diarrhoea. At 2 p.m., he got up, began to dress and collapsed. He was 34, known by the locals as a drunk who escaped his sorrows in pubs along the wharf, but remembered by his people as "a fine young man, plenty beard, plenty laugh, very good, that fellow".

Lanne's death had about it the grisliness of a horror movie. His body was laid out in the morgue at the Colonial Hospital, but that night his head was cut off and the skull of a dead English schoolteacher called Ross inserted in its place. Soon after, it was rumoured that Dr William Crowther of the Royal College of Surgeons had left the hospital carrying a mysterious parcel under his arm. Lanne's skeleton then became the object of a tug of war between two warring scientific bodies, one of which sent his skull back to England while the other cut off his hands and feet. In a sickening note that I found among his papers, Calder wrote that Dr George Stokell of the Royal Society of Tasmania had a purse made out of Lanne's skin, and that Pedder, at one time Superintendent of Police, had called at Stokell's little surgery at the hospital and seen the skin pegged out on the floor. A magpie and a terrier dog were standing by, and there were buckets in the room "chock-a-block" with Lanne's "fat".

LALLA ROCKH, OR TRUGANINA, THE LAST WOMAN.
(Photographed by Mr. C. A. Woolley, 1866.)

Truganini's grief when she heard of his death was "something terrible".
She survived Lanne by seven years, coming to live with Mrs Dandridge
at 115 Macquarie Street along from Kemp's first warehouse. She sat on the
steps smoking a pipe or went walking around Battery Point, her dark face
framed by a red turban, and a necklace of green and white Mariner shells
in her pocket to give to Margaret's grandmother in return for beer. "She
was under four feet in height and of much the same measure in breadth,"
wrote Sir Charles Du Cane, the Governor, who sometimes welcomed her
at Government House, where someone described her as chuckling like
a child over a slice of cake, a glass of wine. On May 3, 1876, she had a
premonition. She gave her pet bird to Mrs Dandridge's son and in the
evening screamed out, "Missus, Rowra catch me, Rowra catch me!" She
did not speak again until shortly before her death five days later, when,
remembering William Lanne's fate, she called, "Don't let them cut me, but
bury me behind the mountains."

XIV

THE CAPTION BENEATH LANNE READ: "LAST MALE DESCENDANT OF THAT RACE who succumbed as the white man advanced. Hastily have they disappeared and left no 'footsteps in the sands of time'." Until 30 years ago, this statement was commonly accepted as true. Aborigines, wrote the anthropologist Bill Stanner in 1968, were regarded as a "melancholy footnote" in the past and no account was taken of their continued presence. In other words, they had become just one more example of what Martin Flanagan calls Tasmania's "convenient silences".

This silence extended to the Aborigines themselves. Patsy Cameron grew up on Flinders, and she told me of the 1978 film, *The Last Tasmanian*, in which her cousin Annette Mansell had made the remark: "I'm not an Aborigine . . . There are no Aborigines now. We're Islanders." Cameron says: "And *then* we weren't. We didn't know it existed – Truganini being the last, we were taught. It didn't really come about till the 1970s."

How people with Aboriginal blood came to terms with their Aboriginality, at first by keeping it hidden and pretending that it did not exist, and then by flaunting it as a badge of honour, is something that perplexes the whole Tasmanian community. But the historian Peter Chapman understands the defensive and contradictory behaviour that has characterised the position of many Tasmanian Aborigines for the last 30 years. "I can remember being told aged nine by some revolting figure out of the RAAF, a schoolteacher, how he'd been in the Northern Territory and he'd get the 'Abos' round the campfire, make them take a mouthful of petrol from a bottle and spit it out on the fire – and whoosh. I can remember as a nine-year-old roaring with laughter at this jocular way of putting down a race. Of course they're defensive, and we expect them to deport themselves with Western rational dignity . . . " He goes on: "Even in the late 1960s the propellers would be going on Flinders – to take the children away from their upset mothers and put them into social care. They were regarded as Aborigines then, all right."

Many of Tasmania's Aboriginal descendants came, like Patsy Cameron, from Flinders and Cape Barren Island in Bass Strait. They were the offspring of European sealers and Aboriginal women – whom the men left behind on the islands to skin the seals and clean the hides – as well as a handful of Maori and Indian women. As late as the 1960s they called themselves Islanders or "half-castes", but were treated – in terms of prejudice – as full Aborigines, and brutalised, insulted and patronised as "Boongs". Cameron said: "My mother grew up when there was a black bar and white bar. She had to go in what was called 'the bull-ring'."

Segregated drinking was outlawed in 1967, but Cameron recalled seeing another cousin, Daisy Maynard, on her first day at school in Lady Barron. "A teacher was putting white powder in her hair for lice. Someone from Sydney, they didn't get their hair white, but all the Aboriginal kids did. At times, I did think: Why are they doing it?" Patsy's father was Italian, her mother an Islander, but Patsy identified only with her mother's side of the family. "We knew that we were different. I always had a sense of seeing these strange people, my mother's relations, speaking in a strange language, with a different melody, wearing headscarves, and lots of frizzy hair. Even though we were isolated from everyone, we did have our get-togethers. The women would bring shells, and the old uncles would play cards and drink and fight a lot – but they fought with each other. It was internalised."

In the 1970s attitudes changed. Angered by the prejudice and by a long-festering sense of grievance that Robinson's promise to Tongerlongetter had never been honoured, the community began to fight for full-blooded recognition. Under the leadership of men like Roy Nicholls and Michael Mansell, they refused to acquiesce in the notion of their extinction. Consciously or not, they were fulfilling the prediction reported by W. Horton, a Wesleyan Methodist who interviewed Aborigines in Bass Strait in 1821, "As to a future state, they expected to reappear on an island in the Straits and jump up white men." This is more or less what happened. All over Flinders and Cape Barren Island, men and women sprang up to speak on behalf of their ancestors. Their calls were heard across Bass Strait and one day they reached Edna Webb in Forget-Me-Not Cottage outside Swansea.

XV

EDNA HAD PINK CHEEKS, DEEP-SET ROUND BROWN EYES AND LION-COLOURED hair. "It's too nice a day to do anything," she said, letting me in. She lived across the field from the Cellar — we could see the corrugated iron roof from her window — and she knew about the holes through which William Lyne poked his gun to shoot Aborigines.

She had grown up in Latrobe in the north-west. Her father was a noisy Irish bushman who sang mad Irish songs and ran a 50-acre block at Dawson's Siding. Her mother was known as "Dellis", and did not talk about her past.

Edna drifted south to work in the Swansea hotel, and was walking home over the Meredith River when a man with a big cheeky grin passed by in a truck. "Hello, love," he called out. They met a few nights later at a picture-show and married soon after. "That was 44 years ago. He was my first love and my last love," and she pointed at a high-backed couch. "He died sitting there six years ago this August. I think about him every minute of every day."

She had been married to Murray 14 years when Bill Mollison, a lecturer at the University of Tasmania, came to stay at Glen Gala. Mollison met Edna's husband and was interested to know whether he had Aboriginal ancestry. "My husband was dark, with a flat nose, and known to all the shearers as their 'half-caste mate'." Mollison offered to find out. "A month later he rang me up. 'It isn't Murray, it's you.'"

The news shocked Edna. "At school we weren't taught nothing about the Aborigine past. That never came to light. We only heard the bad side

– that they were lazy hangers-on and wouldn't help themselves and that sort of stuff. Well, your mind just boggles. I said, 'Oh no, I don't think so.'"

She drove to Latrobe to speak to her mother. "It was news to her as well. 'Well, well, it's there,' she said. 'Nothing you can do about it.'"

Not until her mother's death did Edna discover that her mother had been born with the name Dalrymple, after their ancestor Dalrymple or "Dolly" Briggs – the daughter of a red-haired, freckle-faced sealer from Bedfordshire and the Aboriginal woman, called Woretermoeteyenner, whom he seized from her land.

To Edna, the discovery explained a connection: "When we were kids we never wore shoes, but raced through the bush. I always felt – even when I was a child about the land – that I belonged out in the country, that I was part of it."

"What else did it mean?"

"We were entitled to so much money every quarter for our children."

"How much?" There was a widespread perception in Tasmania that many, as one man said to me, "hauled up the flag when the money came in", and that a lot of people applied for Aboriginality because there were lucrative grants.

Edna said that she had had an allowance of $60 each term for each of her three children to help to pay for their schoolbooks and clothes – hardly an incentive to switch cultures.

"How did you feel all of a sudden to be an Aborigine?"

She thought for a long second. "Proud, I suppose." But she refused to get involved in the cause, unlike her brother Albert, who flew the Aboriginal flag outside his house near Railton, and whose pride in their mother's past had led him to investigate their Irish father's genealogy as well.

"I don't know if there's any truth in it, but he's found out we're related to the Spencers in the UK."

XVI

THE WOMAN WHO DELIVERED THE PEA-STRAW HAD BLUE EYES. SHE REMEMBERED the moment when she became aware that there were Aborigines still in Tasmania.

She was 16, just out of a Catholic boarding school, and fishing with her father for crayfish off Trefoil Island on the far north-west coast. "We anchored right into a very steep rock on the northern side and I looked at these people, and I looked, and I saw that they were black. This old black woman was sitting by a pot, plucking, flicking mutton-bird feathers all over her lap. I wanted to get over there, talk to her, know about it. I ran back to call Dad.

"'There are black people!'

"'Yeh, bloody Aborigines.'

"'Aborigines? What, there's Aborigines?' I was so excited. I didn't know there were such people in Tasmania. I didn't know they existed.

"'Yeh, bloody take all the government money. You know what they bloody do, burn the house down,' and he mumbled away.

"I got hurt. Why does he think they're no good, does he know them? I knew that he had lived at Wybalenna. 'What's your problem, Dad? Why does it upset you so much? I think I know.'"

The idea took root that she might be linked to the old woman. She had hot, strange dreams in which an Aboriginal Elder appeared. She pestered her mother. She pulled out the family album and pointed to her mother's brother, known as "Blackie". "How come he's so dark-skinned? What about his curly black hair, brown eyes, broad nose? Why do you think he looks like the traditional Aboriginal?" At first her mother denied any connection. But one night she remembered something, a detail: "It's a funny thing, but when I was little – you know what it's like with adults talking and you're meant to be in bed. I heard this talk in the kitchen and I hid behind the door. Your Nan wasn't there, and the men were talking about the fact she was a black fella and thank God she wasn't *that* black and no-one had to know."

The woman had since changed her name to an Aboriginal word meaning "near the sea".

XVII

AROUND SWANSEA THERE WERE FEW ABORIGINES, BUT I WAS GIVEN THE NAME of a man who lived 20 minutes away in Little Swanport.

He sounded cagey when I telephoned. His septic tank had blocked and he was waiting for a truck. How did I plan to use my material? Had I read this and that, had I seen Greg Lehman and Doug Maynard? He was reluctant to say anything that would have his name on it. "Everyone looks at it and there are seething arguments."

"I'll call you Jimmy," I proposed.

"What do you want to know?"

"I want to know how you came to realise that you're an Aborigine. Also, how the culture of a so-called extinct race can have been preserved?"

He asked where I lived.

"How far along Dolphin Sands?" a new note in his voice.

I give him the number.

He chuckled. "How's Helen?"

It turned out that he had lived three years in my shed.

"I'm ringing you from there," I told him.

Another chuckle. Once, he said, he found half a pound of cannabis in a hole up the wall where I had heard the scratching. And if I was to go in a diagonal from the kitchen to my desk, and walk outside, about 30 yards, up in the mound behind the big gum tree I would discover the remains of a dope plantation.

"Then you'll talk to me?"

"You should look into your own ancestors."

"That's exactly what I'm doing."

Jimmy lived in a wooden house by a river. He was mid-50s, small, with a long grey beard and brown hair parted in the middle. He caught me looking at him and grinned. "People expect me to be black as the inside of a dog."

He had rented my shed off the man who owned the house before Helen and admitted that he pined for the sight of the sun bouncing off the clouds onto the Hazards. "I see those colours and think Albert Namitjira."

I wanted to know if there was any advice that he, as an Aborigine, would give in connection with the house. He spoke of burial sites near the beach. "Try not to disturb the land too much. And leave the place as it is."

His grudging manner dissolved the more he remembered Dolphin Sands and the shed where I now worked. "The waves, you could feel them. The whole building shook. I'd go down after every storm. A southerly coming up sometimes takes ten years off the shore and rips it off – and all comes back. I'd pick up sea-slugs, like old men's dicks, and feel so sorry and throw them back. I'd take rock oysters to eat. And once I kicked a large shell in the sand, and it was a cowrie shell, that big."

The buff-coloured shell had sat on the barbecue for a year. "But I knew it was a little bit different. One day I took it in my pocket to the Hobart Museum, check shirt and country trousers. I asked: 'Is there a shellologist?' They brought a woman, a marine invertebrate specialist. I told her, 'I've got this old shell.' She back-flipped, pissed herself and turned purple: 'Ah . . . ah . . . ah . . .'

"'Not a bad old shell.'

"'Do you know what that is? Quaternary. 100,000 years old.'

"'Oh, I know it's pretty bloody old, lady.'

"'What do you want to do with it?'

"'I'll give it to the museum as long as you put my name on it.'"

Later, I spoke to Liz Turner at the Hobart Museum. Yes, she confirmed, she had been "very excited" when Jimmy produced the shell. "I hadn't seen a fossil that old before. It's extremely rare to find this type of cowrie, enormously old and robust." She thought it had probably washed from the Aboriginal midden at Brown's beach.

I wondered if this was the beach that had featured in Jimmy's dream.

Jimmy could not remember when he had had the dream, but I spoke to two women who said that he had dreamed it in my shed. They met him next morning in Swansea's main street. Normally, you could shoot a cannon down it without hitting anyone, but on this day you would have hit Jimmy Riley.

He had dreamed he was walking on Dolphin Sands or on a beach near it. Suddenly, he was surrounded by a mob of Aborigines, taunting him. "These young bucks were harassing me: 'You're not Aboriginal.' I said: 'Be fucked I am!' and tore my shirt open. And there on my body were scars – big cicatrices – that only the Oyster Bay people have. 'OK, you are,' they said. I went back to sleep. I started to feel my chest. I still remember the marks. They were my marks. They're the equivalent of body painting: your totem, who you are, who you're related to. Just because the white fellas came here 200 years ago doesn't mean that the dreamings stopped."

He sat back, fiddling with an empty mug. "After that dream, I decided: I'm out of here. It's in front." All his life he had kept his Aboriginality hidden. From that night, he went public.

I asked about his family. His grandfather on his father's side was a member of the Light Horse cavalry. His grandmother was a Purton from Ulverstone who had an old people's home named after her. It was from her that Jimmy inherited his Aboriginal blood.

"Do you see yourself as part-Aborigine?"

"No." He embraced his Aboriginality as a total identity. "Those who don't identify themselves with the struggle are out. Only people who don't understand about being Aborigine call themselves 'part'. You can't be a part Jew. You're either of the Jewish religion or not."

"My great-great-grandmother was Jewish and spoke Hebrew," I said. "But that doesn't make me Jewish. How can you decide to make a $\frac{1}{32}$ of your inheritance your total inheritance?" According to one reckoning, Winston Churchill could have claimed to be an Iroquois on the same basis.

"It's a feeling, a political decision." He lifted the white mug. "If I put in a teaspoon of coffee and add water what do I get? Coffee. And if I put more water in it? Coffee. And if I put this much milk in it?"

"Are you are saying that your Aboriginal blood is much stronger than any of your other bloodlines?"

He put down the cup. "Did you find the dope?"

"No, just some fence stakes and wires."

He nodded. "To stop the wallabies. The plants were already going to seed when I came across them. They're unlikely to have lasted so high above the waterhole."

XVIII

ON THE LIVING-ROOM WALL AT DOLPHIN SANDS WAS AN ORANGE DOT-PAINTING of an Aboriginal waterhole north of Alice Springs. It was painted by an elder from the Stirling community, who one unforgettable day led me through the country of his "dreaming", along a red desert track bordered by dogwoods, to the Anangarra waterhole. Clem had stood on the bank and sung into the water some words from a language that seemed more foreign and ancient even than the landscape. Afterwards, I asked him to paint me his "dreaming". The canvas arrived two years later as my son was being born.

Tasmanian Aborigines today do not have access to the language or "dreamings" that allow mainland Aborigines to connect with their land. They have their dreams, like Jimmy, and an oral history that teaches how to find, trap and kill animals in the bush. And the records of men like Robinson, white fellas who had led their ancestors to their graves. But Jimmy's separation from his lost culture was no less painful and profound than the longing of an Afro-Caribbean for Africa, quoted in an essay by Greg Lehman: "I have come from a place to which I cannot go back and I have never seen. I used to speak a language which I can no longer speak, I had ancestors whom I cannot find, they worshipped gods whose names I do not know."

The little that is known about Tasmanian Aborigines must itself be hedged with caveats. As Lloyd Robson warned, what was recorded of Aboriginal culture and behaviour may have been wildly atypical of them when they were undisturbed. The fact that so little is known means that "quite contrary conclusions concerning motivation may be drawn with equal facility . . . how the Aborigines behaved during the course of their destruction at the hands of the Europeans may reveal little or nothing or be absolutely misleading about practices during the period prior to conquest."

It is possible that each of Tasmania's nine tribes spoke a different language, but the problem is that no Tasmanian Aborigine who may have become educated in English ever produced a dictionary of his/her language. No text or recording exists that might enable linguists to resurrect even one of these languages – as has been done in South Australia, where young Aboriginal girls wrote letters and German missionaries made recordings. In Tasmania, much fund-money has gone into "restitution" and there has been some ambitious linguistic work, but a language remains frustratingly out of reach. Henry Reynolds says, "Putting all the word lists of all the languages together, there is a vocabulary of some hundreds of words. But no grammar, no sentence structure, no pronunciation."

One reason for Robinson's success with the Oyster Bay tribe was that he was practically unique in having learned Tongerlongetter's dialect, and although the vocabulary he claimed to have compiled has vanished (along with Jorgenson's so-called "dictionary"), Robinson did note down in his journal the phonetic equivalent of a number of Aboriginal words as well as accounts of their beliefs and myths. In the absence of a native alternative, his journal has assumed the status of a sacred text. Patsy Cameron says: "The stories they told Robinson were, I believe, for us. We've got to look between the lines and pull them out." But she accepts that it is an excruciating position to be in: to have to count on imperfect mediators like Robinson, Péron and Jorgenson to revive her culture. The inherent contradiction exposes her to historians like Windschuttle, who is quick to point out that the white man's record is quite as much Patsy's inheritance as her Aboriginality. "Most of those who today trace their ancestry to the Bass Strait community must be the descendants not only of Aborigines but also of people who committed atrocities against Aborigines . . . In short the Tasmanian 'Aboriginal community' today embodies both the invaders and the invaded."

A society that accepts its mixed identity is not so likely to be troubled by this contradiction. But in the Dechaineaux Theatre I had seen for myself that Tasmania's Aboriginal community was confused and divided. Two of its most important leaders regularly accused each other of not being Aboriginal nor able to point reliably to a tribal ancestor. I wondered how much of the confusion had arisen from a decision by the political leadership to reject the richness of their background and to embrace Aboriginality as the sum of their identity. The impulse was understandable, a response to a century and a half of brutality and denigration, but it could result in decisions that many perceived to be skewed, unimaginative and confounding. A powerful example was a ruling in September 2002 by the Independent Indigenous Advisory Committee to reject the claim for Aboriginality of Tracey Norman from Snug, but to uphold the claim of her brother, Damien Coulson. "I am not happy at all," Norman said. "We have the same parents."

Doubt was sown not only about who people were, but about who they had been. Talking to Tasmanian Aborigines, it was easy to gain the impression that the fact of their white blood was an inconvenience to be ignored. This willingness to overlook one aspect of their background obscured their project of forming an accurate picture of the past, and helped to recreate in its place a culture in which it was possible to shelter and be vague and secretive.

Even those opposed to Windschuttle's thesis, like the archaeologists Tim Murray and Christine Williamson, agree that "the absence of evidence has made it relatively easy for historians, anthropologists, even archaeologists to construe Aboriginal Tasmania to suit their needs". Nor are Tasmanian Aborigines exempt. Henry Reynolds finds it "consistently fascinating and distressing" to witness how "those who have the least make the claim to most". He says: "There is bad faith on all sides – bad faith in their pretensions, and bad faith in the way people sit around and say: 'That's right.'" Reynolds yields to no-one in his knowledge of post-colonial Aboriginal history. He has championed the rights of the Aboriginal community over four decades. But he is forced to admit: "Pursuing Aboriginality has been a bad thing in a way. It would make much more sense to say: 'Of course, we're mixed.' It would solve the problems about who is and who isn't Aboriginal." He gives the example of the Métis in Canada, another product of the colonial frontier that is proud of its distinctive culture, and that reminds Reynolds of the community in Bass Strait. "The Straits people know exactly who they are, where they come from. They don't have to try and be who they're not. If you say you're a Tasmanian Aboriginal, you are saying that you're something you don't know how to be. You don't know how to live it."

Reynolds is in a good position to make this observation. He discovered five years ago that his late father, whom he believed was Armenian, was in fact Aboriginal, and yet the discovery has not persuaded him to claim Aboriginality. "If you say you're Aboriginal, it makes it easy to assume a position of moral authority and not to have to do the work. It gives an authority that doesn't come from you, but from what you're supposed to be."

My conversations with Reynolds made it clear that an important element of Tasmanian Aboriginality was explained by the need to belong. This explained to him the surge in numbers of those who registered themselves as Aboriginal. In 1976 it was fewer than 3,000. Now the figure has risen to almost 16,000. "I suspect lots of these people once upon a time identified [themselves] as working-class. When you take away class, you need to find some other identity. Many were rural. As the middle class spread, they were removed from a strong working-class identity, and got lost."

But in Bass Strait one cultural activity had survived that most parties agreed was central to defining modern Aboriginal identity.

XIX

THE SMELL HIT ME AS I CAME OVER THE RIDGE, OILY AND THICK, WITH THE smokiness of wet hay. "The perfume is not readily forgotten," wrote an early visitor. I was told that it disappeared with the last mutton-birds at the end of April and returned with them in September, and that fishermen could smell it out at sea.

The only birds in sight were a pair of gulls battling against the updraught. The horizon was dotted with islands, and across it a north-easterly blew clouds the colour of grey down. The path sloped through a field of tussocks and lomandra grass. The burrows lay in a springy labyrinth beneath.

"This field, you're looking at 100,000 birds," said the man taking me to Furley's shed.

The mutton-birds arrived from Siberia, punctual as blossom, on September 27 each year. In 1798, Matthew Flinders was amazed at the sight of a sky black with "sooty petrels", as he called them. They passed over-head without interruption for a full 90 minutes in a broad stream. "On the lowest computation, I think the number could not have been less than a hundred millions." Numbers had dwindled, but an estimated 12 million birds still made the 9,000 mile journey to the rookeries in Bass Strait. With a salmon's accuracy, they returned year after year to the same burrow to hatch their chicks. "If you're standing in front of their burrow," Jimmy said, "they'll fly straight into you. They'll go through tankers if the port-holes are left open." A fisherman who had anchored off Chappell Island during the forest fires of February 2003 told me that Mount Chappell had been alight, and he had watched a thick constant line of birds fly into the blazing mountain.

The wind dipped the tips of the grass into the grey sand. I would not see any birds until dusk. They were out at sea, feeding for krill to regurgitate to their chicks. It was mid-April and the old birds were thinning out. They would come in from the east right on dark, spend the night in their burrow and leave at daylight, and gradually they did not come back. When they returned to find the chick gone, they stayed one or two more days, and then moved on too.

But in thousands of cases, the chick had not flown. Either it had been eaten by a tiger-snake or, more likely, it had had its neck broken by a "birder".

A pidgin language had evolved in Bass Strait using phrases like "curpa china" for cup of tea and "old co", after the Cornish for "old cove". Mutton-birding also combined native and European traditions. The Aborigines had hunted birds for their own consumption. The sealers turned this into a commercial industry. By the 1950s the industry employed 300 people at a canning factory in Lady Barron from which the birds were exported as "squab in aspic". So strong was the tradition that the Islanders demanded control of the rookeries as compensation for the loss of their homelands. Recently, the government had restored control to the community, but the importance of the activity was metaphorical as much as financial, and had come to symbolise the survival of a culture. Patsy Cameron says: "You have a feeling of spiritual communion with the bird. You're thinking of the journey that the bird takes, coming back to the same hole, under the same tussock. While you're birding, you're thinking of that journey."

At last we reached Furley's shed. A teacher stood on the wind-nipped grass, preparing to lead a group of children to the boat. They had completed three days on Big Dog Island, part of a project to bring young Aborigines from the mainland so that they could learn about mutton-birding from the woman inside.

She sat by the fire with her back to the window, olive-skinned with white curly hair and dressed in pink trousers and a home-knitted lavender jersey. She turned to see who had come in, and the lines in her strong face contracted about her eyes.

"Auntie" Furley's son was Michael Mansell, the most active of Tasmania's Aboriginal leaders. He had a flair for controversy. In 1987, he had flown to Colonel Qaddafi's Tripoli to divert attention onto his community. He had not met Qaddafi, as many people thought, but the ploy succeeded. Jimmy said: "There wouldn't be any Tasmanian Aborigines without Mansell." And Furley was his mother.

Tacked to the shed walls were pieces of paper, each with a word printed on it and a translation.

Muna – yes
Nayri – good
Putiya – no

The words reminded me of Robinson's English lessons to the Aborigines in the museum at Wybalenna: "Has not a cat fur? It has and so has a fox. The sun has set. I do not see the top of the hill."

"Ya is hello," Furley said. "And waluka is goodbye. That's as much as I know."

"Did your mother and father use these words?"

"No. They've come out since. They've done research."

I thought of the Scottish lady I was staying with, who was learning Gaelic from cassettes – "something I've always wanted to do." So far she could say: "How do you do?" and "Would you like coffee?"

I asked Furley: "When did you first go birding?"

"I was five," she said. "It's a long, toiling job for little money."

On Babel Island, there had been 27 sheds. She had worked in a group of eight and the highest number of birds they took in a season was 14,500. She said: "Everything of the mutton-bird is saleable apart from its head and feet, which they feed to the flathead."

The feathers were sent to East Germany, the oil to a chemist in Launceston. "We were made to take it for chest troubles, although I can't swallow it without sugar. It's got a certain flavour of its own."

"Can you describe it?"

"A bit chickenish, a bit fishish."

"Are there 'dreamings' associated with the mutton-bird?"

Furley smiled. "I used to dream about looking forward to next time."

She painted the scene: a family gathering, cricket matches and singing at the weekend. "There was always a concert somewhere on Babel, a shed with people playing the violin and accordion and guitar."

"What were the songs?"

"Mainly country and western."

"Which song do you remember?"

"'Blue eyes cryin' in the rain.'"

The net loosened on her face. Her mouth opened and she began to sing. I thought of Clem at the Anangarra waterhole.

> *"Someday when we meet up yonder*
> *"We'll stroll hand in hand again*
> *"In the land that knows no parting*
> *"Or blue eyes cryin' in the rain."*

XX

NEXT MORNING I WENT WITH DUSTY ON HIS TRACTOR, BOUNCING ALONG A sandy path to the rookery where Tas and Angus stood in the tussock grass.

They staggered towards us, two stooped figures in a thunderstorm of feathers. Each carried a spit of 50 birds across his shoulder and the backs of their hands were scratched red. Tas complained that the beaks were starting to toughen up and that the burrows near the shore were occupied by penguins with beaks like pairs of bolt clippers. He said that he had to put on antiseptic cream every night and bathe his cuts in salt water. "Main thing in birding is all the time look after your hand."

He slithered his harvest onto the back of the tractor.

"How many will you catch today?" I asked.

"I reckon if you get a hundred birds a day you're doing a pretty good job."

"If we're not getting them, it's a dirty bastard of a job," Angus growled. "Matter of upstairs agreeing with us." He cursed the work, the distance from the shed, the rain darkening the sand.

But for Tas the rain was a good thing. It made the birds scratch their pen feathers out, and so the flesh was firmer and easier to pluck. "Without rain, they're soft and shitty," and he pulled out a feather and snapped it. A dark colour half-filled it, the shade of ink in a quill. He said: "When they fly, they don't have blood in their feathers. They drink salt water and it dries up the blood."

"Couple of days of this, that's enough for me," grunted Angus. He offloaded his spit and I saw that he had "Hate" and "Love" tattooed across his knuckles. Robert Mitchum in *The Night of the Hunter*.

Dusty started up the tractor, and I walked into the field with Tas and Angus to catch my first mutton-bird.

It was once called a "flying sheep" or a Norfolk Island petrel, but its correct name is the short-tailed shearwater, or *Puffinus tenuirostris*. It lives to an age of 38 and got its nickname after a British officer remarked that it tasted like mutton.

A shearwater is five before it lays its first egg. This takes 53 days to hatch, and until the chick can fly it is prey to water rats that swim over from Little Dog Island to suck its brains out. And tiger-snakes.

The image of a tiger-snake waiting in a burrow for a mutton-bird to hatch reminded me of Kemp. In February 1805 at York Town he had watched Paterson make the experiment of putting a tiger-snake into a cask together with a wounded seagull to see what happened. The snake at first attempted to choke the gull by twisting his body round the bird's neck. Then it bit the gull in the foot and under the eye. "In about two minutes the poison began visibly to operate . . . and in one minute more he had two or three spasms and died."

Tas wore no gloves so that he could better gauge the temperature down a hole. Generally speaking, if the burrow was warm a chick was inside. "Reckon if it's cold, a snake's in there."

"Last half of March is the mating season," Angus said. "They'll chase you down the track for a hundred metres." It was the second week of April, but two days earlier Angus had come across a snake. At first he thought it was a bracken fern root – then it moved across the back of his hand and he felt cold scales on his knuckles. He said: "A copper-head will kill you – you've got two hours."

Already, I had asked the women in the shed if the danger from snakes was exaggerated.

"It is *not* exaggerated," Patricia said. "My nephew was bitten twice, two years in a row. On this island." A man had died on Chappell where her uncle, Wallaby Jackson, had killed 90 snakes in half an hour. Tiger-snakes thick as his wrist.

Frances was Wallaby's sister and had been birding since 1947 and has seen off many snakes in that time. "I've grabbed them in the burrow by the tail and chased them and cracked them." She advised me: "When you grab a snake by the tail, you crack it like a whip, very quickly."

Once on Chappell Patricia saw a tiger-snake swallowing a whole mutton-bird, fully grown. "It was a lump in its stomach."

Not to be outdone, Frances recalled the first occasion when she put her hand down a hole and felt something. It was 1952. The burrow had an awkward turn and there was a granite stone in the way. "As soon as my fingers touched the smooth skin, my hair stood up. I felt this cold scaly thing, and Jesus, I came out of that quick."

I thought of "Auntie" Furley, who two months before on Babel had sat down on a rock. "I felt something go across my leg, and of course I didn't look down straight away, still daydreaming, and when I looked down there was a black snake coiled up right beside my foot." And I thought of the old Scottish lady gesturing at the leaves in her "remarkably unproductive" strawberry patch, where, the same month, she had been taking a break from her Gaelic lessons when a four-foot tiger-snake raised its head. "This is where it bit me. The poor creature was stuck in the nylon netting trying to get the strawberry, foolish fellow. I was picking out weeds and I idiotically put my arm into its mouth, poor thing. It was quite like a needle and I felt pretty queer." The bridge to her farm was down and the ambulance had taken a while. She was eventually flown to a hospital in Launceston where she was bombarded with questions to find out just how bad she was. What was her name, how old was she, what day was it?

She replied correctly: "My name is Lady Mary Mactier, I am 88 and today is February 27, 2003."

Most of all I thought of Fred Willis, an old birder with unlined skin and kind, unseeing eyes that shone like the oil he sipped each morning from a 44-gallon drum. He was going blind and this was the first year he had not been birding since 1920. "I reckon I've caught my last one," he said. "But if you think about snakes, you'll never catch a bird."

Angus had worked in a supermarket in Alice Springs.

"Did you get to know any Aborigines there?" I asked.

"No."

"Why not?"

"Their smell put me off. It's a really strong smell. Not bad BO or anything. But it put me off."

I stopped and looked at him. He had just told me that he came from Launceston and was 20 when he discovered that he was Aboriginal. I asked: "Weren't you interested in their culture?"

Angus stared intently at a lomandra clump. "They've got their own particular way of living. They're different tribes and they talk in Aboriginal lingo. They virtually keep to themselves."

But his mind was not in Alice Springs. He fell to his knees. "I don't worry about snakes, blue-tongues, spiders. All I worry about is the mutton-bird."

"Come on," Tas said.

I followed him between the tussocks, my ankles sinking into the burrows.

He approached a small opening and pushed back the grass. "When the parents come to feed, they regurgitate at the edge of the hole and you can smell it. It's not real good."

Tas stretched out and thrust in his hand. He creased his nose. He was nine when he caught his first bird. "I didn't like putting my hand down a hole like this. I still don't. Jesus, this is a deep hole." Then: "There's one in here. Put your ear to the ground."

I listened to the thump-thump-thump of the wings.

"Jesus, it's nice when you get an easy one. I hate it when there's not a bird down the hole. I hate it. 'Cos it's a bloody effort. Ah, you bugger."

He pressed his thumb and finger to the neck, and flicked. There was a squeak and a quiet clatter of wings as he whirled it. The oil oozed down and blackened the beak. Then he lifted the slack bird and pierced it through the bottom of its mouth onto the spit.

Now my turn.

"This one?" Tas said.

I sensed his impatience. I had rejected a dozen holes. "All right."

The opening in the sand was about four inches wide. I prayed that it would be shallow and warm. I lay on my side and inserted my right arm at a 30-degree angle, stretching forward inch by inch. The wind had frozen my hand and the air that it clutched seemed extraordinarily cold. The tips of my fingers felt for a head, but would it be a reptile's head or a beak? I touched a stone, some roots. Had I moved past him? Or was this a "blind" hole, and if so what did that suggest? My arm was in up to my shoulder and my heart was drumming.

A peck.

"Bring him out slowly so you don't bruise him," Tas said.

We were soon back at the shed. New regulations demanded that no more than 40 minutes elapsed between my catching a bird and plucking it. Tas moved with an urgency he had not shown before. He carried the spits to the gurrying rail and we ripped off the birds and squeezed them, squirting oil and undigested krill into a drum full of the viscous red fluid.

This was the oil that cured Furley of her chest colds and gave Fred Willis's skin the clarity of a man 50 years younger. Patricia, who leased the shed, sold the oil for $20 a litre, and she said that if I doubted its properties then I ought to speak to Bruce Binzemann in Bridport about the effect of mutton-bird oil on his angina, or Harold Hislop in Penguin about his arteries, or Lester Jones, another who, properly speaking, should not be alive this morning. Later, I rang Lester. "I'm still taking it," he said. "Half a cup per day."

"Spoonful in their milk makes a horse's skin real shiny," Tas said. He tossed the last of the gurried birds through a sliced plastic curtain, and jumped onto Dusty's tractor. He was going back to the rookery.

Now that I had caught my mutton-bird I was determined to follow the process to the end. Under the guidance of an old Aborigine called Harry, I sat in the pluck-room and filled a tub with sticky black feathers. In the scalding-room, a large woman with "Joanna loves John" tattooed on her arm showed me how to dip the bird in a basin of bubbling water and to rub off the fine down. Then I went into the opening-room to remove the stomach and guts, and to cut off the head, wings and feet.

"My dog used to eat the legs, used to love 'em," Harry said, his white beard pricking through his dark skin.

For all the mutton-bird's anti-rachitic properties, the men and women in the shed had about them a sadness. This was their most manifest culture, and yet the very tradition that they clung to as defining them was under threat. The activity had diminished enormously in recent years. In 1978, the total harvest was 250,000. This year the number was unlikely to exceed 25,000. The industry was dying for several reasons: a decline in the bird population, the collapse of the feather market in Eastern Europe, internal politics, costly health regulations. But potentially most damaging was a shortage of people wanting to do it. Those in Patricia's shed were distressed that a new generation had little inclination to bird or to join in what had been a significant family occasion. They felt that something vital was slipping away.

"The younger ones are *not* interested in birding," Patricia said. "My children are. My grandchildren aren't. It's tragic."

"It's not tragic," Joanna said. "I wish I'd never learned. Five weeks is a long time sitting on your arse all day."

Harry said glumly: "My son's a good mutton-birder, but I couldn't get him over this year."

"You can't force 'em to come," Joanna said, "and you can't blame 'em if they don't."

I asked the blind man who had caught his last bird: "In ten years' time, do you think people will still be birding?"

Fred Willis had visited his first burrow in his mother's womb. "I doubt it."

★ ★ ★

But Frances was excited. Pelagic shells had come in with the east wind from the open sea. She was heading down to the beach to collect them.

"She gets all my shells," Patricia said. "It takes three months for her to fish them out and clean them."

"Show him, dear," Frances said.

"No."

"Show me," I said.

With reluctance, Patricia produced a plastic bag and drew out a necklace. She had threaded it from green Mariner shells and I remembered that the last time I had seen such an object was in Margaret's cutlery box. I didn't feel that I ought to ask, but I asked anyway.

Patricia thought about it. "All right."

It was time to go. Frances offered to walk to the end of the beach and point out a short-cut to the jetty. Within moments she had picked up a spirula covered in barnacles, and a blue and white pelagic shell. It had floated in on a raft of bubbles, and when she waved goodbye I saw that it had stained its purple dye on her palm.

I left her on the beach collecting shells for my wife's necklace and hurried up the dune swale towards the boat.

XXI

THE CAPTAIN WAS DROPPING OFF SOME CHILDREN ON CAPE BARREN, AND I took the opportunity for a walk. There was a line of ti-trees above the sand, with a matchless view over Flinders, and further back in the grass a monument.

The war memorial commemorated 18 men from Cape Barren who had fought for King and Country in the First World War, two of them giving their lives. Reading the names of these Mansells, Browns, Everetts and Maynards, I thought of the sacrifice they had made to safeguard a society that persistently ignored them, and I remembered a story that the captain told me on the boat, about a Cape Barren lad who had worked on his farm and Viscount Montgomery of Alamein.

As a boy, Bernard Montgomery used to visit this island with his father, "the mutton-bird bishop". Bernard would climb in the hills and swim in the sea with his friend Cecil Williams, and Cecil took him birding. By the time he left Tasmania at the age of 14, Montgomery wrote, "I could swim like a fish and was strong, tough and very fit." Their paths crossed once again, in North Africa. Bernard was then a General and Cecil among one of the ranks in the ninth Australia Division that he was inspecting in Alamein. Monty walked slowly along the line of troops, stopped before Cecil, straightened his collar, looked him in the eyes, and walked on.

We head back. A big swell thumps the boat. The sky has grown darker and I see the mutton-birds skimming the waves. I watch them dipping up and down, and I know that because of me one of them is returning to a burrow that is empty.

XXII

I FLEW BACK TO TASMANIA TO MEET GREG LEHMAN AT A RIVULET NEAR HOBART. It was a hot day and he waited for me on the grass, slapping mosquitoes from his face. Ducks bobbed their heads under the water, and across the bridge was the place where all this began.

I recognised Lehman from the debate in the Dechaineaux Theatre. I had wanted to speak to him after listening to his talk, and since no-one was able to visit this site without the community's permission, I asked if he would be prepared to show me around Risdon Cove.

We crossed the bridge, and I told Lehman about my mercurial ancestor and the discoveries I had made since coming to live in Tasmania: how Kemp had condemned the massacre, his travels with Bennelong, and how his long life in Tasmania had tracked the extinction of the native population.

Lehman agreed that the Aborigines would have perceived Kemp at first as one of themselves. "The old fellas didn't recognise an Other. They didn't see a Black or a White. They lived in a world where *Homo sapiens* was all created out of the tail of a kangaroo." A guiding dictum of Lehman's was a remark by a Cherokee Indian: *There is no such thing as a non-indigenous person.* "The basis of my belief in identity is that there was never in this land any distinction between black and white."

With his ghost of a grey beard and his father's complexion Lehman was, he agreed, an improbable-looking Aborigine. His father was descended from Bavarians from the Black Forest; his mother from a convicted Irish axe-murderer called Chugg. But Lehman identified with his paternal grandmother, an Aborigine called Molly Kennedy who had lived in the hamlet of North Motton in Tasmania's north-west. "I am so lucky," he said, "to be living in a landscape that my family has inhabited for 2,000 generations."

We stopped before a rock where a plaque commemorated the first English settlement. Somewhere not far from these trees Kemp's regiment had shot Robert Hobart May's parents dead.

In his autobiography, *Living to Tell the Tale*, Gabriel García Márquez writes of a "massacre" that took place in 1928 in the Colombian coastal town of Aracataca when soldiers protecting the American-owned United Fruit Company opened fire on striking workers from the local banana plantation. The episode came to occupy a significant place in the consciousness of his nation and in his fiction. Later, Márquez tried to piece together the events of that day. "I spoke with survivors and witnesses and searched through newspaper archives and official documents and I realised that the truth did not lie anywhere. Conformists said, in effect, that there had been no deaths. Those at the other extreme affirmed without a quaver in their voices that there had been more than a hundred . . ." Márquez inflated this in a novel to 3,000 dead, and in the end, he wrote, real life did him justice when the speaker of the Senate asked for a moment's silence in memory of the 3,000 anonymous martyrs "sacrificed by the forces of law and order". Aracataca seemed to have a lot in common with Risdon Cove.

"What does this spot mean to the Aboriginal community?" I asked Lehman, who worked as Head of the Centre for Aboriginal Education.

"For the Aborigines," he said, "it became important because of the invasion history. It was the first place where the British set up camp, the first place where there was a record of British killings."

Lehman was regarded in Tasmania as a leading Aboriginal voice. After taking a first-class degree in zoology, he had become one of the instigators of the Tasmanian Aboriginal Land Council, and had played a prominent role in restoring this, Tasmania's most contentious site, to his community – although Lehman's claims about what had occurred at Risdon had been challenged by historians, including Windschuttle. In a handout given to Aborigines attending a memorial here in 1993, Lehman had written that "close to a hundred were killed that day". This was at variance with previous estimates that ranged from three to 50. Reading from his laptop in the Dechaineaux Theatre, Lehman had told the audience that he had since dropped the phrase "close to a hundred" because it seemed "unnecessarily strident", and had replaced it with "whole families were killed on that day". He had concluded: "The exact number will never be known, but the exact number was never very important." What was important was the fact of innocent deaths.

He kicked some bark on the ground. "I then saw Risdon as encapsulating injustice and the bloody manner in which the British had invaded. It was the intent rather than the extent."

"What was the intent?"

"The intent of the British to establish themselves here and the action to use firearms to deal with a situation they didn't understand. But it became a metaphor for a broader political campaign."

Lehman's preference for metaphor over historical truth had fallen on stony ground in the Windschuttle camp.

"Have you ever met a Pentium primitivist?" Lehman asked. And he told me about a review in the magazine *Quadrant* of an essay that he had written in response to Windschuttle's *Fabrication of Aboriginal History*. Entitled "The Pentium primitivism of Greg Lehman", the review accused Lehman of openly rejecting the search for objective truth. It quoted him: "For us, the 'truth' is made up of countless contradictory, ironic and provocative elements, woven together into an allegorical, sometimes fictive documentation of what it is to live our lives." The reviewer ended with the assertion that Lehman's essay presented a threat "potentially more destructive" than September 11.

He led the way up the hill. There was a fine view from the summit through the cleared bush, and behind us young trees were planted in tidy rows. We sat down on the grass and I asked the same question that I had asked Edna and Jimmy and Angus:

"Can you tell me how you discovered that you are an Aborigine?"

Lehman's parents had worked in Ulverstone, in a factory that processed peas and potatoes, and his father also bulldozed for the public works department. "My family didn't talk about Aboriginality till I started asking. They were typical of a number who'd become isolated. They had done what a lot of families had done – attempted to disappear."

He had not known he was Aboriginal till he was ten. Again, Bill Mollison was central to the discovery. "Mollison was doing research, speaking to families, and people started to talk." Lehman remembered conversations around the kitchen table, about how his grandmother was related to "Dolly" Dalrymple Briggs whose grandfather was a chieftain. "This was amazing stuff for a ten-year-old. I got hold of Mollison's chronology – and there was my family. Bang. This world I knew nothing about." He said: "If this conversation had come up in the 1940s it would not have been conducted at the kitchen table, but in the 1970s things started to open up."

Unfortunately, his grandmother Molly Kennedy was not interested in talking about it. "You'd say to her: 'What can you tell me about Aboriginal culture in our family?' She would say: 'Don't worry about that stuff.' It wasn't part of what she wanted to pass on – and she was fairly strident." Nor did he feel able to interrogate his father: "I was too frightened. It tended to be me going out finding things for *him* to read. He was aware it was a dark secret, something you kept a lid on. He wouldn't have heard of chiefs like Mannalargenna or Tongerlongetter. He was suffering from an interruption to oral tradition. I had to go out and put together the jigsaw for myself. It's taken 30 years."

"How did you begin?"

"When I was at high school trying to make sense of this strange ethnic tension, I would describe myself as ¼₄ Aboriginal. That was the best way I could make sense of it. The fact that I looked like someone who had walked out of the Black Forest didn't prevent my peers from calling me Nigger, Coon, Abo. I got grabbed by the master of discipline and marched off to receive a caning. 'Lehman, being an Aborigine is nothing to be proud of.'"

But he *was* proud of it and he determined to stand up for the rights of those who had been held down as half-castes and trouble-makers. "The totality of my identity occurred for me when I went to Hobart – I became political. I said: 'Don't call me white, I'm black. Don't call me part-Aborigine. I'm Aborigine.'"

"So it was a political decision to say 'total'?"

"Shit, yes," he said, batting away a mosquito.

But I needed his help. How could someone who was ¼₄ Aborigine – like, it appeared, most of the leaders in the Aboriginal community – choose this fraction of his ancestry over and above the rest?

He took my pad and drew a family tree. He sketched a trunk, then a branch that veered left – his Aboriginal branch. He wrote down the names of his grandmother, her ancestor "Dolly" Dalrymple Briggs and then her grandfather Mannalargenna ("a fine man, a great warrior").

"What about this?" and I pointed to the rest of the tree. "What about your German roots? What about your Irish roots?"

"That's mongrel," he said.

I looked away, frustrated by my inability to understand.

At the top of the field the community had planted saplings in plastic protective tubes. I pointed to an older, larger, dense-leaved conifer.

"What do you see?"

"A tree," he said.

"Exactly. You don't see just one branch. Aren't we made up of all the leaves and branches?"

He looked at me, and in his eyes was the expression of someone who doubted that I would ever understand.

I felt out of my depth. I felt that Tasmanian Aboriginality had elements of a faith, and that facts counted less than feeling. It was hard to think it through: I had to imagine it through. But I felt chained by the Western, linear, rationalist tradition of my English culture, and in the end it was impossible to let this go.

We saw that there was an impasse. He handed back my notebook, and we went on talking in an amicable way, one of us a white colonising bastard, the other an Aboriginal warrior from the Trawlulwuy nation, who had lived here for 2,000 generations. As Lehman had said in the debate: "Your 200 years of history are like yesterday for us."

We were walking back across the rivulet when I remembered that there was something I had been meaning to ask.

He had mentioned that his Aboriginal grandmother came from North Motton and I asked if he knew a couple of old ladies there.

"What's their name?"

I told him.

He stopped and touched the ring in his ear. "I think I might be related to them. Why?"

I said: "They're cousins of mine."

Part III: Elysium

"Apparently warm weather is coming. Here are some predictions that might happen and affect you in no particular order. Warm weather, sunburn, no seat-belt, Grand Final day, parties, good times, accidents, sunburn, no seat-belt on your kids, golf, mother-in-law comes to stay, drink-driving, parties, good times, accidents, drink-driving, no seat-belt, accidents, flashing lights, screaming people, ambulance, SES, police, knock on the door – and it's not the mother-in-law. Do you want to take a chance on what comes next? Please consider others if not yourself. Your licence is not the only thing you should consider. Think ahead and make arrangements."

Sergeant Rob Reardon, Swansea newsletter,
September 24, 2002.

I

WE WERE IN OUR SECOND YEAR ON DOLPHIN SANDS WHEN MY MOTHER telephoned from England.

"You may have other relatives in Tasmania."

"Are you sure?" I said, warily.

She had just discovered in her father's autobiography a mysterious reference to a favourite uncle who had emigrated to Tasmania in 1900. He came from Devon and his name was Hordern. "He sounds extravagant," she said. It puzzled her that her father had never spoken of him.

I looked up Hordern in the telephone book. There was one entry. I rang the number and found myself talking to Hordern's granddaughter, Ivy. She lived with her sister Maud on the smallholding where they had been born, 80 years ago, in North Motton in the north-west of the island.

Ivy declared herself in "a state of shock". She had lost hope of tracking down any Hordern descendants in Britain after years of fruitless research. She had followed the lives of my mother and grandfather through my grandfather's books, copies of which she owned.

"Your grandfather was," she told me, "a very famous writer."

He was also partly to blame for my living in Tasmania.

II

HIS NAME WAS STUART PETRE BRODIE MAIS, BUT EVERYONE KNEW HIM BY HIS initials. He was the first writer I ever met, and the reason why I never wanted to become a writer myself. The author of more than 200 books, he died in his ninetieth year, bankrupt and heartbroken, shortly after my grandmother ran off with a man who first proposed to her when she was 17. His sorrowful end has continued to haunt me.

He was the only child of an impoverished Devonshire clergyman and a snobbish mother – "an abominably stupid woman", he called her – who was more than 40 when he was born. Hannah Mais never wanted children, and since she was married to a man too poor to afford holidays she farmed SPB off to her brother, an enchanting but profligate Devon landowner, whose proudest boast was that he had played tennis with the Kaiser, and who rattled between his two estates in a dogcart. So North Devon became my grandfather's preferred place in the world – the location of his "earliest and easily my most carefree memories" – and Petre Hordern his "boyhood

SPB Mais

hero". Hordern paid for SPB's education and enabled him to go to Oxford. He wrote of Hordern: "I had a deep affection for him and he for me and I was very sorry when he disappeared from my life." This was how I felt about SPB.

My first recollection of him. I'm nine, recently arrived from Singapore, and in my first term at my prep school in Oxford. I sit on top of a red letter-box in the Bardwell Road, waiting for my grandparents to take me out for Sunday lunch. I am eager to see them. My parents have dropped me off here and immediately boarded a ship to a new home in Rio de Janeiro.

SPB arrives sooner than expected, in a deer-stalker hat with a number of scarves draped around his neck, each a different colour. ("He was fanatical about time," my mother said.) All the way up both arms he wears a number of Rolexes, which he later pawns, and a billowing black coat, which anon I inherit, and he seems to be gruff, intolerant and rather terrifying.

My grandmother was a former model who would never leave her bedroom without make-up on. Already immaculate, she spends a lot of the meal vetting her perfection in a tiny mirror. When she tucks her compact into a bag, I cannot help noticing that the bag contains two wrapped gifts. For me, I hope.

Some days later, my grandfather writes me a letter. The handwriting is so minuscule and untidy that I cannot decipher a word.

His handwriting was the only small thing about him. He filled the room, as if he had rambled in not from the bus station – he never drove – but from the pages of the stories I was then reading: *Greenmantle*, *Mistress Masham's Repose*, *The Prisoner of Zenda*. It didn't surprise me to discover that after coming down from Christ Church, he claimed to have received "an offer from Sir Eyres Mansell, who wanted me to become King of Albania. I should have liked that, but my mother, in spite of her snobbishness, could not bear the thought of my going so far away."

Instead of a Balkan king – a role which would have suited him since he was emotional, driven and excitable – he became a schoolmaster, teaching English literature by turns at Rossall, Tonbridge and Sherborne. He was by all accounts a remarkable teacher, already practising in 1913 a student-based philosophy that did not become common till the 1960s. He flung the set texts out of the window and divided his class into teams to debate the merits of Wordsworth, say, over Byron. At Sherborne, he became mentor to Alec Waugh and encouraged him to publish *The Loom of Youth*

– a novel that Waugh wrote after his expulsion and in which SPB is cari-
catured as always rushing about with an armful of books.

In 1917 – "to my great surprise and dismay" – SPB himself was sacked
from Sherborne after Chapman & Hall, the firm managed by Waugh's
father, published his novel *Interlude*, about a married schoolmaster who
elopes with a shop-girl. He fell back on his pen. He went to work for the
Daily Express and then as fiction reviewer for the *Daily Telegraph*, also
contributing regular broadcasts to the BBC. He had a rich, irate voice and
was renowned as an unrepentant Englishman: in 1940 he received up to
500 fan letters a day. Winston Churchill said of him: "That man Mais makes
me feel tired."

As his fame grew so did the procession of visitors to his home in Sussex.
My mother remembers George Bernard Shaw, J.M. Barrie, H.G. Wells, John
Betjeman (he gave the speech at her wedding) and Henry Williamson (he
slept on the floor). I used to wonder if my mother was not guilty of inflating
SPB's reputation, but then I read Julie Burchill enthusiastically quoting him
in the *Guardian* ("Anyone who does not live in Brighton must be mad and
should be locked up"). Graham Greene and Anthony Burgess told me that
they had made the pilgrimage to Hove. A scourge of old fogies, he had
been kind to them when they were young writers and they felt genuine
gratitude – which Greene subtly acknowledged by using his name for a
character in *Brighton Rock*: "See that man going to the Gents'? That's Mais.
The brewer. He's worth a hundred thousand nicker."

SPB was, on the contrary, famously worth nothing of the sort. His
personal life came to replicate certain passages of his risqué novel *Interlude*.
In 1913 he married Maud Snow, a girl with a taste for schnauzers, sweet
biscuits and dry gin. He threatened to kill himself when she wanted to
cancel the wedding, and on their honeymoon he took her to his uncle's
haunts – and "on foot almost every day" compelled her to follow the
Devon and Somerset stag-hounds. Neither had a clue about sex. After two
years he sought enlightenment from a doctor and then Maud ran off to
Paris with a gossip columnist.

Meanwhile, on a catwalk at the Savoy, SPB had met a beautiful 17-year-
old Irish model, Gillian Doughty. An enthusiastic rambler, he invited her
– over a lunchtime grapefruit in the Savoy Grill – to see the total solar
eclipse on top of Mount Snowdon. She was my grandmother.

Nowadays, his might seem a desirable way of life, but in the 1930s he
was paid a pittance by his newspapers and the BBC, and for the next 51
years he struggled to ward off penury and bailiffs. He supplemented his
efforts to support his new family by writing books, sometimes six a year.

I remember the surprise with which I stumbled on one of them, in a second-hand bookshop in Abergavenny. It was entitled *Some Books I Like*. This seemed self-indulgent until a yard along the shelf devoted to his works I discovered its sequel: *More Books I Like* (total sales: 696).

Apart from books on books he liked, my grandfather wrote novels, children's stories, school texts. Not one of his novels sold more than 5,000 copies. His most successful book, *An English Course for Schools*, sold 21,000. The most he earned from any book was £850 – for *I return to Scotland*.

He lectured widely, especially on books about the English countryside. My grandmother liked to tell of the occasion when he was invited to give a talk at Lewes Prison. He became so excited and enthusiastic about the South Downs in Sussex that he found himself telling the inmates that they must get out more, see it for themselves.

By the time I came to know SPB, his rambling days were over and his income derived chiefly from leisurely travel books. Every summer his publisher Alvin Redman dispatched him on a different cruise. The result was a series with titles such as *Mediterranean Cruise Holiday*, *South African Cruise Holiday*, *South American Cruise Holiday*. These cruise books never made him much money (about £100 each), but they made him all he had to live on. This, I suppose, was the reason I was put off by his profession.

My last image of SPB. It is the school holiday and I am visiting him in Bliss House, Lindfield, where the Samaritan Housing Association had offered him a tiny first-floor flat for £4 a week. The man who could have been King of Albania sleeps below my grandmother in a bunk bed. There is room in the kitchen for only one of them at a time. Furniture is stacked on top of the fridge, including a trolley and a child's chair for me.

A description that he wrote in the *Guardian* tallies with my recollection: "The living room measures 12 foot by 14 foot plus a small alcove, and this room contains three desks (two of them mine), a large inherited chest of drawers which holds my sweaters, socks and underclothes, a glass-fronted bookcase containing my remaining first editions, some glasses and decanters . . . Add to this our beloved miniature dachshund and painfully thin walls so that the widow below bangs with a stick every time he dares to play with his tennis ball and the fact that I do not sleep very well." The article concludes: "Do you wonder that we get on one another's nerves?"

I could not wait to leave. Nor, it turned out, could my grandmother.

When it first happened he went roaring through the village: "My wife has left me for another man."

In 1974, their mutual friend Dudley Carew had knocked on the door. His second wife had died and he was depressed. His doctor had told him to get out, meet friends. He thought: "Petre and Gillian, I'll go and see them." Whereupon he and Gillian fell for each other and Carew, under the impression that he was rescuing my grandmother from a very unhappy relationship, proposed. She was almost 70.

They married and Carew bought a house nearby. A year later SPB died of a shattered heart, still in love.

My mother never liked to read her father's books. It was her sister who had alerted her to the reference to Tasmania. I too had avoided them, until, on a subsequent visit to Kempton, I stopped at a second-hand bookshop in a field, and there on a shelf at the back I found a book that SPB had published in 1965, and dedicated to his grandchildren. On discovering with a jolt that *Round the World Cruise Holiday* was written for Nicholas "who will one day, we hope, follow in our footsteps round the world", I bought it.

It occurred to me that my grandfather's wish had come true. My father being a diplomat, I had been brought up in France, Cambodia, Brazil, Argentina, Portugal, Peru and Morocco. There was a further coincidence: I, too, had married a girl called Gillian. And I began to wonder if perhaps some of the reasons that decided me to settle in Tasmania had to do with not wanting to follow too closely in the footsteps of SPB. Directly facing the South Pole, and 13,000 miles from England, our house was as far away as I could travel from Bliss House, Lindfield.

Except, of course, that it was not.

III

I OPENED *Round the World Cruise Holiday* AS SOON I GOT BACK TO DOLPHIN Sands. I had only read a few pages when I felt my heart drumming.

Round the World Cruise Holiday was co-written by my grandmother Gillian, who had embarked on the cruise on the *Southern Cross* without her husband. SPB explained his absence in a short preface: "On this occasion owing to heart trouble I had to stay behind and while she wrote the story of her very exciting voyage I wrote notes on the historical background of the places she visited."

Gillian was nervous travelling on her own: "For so long now, 41 years to be precise, Petre has been my guide, philosopher and friend, in fact my all, and we have never been separated for more than a week . . ." Among the items she took with her to keep her company for the next three months was a photograph of her eldest grandson that she pegged to a board in her cabin beneath a brass dolphin.

It was amusing to read how much of my grandmother's time in Australia had been taken up looking for a suitable present to bring back for me. In Melbourne, she fingered a boomerang. But after feeling its hard edges, she decided that I might do untold damage to my sister. (The Aboriginal owner gave a demonstration, throwing it across the road. It dropped short on the return and a car deliberately "swerved to run over it and break it in half".) In the Barossa Valley, she gripped an Aboriginal spear that was intended to pass through the body with a single thrust. "I was more sure than ever after handling these weapons that Nicholas should not have one." When I read what present she did buy me, a memory came spinning back. A strange boarding house in Oxford. My grandfather impatient to get to the bus station. My grandmother plucking two packages from her bag: a curved piece of wood with odd-looking scribbles burned into it, and a peculiar animal, flat-nosed with claws, which the boys in my dormitory would take fantastic pleasure wedging between the roof beams.

The boomerang and the toy koala helped to staunch my peculiar form of homesickness, which could not be truly described as homesickness since I had no home. They were also, as I understood, nearly 40 years on, my first contact with Australia. And why, since a boy, I had felt an emotion comparable to the one which Andrei Sinyavsky describes in *A Voice from the Chorus*. "Whenever one sees Australia on the map one's heart leaps with pleasure: kangaroo, boomerang!"

IV

MY GRANDFATHER WAS SENT TO STAY WITH HIS RECKLESS UNCLE IN DEVON AT the same age as I was when I went to the Dragon School in Oxford.

Hordern's two estates were on the fringe of Exmoor. Yarde, near Stoke Rivers, lay in a hollow with no view of the sea, a long low white house with a hornet's nest right outside SPB's window. The hall gave off the odour of old timber. "Ever since I first smelt that strange unanalysable smell," SPB wrote, "I have been under the spell of Devon."

Yarde was occupied by Hordern's maiden sisters, who, in their relations with SPB, pursued what he called "a consistent policy of 'No!'" He wrote: "I wasn't allowed to play even solitaire on Sundays and no book was allowed to be opened except *The Quiver* or *The Sunday at Home*." Conversation at meal times was never lively. "I remember that in the evening Fanny and Bertie used to rise from their seats exactly as the clock struck ten and without a word of 'Goodnight!' would disappear to their respective bedrooms."

Hordern

Into this world stormed their brother in his dogcart, popular and spirited, who liked to dress well, even nattily, in white spats, with a gold
toothpick flashing from his mouth and smelling of milk to disguise whatever he had had to drink.

Hordern rode SPB back the 17 miles to Boode House, near Braunton,
whipping his horse on with a silver-handled crop – a drive not without
hazard since at a certain point Hordern preferred to sleep and leave it to
his horse to pick its own way along the high-banked Devon lanes. "So
great was my confidence in my uncle that I, who always accompanied him
on these trips, which were usually in the dead of night, also went straight
to sleep soothed by the rhythmical jog-trot of the horse."

Their destination – Boode – was Hordern's headquarters and the birthplace of SPB's mother: a rambling whitewashed farm with a huge garden
that stood at the top of a narrow coombe. The two lighthouses that SPB
claimed he could see from his bedroom window cast the same spell over
him as the entrance hall at Yarde. He spent, he wrote, "joyous hours"
looking out at night over the sandhills and the flashing lights of Lundy
and Hartland Point to Westward Ho!, the place named after Charles
Kingsley's novel, and where Rudyard Kipling had been at school, and
which he wrote about in *Stalky & Co*. Hordern took both books with
him to Tasmania.

At Boode, SPB met his first author: a fruit-grower who had written
the popular Exmoor romance, *Lorna Doone*. Richard Blackmore, he wrote,
was "a large-hearted, lovable sort of a man" with broad, sagging shoulders
and a benign, rosy face, whose uncle had the curacy of Charles, ten miles
away. He did not look like a novelist and he shunned society. "An air of
rusticity enveloped him," remarked a contemporary. "Not the material
rusticity of the farmyard, but that of the wind and the scents and the voices
of the open spaces . . . he seemed to exhale the very presence of the moorland and coombes he loved and interpreted so well." Blackmore had tried
school-teaching and market gardening before taking up historical fiction,
and Hordern regarded him as his mentor.

Blackmore often strode up the muddy lane to visit Boode. He sat SPB
on his lap and in a memorably low voice told stories of *Lorna Doone's*
hero, the young farmer John Ridd, and of Ridd's love for a well-born,
black-haired girl he had encountered in a moorland pool, and of the band
of wild desperadoes who had kidnapped her, whose lair was in an unget-
at-able place in the hills among the rocks of Exmoor. When SPB came to
describe his upbringing, this was the experience he singled out. "Nothing
can destroy the fact that I spent an idyllically happy childhood on these

two farms. Nothing can destroy the
fact that R.D. Blackmore with his
strong Devon 'burr' used to come over
from Charles and dandle me on his
knee."

Blackmore was not the only influential figure at Boode. There was
Hordern's wife Penelope. Hordern had
courted her assiduously and talked of
her as his own Lorna Doone. "She was
one of the Downings of Pickwell
Manor, Georgeham," SPB wrote. An
elegant, large-nosed lady with a direct
gaze, she was never heard to say a bad
word about anyone, least of all her
husband, but because of him she would
end her days a long way from Georgeham,

Hordern's Wife

perpetually dressed in black, sitting bolt upright in a rented dining room,
knitting cardigans and praying. Once upon a time, when Hordern had
courted her, she had loved to dance, but religion had become her tipple.
When her brother drowned in the *Stella* off the Channel Islands, it was
felt that he deserved his fate "for travelling on so holy a day".

The Hordern Family

Less pious were Hordern's eight children. "My cousins were a rackety crowd, and we were allowed more or less to run wild at Boode, of which I remember best the fragrant smells of the stables and the harness room, the peaches on the south wall, the gaily coloured if somewhat crude glass in the front door and greenhouse, the thick laurel bushes in the drive . . ." SPB was an only child of remote parents. It was easy to understand why Boode became his second and happier home, and Hordern's children his earliest friends. They formed, he wrote, a self-contained and completely content unit. Best of all his cousins, SPB liked Hordern's youngest son Brodie, who everyone agreed was a dead ringer for him. He and Brodie used to play hide and seek in the laurel bushes. "Looking back, I find these were days of pure enchantment."

On hot summer days Hordern rode them in his large hay-wagon down to Croyde Beach where they bathed and raced each other on surfboards. SPB's description evokes the feeling that I had when walking with Max along Dolphin Sands: "My cousins and I used to walk along the banks of the Pill, climb on round the old wooden hulks, bathe naked from the sand dunes in the Estuary, set fire to the marram grass, which screams like a child in pain as it burns, play hide and seek in the vast solitude of the Himalayan sand dunes, watch fishermen pull in the salmon in their nets . . . and sometimes halt to remove the thorns from our bare feet. I seem to have spent the greater part of my Devon childhood days barefoot."

If SPB's cousins were his best friends, then his spirited uncle took the place of a father. In autumn, under Hordern's tutelage, SPB followed the stag-hounds on foot through North Molton; and on Fridays drove with him into Barnstaple market where Hordern bought and sold cattle. Hordern's herds and flocks were among the finest in the country, winning prizes at agricultural shows from Launceston to Norwich. Sounding a premonitory note, SPB remarked that after market was over his uncle "invariably bought me some outrageously expensive present. His generosity was not confined to me. He went bankrupt because he could not find it in his heart to refuse anybody anything. He was the kindest man I have ever known."

Hordern passed on to SPB his taste for books, his love of Devon, and his talent for extravagant living. He was perpetually hosting large parties at Boode at which champagne freely flowed. "He enchanted me by his behaviour," SPB wrote. "I can't remember whether he drank champagne for luncheon regularly, but I do remember how delighted I used to be when he took up empty champagne bottle after empty champagne bottle and hurled them one after another through the large dining room window

on the lawn outside. I remember this lawn contained more broken glass
than grass because we used to try to play tennis on it."

One day in 1900 the champagne ran out. Cleaned out by his generosity,
Hordern put the two estates up for auction. They had been in the family's
possession 700 years, since the reign of King John. Four months later,
having earned his sisters' "lasting enmity" for going through their money,
he booked his passage for Tasmania.

V

"I HAVE NOW RECOVERED FROM THE SHOCK OF YOUR PHONE CALL & WOULD like to thank you so much for being in touch . . . There are so many things that I would like to ask you that I am hoping you will have the answer for."

Five days had passed since Ivy had written, enclosing directions to the farmhouse. I drove up the Midlands Highway to Launceston, and west along the coast, past a gigantic white board – "Have you missed Ulverstone, the centre of attraction?" From Ulverstone, the road dipped and rose through potato fields and lines of towerering macrocarpa, and along the horizon the Dial Range slid away in a sharp band of blue.

The farmhouse lay a mile or two beyond North Motton on the lip of a valley overlooking Gunn's Plains: a neat white weatherboard bungalow set in beds of red carnations and dahlias. Ivy's parents built it after their marriage in 1921 and named it for Hordern's property in England. "We're Boode House," Ivy said on the telephone. "They used to use the name, people did."

There was no car in sight, and it crossed my mind that the sisters had gone out or even forgotten that I was coming. I walked through the neat front garden planted with pink lilies and rapped on a chocolate-coloured door. Silence. I thought, peering through a window, I saw a shadow getting up from a large bed. When I looked again, the room was empty.

The door cracked open. Presently, two tiny old women emerged, in unbuttoned hand-knitted, turquoise cardigans and matching fluffy slippers, and shielded their eyes from the sun. They seemed frail, and I had the impression that if I hugged them they would crackle like two poppadoms.

★ ★ ★

"It's called the Garden of Eden up here," Ivy said with pride. "Did you see the turn off to Gunn's Plains? It begins round there, Dad reckoned." She was wiry, with a thin, wrinkled face that made her nose look sharp, and her small eyes more bloodshot. Her hair was long and grey and she wore it parted in the middle in the style of the 1930s.

Maud had a plumper face and smooth straight hair, and appeared agitated.

They led the way down a dark corridor of slot-and-groove walls, past a silver-framed photograph of Lady Diana, in pride of place beside the telephone. Past a bedroom with a cupboard from which ranks of bridal dolls stared down at me through veils. Into a kitchen.

The wood-patterned vinyl wallpaper was hung with plates of young girls with posies in their hair and a ceramic prayer to "The Miracle of Friendship", and on the table there were plates heaped with food.

"How long have you lived in this house?"

"All our lives," Ivy said.

"Except one or two days," Maud said.

"How many days?" I asked.

Ivy counted on her fingers. "Three weeks for me, near enough. Maudy would be longer. You had a fair while in hospital, didn't you?"

But Maud was keen for us to eat. She poured me a cup of tea and soon I was settling into a plate of spam and a meat-loaf that tasted with the sweetness that comes of being cooked in apricot jam.

"Not like what we served up when we were all younger, but we can't digest what we used to."

"Don't put that there," Maud said.

"Oh, sorry," Ivy said and moved the jug. Then smiled at me: "She's too slow and I'm the opposite." She tapped her tiny head: "So far I'm pretty good up here. Like the insurance fella said: 'It's in there somewhere, but you've got to get it out.'"

Ivy was impatient to show off the fruit of her research into our common family tree. She darted in and out of the room as I ate, each time returning with a letter or a photograph that she wanted me to look at, finally a sheet of paper six feet square with a forest of names entered in microscopic hand. Beneath the names of my grandparents, it was strange to see my name.

"We felt we already knew about them before you were in touch. Of course, we are sorry about the sad parts, but seems we all have those."

Once, she came back holding a calf-bound photograph album. She did not know who the people were. Had I any ideas?

It was the usual thing: studio portraits from the Victorian and Edwardian eras of men with wax-tipped moustaches and women with round, puddingy faces.

"No," I said. "I don't think so."

"They didn't think enough of themselves to write down who they were. *They* know who it is, but what about the next generation?"

After I had eaten, she took me into a little light room adjoining the kitchen. This was the Sun Room, where she had compiled her chart.

There was a framed photographic portrait of a good-looking man dressed in a jacket tight-buttoned at the neck. I had a fleeting impression of intense fiery eyes, a black moustache, a small goatee.

"That's grandfather Hordern."

Facing him was a sepia photograph of a substantial ivy-covered country house. It was taken from across a grass tennis court and was of a family gathering on a summer day in the 1890s. Wide open on the ground floor of the house were two sash windows, and beside the court, beneath a parasol, sat a bonneted woman in a black bombazine dress, and two other women. They were watching a young man with a blurred face who wore white trousers and was gripping a tennis racket. The woman in black was Hordern's wife and the two women, I suppose, were probably Hordern's spinster sisters. I was wondering if the blurred figure could be SPB when Ivy said: "We reckon your grandfather sent that."

She knelt by a canvas trunk that her grandfather had lugged halfway across the world. The shipping company had stamped the figure 8 on the outside, and the trunk was fortified with wooden slats and metal hinges, and still had stickers on it: PLYMOUTH, MELBOURNE, PASSENGER'S LUGGAGE ULVERSTONE.

She opened the lid and dipped her little hand underneath. This was where Hordern had stored the things that mattered to him most.

Either from this trunk or from another part of the house Ivy brought forth the relics: Hordern's riding crop; his gold and porcupine toothpick; a copy of *Tom Brown's Schooldays*, dedicated to Thomas Arnold's mother and with Hordern's neurotic-looking signature; and *Lorna Doone* in a red binding, dated 1883 and with Hordern's name on the title page in pencil.

Then the trophies. Red rosettes like flattened carnations for his prize bulls. Plus blue cardboard placards.

- First prize Devon bull, Launceston, 1894
- First prize, Devon County agricultural show, 1896
- First prize, Barnstaple, 1897
- Certificate of merit, Best Mixed Breed Pig, 1885

More photographs: my grandfather's room at Christ Church, in which, above a velvet sofa, hung an oil painting of Lorna Doone; a portrait of SPB's mother sitting surrounded by potted ferns and gazing up at the Reverend Brodie Mais; another large country house – Yarde; a second portrait of Hordern.

The studio photograph was taken several years after the one in the frame. Hordern's tie was loose round his neck, his lips were slightly open, and he had lost his vigour and his hair. His face was turned from the camera and his eyes, downcast, followed the melancholy angle of his moustache.

From near the bottom of the trunk, Ivy drew out a sheet of stiff paper that she unfolded and spread on the floor. A black and red poster announcing the sale at 3 p.m. on June 29, 1900, at the Golden Lion Hotel, Barnstaple, of Boode House – a "well-built and conveniently-planned" residence set in 140 acres with a summer house, coach house, conservatory and four-stall stable. And a tennis lawn that, until very recently, had glittered with broken glass.

VI

"WE HAVE THOUGHT FOR A LONG TIME THAT YOU DON'T LEARN ABOUT THINGS until you are meant to," Ivy said.

I came by a more or less credible, satisfactory version of Petre Hordern's story in part from what Ivy told me and in part from others, and also from what SPB had written about him.

The empty bottles sailing through the open sash windows had presaged the sale of Boode. As a young man, Hordern had modelled himself on John Ridd, the honest yeoman farmer summoned to run the family estate after his father was murdered by the Doones, a family of outlaws living in a moorland valley. But he was more like Anthony Fenn Kemp than John Ridd.

Hordern was 28 when he inherited the two estates; the famous herds that his father had managed for 70 years, ever since he was fourteen; and £30,000. This was a hefty sum, but Hordern spent it briskly, and even had to borrow a further £10,000 from his sisters. "He was too good-natured," Ivy said in his defence. "Mum said that he packed up hampers and sent them to people at Christmas. They used to have champagne parties in Boode and if Auntie Ethel behaved she was allowed to the banisters to watch." Ivy clung to the belief that her grandfather had invested a large proportion of his fortune in cattle-feed.

"He used to mix with those higher-up ones – like the Kaiser. He used to play tennis with him. We got a book from the library because we weren't sure who the Kaiser was." Hordern was known as "the Lord of Gratton", although Ivy could not explain the reason.

At Boode, there were parlourmaids and cooks and a governess ("Miss Tatum") for the children. The walls were hung with oil paintings from floor to ceiling. Ivy had a cutting from the *North Devon Journal* of February 13, 1877, a report on Hordern's coming of age for which his father had thrown "a grand dinner" for 100 farmers.

But 15 years on, many of the farmers who had toasted Hordern on his 21st birthday congregated in a field adjacent to Boode and watched him raise the hammer at the first of four enforced auctions.

In 1892, he sold a flock of 1,000 Devon Longworth sheep and a whole herd of pure-bred Devon cattle. Another cutting, this one from the *Live Stock Journal*, remarked that Hordern "may fairly boast that he possesses one of the best herds of the breed in the kingdom in that with which he is about to part". The animals included the sire Quartly, winner of Royal Agricultural Show's First Prizes at Shrewsbury and Norwich, "a neat, small-boned animal of almost faultless symmetry".

Three years later, Hordern sold a further 62 pedigree cattle, 788 sheep, 60 pigs and ten horses; and in 1899, a year before he emigrated, he disposed of the balance of his livestock.

The advance notice for this, Hordern's penultimate auction, was the most effusive of the lot. "No more noted herd of cattle has come before the public than the old-established one of Mr P. Hordern of Boode." The prizewinners included Johnny-Come-Quick and Fireaway ("with regard to this last bull a competent critic has declared that there is not a weak point in him"). News of the auction of 96 "superb Devon beasts, including all the prizewinners" spread rapidly to the country's prominent breeders, among them Queen Victoria, who sent a representative to bid for a bull called Joy. But competition was keen and Her Gracious Majesty, said the *North Devon Journal,* lost out to the President of the Devon Cattle-Breeders Association, and was obliged to content herself with Hordern's two sires, Peace and Plenty. "I have never seen a better lot of stock," remarked Hordern sorrowfully in the course of an excellent lunch.

Joy went for 45 guineas; Curly, a famous milker, for 25; and Johnny-Come-Quick for 21. But the auction – and the cheers that were called for him – did nothing to improve Hordern's situation. At the age of 43 he was broke and disgraced. There was only one option left. "He was too much imbued with the spirit of his class to hesitate in the choice of his next step," Somerset Maugham wrote of Warburton, a character in one of his stories. "When a man in his set had run though his money, he went out to the colonies."

"WHY TASMANIA?" I ASKED IVY.

"He was reading things, Mum said. It sounded nice. He used to study it."

It was not too hard to piece together the books that Hordern might have studied. He knew several families in Devon who had been hounded out of England by the weather and drawn to Tasmania by the eulogies of Anthony Trollope. In *Australia and New Zealand* (1873), the novelist had fondly characterised Tasmania as a listless Sleepy Hollow and its people as slumbering Rip Van Winkles, being eaten out of house and home by rabbits imported from Europe. And yet Trollope's admission that if he had himself to emigrate he would choose Tasmania encouraged a flotilla of English settlers, including his cousin the Reverend William Trollope (who ended his days in Kempton of all places, and was buried against the east wall of Kemp's church). "It is acknowledged even by all the rival colonies that of all the colonies Tasmania is the prettiest," Trollope had written. "It is a Paradise for a working man as compared with England."

Another text was *My Home in Tasmania, during a residence of nine years*. Its author Louisa Meredith had stayed with friends of Petre Hordern in Devon ten years before. She may have planted in his mind the notion of Tasmania as a destination.

Meredith was a Birmingham poet and the niece of Kemp's friend George Meredith. She had married Meredith's son – her first cousin Charles – and in 1840 settled near Swansea in a house on her uncle's estate. He also owned the land on which our house stood. While living on the

East Coast, Louisa Meredith had gathered material for her book, in which she observed the transforming effect that moving to the opposite end of the world had had on some emigrants she had met there, particularly those in abruptly reduced circumstances: "Here, removed from the first crushing grief of disgrace, and seeing before them the prospect of rising again, and of building for themselves a new character above the ruins of the old, all the latent good in them springs into action."

Did Hordern remember these words as his creditors swarmed? The role of bankrupt squire cannot have been easy to conduct with élan. And it is possible that Meredith had further pricked his curiosity by mentioning the Castra settlement: a scheme in which her husband Charles Meredith had been involved, to create a utopia in Tasmania's north-west for retired Indian Army officers.

VIII

IN ITS SECOND HALF–CENTURY AS A COLONY, TASMANIA WAS A RELIABLY FATAL
destination for those who no longer saw it as a "hell on earth" but as a
Valhalla. Often the same site that had provoked frissons of horror was held
up as an example of the abundance of God's earth. From the time of
Kemp's death, Hades was the new Paradise.

Opposite our house, on Maria Island, an egotistical Italian silk-
merchant gave his own name to the convict settlement at Darlington. In
1884, Diego Bernacchi converted the 208 cells into a Coffee Palace and
advertised San Diego as "the Sanatorium of the Sunny South" with a
climate "comparable only to the famous Riviera in Europe". On the site
of the old penitentiary, whose inmates had stirred Judge Montagu to tell
a jury in Hobart that "a worse community . . . never existed on the face
of the globe than on this island", was erected a 30-room temperance
hotel with French cooks and Swiss and Italian maids "attired in the
costumes of their native lands".

The collapse of Bernacchi's enterprise within a few years did little apparently to dim the spirits of other visionaries. At the far end of Maria Island,
I made a pilgrimage to the deserted shed of the farmer John Vivian Robey,
a member of the New World Reconstruction Movement. In August 1965,
Robey, a fastidious South African who quarrelled with everyone, was
carried off the island suffering from severe malnutrition. Discovered in his
shed was a table laid for dinner: ivory-handled cutlery, white linen cloth,
and in the cast-iron oven a rice pudding. Robey's neat, modest shed
reminded me of the small deserted farmhouse that Garibaldi had visited

in Bass Strait en route from Canton to Lima in 1852: a one-storey dwelling, rough but comfortable, carefully built and furnished with tables, beds and chairs. "How often has that lonely island in Bass's Strait deliciously excited my imagination," wrote Garibaldi, "when, sick of this civilised society so well supplied with priests and police-agents, I returned in thought to that pleasant bay, where my first landing startled a fine covey of partridges, and where, amid lofty trees of a century's growth, murmured the forest, the most poetical of brooks, where we quenched our thirst with delight and found an abundant supply of water for the voyage."

In 1942, round about the time that Robey joined the NWRM, in order, as he hoped, to give "economic security and social justice to everyone", another tragedy was unfolding on the south-west coast in Bathurst Harbour.

In September 1942, a fisherman who had gone ashore to shoot kangaroo stumbled on a sleeping bag at the foot of Mount Mackenzie. Inside was the three-months-dead corpse of a 31-year-old Melbourne man, Critchley Parker. Unable to persuade anyone to accompany him on his ambitious trek, Parker, the son of a wealthy mining engineer, had died of starvation and exposure while surveying alone the site of a "Promised Land" on behalf of the British Zionist League.

His tent had blown away, but in the button-grass was found a diary in which Parker expressed his hope that "the little Settlement of Poynduk will be the leaven which will completely change the economic and financial system of Australia".

A year or two earlier, Parker had written in enthusiastic terms to Isaac Steinberg of the Freeland League, then looking for a site for a possible Jewish settlement in the Kimberleys. Parker wrote that Steinberg was wasting his time on the mainland. He urged him to look further south: "You must come to this country and see the mountains of Port Davey as I have seen them, now clear and shining in the summer sun, now enshrouded with mist and snow. You must see, too, the inlets and bays, the five rivers that flow into it, and climb Mount Mackenzie, at whose foot I camped. You will soon realise what a magnificent centre this will be for a settlement, one of the finest harbours in Australia, a country rich in mineral wealth and water power . . . "

Trooper Arthur Fleming recovered Parker's body and diary. "He had written in his diary how [the Jews] were going to grow timber there, and start a fur industry and tin mining, and there were all sorts of other things he had set out for them to do." Among several more fantastic schemes, Parker envisaged an annual Jewish/Tasmanian trade fair – "the equivalent of the Leipzig Fair" – to be called the "Pacific Fair". One of the dying

Kafka's three wishes was to go "to a foreign land in the south". Parker's final entry read: "It is at Port Davey that I hope the Jewish settlement will start, not far from where I sever all connections with it . . . to die in the service of so noble a cause is to me a great satisfaction and if, as I hope, the settlement brings happiness to many refugees and in doing so serves the state of Tasmania, I die happy."

His plan had been to walk for ten days, but bad weather and sickness forced him back. No-one knows how long he waited for help. He had arranged to light a fire on Mount Mackenzie when he was ready to be collected. But either his six boxes of matches had got damp or he had burned them in an accident.

One man scanning the horizon for a smoke signal was Ernie Bond, who had put Parker up the year before in the Vale of Rasslea. Bond wrote in his diary: "26 May, 1942. No sign other than a biscuit carton near the Arthur Range has been found of CP." Eventually, Parker became so hungry that he ate his aspirins. He had told Steinberg: "I have said to Mother that I hope my name will live in this project." It does so in two sites named after him: Critchley Creek and Parker Bay.

But one project did get off the ground, the brainchild of a friend of Louisa Meredith, a splendid optimist from the 3rd Bombay European Regiment called Lieutenant Colonel Andrew Crawford.

IX

THE HAMLET OF SPRENT LIES FIVE MILES SOUTH OF IVY'S AND MAUD'S FARM and was once called Eden. In the cemetery, a lopsided tomb hedged in by rusted ironwork commemorates the author of the pamphlet that may have tilted their grandfather towards Tasmania.

"I could not have selected a Colony wherein I could hope to prosper better than this one." Crawford's *Letter to the Officers of H.M. Indian Services* went into three editions between 1865 and 1874, and was addressed to those who felt themselves "unable to mix in society and to reciprocate hospitalities as has been wont, to travel, or in short to do anything but vegetate". After retiring from the Indian Army, Crawford had lived in England, where the expense of everything appalled him. "The very greatest difficulty exists in all classes to provide for their families *without descending in the social scale.*" His *Letter* advertised itself to Gentlemen who were debating the wisdom of "throwing themselves among strangers and exposing not only themselves but their wives and children also." It would have been perfectly adapted to Hordern's case.

Like many of his colleagues in the Indian Army, Crawford had first come to Tasmania on leave. The island was less than one month by steamship from India, and following the Mutiny in 1858 Tasmania's popularity had grown as a destination for wounded troops who were attracted there by the "extraordinary equability" of the weather. As early as 1810, John Oxley, a dull naval officer who became Australia's surveyor-general, marvelled at the climate, "as fine and equable as can possibly be imagined . . . in truth, few places in the Southern Hemisphere can boast of being more congenial to the human frame." In 1823, *Godwin's Emigrant Guide to Van Diemen's Land* described it as "perhaps, the most salubrious and congenial climate of any in the known world for an European constitution. It has been ascertained by the thermometer to be similar to that of the south of France." Captain Roe, on sick leave from the Bombay Army, was an early beneficiary of the effect that being in Tasmania could have on the spirit. In 1831, according to the *Hobart Town Courier*, Roe "recruited his health and completely restored his constitution by a few months among us". The air was so healthy that medical officers, noting the swift

Col Andrew Crawford

recovery of invalids like Roe, reported to London that "mortality amongst the men stationed in this colony has been considerably less than in England".

By the 1850s, its health-restoring air was Tasmania's principal attraction. "A more salubrious climate than ours it would be difficult, if not impossible, to find," declared the *Mercury*. "The air of Hobart Town is perfect air," was Trollope's opinion. "The air of Tasmania was to that of England as cream to skimmed milk," echoed Edward Braddon, a civil servant and former indigo farmer from Oudh who read Crawford's brochure and promptly packed his bags for Launceston.

Nor, as it turned out, were Crawford, Trollope and Braddon mere propagandists.

X

I GO TO THE NORTH-WEST TOP OF THE ISLAND TO FILL MY LUNGS WITH WHAT, officially, is the purest air in the world.

Cape Grim falls 308 feet of basalt cliff to a beach speckled with black domes – Aboriginal middens composed of charcoal and seashells. Lumps of brown kelp rise on waves that explode against lichen-covered rocks and leave behind rags of hissing foam. Cape Grim lives up to its name. It was christened on December 10, 1798, by Matthew Flinders, who, sailing with his friend, the surgeon George Bass, in what was hitherto supposed to be a huge bay, perceived a long swell to come from the south-west. "Although it was likely to prove troublesome and perhaps dangerous, Mr Bass and myself hailed it with joy and mutual congratulations." The swell proved once and for all that Tasmania was not part of the Australian continent, as Abel Tasman had speculated in 1642, but an island.

I breathe in. The stiff southerly has blown across the ocean from Patagonia, 10,330 miles away. (In July 1998 it recorded a gust of 177km/h). That I cannot smell anything this morning is no surprise. In 1970, the Cape Grim Baseline Air Pollution Station judged the air here the "cleanest ever measured on earth". On the rocks below, the orange lichen, known as *caloplaca* and the colour of freshly cooked crayfish, is a barometer of the healthy atmosphere.

The scientist in charge, Jill Cainey, does not exaggerate when she calls the view from her desk, five yards away from the top of the cliff, "one of the most stunning office views you can possibly imagine". The station began in 1976 in a NASA caravan and is now one of 22 set up to assess the

changes in our atmosphere. It is funded by the Bureau of Meteorology in Melbourne and operates jointly with CSIRO (Commonwealth Science and Industrial Research Organisation). Cape Grim may feel like the edge of the world, but the information sifted on this clifftop has implications for our planet.

Cainey's team of seven trap the wind in flasks "like fat glass sausages" and analyse samples taken from the top of a 230-feet tower that enable her to monitor global levels of pollution. From her desk, Cainey is in a prime position to observe the effects on the earth's atmosphere of a volcanic eruption or a nuclear detonation: "The signatures are all there; they can be detected." More significantly, she has a ringside view on the vanishing ozone layer, an Africa-sized hole that hovers every springtime above Antarctica.

When she first came to Cape Grim in 1993, ozone layer recovery and the greenhouse effect were considered to be separate issues because they occurred in different layers of the atmosphere. There appears, however, to be a connection. "Things are far more complex," says Cainey, showing me the graphs, "than we naive little scientists believed."

The good news: since the Montreal Protocol of 1987 banned the use of ozone-depleting substances there has been a 30% reduction in the concentration of chemicals like methyl chloroform (used, for example, as a solvent for dry-cleaning). What worries Cainey is that greenhouse gases like methane and CO_2 are showing little sign of abating, with concentrations of CO_2 rising 10% (from 330 parts per million in 1983 to 372 per million). "They're not dangerous in the sense they're going to kill us, but the changes that CO_2 has wrought are reflected in temperature change." It is no coincidence to her that as we speak Australia is emerging from its worst drought in a century.

Australia not having signed the Kyoto Protocol, Cainey is not at liberty to make a statement on climate change, but she does say this: "If they look at the scientific evidence, a large majority of scientists would agree there is human-induced climate change."

On bad days, when a northerly carries Melbourne's plume of pollution across Bass Strait, the number of particles in the air measures 10,000–50,000 per cubic centimetre, a cocktail of vehicle fumes and carbon-based solids.

On these days it alarms Cainey that *Homo sapiens* is going to continue to modify the atmosphere to a point where the natural systems cannot cope and we will render ourselves extinct.

On good days, such as today, the winter air blowing off the Southern Ocean has had no recent contact with man and contains only 20 particles per cubic centimetre, most of these being ammonium sulphates or sea salt. This is what gives Tasmania's rainwater its exceptional cleanliness, its oysters and wine their freshness and the air its spectacular clarity.

"There is a real, different intensity in the light," Cainey confirms. "It is filtered through fewer particles, and those are predominantly from tree and marine-generated gases. Plus being near to Antarctica we come under the thinning ozone."

Cainey endorses Colonel Crawford's claims for Tasmania's climate. She grew up in England's industrial north, where the nitrogen oxides in the air caused her to develop a theory that she raises at conferences. "When you go back to England, your nose becomes chunky and coloured, doing its best to filter out gases. But when you're somewhere clean, your nose is clean. As an atmospheric chemist, I have to wonder: does air quality have anything to do with the dramatic increase or vice versa of asthma and certain cancers?"

Set back in pines down the road from Cape Grim lives a man who has no doubt about the answer. Bernard Eisele is a builder from Michigan who was attracted to Tasmania because of its air. "I had lung problems pretty bad after working in concrete and the various dirt that goes into building. I felt like someone was sitting on my chest and I figured I wouldn't live too long if I stayed in Michigan." One day his metallurgist son brought home a copy of *Scientific American*. "I read that Tasmania had the cleanest air and I thought, boy, it sounds like the place I'm looking for. The other place was Tierra del Fuego. I spoke pretty good English and didn't speak Spanish and so I came here." On September 26, 1982, two weeks before his 50th birthday, Eisele bought 87 acres as close to Cape Grim as he could get. He put in a blueberry plantation and then 80 apple trees. "When I arrived, I could work maybe an hour and then I'd sit down and huff a little. I'm 70 now and I'm working six hours and trimming trees pretty well every day. I eat 50 kilos of blueberries a year," he says, "and am probably in better shape than most 70-year-olds."

XI

IN COLONEL CRAWFORD'S OPINION, TASMANIA OFFERED SO MUCH MORE THAN a health resort: it was a place to put down roots. Another factor ardently promoted by him in his brochure, and liable also to have found favour with Petre Hordern, was the quality of the soil, especially in the north-west. Scrupulously abstaining from "any fancy-painting", Crawford included a report by James Erskine Calder, then the Crown Surveyor, on a tract of 32,000 acres that Crawford had earmarked between the Mersey and the Leven rivers. Calder gave this ringing endorsement: the spot where Crawford proposed to found his settlement for retired officers, to be called Castra, was, he wrote, "a most magnificent country, an expression by which I mean you to understand that its soils and forest are not to be surpassed in Tasmania." Planted in its rich red soil, trees would bend under the weight of all kinds of fruit and vegetables – the same vision had so enticed Anthony Trollope and Thomas Arnold – quince and pear trees, luscious strawberries, gooseberries, raspberries. "It almost makes my mouth water now to think of them," Arnold wrote on his return to England. Trollope was almost more enthusiastic. "The fruit is so plentiful that in many cases it cannot be picked from the trees."

Crawford had only two caveats. "I would most earnestly deprecate the idea of any gentleman plunging alone (or with a family) into the backwoods, however good might be the soil, however tempting the situation. Union is Strength." For this reason, he proposed "a body of gentlemen" to live together in a community with their own church and school. Essential to the execution of his plans was a road from the coast into the interior. But on this matter Crawford had received guarantees from Louisa Meredith's husband Charles Meredith, then Minister of Works, that the government proposed to build a tramway from Ulverstone.

One reader of his pamphlet, Colonel Michael Maxwell Shaw, was so bowled over that he started to organise a scheme to induce a body of Glaswegian mechanics, artisans and labourers to emigrate. It seems more probable that Petre Hordern read and learned from the *Letter to the Officers of H. M. Indian Services*.

I had an instinct that Crawford's recommendations on their own would not have been enough and that Hordern needed a further sign. When Ivy retrieved from the bottom of his trunk a book with a jade-coloured binding, I suspected that this was it.

The book was the 1896 edition of *The Orient Line Guide: Chapters for travellers by sea and land,* by W.J. Loftie. Hordern had bought it to study on his sea journey.

Few can have read Loftie's chapter on Tasmania without wishing to book their passage on the next ship. It reads like a prospectus for the island paradise portrayed in Matthew Kneale's novel, *English Passengers,* in which a Victorian clergyman, under the illusion that it was the original Garden of Eden, sets sail for Tasmania. The island was praised by Loftie's contributors alternatively as "the garden of Australia" and a gem suspended from its neck. "How shall I describe," writes the now knighted Edward Braddon, "the balminess of that air which makes him who breathes it feel a pleasure in merely living?" A seductive claim was made for the vitalising power of the atmosphere and its effect on Tasmania's fortunate population of 150,000, among whom "zymotic diseases hold a very obscure place in the bills of mortality". Her unrivalled climate and beautiful scenery made Tasmania's prospects for the enterprising immigrant vastly encouraging. Hobart was billed by Loftie as pre-eminent for beauty among capitals, "being built on more hills than Rome herself", while the snug homesteads, the orchards, the fields rich with wheat crops, the hawthorn hedges, with here and there a small plantation, "were charming duplicates of England".

The clue was in the map of north-west Tasmania. I read the name and saw it quite well. A chance meeting with Louisa Meredith. A glance at the atlas. An island remote from the scene of his disgrace, and where he could breed prizewinning cattle and plant mulberry trees. And the racing of his pulse as he absorbed place names that duplicated the villages and districts of his childhood: Launceston, Bridport, Appledore, North Devon – even a North Molton (although this seemed to have been spelled incorrectly in Loftie's map). "It is the Devon of Australasia," Braddon wrote, "a happy mixture of Elysium and a lesser Eldorado."

Hordern felt a twinge of destiny. He saw this antipodean Devon and, with all the romanticism of his hero John Ridd, persuaded himself that here was one place where he might begin afresh.

On November 12, 1900, Thomas Arnold was reported dead. In the same week, Hordern packed his belongings. He put his books, his spats, his silverware, his sterling riding-crop and a cutting from a laurel bush in the drive at Boode into a trunk. Then he had his stockman, Mr Eastbrook, drive the family to Plymouth to board the Pacific Navigation Company steamship *Orizaba*.

XII

THE *Orizaba* DEPARTED PLYMOUTH ON NOVEMBER 24, 1900. HORDERN COULD only afford second-class tickets for himself, his wife and their seven children – they had left behind their eldest son Will. The four sons and three daughters were of ages from two to 17. They had been at sea a week when the family assembled on the promenade deck to listen to a concert of songs that included the duet "Life's Dream is o'er". Few passengers noticed the 44-year-old father of the group, silent and morose, with his nose surprisingly mottled, his face sagging a little and no longer exhilarated by champagne. Richard Blackmore had died ten months earlier. Never had Hordern felt so unmoored.

The steamship touched at Gibraltar, Marseilles, Naples, Suez, Colombo, Fremantle, Adelaide and Melbourne, where the Horderns changed onto a packet to cross Bass Strait. They travelled saloon class for the overnight journey. Hordern may have lost his fortune, but he was damned if he was not going to arrive in his new country in style.

On January 6, he stood on the deck of the *Pateena* as she steered past George Town, up the Tamar and towards Launceston. Deep in his sad thoughts he looked at the passing creeks. The consensus on board was that the rain would immensely benefit the potatoes. Ninety-seven years earlier Kemp had watched the same hills solidify in the same steady wind.

Talk on deck that Sunday morning, according to the *North-West Post*, was of the murder of a girl at Oyster Cove by a jealous teacher. She had been engaged to a returning soldier from the Boer War called Potter. On board the *Pateena* eight Tasmanian soldiers invalided home from South

Africa, some with their arms in slings and one with his little finger amputated following an ambush on the Marico River, discussed poor Potter and his homecoming.

Another topic of conversation was the new Commonwealth of Australia, ushered into being five days earlier. The announcement of the cabinet, said the *North-West Post*, had "caused a thrill of disappointment in very many minds in Tasmania, for it was naturally enough expected that as one of the oldest states and as one that had laboured long and hard to bring about the much desired union of interests, her claims to be represented in the initial ministry would be fully recognised." But once again Tasmania had been ignored.

And Hordern – what intricate regrets did he have? And had he given up alcohol? If he had opened that day's paper, he would have read an advertisement for a herbal remedy that a roster of satisfied customers affirmed as an effective cure for chronic enlargement of the liver. ("Sir, I have been a great sufferer the last four or five years from Liver Complaint . . . I have been induced to try Vitadatio and it has acted like a charm on me . . . You are at liberty to use this memo as you think fit.") One letter of endorsement read simply: "I am cured and I feel quite 'a new man'." The hope of his family was that Tasmania would act on Hordern like Vitadatio.

At 9.18 a.m. the *Pateena* docked at the Launceston wharf where a crowd waited to welcome the wounded soldiers. In a sharp shower of hail, Hordern led his wife and children down the gangplank and disappeared into a sea of white flags that swayed back and forth, back and forth.

Barely had the Horderns retrieved their luggage from Customs and settled at a hotel in Launceston when there was news from the Isle of Wight that saw shops shuttered, flags at half-mast and churches draped in black. In Hobart, the telegram arrived mid-Regatta Day. The band stopped playing. The Kaiser's grandmother, Peace and Plenty's new owner, had died from a blood clot on the brain. "There is an atmosphere of mournfulness prevailing such as was never experienced before," commented the *North-West Post*.

As Queen Victoria's body was escorted by her fleet to Portsmouth, Hordern began to look for a property to buy.

Against Kemp's noise, Hordern's silence.

Kemp pitched his Regency house in the centre of Tasmania in open landscape. Treeless pastures that required no great agricultural expertise, and from where, at the smallest provocation, he could gallop into town to stir up trouble.

Hordern, by contrast, elected to lose himself beyond a virtually impene-

trable maze of blackwood and myrtle forests on the north-west coast. After
his landing in Tasmania, no-one in England heard from him again. Save once.

The clipping that Ivy produced was from the *North Devon Journal* and
dated 1904. "A Tasmanian paper just to hand shows that Mr P. Hordern
still worthily holds his own in his new home. Some fat sheep of his sold
at auction (everything is sold by auction in Tasmania), topping the market
. . . Mr Hordern's many old North Devon friends will be delighted to
hear that he is in good health and doing well."

I returned her the article. "Then he made a success of things?"

"We weren't told much."

"Did you go to his house?"

"I once went. It wasn't very big."

I did not know why, but I had the impression that behind Ivy's answers
was a feeling of shame. And yet each time I tried to bring the subject back
to her grandfather, she was not forthcoming, and without her guidance it
was impossible to track Hordern through the dense scrub into which he
had vanished. Not until my third visit did she produce the image that
encapsulated the many surrenders that he had made in coming to Tasmania.

"You wanted to see where he lived," and she showed me a photograph
– the only one she possessed – of the dwelling that Hordern had built in
North Motton.

Stoke Rivers

The legend on the back said "Stoke Rivers", which was the name of Hordern's birthplace. I drew breath when I turned it over. The building stood in pathetic contrast to Boode and Yarde, where S.P.B. Mais, my grand-father, had passed his enchanted childhood. Single-storey, of weatherboard with a corrugated iron roof and a brick chimney, Stoke Rivers would have fitted into any of the stables on either one of Hordern's estates.

The crude construction was made to appear bleaker by its setting. On all sides, a forest of bare white tree-trunks receded in ghostly files, branch-less and leafless, while a mass of creeping vines and fallen eucalyptus obscured the front deck. It did not resemble a property on which a man could graze fat sheep. The scene was the image of poverty – a shack in the bush for a man who had once entertained royalty. At Boode, each of his eight children had had their own bedroom, plus a governess. How happily the family squeezed into Stoke Rivers, I could but imagine.

Ordered out of doors by the photographer, Hordern's wife and chil-dren had assembled like the other ranks of a routed army to defend him from a sniper. They took up position in a loose line – on the deck, behind a tree, against a single-beam fence with white roses growing over it. The youngest girl was dressed in a large cream hat and held a Hereford calf by the halter. Her wintry smile suggested that she and the animal had been asked to stand still for far too long.

"That's Aunt Dorothy," Ivy said.

I was still trying to take on board that these were SPB's cousins who had not long before played hide-and-seek with him in the laurels at Boode.

"Where's Hordern?"

"Grandpa? He's inside, I suppose."

The front door to the house was slightly open. I held up the photo-graph to the light and looked through the pane of glass and the reflection of tall white gums that had been either burned or ring-barked, but I could see no-one.

XIII

ON SPB'S BEHALF I STARTED TO GO AFTER A LOST UNCLE OF WHOM MY grandfather had been fonder than of his father or mother, and the cousins who had been his best friends.

Their story emerged confusedly. The first reference to Hordern came two years after his arrival in Tasmania. In 1903, he was listed in a register of local residents as "Horadern P. farmer, North Motton". He never bothered to correct the mistake, and I discovered that it was the first of several.

Another misprint was the name of the hamlet to which he had been drawn as though by a potion. It was obvious to the meanest intelligence that the cartographer had intended North Molton – the village in which Hordern used to take my grandfather stag-hunting, and where SPB had spent his honeymoon. But when Hordern got there, he discovered that North Motton was the preferred spelling, even though it might have originated as an error. He was given the garbled explanation that people had always asked "Where's Motton?" – and gradually the name North Molton had become North Motton.*

In Launceston, Hordern's enquiries about North Motton had been met with endorsements of "the wonderful fertility of this hill-locked, river-traversed area". An article about the neighbourhood, written a year before,

---

* North Motton's most famous son is A.W. Knight, an engineer of surpassing ability, who in a paper before his death remarked on the oddity of "*North* Motton" in the absence of any other "Motton". The name posssibly derived from one William Walter Motton who settled thereabouts in 1854.

spoke to his heart. "What parent could leave to his children's children a more goodly heritage than an area of such land, in a perfect climate and within easy reach of great centres of population, yet remote enough to enjoy perfect tranquillity?"

Unable to buy land in North Motton itself – it was all sold – he settled for a plot six miles from the village in a tract of dense virgin scrubland. He paid £45 fourteen shillings and two pence on a 14-year mortgage for 100 acres. It might not have escaped him that this was almost the same sum that he had received at auction for his sleek, glossy bull Joy.

Two phrases, he was told, summed up the district where he was heading. The people were hospitable to the last degree. And his property was situated in some of the best agricultural country in Tasmania. The rich chocolate soil was valued up to £30 an acre; the potatoes brought the highest prices in the Sydney market ("For potato growing, North Motton has the palm"); the turnips and marigolds were of excellent size and quality; and cattle fattened into beef very readily. As for the scenery – magnificent. "It is the English trees which make of North Motton such a pretty spot," remarked a journalist who travelled through the village at this time. He described an idyll lined with silver birches, poplars, mountain ash, blackberry, nasturtiums, columbine – and added that that year lupins "have been especially fine and gladioli a joy".

Despite Charles Meredith's assurances to Colonel Crawford, no road had yet been built to North Motton. The Horderns had to travel from Launceston to the coast and follow the river down. At the small port of Ulverstone, they paused to breathe the sea air and found themselves gagging. The wharves were coated with phosphorus paste and strychnine, and from the sidewalk there rose the stringent whiff of sulphur.

Their journey to Elysium coincided with an outbreak of bubonic plague in New South Wales, and the setting up in Tasmania of hastily assembled committees to prevent the epidemic from crossing Bass Strait. In Ulverstone, a bounty of four pence a head was paid for every rat. The carcasses were dipped in kerosene. Poison was issued free.

The family loaded their bags into a bullock dray and floated the vehicle upriver on a steam-powered hardwood punt. The weather was still boisterous, and from under a tarpaulin the young Horderns peered at the strange trees that grew to the water's edge.

Six miles inland, the punt stopped at Mannings Jetty and they disembarked. Overhead, a wire cage required more persuasion to move than "the proverbial mule", according to one local. Visitors to North Motton from the opposite bank had no choice but to sway over the river in this squealing contraption.

Hordern laboured from the jetty up a track ten feet wide that was in shocking condition. He struggled to wrap chains around the cart's wheels. Thick volcanic mud clung to his boots, the mud so deep that the cart sank up to its axles. There was no room to walk beside it, and the family squelched behind, scrambling and struggling from log to log. Like this, they trudged parallel to Skeleton Creek, where, half a century ago, two early settlers had come upon some human bones attached to a rusty chain. The disastrous effects of the hail were evident on all sides: paddocks strewn with fallen timber, the grain sodden and but one or two livestock standing miserable. The captain of the punt had told them that a few days earlier lightning had struck a bullock in North Motton. When found, it was still standing by a tree, quite dead.

XIV

REPORTS EXTOLLING NORTH MOTTON'S "WONDERFUL FERTILITY" WERE OF recent origin. Among the first white men to set eyes on this landscape were Kemp's shipmates Bass and Flinders, sailing by in 1798. In 1824, another sailor, Captain Hardwicke, made a bald assessment: "The land is mountainous, extremely barren and totally unfit for habitation" – an opinion shared by a surveyor for the Van Diemen's Land Company, who in 1826 left George Town to explore the coast. "So entirely wretched is the country in this neighbourhood that were I to attempt to describe to you the dreary and desolate tract which extends along the coast 40 to 50 miles as far as Rocky Cape and thence to Circular Head, it would cost you more time to read than the whole place is worth." Two of Devon's earliest pioneers ignored these warnings to their cost and suffered the peremptory fate of the convict who had given the name to Skeleton Creek. The sensitive surveyor Henry Hellyer committed suicide and Captain Bartholomew Thomas, veteran of Bolivar's army in Peru, was speared to death by Aborigines.

The settler who did most to open up the area was an Irish immigrant, James Fenton. He had spent part of his childhood on the east coast, in Swansea, and first came to the Forth Valley in September 1839. "We saw no vestige or mark of anything that indicated the existence of mortal man, unless it were a few little heaps of time-worn shells on the sandbanks, left there by the aborigines in former times . . . " The country was densely scrubbed, broken by hills and gullies: "In short, a desolate, howling wilderness." Tempted into speculation, Fenton bought 640 acres in North Motton, but sold his land after spending a long day walking through the scrub and getting "fearfully stung with nettles, which were indigenous to that quarter". His death in 1901 coincided with Hordern's arrival.

Louisa Meredith had also, many years before, lived in the neighbour-hood, and her experience was not more pleasant. In 1845, she left Swansea for Port Sorell – about 20 miles north-east of North Motton – where her husband had been offered the post of police magistrate. Her glass and china from England arrived in fragments, and she spent her first winter shivering in a split timber cottage through which the wind snarled. Stepping outside, she was hemmed in by an oppressive screen of gigantic trees covered in fungi, and when she followed a cattle path "the shrubs gave way on being pushed, but instantly closed again". Her husband was unable to afford to rip down this tangled curtain. "The mere clearing of the timber from such land usually costs at least £10 an acre and the impracticality of a man without capital clearing it, paying rent for it all the while, and maintaining himself and family till the crop comes in, is too evident to any rational mind to need a comment." Until she arrived in this district, "I could not conceive such poverty as I saw there to be possible in this land of plen-teousness; nor is there, I imagine, in the whole island a similarly condi-tioned neighbourhood." Nor was that all. It rained for nine months out of twelve, turning the roads into bogs and planting hostile surprises in the undergrowth. The nastiest of these were the nettles that had tormented Fenton, and also Kemp in York Town, 40 miles east. "The nettles in the colony are the most formidable I have ever encountered, both in size and venom," she wrote. "A friend's horse threw himself down to roll in them. The creature was rendered mad and furious by pain, and in a short time died in convulsions."

Little had changed by the time a bullock cart crashed through the gums in a 100-acre title of drenched scrub. Through the dripping leaves Hordern could see that he had come to a halt right under the Dial Range and a cliff-face known as Old Sawn-Off. He heard the traffic roar of a distant river and down many hundreds of feet glimpsed a stream winding through a dense tangle of forest dogwood, sassafras and musk. It was the kind of place which the Doones might have chosen as their hideout. On summer days the scenery was awe-inspiring, but it looked in the rain more like Wizards Slough, the slimy dreadful bog through which Carver Doone, having shot Lorna, disappeared.

XV

THERE WAS SO MUCH I DID NOT KNOW. WHERE HE STAYED – IN TENTS OR A bark hut. Where he kept his possessions while the house was being built. Who built it.

Seventy years earlier, Kemp had put together the stone walls of Mount Vernon with the assistance of 18 assigned convict servants who cost him nothing but food and clothing. Hordern most likely erected Stoke Rivers with his bare hands.

First, the land had to be scrubbed and the timber cut. The dogwoods grew to a density of 3,000 an acre. The choice that faced him was to let the trees fall over and rot; or axe them; or follow the example established by Fenton and cut a narrow circle in the trunk when the sap was up in the tree, a procedure known as "ring-barking". To judge from Ivy's photograph, this was Hordern's preference. He then needed a team of bullocks to drag out the wattle scrub by the roots, but he had his sons to help him. They bought palings and cut posts and sank them into the red soil.

Only after the skillion roof had been nailed into place did Hordern unpack his trunk. He took out the two silver cups, the rosettes, the wine salver awarded for his pure-Devon sires, and arranged them on a black-wood shelf. Behind the cups he stacked his books – *Lorna Doone*; *Westward Ho!*; *Stalky & Co*; *Tom Brown's Schoolboys*. And on the wall he pinned photographs of Boode and Yarde. Plus one of Mr Eastbrook, his stockman, dressed in a bowler hat and poking a stick at his prize bull Union Jack outside one of Boode's ever-open windows. The force of the wind barrelling up the Leven meant that the windows of his new home he had to keep fastened.

I pictured the former "Lord of Gratton", his pious wife and seven children struggling to cope in their remote surroundings. Because Stoke Rivers
was certainly remote.

On still days, three cracks could be heard from the top of a hill – a
bullock-whip signal to settlers that a ship had arrived on the Leven. But
on most other days the wind that swept over North Motton was the only
sound, gusting clouds of heavy rain from Bass Strait. More than 40 inches
fell on average each year, turning the fields into a thick chocolate spread
and making next to impassable the rough tracks that linked the outlying
farms. Louisa Meredith's horse had disappeared in a broad stream of dark
liquid in a creek called Dead Cow. North Motton's mud was celebrated.
There was a saying: North Mutton mud "sticketh closer than a brother".
Hordern's children walked across the paddocks to get to school and often
plunged up to their knees in it.

Even on dry days, the bush track to Ulverstone had, according to the
locals, "to be used to be understood". Part of the way was "corduroy",
constructed from felled trees that were placed side by side and had a ridged
surface like corduroy velvet. There were no cars and it was a common
sight to see a woman on foot carrying a baby. Ivy's great-grandmother
used to walk from North Motton into Ulverstone, a basket of butter on
one arm and a basket of eggs on the other, singing "It's the Army and
Navy for ever, three cheers for the Red, White and Blue."

The Tasmanian author Pete Hay had a grandmother who lived on the Gawler Road. He wrote in *Vandiemonian Essays*: "One of the tasks of the women of the north-west was to keep the stories, the stories that bind the generations one to the other . . . 'Story', then, was the new story of one's immediate family." But Mrs Hordern's story was a hot, smouldering coal that nothing could bring her to touch.

Hordern had flown through his wife's money, too. In England, she was accustomed to servants: in Tasmania she had none. "People don't here," Ivy said. "Poor old Granny, it was terrible for her. She used to bring us a jelly bean at night, poor old Granny."

In Devon, she had watched Mrs Eastbrook in the dairy. She now threw herself into milking the cows. The woman who had loved dancing taught herself how to skim cream, adding hot water to speed up the turning. She reared poultry, cultivated vegetables, kept the house warm. Their four-roomed "Castle Dismal" was so cold in winter that her son Nigel went down with rheumatic fever and had to spend seven months in Launceston hospital, an experience that left him with a twisted foot.

Life at Stoke Rivers was never so unforgiving as in those early months. Provisions had to be punted from Ulverstone to Mannings Jetty and the expense of bringing them upriver was prohibitive. Candles cost one shilling and six pence, tea three shillings and sixpence to five shillings, treacly sugar sixpence. Hardly any currency was in circulation and the normal method of paying for purchases was by barter. But first Hordern had to produce something.

Once the underwood was cleared and burned, he sowed potatoes in the ashes between the skeletons of the dying trees. He took out his laurel cutting and planted a hedge of laurel bushes in imitation of the drive at Boode. The rest of his fast-draining energies he put to the service of his sheep and cattle.

I assumed that I would find him mentioned in the annals of local organisations like the West Devon Agricultural Association (ex-President: Colonel Crawford). Hordern was fêted throughout England as a "well-known agriculturalist and successful stock breeder". Yet at the Ulverstone museum he appeared in none of the records for agricultural shows. He was nowhere listed as a breeder, buyer, steward or judge.

"I've never seen his name in anything," said a woman who worked at the museum. She had researched the history of the area. I need not bother to look in the Historical Families of Ulverstone series – the Horderns did not feature there either. Even so, she had gained a definite impression of them.

"I thought they were a very funny family."

"In what way?"

"They were very private. They kept their mouths shut."

United in their indebtedness, Hordern was in most other respects the reverse of Kemp: generous, kind, romantic. And determined at all costs to maintain a low profile. But why? I questioned Ivy.

I had started to notice that she was keeping stuff up her sleeve, and that whenever I came to the farm, she produced a new scrap of information. To my delight, she brought out a letter that had been stamped at North Motton post office in 1907, and which offered a tantalising glimpse into Hordern's circumstances.

The letter was posted from North Molton, England, and was written by Mrs Eastbrook, the wife of Hordern's former stockman, in reply to a letter from SPB's favourite cousin Brodie, Hordern's fifth son. "We were all getting ready to take Annie to the station when your letter arrived and of course must drop everything to see its contents. After that we had a good cry for we felt it a bit." Evidently, Brodie had painted a sorrowful picture of the family's first seven years in Tasmania. Mrs Eastbrook wrote: "It makes the tears come in my eyes when I think how hard your mother must work to keep all straight, and no girl. It does seem a shame. I wish I could fly and help her a bit, but that's no good for I can't help over at the farm owing to the fits." She went on, as the English do, about her medication ("no meat") and the weather: "It has been very wet and cold, very sharp frost and snow as it has not been for many years. Outside our door is a perfect glitter just now." She makes no reference to her former employer. The only mention of Hordern I was able to find was a post-script in a letter to Brodie. "PS Had a letter from your father. He was not too well."

Brodie's father must have suffered extremely from the moment he set foot in Tasmania. Consumed by the disgrace and poverty he had brought upon his family, he could not even look his sons in the face. The truth was that his hopes of founding a new life on the model of Colonel Crawford's settlement up the road had gone the way of Castra.

XVI

FORTY-ONE RETIRED OFFICERS HAD FORMED THE BUDDING NUCLEUS OF Crawford's utopia. They had paid £640 each for a 300-acre plot, sight unseen, but when they disembarked from India to enjoy their retirement they discovered that the promised tramway remained but a chimera and they were expected to bust their guts "reclaiming the jungles of Tasmania", as one Calcutta newspaper described the enterprise. "Settlers with the hearts and muscles of lions were able to clear a small acreage in their lifetime." So recorded Frank Penn-Smith in his autobiography. Even after he had cleared the jungle, he could not guarantee that crops would flourish. A woman whom he met in Paradise told him: "Every bit of food has to be dragged in."

The spectacle of elderly Indian officers in the backwoods with their hatchets and saws, vainly clearing land that they had purchased cheap, suggested to one commentator that the Castra scheme had been a sad disappointment if not an absolute failure. Often unable to cut down the bush themselves, they found it too expensive to hire servants. "They are a poor dirty lot when you do get them," a disgruntled officer complained. "And mostly thieves." Another officer wrote: "Some of the inhabitants here deem the settler from India much in the light of a good milch cow to be cleaned out whenever the opportunity arose." One retired General erupted when consulted by his sister-in-law for his overall impression of Castra: "Jungle, my dear, nothing but jungle."

By 1880, only 20 of the original nucleus remained. It was not enough after a hard day's tree-felling to play tennis at Captain Sage's or to admire

Miss Hodder's shell collection or to reminisce with Colonel Crawford on his veranda at "Deyrah" over a cup of Kangra Valley tea. For most, the old days had been immeasurably superior. Today, all that remains of Central Castra is one purply-brown brick bungalow, and, inside, the objects tumbled high as if a burglar had ransacked the house and found nothing.

Ten miles away, Hordern's experience was no less disconsolate. Stoke Rivers never developed beyond a subsistence farm. Strewn among the papers in his trunk, I came across the bill for the sale of his ten "fat sheep" at the Tasmanian Auction Rooms on March 5, 1903. Hordern had been so delighted to receive £61 that he made certain the news reached England, where his sisters had had it printed in the local newspaper – evidence to his many friends there that he had found his feet. But the sale was Hordern's last.

His early hopes had been to start a dairy herd, supplying milk to the Tongs' butter factory in North Motton. But this was not the soil that he had been accustomed to in England. Though good for potatoes, it lacked the minerals necessary for his livestock's health, and the deficiency resulted in some unexpected behaviour. It baffled Hordern to observe his cows and sheep chewing the bones of dead possums and rabbits. He did not realise that they were desperate for zinc. What they swallowed instead tended to make his sheep a liability at auction. Louisa Meredith steered clear of eating mutton that came from her neighbourhood, as it had a "particularly unpleasant flavour, probably from some prevailing plant eaten by the sheep".

Then there was the mysterious disease that swept through Hordern's district and was reported in the *North-West Post*. "The first symptoms appear to be shivering, with frothing at the mouth, and the course of the disease (locally called diphtheria) is so rapid that there seems to be no effectual remedy and death very speedily ensues." The disease was fatal to calves. I wondered how quickly Hordern's Herefords had succumbed, whether the calf in Ivy's photograph was the only animal left.

XVII

HE TOOK UP MARKET GARDENING. HE HAD ALREADY FAILED AT CATTLE-BREEDING. His maxim now would be: "Plant pears for your heirs."

Hordern was 17 when, astonished by the size and quality of Tasmania's strawberries, mulberries and cherries, Anthony Trollope proposed that Tasmania ought to make jam for the world. Hordern took for his model the author he had looked up to since childhood, his late friend Richard Blackmore who had been at his happiest when talking in his low Devon burr about young pear trees, or in his greenhouse stroking a vine. "Any ass can write novels," Blackmore said. "But to make a vine needs intellect." Blackmore's favourite vine was a Black Hamburg, which he called a John Ridd – because of its "great strength and large proportions".

Before publishing *Lorna Doone*, Blackmore had laid out a market garden where he experimented with 20 varieties of peach and 79 of pears. To subsidise his writing, he raised crops of large fruit that he sold at Covent Garden "at profitable prices" – sometimes earning nine shillings for a dozen peaches. This is what Hordern now attempted in North Motton. If he knew of Blackmore's failures, he ignored them. "You know my opinion about 'gardening for profit'," Blackmore wrote to his sister. "The profit of rogues, & the ruin of oneself."

In 1905, Hordern paid a deposit of £35 on a further 105 acres. He laid out 45 acres of orchards in neat divisions. An old panama on his head, he passed from tree to tree with his shears and pruning knife. He nailed up the berries and planted his John Ridd cuttings in pots. Among vegetables he preferred cardoon and Bismarck potatoes, named after a village near

Hobart. He also planted apricots, strawberries and plums – lavishing them with Mount Lyell manure from the west coast. Perhaps Hordern was the mysterious, unnamed figure who endorsed their advertisement: "An English gardener on being asked his advice as to cultivation said the first thing essential was to manure, the second to manure and the third to manure."

Many of his seeds came from England: Beurré Hardy pears and Galande peaches and clumps of cyclamen and little blue scilla and pansies. "Mum told us he had a lovely garden," Ivy said. "People used to come for miles to look at it because it was so beautiful."

When the wind rakes through the casuarinas it makes the sound of people talking. Hordern hoped to earn his fortune by selling his Bismarcks and his flowers to G. & A. Ellis in Ulverstone; his fruit to Jones & Co. in Hobart, who had supplied nearly two million pounds of jam for Allied troops in the Boer war.[*] Very likely he followed Blackmore's example, collecting his pears in round wicker baskets perhaps with his name in black letters. And no doubt remembered Blackmore's words: "To gather fruit a day too soon, withers it; a day too late, and behold it is gone! Also the fowls of the air drill holes." But North Motton was not Teddington. In place of crows, Hordern had to contend with squadrons of voracious parrots and locusts, as well as ring-tail and brush possums. His fields and orchards were ravaged by a plague of rabbits and, in 1913, by a potato blight. Bit by bit he came to know what Blackmore had meant when he warned: "It is true that I carry on the business of fruit-growing, but it never covers expenses."

The unique surviving record of Hordern's fruit farming venture was an article by a journalist who visited Stoke Rivers in Hordern's fifth year in Tasmania. The property, he wrote, "is situated in the prettiest part of the parish, abounding in picturesque ferny glades, which the owner is doing his best to preserve, but very often fishermen forget to put their fires out, and many beautiful places are thus destroyed."

The article described the owner of the property as "Mr P. Orden."

There was something poignant about Petre Hordern's dissolution into P. Orden by way of P. Horadern, and at first I took it as a coincidence. After all, I told myself, the playwright who lent his name to a fishing-tackle manu-facturer was accustomed to sign "Shakespeare" in a variety of ways. Then in an old telephone book I found a third reference to my great-great-uncle. This time he is listed as P. Horde. The inference was impossible to ignore: he had not made much of an impact on the community.

---

[*] Part of the reclaimed land on the Hobart wharf is made up of millions of apricot stones from the jam factory.

XVIII

TASMANIA'S NORTH-WEST WAS A LATE-SETTLED FRONTIER AND A POPULAR destination for those seeking to hide from something. "Much of its pioneer stock was on the run from the stigma of convictism," writes Pete Hay. A person of Hordern's background and education was liable to be someone down on their luck, a remittance man or a natural outsider seeking, in Hay's words, "a place beyond the hard judgment of others' memory".

Nonetheless, this does not account for the variety of references to Hordern, leave aside to Orden, Horadern or Horde.

In his English Devon, he had cut a prosperous figure parading his prize cattle through the streets of Braunton. He had taken a lively interest in local government. He was on the school board and was a member of the parish council and also of the Rural District council. And there were the county set he mixed with.

In Tasmania, there are no secondary characters. Reasonably well known in England, Hordern ought to have been quadruply so in North Motton, a place where news of the health of the most unassuming person was published. The following was a typical item in the local paper: "The many friends of Mrs Elliott (Sprent) will be pleased to know that she is recovering from her recent accident." Nor was unpopularity an impediment to a kind notice. A man who died in Hordern's neighbourhood in 1906 was described as "the possessor of a blunt manner", but was still thought "very highly of by those who knew him well". The "Lord of Gratton" was precisely the sort of person that there should have been stories about. Why were there none?

The greatest asset an immigrant can possess is the ability to get on at once with his neighbours, but at the Ulverstone museum Hordern appears in none of the records. He was not a member of the Ulverstone Gentlemen's Club (for "social intercourse and mutual recreations during the long winter evenings"); nor was he invited to play in the North Motton Ladies' and Gentlemen's cricket match, batting with a broom handle and fielding with his left hand; nor was he listed as a participant at any of the knick-knack parties at the North Motton Church, nor among the congregation gathered to hear the Reverend J.S. Miles's address on the The Rock of Creation or, on the following Thursday evenings, his series on the Apocalypse. He was not even a member of the North Motton tennis club. He does not appear to be known by anyone. I cannot even find a record of his death.

"I find it very strange," said the woman at the museum, "because they did an obituary for every man and his dog. He must have done something horrific."

It might have meant, of course, that he had developed the same reticence as Richard Blackmore. But this was not quite true, as I found out from Ivy.

"Grandfather would go wearing spats to collect the mail" – six miles to the post office in North Motton, across muddy fields – "which was a bit of a novelty round here."

It is a vivid image. Hordern walking through the paths to collect his letters. Wearing white shiny spats. I wondered what on earth this once kind and hospitable and nattily dressed man had done to make himself a pariah in the local community.

At Boode, he had been carefree and generous. The most generous person my grandfather had ever known. Marooned in Stoke Rivers with nothing left to give away, he clung morbidly to the few relics of the life he had lost.

Seldom absent was the image of the perch from which he had tumbled: the two estates in his family's possession since the Middle Ages. Ivy showed me a letter from Laurie Tongs, a cousin who used to farm Hordern's land at Stoke Rivers. Tongs sometimes had meals with Hordern and his wife. They ate off Hordern's silver service and afterwards Tongs would be shown "the lovely homes on photographs of where your people were born". Tongs described the couple as "so very interesting", and said of Mrs Hordern: "Your grandmother although not accustomed to domestic duties was a wonderful cook and housekeeper." Tongs was more circumspect when it came to Hordern. Between the lines, the former landowner emerges as a Coleridgian mariner desperate for company, whose friends were either dead, fictional or beyond the pale. "Your grandfather was an inspiration, telling me of his experiences and lending me books. He loaned me *Westward Ho!* and said that the church dignitary mentioned was one of their previous families." Hordern also lent Tongs his treasured red-bound copy of *Lorna Doone*, saying that "half of it was written in his home and he had himself accompanied the author gathering information". He showed Tongs a photograph of the church where Lorna and John Ridd married. He was obsessed with the book. "Mr Hordern told me that he rode to the hounds with a descendant of John Ridd's," and – the familiar boast – "that when young he played tennis with the German Kaiser."

So – why the pariah? In 1907, at the Devonport annual show, a Shropshire ram was sold whose sire was "Kaiser William". This was the last trace that I found of Hordern the breeder of champion stock. The newspaper did not give his name, only that of his ram. Then it struck me: Kaiser William was a piece of the jigsaw.

In the Tasmanian bush, stories that Hordern had told about his friendship with the German Emperor boomeranged back to haunt him. In the opinion of Tasmania's chief justice, the Habsburg and Hohenzollern families were afflicted with hereditary insanity and notorious throughout the world "for evil and eccentric living, fouled by disease and debauchery".

Nearly 2,500 Tasmanians were killed in the trenches of the First World War, more than a third of all males between the ages of 18 and 44. Tasmanian parents expected of their children the sort of consoling courage displayed by Sergeant Stanley Robert McDougall, a 27-year-old blacksmith from Recherche. He was awarded the Victoria Cross after he attacked an enemy post alone, killing seven men and capturing a machine gun. "He turned on the enemy firing from the hip . . . seized a bayonet and charged other advancing Germans, killing three men and an enemy officer who was about to kill an Australian officer. He subsequently used a Lewis gun on the enemy, killing many and enabling many others to be taken prisoner." Returned soldiers were invited to recruiting parties at which films of battles were screened. Afterwards they rammed home the message that Tasmania was no place for a healthy young man. "We have not room in Australia for fit flag-wavers," called out a hefty lad at a meeting in Ulverstone, "but there is still plenty of room in France for a man with a rifle."

North Motton alone sent 49 men of whom 14 paid with their lives, among them Corporal Arthur Baker. In 1914, Arthur married Hordern's daughter Ethel. Three years later he was shot dead at Passchendaele. His grave was never found.

The same year saw three of Hordern's sons fighting in France. Ivy brought out for me some of the silk cards, decorated with purple and green pansies, that her uncle Brodie had written to her mother from a muddy field in Europe. One silk card was stamped "Love from the Front": "Expect by the time this reaches you all hands will be busy preparing for a picnic on the Leven River. How we boys would like to be with you." He was writing from the battlefield. "I can see the shells bursting behind the firing line. I can see an aeroplane not far from here, but we all like France tip top." In another letter Brodie mentioned having spent his leave in "Dear Old Blighty" where he had seen their wounded brother Joe in a rest camp. He was unaware that in Tasmania their eldest brother Will had died, aged 35, of tuberculosis.

Will had contracted his illness in the Boer War where he fought before sailing to join his family at Stoke Rivers. He was buried at Sprent, some-where near the hulking tomb of Colonel Crawford, whose coffin the No. 1 West Devon Company had escorted here through the village that was once called Eden. When I asked about Will's grave, the woman in the Ulverstone museum said: "It's a simple grave. Unmarked. All on his own. But he has no headstone. No obituary. No nothing. He's not even regis-tered in the cemetery."

XIX

THOMAS MANN IN A LETTER ALLUDES TO THE DEPTH OF HOSTILITY THAT HIS countrymen experienced in the antipodes. "Another is held prisoner . . . in Australia. He has the hardest time of it, although not physically." An anti-German mania raged through Tasmania before and during the First World War. More than a thousand Tasmanians had been born in Germany, including 340 emigrants who came in 1870 by bounty. Many of them lived in Bismarck. The village swiftly changed its name to Collinsvale (although maintaining the name of its potatoes). In Launceston, naval reserves with fixed bayonets encircled a building hoping to smoke out a reported spy. When a terrified Karl Haverland emerged from the Commercial Travellers' Association, he held up documents to prove that he was exempt from German military service.

Meetings were held in Hobart to discuss Germany's use of poison gas and the rape of women by Prussian officers. Homing pigeons were confined to their cages; and in this paranoia informers and nosy parkers flourished. Tasmanians were urged to treat Germans as a race apart. "Cut off their telephones, close their businesses and cease social intercourse with them," wrote "Briton" in the *Mercury*. The same paper carried headlines like: "Men and Women Torn Open with Bayonets and Roasted to Death." A. W. Loone of the Legislative Council recommended that Germans be torn limb from limb. Anti-German attitudes were particularly strong on the north-west coast where those alleged to be "pro-German" became prime targets. Down the road in Ulverstone, the Austrian Gustav Weindorfer, a solitary-minded naturalist and founder of the Cradle Mountain National Park, watched his dog die from strychnine poisoning after vindictive rumours that his kitchen stove (carried up to his chalet by Errol Flynn's father) was in fact a wireless transmitter for establishing contact with enemy ships – and his clothes-line an aerial. A figure such as Hordern walking on his own in a sparsely populated area in the dress of an English country gentleman was a strong candidate for suspicion. That he might have named a ram after the emperor of the enemy was a matter for franker concern. The discovery that he had been "a bosom friend of the Kaiser" – that clinched it.

No wonder he was cold-shouldered. No wonder he kept to himself. No wonder he did not have an obituary. And there was another reason.

Crawford had warned that Union was Strength. "Individual unsupported action in such enterprises is erroneous and too often the forerunner and the cause of failure." Down in his Sleepy Hollow, Hordern was all alone.

A clubbable man, to whom a good dinner and riotous party were necessities of life, he had chosen in North Motton a society that was limited. "In England, he had partied, partied, partied," one of his descendants told me. In Tasmania, he barely left his front door. As Edward Braddon had found out, living a few miles away: "dinner parties (those saddest of festivities) do not trouble the Tasmanian". Braddon's struggle to combat tedium would have been Hordern's. "If, when some neighbour tells me of his Brahma hen laying a score of unexpected eggs, a cynical feeling shows itself in me, I check it in its birth and am all interest." Compelled to take comfort in "homely pleasures", Hordern withdrew more and more into himself, his books and his bottles.

Broadly confined to Stoke Rivers, he cannot have found his memories excellent company; nor his neighbours, who would not have cared a fig for *Lorna Doone*. Laurie Tongs was an exception: he could read and write. Many in North Motton could not. They could not tell the time by a clock, but relied on the morning and evening star. They planted crops according to phases of the moon and buried their dogs and cats facing east. They ate off earthen floors from handleless bowls and spoke in an ancient dialect with words like "teem" meaning "to drink".

"You don't meet anybody here who's read anything. They think it's swank," says a Somerset Maugham character stuck in Samoa. He could only face the evenings, wrote Maugham, "when he was fortified by liquor".

And drink is what I suspect Hordern did.

One day in the Ulverstone museum I let slip to the archivist about champagne bottles hurtling through the window. She gave me a sharp look.

"You do realise we are in the Bible belt. If you were a drinker that would really put you on the outer. And may I say that no matter we're a hundred years down the track, we're no different. If anyone comes in here with yellow hair and a ring in his nose, he'd never get in. Terrible, isn't it?" She looked around. The room was empty. Not a ring in sight. Even so, she felt the need to bend her head and speak in a low voice. "My grandfather – because he was a drinker, they never helped him *one* bit. That's not what I call a good Christian society."

The pieties of a place increase astronomically the further you are from home. North Motton had a Methodist and an Anglican church – St John's Church of England, consecrated in 1889 by Bishop Montgomery. "Church would be full," remembered Ivy, whose family filled a pew "back a bit on the left". The church was more than the spiritual centre of the village. It was the focus of its social life; the venue for dances, tennis matches and knick-knack parties. The woman in the museum told me: "That's all they had – the church."

The intensity of religious feeling was characterised by one lady in Wynyard who crossed out in her Bible anything she found objectionable, deleting the entire "Song of Solomon" and any reference to biological functions. Hordern's wife was a similar case. Her Christianity, already muscular, had toughened since coming to live in Stoke Rivers.

Ivy remembered her grandmother getting in a horse and cart to go to St John's. On Sundays she went twice. Mrs Hordern was so religious, Ivy said, that she did not allow a daily paper in the home, only the weekly *Sunday Companion*, old copies of which Ivy pored over as a child.

"We read and read them, lovely stories."

"What kind of stories?"

"How the sins of the fathers were visited on the children."

It was Hordern's misfortune that he had not migrated to Tasmania during Kemp's time, when alcohol and not potatoes was the currency. It was unfortunate, too, that out of all the places in Tasmania he could have chosen to live he had selected a temperance zone. North Motton was no place for a drinker, even a reformed one. During the First World War it was even less tolerant.

Lloyd George's conviction that strong drink was a far greater foe than Germany was boosted by George V, who ordered the royal household to abstain from alcohol during hostilities, save for medicinal purposes. In Tasmania, his bold example was followed by plenty in the north-west. Temperance and Total Abstinence societies sprang up faster than thistles.

The Early Closing of Liquor Bars League, a campaign to stop hotels and bars from serving alcohol from six o'clock in the evening, won an overwhelming majority and was stoked by enthusiastic Baptists like Harry Benjafield, who believed that drink caused men's wounds to reopen. In letters to the press, the white-bearded Benjafield – prize pear-grower, vaccination expert and author of *Bimetallism: a remedy for our depression* and *How and why do I breathe?* – estimated drink to be "ten times worse than the Devastating Hun". It was in the evening, he warned, from the hours of 6 p.m. till 10 p.m., that Drink linked arms with the Kaiser to wage his infernal war against the human race.

As a childhood friend of the Kaiser and a drunk who had lost heart Hordern would not have stood a chance.

Geoff Williams was a churchwarden in the area for 42 years. He confirmed to me: "I heard he was a drunkard."

I had another question. "I have a perception that the Horderns thought of themselves as better than anyone else."

"Spot on."

And I realised that Hordern had suffered the fate of the man in the Somerset Maugham story: "They resented his attitude of superiority . . . and they did not see why he should put on airs." I could see him with a disappointed expression that his natural kindliness made off-putting, staring at his wife and family with glazed eyes, swaying slightly on the veranda and clutching a six-week-old copy of the *Live Stock Journal* that emphasised his exile.

XX

ON ONE OF MY VISITS, IVY AND MAUD TOOK ME DOWN THE HILL TO SEE Hordern's grave in North Motton.

The cemetery was reached past a weatherboard house. A luminous skeleton dangled against the window and over the fence a polo match was going on. Hordern's was the first grave we came to, a grey slab of weathered marble set on a concrete plinth. Some of the lead letters spelling his name had been removed or bent back by young fingers. His name in its final misspelling read: DERN.

"Real young tinkers!" snorted Ivy, ashamed not to have come here in a while.

Nettles grew along the side of the grave which abutted a red granite memorial to Hordern's wife, who had died in 1939.

There was a whinny and from over the fence a piebald head looked at us. Glancing back at Hordern's gravestone, I saw that the absent metal letters exposed a pattern of nail holes like woodworm. A jack-jumper ant crawled over his age – he was 63 – and disappeared into the nettles.

"When did he die?"

Ivy, the archivist, retrieved the date from her head. "He died on August 16, 1918."

"Mum – did she go to the funeral?" Maud asked.

"I think she couldn't. She was working at the post office."

"How did he die?"

Ivy ripped off a nettle. "With the drink, wasn't it? He asked Granny to forgive him before he died, for what he'd done to her, losing her that money and what they had to do coming out here. He must have died a happy man to be forgiven, and then he must have died a horrible death."

"Cirrhosis?"

"That's right. He was like that before he ever got in with Granny. He only drank milk when he used to go courting her. Didn't want her to know, I suppose. It was the life they lived. You know those rich people, you start socially – and then . . . "

Another of Ivy's relatives was partial to alcohol. "I said: 'Send her up to us. She wouldn't have time to drink.'"

I dug out the edition of the *North-West Advocate* for Saturday, August 17, 1918.

There is nothing like reading a newspaper on the day after a death to remind you that life goes on; that the skeleton in the cupboard is also a jumble of harmless bones. The local temperance branch meeting had decided to form a Band of Hope. The North Motton tennis club was seventeen shillings and fourpence in credit for the season. The film *The Great Secret* was playing at the Majestic Theatre in Devonport. And a new advertisement: "Worms: the children's enemy". Comstock's Dead Shot worm pellets were a safe, sure and reliable remedy in the shape of a lolly and children could take them without hesitation. Plus of course Vitadatio: "You may publish this as you think fit . . . I never felt better than I am today."

In North Motton church, the Honour Roll committee had met to organise the unveiling ceremony for the 14 men who had passed into the Great Beyond, and to plant memorial trees. At the ceremony on August 29, the Reverend R. H. Roberts urged parents whose sons had fallen not to sorrow because with them it was not night but the morning of Glory (applause). After the singing of "God Bless Our Splendid Men", an old soldier got up to say that the lion was stirring and would soon give the Kaiser all the fight he wanted. Not a mention of Hordern.

Up until a few months before, I had never heard of Hordern. But it upset me to think that this distant relative had died utterly forgotten, not even his religious wife seeing fit to mark his passing with a notice. Out of habit, I went back through the newspapers for the month prior to his death. The very least I could do was to try and put his final days into context.

As he lay dying, Hordern's neighbours were preoccupied with a black-berry pest that was spreading up the Leven at such an alarming rate that they had formed a Pest Committee and raised almost £600 to eradicate blackberries. The amount matched the value of Hordern's worldly possessions: his lands, goods, chattels, rights and credits not exceeding in value "the sum of £592".

Hordern had not merited an obituary. All the same, the old stockbreeder in him might have appreciated the lamentation in all quarters that greeted the passing of the mammoth Tasmanian bullock Stock and Hand, who had died of tick disease shortly before appearing at a show in Queensland ("he was fattened to the limit"). The weather, too, I thought, would have reminded him of home. The worst gales in twenty years had felled the wall of the Gaiety Theatre in Zeehan, blocked roads, killed stock and caused three inches of snow in Paradise. "There is a decided 'nip' in the atmosphere."

And not looking for it, I found it. I was reading about the progress of the War – "Never before in the world's history has so much been at stake . . . " – when my eyes strayed, and there, sandwiched between advertisements for Mount Lyell manure and a Russian hair restorer, was the name of my great-great-uncle.

"Saturday July 20 1918

"The funeral of the late Mr P. Hordern took place on Wednesday, the Reverend E.A. Salisbury, Anglican minister, officiating. The late Mr Hordern was a native of Devonshire, England, where he followed grazing pursuits before coming to Tasmania some years ago. Although of a retiring disposition, he was an excellent companion, being well educated and endowed with intelligence above the ordinary. The sympathy of the community is extended to the widow and bereaved family."

He had died a month earlier than Ivy had thought. Swallowed into Fitzroy's crack.

XXI

BRODIE WAS ON THE BATTLEFIELD IN FRANCE. HE WROTE TO HIS BROTHER Petre, who had been invalided home with ruptured eardrums: "You ought to have seen some of the bombing raids we get mixed up in here at times, Petre. Talk about Ypres, it was a 'wasp fight' to the raids now. I have had the 'wind up' in the true sense since then. Such awful great things they carry. You would think it was an ammo dump." He was sorry to learn of their father's death and "that things were not a little brighter", but at least it would free the family to sell up Stoke Rivers. Unable to bring himself to write the name of the house, he called it, as if it were a curse, "that place". He wrote: "It is time all were away where they can get a little encouragement for what they are doing. A change away from everything is what our dear old mater wants."

Back in Stoke Rivers with her wounded sons, the widowed Mrs Hordern was never separated from her Bible.

Ivy showed it to me, plus the three pieces of paper that her grandmother had tucked into it. Her grandmother was always taking them out and reading them for consolation.

– A sermon delivered two months after Hordern's death: "When people are 'dead' they are able to see what is taking place in this world. They are really more alive than ever they were when they were with us. They watch us most tenderly."

– A quote from Patience Strong: "Forgive! The years are slipping by and Life is all too brief."

"Did she ever talk about her husband's drinking?" I asked.

"Granny Hordern wouldn't say anything nasty," Ivy said. "She'd make excuses for anyone, not like me. I'd say something horrible if they need it."

After the funeral, Hordern's widow stayed with Ivy's mother on Mannings Jetty Road not far from the riverbank where she had landed in the mud 17 years before; and then, in 1921, when Ivy's mother got married, she went to live in Devonport with her widowed daughter Ethel.

"Poor old Granny, she used to keep us going in clothes," said Ivy, who recalled a reserved, sedate woman, not saying much except "My dear" and permanently dressed in black. "If Maud puts on black, I don't like it." When not in church, her grandmother sat knitting in the dining room in East Devonport, straight-backed, and the high neck of her dress fastened with a mourning brooch inlaid with seed pearls. "She had plenty to think about, plenty of regrets, poor Granny. You couldn't have fun with her. What happened in her life made her like it." Ivy folded back the sermon between the gilt-edged pages and looked at me. "You see, when she was young, she would go out dancing." As a child, Ivy had been allowed to touch it: a black silk dancer's shoe streaked with gold. After her Bible, her grandmother's most precious possession.

In old age, Mrs Hordern could be observed striding up Preston Road with her walking stick, one hand in the pocket of her wind-whipped long black coat, and lamenting the state of the orchard at Stoke Rivers which her husband had laid out with such patience and into which the new owner had disgracefully allowed his cattle. In 1921, Stoke Rivers was sold to the Owens and subdivided into five plots. The Owen bullocks had crashed through the cyclamen and cardoon, trampling the "John Ridd" vines to smithereens.

The lines on the third piece of paper read: "Oh! That my eyes might closed be/To what becomes me not to see!"

XXII

"IS THERE ANYONE ALIVE WHO MIGHT REMEMBER STOKE RIVERS?"

Ivy had a telephone number in Melbourne for Brodie's son and I called him.

"They reckon I look like my father," he said.

"What did he look like?"

"Not a bad-looking bloke. Tall for the time, about five foot eleven. Brown hair, greeny-blue eyes, and a fair-sized bit of sniffing gear."

He was describing SPB, I told him.

In 1938, when he was nine years old, Brodie's son visited Stoke Rivers with his father, who had taken over the property on his return from the trenches until it could be sold. They had met Granny Hordern, "a real English lady", and then they walked to the farm, Brodie hacking a path ahead through the bush and killing a four-foot tiger-snake that he hung over the fence. They emerged into a clearing where there was a small bush cottage made of sawn timber. "I don't think it had ever seen paint." Brodie pointed out to his son a horse trough that he had carved from a log, and a large table in the kitchen where the family used to eat their meals. Brodie was not a backward-glancing man – "the past held nothing for him" – but the experience of returning to his adolescent home flushed out an unwelcome memory: the memory of Brodie's father, Petre Hordern, eating his meals in this cramped space, separate from the children. The kind, gregarious John Ridd had become a tetchy recluse.

Brodie's son said: "My old man wouldn't run his father down to me, but he announced – which I thought odd – that he counted on both hands the number of times that he sat down to a meal with him." He went on: "My father didn't have much time for Petre Hordern. He was a pompous bloke that hadn't realised circs had changed. He didn't adapt to the new life. He still liked to play the image of a country squire and it didn't work. When you're in Rome you ought to adjust a fair bit to what Romans do." And then he said: "I think Petre Hordern was unlamented, much so. I don't think any of the sons had much time for him."

After his death, Hordern's sons scattered as pigeons from a blast. Brodie sold Stoke Rivers within three years and went to live in Melbourne, becoming a salesman of sewing machines; his deaf brother Petre worked as a dairyman on King Island and became known as "the old hermit". The club-footed Nigel went to live in Queensland where he grew tomatoes and was eventually buried in the biggest cemetery in Australia; the quiet, gentle Joe worked in a munitions factory in Footscray, marrying the woman who ran his boarding house. He died in his eighties, of liver cancer. Ivy said: "You could hear him I don't know how far off, trying to breathe, and he didn't deserve it, poor Uncle Joe."

But Hordern's daughters stayed on in Tasmania.

I spoke to a woman married to a Hordern descendant who had made a distressing visit to Stoke Rivers. One day in the 1950s her husband decided that he wanted to show off his family's first home in Tasmania. He drove her in a green and cream Holden along the Arnoll Road where the long arm of the Leven Blackberry Pest Committee had failed to reach. She said: "We came to the end. And there was this four-room sort of veran-daed house covered in blackberries – just overgrown with them. It was a shocking sight." Her husband had known the original Boode from when he was a Lancaster pilot stationed in England during the Second World War. "It upset him to think what they came to from that. It was a big step down. Definitely a big step."

"Did you see inside the house?" I asked.

She said: "He was so upset that we didn't get out of the car."

I wanted to see Stoke Rivers for myself, but Ivy said that it had been razed to the ground, and she could not be sure whether she would remember the site, even though it was only a few miles away. She telephoned her brother-in-law, Teddy, who lived in the next field. As a boy, he had worked on Hordern's farm, planting potatoes for its new owners. Teddy was probably the one person alive who knew the exact spot where the Horderns had lived.

Teddy arrived moments later, a tall, cheerful man with red-veined cheeks who told me that his family had once owned a grand hotel in Cairo.

I followed his car in the Peugeot through North Motton, past the cemetery and along Arnoll Road. After a few miles we passed a blue board
nailed to a tree that read "Not far now". The fields rose steeply into the
Dial Range and I recognised the shape of Old Sawn-Off from Ivy's photograph, but that was all I recognised.

Then Teddy drove through a gate and came to a halt in the middle of
a grassed-over field on the summit of a hill. I parked beside him and he
called through the window: "Here we are."

I climbed out, looked around. The field sloped down to Library Creek
where Teddy had once overturned his tractor when ploughing potatoes.
It made me wonder if Hordern's books had anything to do with the name.
All that remained of the forest of ring-barked white gums was a line of
four macrocarpa and two pines. All that remained of Hordern's proud
garden and orchard was an old laurel tree fenced in with galvanised tin.

We paused beside the laurel and Teddy pointed to a bump in the grass
50 yards away. "That's where the house used to be," and I saw that it was
right here, under this laurel, that the photographer had stood to take his
picture of Hordern's wife and children.

I walked over to the bump – covered in dandelions and cowpats – and
stood for a minute, looking down to Library Creek, and imagined SPB's
cousins playing hide-and-seek in the shadow of the dying gums and stopping to remove thorns from their bare feet. I was reminded again of
Somerset Maugham: "It seems to me that the places where men have loved
or suffered keep about them always some faint aroma of something that
has not wholly died."

I plucked a small branch off the laurel tree and left.

XXIII

A MILE BACK DOWN THE ROAD WAS A SIGN: PURTON'S CORNER. THE NAME RANG a bell – and I remembered that Jimmy, the Aborigine who once lived in my shed, had mentioned that his grandmother was a Purton.

I only grasped after visiting Stoke Rivers that Hordern had settled – unwittingly, I am sure – in the heart of a significant Aboriginal community. Next to the Purtons were the Hearps family, and next to them – in a property directly opposite Hordern's house – the Kennedys.

I could not wait to tell Greg Lehman.

It was hardly surprising that the families along Arnoll Road should have intermarried and formed a tight community, working on each other's land and helping out with washing and cooking. The Hordern children were no exception. Disgrace and bankruptcy had pushed them from Devon and down this road. Stoke Rivers lay at the very end. It was not the back of beyond: it was further. But here, in the middle of nowhere, where the red track petered out in the bush, Hordern's son Brodie was thrown together with Greg's grandmother Molly Kennedy and her brothers Cyril and Gilbert.

The pursuit of a lost uncle had led me into a territory where family earned me, in my head, the right to ask more questions. If I was not able to tell my grandfather, at least I could share with Greg what I had learned. How his uncles had supplanted SPB in Brodie's affections. How right up until 1916, when Brodie went to fight in France, the Kennedys were Brodie's best mates. And how they were drawn closer still by the violent death of Chrissie Venn.

XXIV

"MUM SAID IT CHANGED THEM WHEN THEY CAME BACK FROM THE WAR. THEY were different people."

Still, it did mystify me. Why so soon after Hordern's death did all four of his surviving sons plus his widow abandon the district? Had they really so hated living in North Motton? Ivy's answer did not make sense. In the Ulverstone museum a casual enquiry threw up an explanation.

"Is North Motton famous for anything?" I asked the archivist.

"There's the North Motton murder," and she brought out a newspaper, 80 years old, in which not one headline but four were stacked above each other:

"MURDER MOST FOUL"

"SHOCKING NORTH MOTTON TRAGEDY"

"GIRL'S BODY FOUND IN STUMP"

"GAGGED AND HORRIBLY MUTILATED"

Ivy had not mentioned this.

"Thought you knew all about *that*," she muttered.

"Who was she?"

"She's related, and the one they reckon did it is related too," and went to fetch something.

There is the Tasmanian light, and then, all over the island, there are pockets of extraordinary darkness. If a single reason determined Brodie once and for all to get rid of Stoke Rivers, and mobilised the Hordern diaspora, it was the desire of SPB's cousins to flee a place that had become inseparably linked to a shocking event. What occurred on Hordern's road in the space of a few minutes one February afternoon in 1921 was, for months afterwards, the main topic of conversation in the north-west. Mention of "North Motton" carried the same impact as would the words "Port Arthur" in 1996 when Tasmania woke up to the news that Martin Bryant had coolly mowed down 35 people outside the Broad Arrow Café. The *Advocate* of March 3, 1921, put it in context: "It has been reserved for the quiet and peaceful hamlet of North Motton to place upon the criminal records one of the most cruel and brutal of the murders that stain the annals of crime in Tasmania." The crime, in the reporter's opinion, was a ghastly exhibition of how low civilisation could stoop and how much the human could be made to resemble the lowest beast of creation.

Lorna Doone begins with a murder. It was apt that a murder should put a full stop to the precarious existence that the Horderns had carved for themselves in North Motton.

It happened on the Arnoll Road, down which Hordern used to amble to collect his mail. He had known the victim well: the young girl had lived less than a mile away. Shortly after 5 p.m. on Saturday, February 26, 1921, she left her two-windowed, shingle-roof shack, waved her mother goodbye and set off on an errand to North Motton, three miles away. She headed downhill along the horse-and-cart track, running her hand against a bank overgrown with bracken and blackberries, and was entering a thickly timbered gully when a man stepped into the road.

The following afternoon, Brodie pulled up on his motorbike at the house of Chrissie Venn's mother, Eva Dawes, who lived in the next property to Stoke Rivers. Eva was separated from her husband, who had belted her "from the day he met her until the day he left". Chrissie was their daughter. To Brodie, who had watched her grow up, she was more younger sister than neighbour.

A distressed Eva told Brodie that Chrissie was missing.

To begin with, Eva had hoped that she might have spent the night at her uncle's house. She was now less certain.

Chrissie Venn

Chrissie was 13 years old and, as the doctor observed at the inquest, "a particularly well-developed girl". When she left home the day before – to get some meat and groceries, and to fetch the post – she was wearing a cream-coloured dress with a green sash around it, a white calico petticoat, white stockings, black shoes, black garters, and a gold bar brooch. It would have been impossible to miss her.

Brodie offered to drive to the post office where his sister – Ivy's mother – used to work behind the counter and send a message to the police. Just then John Hearps appeared, who owned a farm above the Arnoll Road. He, too, was worried about Chrissie. His son Jack had said something the night before that he could not stop thinking about:

The previous afternoon Hearps's son was ploughing a steep paddock with a team of horses when, about a hundred yards below, he noticed Chrissie coming along the lane towards Dead Horse Gully. She "had a lean on her" and seemed in a hurry. That was the last Jack saw of her.

But it was not simply Chrissie's failure to reappear further along the road that had nagged at Jack. Later in the evening when his father came home, he asked: "I say, Dad, did you see anyone kicking about or dead down at the turn-off?"

"No, don't be silly, why?"

"I heard a squeal down there."

And out it came, how Jack's brother Tom, also ploughing the field, had heard it too, a terrible scream that sounded like a girl who had trodden on a snake "and got a fright", or was reacting to a horse bolting along the road.

"A pity you did not run down," Jack's father remarked.

Jack's excuse was that he was waiting for another scream. He did not think it could be serious with only one scream. He told his brother that if it was a bolting horse they would have heard the cart rattle. He had listened again and when they heard nothing, he went back to his plough. "I didn't think there was anything there to harm her."

On the same afternoon as Chrissie had disappeared, at about 6.20 p.m., Brodie had ridden his motorbike home along Arnoll Road. His friend and neighbour Gilbert Kennedy was behind him on the pillion. Brodie confirmed to Eva that neither he nor Gilbert had seen Chrissie. All agreed that Brodie must now drive to the post office and wire the constabulary at Ulverstone. At 7 p.m. the police received the message.

The following morning a search party that included Brodie and his brothers Nigel and Joe fanned out along the potato and pea fields, converging into the gully. They looked all day without finding anything.

The search resumed on Tuesday morning. At 11.30 a.m. a fettler called Charles Taylor, following Jack Hearps's casual suggestion, approached a huge tree stump 40 yards above the road. The stump was nine feet high and burned around the base, and Taylor noticed that in several places the charcoal was crushed. He hoisted himself up by a sapling and as he neared the top he heard "the buzzing of a blow-fly". The stump was hollow. Peering down, he saw, about six feet below him, a body thrust head-first into the cavity. The buttocks were naked and bruised, the legs had white stockings on and there were shoes still on the feet.

Taylor coo-eed: "Hey! She is here."

The search party had sat down to rest.

"No fear," someone said.

"Too true. She's here."

Brodie, Nigel and Joe jumped up, and all took turns to have a look.

Chrissie Venn had been dead three days. Her face was "swollen, livid and bloodstained", according to the doctor who examined her two hours later, and there were maggots on her eyelids and in her mouth. Her dress and petticoat were torn and dirty. A foot of wire of the sort used for tying hay bales was twisted round her neck, and stuffed into her mouth was a piece of cloth ripped from her dress with a gold brooch pinned to it.

For the rest of his life Brodie remembered the blow-flies coming out of the stump. Another man who saw the body that morning lost his faith in God and never regained it. "If one were to search the world," read one of many editorials, "it would be impossible to find a more unlikely spot for such an awful thing to happen, here, in a district inhabited by quiet law-abiding farmers noted as they are for their hospitality and good nature, surely the last place that a young girl should be fatally murdered in broad daylight." It was the newspaper's position that no-one hearing of the fate of Chrissie Venn could fail to have a sense of righteous wrath against some person.

North Motton was a tight-knit community. Most of the searchers were related. But one person who sprang up when Taylor coo-eed was a newcomer to the area. George King, six foot four, 35, ex-miner, ex-policeman and a Catholic, was married to an attractive wife and farmed the land up the road from the stump. While they waited for the body to be removed, Jack Hearps's father noticed that the flies had started to buzz around King's large hands and that his right hand was bleeding.

"Look what I done in the search," King grumbled, and told Hearps how he had trodden on a rotten log and fallen backwards, catching his hand on a stone and injuring it.

"Oh bugger it, that's nothing," Hearps said.

But King's bleeding hand would be remembered. As would the scratches on his face.

Half an hour later the police arrived.

"What's this?" I asked.

"That's the murder," Ivy said, and spread out the photographs.

I picked them up and saw that they were taken by G.P. Taylor who had photographed the Horderns outside Stoke Rivers.

"Uncle Nigel gave them to me."

They were: a group portrait of North Motton school with Chrissie Venn in the front row; a studio portrait of Chrissie Venn's mother, Eva Dawes; and a photograph taken at the crime scene. Sergeant Tomkinson, in hat and shirtsleeves, kneels on top of the elephant-sized stump, looking down into the cavity that still contains Chrissie Venn's body.

"Did you know about the murder?"

"Oh, we could see the stump. That's where grandfather would be walking past. We'd go on the road and mother would tell us about Chrissie Venn."

And another portrait. A tall, athletic-looking man with a receding hairline and enormous hands.

"That's the one, but he wasn't the one. They accused the wrong man."

"Bossy" Jones, the smallest present, was lowered into the cavity to tie a rope around the body and it was pulled out. Wedged underneath was found a basket with a bottle of kerosene, a pudding cloth and the girl's underpants. But the coins that Eva had given Chrissie, amounting to nine shillings and sevenpence, were missing.

Her body was laid on a dray, covered in hessian bags and taken to the cold room of the Seaview Hotel in Ulverstone, where Doctor Fred Ferris, Hordern's GP and a man with no expertise in forensics, conducted a post-mortem.

Ferris established an order of events. Chrissie Venn had been attacked and raped after a violent struggle. Her right sleeve and the back of her dress were torn, indicating that someone had grabbed her from behind. Her left breast was bruised and her cricoid cartilage fractured, suggesting that she had been strangled. She had suffocated to death probably about five minutes after the gag was jammed into her mouth – following the piercing scream heard by Jack Hearps, ploughing his field 100 yards away. Her body had then been hauled into the cavity of the stump by the hay-wire around her neck. Bloodstained pubic hair ("short human hair") on her calico sanitary cloth confirmed that she was either beginning or completing her menstrual cycle. Two smears showed traces of spermatozoa in her vaginal passage.

Over the next six months, Doctor Ferris altered his initial testimony ten times as the coroner's inquest led on March 22 to committal proceedings and finally, in August, to a criminal trial. At first, he believed sexual intercourse had taken place shortly before her death. Then he thought her hymen might have been ruptured at any time during the two weeks leading up to it. Then he recalled that she could not possibly be a virgin because he had examined Chrissie two years earlier following a charge of rape. When, 36 days after inspecting the body, he realised that he had forgotten to take scrapings from under her fingernails, he arranged for her coffin to be dug up. But Chrissie had been buried in a waterlogged cemetery: her body had decomposed.

Ferris's testimony was so contradictory that it stoked "reports of a startling character". Rumours of arrests and discoveries exhausted the village. Chrissie had known her attacker . . . She had made an assignation with him . . . When she explained that she could not make love because it was "her time of flowers", he refused to listen . . . But who was her attacker? And why had Jack Hearps not come down to the road?

Hearps's neighbour George King considered it all very odd and was overheard to say that he would not care to be in Jack Hearps's shoes. In the event, it was King, not Hearps, who was arrested.

The detective in charge of the police investigation was Fred Harmon from Devonport, a zealous hypocrite with a record of incompetence and dishonesty. Harmon would be dismissed from the police service following his part in bringing George King to trial.

Harmon was so convinced of King's guilt that he saw no need to detain suspects like Patrick Williams, a tramp who had been working on a farm half a mile away and who walked past the stump on the afternoon following the murder. Two days after reaching Ulverstone, Williams was arrested on a vagrancy charge and briefly locked up for his own protection. His manner was described as "peculiar". Odder still was that he had sixteen shillings on him. But Harmon never asked where he had got the money. The murderer was clearly George King.

On March 3, Harmon called at King's house in an aggressive mood and tore out some of King's hair – "far more than he should have", complained King – to compare it with some coarse black strands he had in his notebook. Rudely, he asked King if he had ever cut wood for Chrissie's mother. King said that he had, and once had made her a barrow. Leering, Harmon asked how she had paid him – with sex? Offended, King replied that if that was the kind of man Harmon was, he didn't want to be thought of in the same breath.

Two days later, King received an anonymous envelope containing the drawing of a gallows and a man being hanged. Underneath, in a plain angular hand, but "rather rough as if disguised", were the words: "Beware – I saw you murder Chrissie Venn. If you don't confess, I will tell the police."

King gave the letter to Harmon saying that he had a good idea who wrote it: Jack Hearps. But Harmon's superior, Detective Oakes, said that he had lots of experience tracing anonymous letters and this was obviously written by a woman. A few days later the drawing vanished. Harmon made no further effort to trace the author.

On March 7, Harmon returned to interrogate King. He was angrier than before and brought with him the hay-wire from around Chrissie's neck and some of her bloodstained clothes. He shoved these up against King's face, practically stabbing him in the eye with the wire.

Harmon was accompanied by Doctor Ferris and George Taylor, who asked King to sit still while he took photographs of his face and hands. Ferris examined a healed scratch on King's upper lip and a scratch on the back of his right hand near the base of the middle finger. The wound on King's hand was lacerated and slightly festering.

When Harmon knocked on the door the following day, King, a man with no prior convictions, said: "I expect you will arrest me. I will not run away." But before Harmon led him off, he had a request: "I would like to dig some potatoes for my wife."

Brodie and his brothers walked eleven miles to Ulverstone to hear George King give evidence, booking into a local hotel and leaving behind a deserted village. "It would be impossible to describe the state of nervous excitement in the North Motton district," wrote the *Advocate*. "It was safe to say that not a farmer was on his farm that day." A travelling salesman who passed through North Motton complained that he was unable to do any business: the entire population had decamped to Ulverstone where they crowded outside the court house in Reibey Street, peering over each other's shoulders and climbing onto window sills, desperate to get a glimpse of the witness.

Of those who testified at the coroner's inquest, King deviated least from his original story. Clean-shaven, with neatly brushed hair and wearing a raincoat, he was described as cool, self-possessed and of "a bright and intelligent appearance". But his manner had changed by the time of his trial in August. He repeatedly burst into tears as he protested his innocence and once more rehearsed to the jury – who numbered among them a Macbeth and a Chatterton – his recollection of Saturday, February 21.

On the afternoon of Chrissie's murder King had been digging in his potato patch. At about 3.30 p.m., after having a pipe, he left his hoe against a stump and made for home, cutting up through a pea paddock and onto the road. A quarter of a mile from his house he spotted his wife's pregnant black pig trotting below him towards a waterfall in the gully. There was no water at King's house and he said that the pig – a two-year-old Berkshire sow – was always escaping to the waterfall. He shooed it back along the road and shut it in his yard.

He then spent 15 minutes talking to his wife in the shed where she was washing clothes. He went to the toilet – a hollowed-out stump; drank a cup of tea, went to collect some thistles for his cow, and at the time that Chrissie Venn was walking along the road was down in his paddock, tying stalks. He didn't have a watch, but he estimated that between 4 p.m. and 4.30 p.m. he saw a motorbike pass with two people whom he did not recognise – possibly Brodie and Gilbert Kennedy. But it was the next group of people who became the focus of his lawyer's special attention.

King said that he saw Chic Purton pass by on horseback between 5 p.m. and 6 p.m.; and he saw Chic's sister Florence and Cyril Kennedy pass by a little before 6 p.m. in separate traps heading towards North Motton. So far as King could remember, Kennedy was in front.

There were plenty who agreed that Detective Harmon mounted his case against King on tenuous evidence: the whereabouts of his wife's pig, about which three pig experts were called to give opinions; whether Florence Purton or Cyril Kennedy was in the lead riding up Badcock's Hill; and the scratches on the side of his face and right hand. Harmon claimed that they were marks gouged by human fingernails. He distributed Taylor's photographs to the jury.

King said that the scratches were easy to explain. He had injured his hand when cutting bracken on the Thursday prior to the murder. The wound had reopened when he was looking for Chrissie Venn: in falling over the rotten log, he had torn off the scab. When King got home his wife noticed and said, "You have been cutting your hand again." He was never free from scratches.

Questioned about the wounds on his face, King said they were made by his wife "skylarking" while in bed when they were trying to see who could kiss their little girl first. It was a game many had played who listened to him. On Sunday mornings before he got out of bed, his little girl Eileen always tried to "annoy" him by giving her mother the first kiss as a joke. That Sunday morning, as usual, she ran across to the bed towards her mother, but this time King decided to compete for his daughter's kiss. They had a tussle and in the giggling struggle his wife accidentally caught him on the side of the face. The scratch was not intentional.

Doctor Ferris, called for his expert opinion, said on balance it was equally likely that the scooped-out appearance of the wounds might have been caused in this way as not, but unfortunately he had been unable to examine Chrissie Venn's fingernails. Listening to his evidence, the solicitor-general, L.E. Chambers, scribbled himself a note that summed up what many felt in the court. "The slight variations point to the veracity of the witness."

Slight variations marked the testimonies of other witnesses who had provided the only alibis for each other. To the jury it became daily more obvious that discussions had gone on between Chic Purton and his sister, the Kennedys and the Hearps brothers – all related to each other or friends since childhood, all apparently anxious to protect one of their number. Some of the times they presented at the inquest were tightened at the trial. In other instances no estimate at all was given. When asked, for instance, what he was doing between 8.45 p.m. and 11 p.m., Chic Purton answered in a meek voice: "I had no time," meaning that he, like King, had no watch.

It was the inability of King and other witnesses to remember what they were doing when that moved Chief Justice Nicholls to make to the jury his disquisition about the attitude of Tasmanian farmers towards time. "It is no slander, possibly, to say that when he looks at the family clock and his watch they don't agree, and probably they are both likely to be wrong."

Chic Purton, a young illiterate labourer who signed his depositions with a cross, was of all the witnesses the most "reticent". King's lawyer, A.G. Ogilvie, judged his evidence "contradictory, questionable and suspicious". He had no doubt: Purton, not King, ought to be standing in the dock.

Purton claimed he had left his house on horseback at about 5 p.m., although he couldn't say for certain. He had ridden to the North Motton store and returned home at 11 p.m., he said, but later changed this to 10 p.m. and then to 8.45 p.m. Asked several times why he had altered the time, he stood mute. He could not answer.

In summing up, King's lawyer said the theory about scratches was "absolutely battered to pieces" and suggested that there was one person Purton ought to have seen, or at the very least heard: Chrissie Venn. Purton must have been passing within 40 yards of the girl when she was murdered and he had not heard her scream, while Hearps 300 yards away did hear it. His eyes fixed on Purton, he asked penetratingly: "Who was the most likely person to commit such a crime – a married man with an attractive wife or a young man of the locality?"

The jury was persuaded. After deliberating for six hours they delivered a verdict of Not Guilty. The court greeted it with cheers.

King was a free man. But the trial had destroyed the ex-policeman. He had spent 157 days in prison, his home had been broken up, his furniture sold and his wife Ruby admitted to Hobart General Hospital after suffering a mental collapse. Unable to pick up the pieces of his life in Arnoll Road, he changed his name and became an itinerant knife-sharpener.

In North Motton, no-one was found guilty of the crime. But Chrissie Venn continued to throw her shadow. The ghostly shape of an axe was seen to hover along Arnoll Road (even though she had not been killed with one); horses would dig in their heels at the stump where her body was found; motorbikes refused to start. Her murder paralysed the lives of those she had touched and they detected her restless spirit behind the most trivial incident.

Brodie was not summoned to give evidence – he was told that his testimony would merely duplicate Gilbert Kennedy's – but the repercussions of the case marked him as deeply as anyone. At the time of Chrissie Venn's murder he was engaged to the cousin of Chic Purton, the man who became prime suspect after King's acquittal. He married her two months before the trial. Soon after the verdict, Brodie's new wife was cooking dinner on the wood stove at Stoke Rivers when she discovered that she had closed the oven door on her cat, which sometimes crept inside for warmth, and incinerated it.

For Brodie, the burned cat was the final straw. Abandoning the farm that his father and brothers had wrestled from the bush, he left Tasmania for Melbourne, where to the end of his days, his son told me, he was firmly convinced that "the policeman had killed her".

★ ★ ★

But a 70-year-old man who lived on the edge of Hordern's property was not so certain.

"Who do you think did it?" I asked.

He told me the name. "I think *he* did it. Though you have to be careful who you say it to. The amount of lies that were told," and he rolled his eyes. "Old people swear King done it because they're related to Purtons."

He took me a mile down the road to the site of her murder, on the way pointing out a daffodil patch. "That was Chrissie Venn's house." The road descended through dense bush and between the peppermint gums I saw the steep field where the Hearps brothers were ploughing when they heard a scream. "Fifteen years after, when I was a kid, I used to hear old people still talking about it. I wondered, 'Where's North Motton? Who's Chrissie Venn?'" It had taken him another 50 years to winkle out the detail that he was about to share. Eighteen months before, old Lester Shadbolt had led him to the spot where her body was found.

There was no longer a stump, they had grubbed it out, but he knew its position down to ten yards. "See those big gums?" Up a red bank, behind a mass of blue hydrangeas and white agapanthus, were two eucalypts. "One of them trees could have grown over the stump. If he'd done it down there," he said, gesturing, "he could have dragged her back."

We walked a few more yards, towards the creek where the pig had trotted. Someone had splashed paint across the tarmac. I took no notice until he stopped and pointed at the paintmark, the crude yellowing shape of an axe. This was where her murderer had stepped out. "I know a fella, 42, he won't drive down this road at night."

Back at his cottage, I asked about the first settler who had farmed his land. He had not heard of Hordern, but knew well enough where Hordern's house had stood. Sometimes his plough went over the foundations, raking up stuff.

"What kind of stuff?"

"That much bloody glass," he laughed. Alcohol, but also little perfume bottles and bottles for gut ache. "You can have some if you like."

He took me into a shed built with rocks salvaged from Hordern's old water tank. When he took over the property, his plan was to leave the stone base as a memorial. "But when I removed the tank the whole thing crashed down."

Shelves inside the shed were stacked with bottles of different shapes, colours and sizes that he had rescued from beneath Stoke Rivers. Iodine; chicory essence from Edinburgh; chlorodine.

I chose a small green perfume bottle and another of clear, thick glass that had contained some kind of medicine. I would give the bottles to my mother.

Before I left I asked if any fruit trees remained on the property.

He shook his head. "I cut the last two plum trees down. One was hollow in the middle. I lit a match and he burned right down to ground level, that's how dry he was. I reckon the ants been through him."

He promised not to cut down the laurel.

XXV

SOMEONE HAD LEFT A ROW OF SILENT MESSAGES ON THE ANSWER-MACHINE. I traced them to Ivy, who said that she had something of Hordern's that she wanted to give me, although this was not the only reason for her call. In less than a fortnight she and Maud were selling their farm and moving to a bungalow in Ulverstone that they had set their hearts on.

"You don't do the same thing all your life. You got to do something different."

I went to stay with them on the eve of their departure. The distance between Boode House and their new home was less than nine miles, but for "the girls", as a local woman referred to them, it was a journey as distant as if they were setting sail to Australia two centuries before.

The silver-framed Lady Diana was still in pride of place beside the hallway telephone, protected by a posse of stern-looking dolls. Ivy said, seeing my face: "And there are some dolls where you're going to sleep, whether you like it or not."

In the kitchen, the walls were stripped of ancient photographs and ceramic plates. The sisters' belongings were packed in cardboard boxes, awaiting the arrival of various cousins to transport them by car to Ulverstone. They had sold the farm to their nephew Bill, the son of Teddy who had shown me Stoke Rivers.

Ivy was trapped between her wish to leave Bill a good garden and her determination to transplant every leaf in it. She and her sister had potted hundreds of daffodils and dug up seven cases of potatoes. Outside the kitchen, all ready to go, were tubs of soil spaded from the farm and originally ordered by their mother. From one tub I picked out a woman's stocking stuffed with Maud's tulip bulbs. A label tied at the neck read: "White Dreams".

It had taken three nights to burn the rubbish of a lifetime. "I stayed one night until 10 p.m. then carted six buckets of water to put the fire out," Ivy said. She had poured on a further 14 buckets the following evening. And watching the smoke rise from the damp ashes it had dawned on her: the date they had fixed to leave Boode House – February 13 – was their grandfather Hordern's birthday.

The business of packing-up had made the sisters nostalgic, Ivy especially. "A lot of things you don't realise, do you, what your parents do for you when you grow up?"

In the kitchen Maud was busy preparing tea. On blue Wedgwood plates she had laid out buttered fingers of malt bread, and covered them against the flies with cream-coloured tin cups.

"What regrets do you have?" I asked Ivy.

"I suppose there are silly things in your life you wish hadn't happened. But I don't know if I'd have done any differently. It just sort of happens, your life. They reckon it's mapped out when you're born. People can be in a car in an accident and some are killed and some don't even get a scratch on them."

"Have you treated anyone badly?" I suppose I was thinking of Kemp.

"Don't think I have."

"So you've led a blameless life?"

"Looks like it, doesn't it?"

Maud snorted. "I get told off."

"I tell you off, yes, because you do silly things you shouldn't, like you thought I'd gone into the garden but I was sitting in there reading one of those rubbish things in the mail."

"I didn't say a thing!"

"You were talking to yourself. You said 'bloody'."

"I didn't say –"

"Yes, you did, I heard you. I tell you straight to your face what I think of you."

Both were sobbing with laughter.

Ivy turned to me. "Tell me the truth. No two people can live together they don't have words," and rubbing her eyes she went outside to get me some potatoes that she had promised.

She dragged back in a large paper sack brimming with Pontiacs and Red Rascals. Next, she insisted on cutting for my wife a bunch of dahlias, pink lilies and carnations that she wrapped in damp newspaper. Then she gave me a bundle tied in a cloth. "I packed up some silver last night for you, but I don't want you telling anyone."

The bundle consisted of two of her grandfather's prize cards for breeding; his brass inkwell; and half a dozen silver knives and forks stamped with his initials and those of his wife.

Before I went to bed, I telephoned Gillian. There was no answer

"Perhaps she's walked out on you," Ivy said. "That's what they do nowadays."

I slept very well in their mother's bed under the strict ministry of their dolls. And in the morning found them sitting in a dark kitchen, curtains drawn, Maud eating in silence – her dried chicken covered in bacon – while Ivy, sitting by a solitary sunbeam, read a small pocket diary in which she had recorded the most important moments of her life.

She handed it over without hesitation, the shiny black notebook from her grandfather's trunk into which she had entered her 78 years on earth with the born archivist's lack of embellishment.

"War declared between England and Germany, July 1914"

"Mum and Dad marry, June 14, Tuesday 1921"

"Maudy born, July 6, 1922"

"Twins: Heather and Ivy, May 15, 1926"

"We bought our wireless set, September 13, 1939"

"Cow shed started, June 6, 1940

"Maud got her false teeth, September 22, 1941"

"Gwen and I went to Devonport to stay, June 14, 1943"

"We had electric light put through, July 9, 1943"

"We had the telephone in, August 2, 1944"

"I got my top and bottom dentures, July 1945"

"We went to Launceston, Sunday March 16, 1947"

"We bought our radiogram, April 30, 1947"

"1950 I weighed 7 stone 10lbs"

"Went to pictures January 2, 1950 'Good Sam' and 'Dick Tracy vs Cueball'"

"January 7, 1950, 'The Lost Moment' Robert Cummings and Susan Hayward."

"We bought our fridge, 20.2.1964 £150"

"We bought our washing machine £102 24.4.64"

"Uncle Joe passed away, December 17, 1969"

"Mum died, July 3, 1976"

"Uncle Brodie passed away, Wednesday July 4, 1979 (evening)"

Near the end of the diary were two notes on their own, without dates: "During 20 years Stuart Mais (Mum's cousin) made nearly $70,000 out of literature."

And: "G. went through £40,000".

"Who's G.?" I asked.

"Grandpa."

Boode House had been built following a week of Hordern weddings. Brodie married Chic Purton's cousin on June 22, 1921. Seven days earlier, Brodie's sister Mary had married Harry Rose, a farm labourer and accordion player, who had courted her in the post office with polka tunes. They erected the weatherboard bungalow as King's trial was going on in Hobart.

Maud, the first of their daughters, was born the following year; Gwen in 1924, and two years later Ivy and her twin Heather.

"No boys, so we had to be boys, didn't we, Maudy?"

Ivy's first bed was an open drawer, her first vehicle a horse and cart. She thought nothing of walking five miles a day. In the morning she walked 45 minutes to the primary school next to the cemetery and in the afternoon walked back up the hill. On Sunday, she squeezed with her sisters into the family pew in North Motton church.

"Do you still believe in God?"

"Yes. But don't think going to church makes you Christian. They use that for cover. It's how you live your life. It's how you treat other people. As far as we know, Maudy, we haven't caused anyone any harm, have we? We've tried to behave ourselves, lead good lives."

They had left school at 14 to help on the farm. In due course their sisters married, and Ivy and Maud made each a four-tiered wedding-cake. After Gwen's marriage, they stood in the front garden and watched Teddy wheel her belongings down the hill to his house. Then they went back indoors.

"Did you always know you'd be farmers?" I asked.

"No, you don't do you?" Ivy said. "Our parents might have liked us to get out, but they never said. Not like the birds – kick 'em out, don't they?" She had experienced only one flicker, one moment when she pictured an alternative life. "In a penny concert, I was dressed up as a nurse. But that was make-believe stuff."

The 48-acre farm consumed both sisters' energies. Their mother taught them how to make "eggie" cakes and to sew their own clothes; their father how to set traps for rabbits, cut fences from palings and to operate the thresher and stone-crusher. "Whatever the season brought, we were mixed up in." They continued where their grandfather Hordern left off: growing crops and flowers; breeding cattle; selling eggs, butter and cream that they trundled to the road where a truck collected it.

The crops were mostly potatoes, but they also grew oats, hay and peas, tearing outside in thunderstorms to cover the young pods with the tarpaulins that they would later thrash them on. Like Hordern, they operated a barter system with G. & A. Ellis in Ulverstone. "They had three stores under one roof – grocery, drapery, hardware," Ivy said. "A man came on Monday to take orders for delivery on Wednesdays. Never much money changed hands. They'd take all we had."

Ivy had kept the receipts. In June 1937, for instance, was delivered one coil of cyclone wire (value £1 four shillings and ninepence), 25 sacks (value nineteen shillings and ninepence) and various groceries (five shillings and sevenpence). In return, the Ellis brothers took away potatoes worth £4 four shillings and fourpence, plus seven bags of onions and 15 and a half dozen eggs worth £2 eleven shillings.

In this way they had bought a battery-powered radio set in September 1939 to listen to Neville Chamberlain. Later, they congregated beside a kerosene lamp to hear the names of the fallen reeled off, among them three schoolfriends from North Motton primary. It was a time of ration tickets for meat and extravagant rumour. Up the road, Bebe Close's husband had told her that if the Japanese arrived she was to go with the children to the wharf and jump off.

The Second World War also brought electricity. Until then they had had to read in bed with candles, and soap their cardigans by hand. "We had no washing machine – we used scrubbing boards." Once electricity was installed in 1943, they bought an electric iron, pinning neat pressed blackouts over the windows and obscuring the headlights of their father's fawn Chevy with black strips. "We still use that iron," Ivy said. "And we've had two washing machines in our lives. Not like the next generation that gets a steam iron and forgets to pour water in it and it blows up."

In the late 1970s, Ellis's refused any longer to pick up the cream and the sisters switched over to breeding. They bought in day-old Jerseys and Herefords, hand-fed them milk from buckets and sold them as yearlings, about 25 in any one year.

Flowers were another source of income. "We couldn't have afforded what we did without cut flowers," Ivy said. Auntie Ethel, who was known to walk miles for one rose, had started her off. From the age of 16, Ivy sold cut carnations, chrysanthemums, violets, polyanthus, iris, phlox, lily of the valley, dahlias, daffodils, tulips and peony roses. Mrs Pearce's van came nearly every day for funerals. "I'd be in the cowshed and Maudy would come over with the secateurs and we'd go and fill her car with flowers. I reckoned we earned $26,000 in 60 years."

It is difficult to be wise and serene in midst of the things. But it seemed to me that these sisters had achieved serenity by narrowing everything in; by not going beyond the front gate; by removal. The only picture left on the kitchen wall – a coloured print, titled *Wishing-Well Lane* – was of a thatched cottage with a flower garden.

"I said to Maud we could do our house in Ulverstone like that."

Maud laughed.

"We could!" Ivy insisted. Then noticing my cup she said sternly: "You haven't had yours, have you?"

XXVI

THERE WERE A COUPLE OF ENTRIES IN IVY'S DIARY THAT I DID NOT understand.

Ivy reread her young girl's flowery handwriting. "W. Delaney arrested, August 7, 1938." She looked at her sister. "That was sad, wasn't it?"

She was twelve when a family quarrel stopped her attending North Motton church. The diary suggested that it was one of two defining events in her life.

On August 7, 1938, their father's first cousin and neighbour, Bill Delaney, was caught stealing eggs and wheat from their shed. ("Mum got all the bad news in the cowshed – where she read the mail.") Already Delaney was suspected of taking timber and scratching a few of their potatoes out of the ground. This time they surprised him red-handed, Gwen and their mother having hidden in the bathroom with the local policeman.

"Just getting a bit of wheat, sir, to feed my chicks," Delaney said.

Ivy's father agreed not to press charges so long as Delaney returned the timber.

"He couldn't help himself," Ivy said. "He was a kleptomaniac. After that, the kids would tease him if he had a basket. They'd say 'Any eggs in it?' He was that thick in the hide, he'd just take it. He had four girls and they were the same. One was had up for thieving in a store. Another stole clothes off a dog. Off a dog!"

They had stopped attending North Motton church because of Delaney's wife. "You wouldn't be enjoying yourself much, the things she came up

with. She'd do it to your face, no matter where you were. She'd ruin everything you went out to do with the horrible things she'd say."

Instead, they worshipped at the church in Gunn's Plains, but the fear of
meeting Delaney or his wife made them reluctant to leave their property.

"It stopped us going out because she'd say something," Maud said.

"Dishonesty! I can't stand dishonesty. Or meanness!" It was the first
time that I had heard Ivy raise her voice.

The second incident was reported in a newspaper cutting that Ivy had
glued to the front flap of her diary.

In the early hours of April 23, 1946, their 18-year-old cousin and former
classmate Margaret Viney died after a strange head-on collision between
two motorbikes. The cutting described Margaret as "an active worker for
patriotic organisations and church". But elsewhere her affections were the
object of fierce competition.

At 2 a.m. she was riding on the pillion behind William and Kenneth
Lee on a level stretch of the Gawler Road. Driving on another motor-
bike in the same direction were two more rivals for her love, Clement
Dolbey and Thomas Cassidy. The two motorbikes accelerated past Lovett
Street and then one of the drivers decided to overtake.

Shortly afterwards, Mr and Mrs Horace Whiley were awakened by the
sound of the machines which they heard stop suddenly. Going outside to
investigate, they found five young bodies scattered on the road. "A mysterious feature is that although both motor cycles are believed to have
been travelling towards Gawler damage to the machines indicates that they
met head on."

Viney and Dolbey died a few hours later, the victims of a game of
Tasmanian "chicken" that had gone terribly wrong.

"Too many blokes wanted the same one," Ivy said. "There were plenty
of others about and then none has it."

XXVII

"IS THAT WHY YOU DIDN'T MARRY?"

Ivy stared into her teacup and the reflection played over her face. "Our cousin Betty said: 'You've had everything but a man.' And I said: 'I don't want one, either.' Mum always said that once you got in with the opposite sex that's when your troubles start. What you never had you don't miss," and glanced at her sister.

Maud said after a long moment: "We didn't marry because we had plenty going on. All work and no play. Dash upsetting times we had."

Ivy said: "We were helping other people. And we saw too much of the others, what they was doing. Dear, oh dear. Gwen was pretty useless with the little fellas, wasn't she, Maudy? She'd be getting sick all the time and everyone here got sick of it. She's in bed sick and I'm trying to clean the house up, Good Old Faithful."

And so the two sisters had stayed in paradise, milked the cows, cut their flowers, reared their Jerseys and Herefords, and only ever brought in men to do the fencing and for harvest. "Men came to help with potatoes, young fellas. Useless looking bags," Ivy said. "You want paying to have them around, useless things."

"Do you wish you had descendants?" I asked.

"Not now, when you see the way things go on. Only when you're really young you'd be thinking about it. But you get a bit wise, don't you, when you see a bit? It's easier to live life how you are. Cousin Betty reckons we're the lucky ones now – that's what they're all saying."

"Is there anywhere you'd like to have seen?"

"I suppose I would have liked to have gone back to England, wouldn't we? I would have liked to see where the Horderns used to live. 'Course that would have been nice, but you can't do it, can you, when you're tied up with things you've got to do. You couldn't leave this."

"Where's the furthest you ever travelled?"

"Launceston. That's as far as we ever got," Ivy said. "But that was years ago."

Launceston was no further than 70 miles away. "When was this?"

"Oh, 1947." Ivy had taken the train when they ran cheap excursions from Ulverstone. Her father arranged the tickets. It was a day trip with her mother and sisters and they came back late. "We looked round the parks. Mother took us on a tram. We went up the main street. Not much else. It wasn't frightening. When you're young you do a lot of things. You gad around."

"So how many times have you left here?"

"About half a dozen." She and Maud used to go on expeditions to Devonport to buy their dolls. "We were well known. There'd be good smiles on their faces when we walked in!"

"And the last night you spent away from this farm?"

There was some discussion. Ivy thought it was when she went to stay with Aunt Ethel in Devonport. "That would have been in 1943."

Otherwise, they had not travelled further south than the farm or further east than Launceston in their lives. Reports from family who had ventured further afield had not, they implied, been enticing.

"Dad never went to Hobart. He took mother to Melbourne for their honeymoon and wished they hadn't done."

There was also the experience of Ivy's twin Heather. She had never left Tasmania, but when she was 54 she did make a visit to Hobart, 120 miles south, with her husband.

Maud giggled. "She was taken to a shoe shop and he couldn't get her out."

"*A frock shop too,*" Ivy said disapprovingly. "I shouldn't say it. She's a snob. There are more ways of keeping up your appearances than how you dress. It's how you behave."

But I still could not believe that the last time they had spent a night away from Boode House was 60 years before.

Ivy tried to explain. "It's not so easy to get away on a farm."

Even so, she and Maud made Bruce Chatwin's brothers in *On the Black Hill* look like frequent flyers. I added it up. In a span of almost 80 years the sisters' ventures outside Boode House seemed to have consisted of half a dozen doll-buying excursions, the Sunday morning walk to church and an annual visit to the local Daffodil Show, held in the Leven Theatre opposite G. & A. Ellis's store.

"Is that it?" I wanted to know. Was that the total extent of their exposure to the world?

"Didn't we go to the cinema?" Maud remembered.

Very occasionally, as a special treat, their brother-in-law would drive them to the Leven Theatre to watch a film.

"We don't go now," Ivy said. "You got it in your own house. We don't look at that either. Not fit to look at, what they have."

The nine-mile journey to see *Dick Tracy* or *The Lost Moment* took them to another situation. They would sit down in the dark dress circle, where they had won prizes for orange cakes and knitting, and look at stories that had the effect of validating their lives. If they needed confirmation of their mother's belief that all troubles emanated from the opposite sex, it was there in the Leven Theatre in flickering horror.

"It would be late when we finished. Time to go home."

I thought of Ivy on the road to North Motton, at night, her mother's advice coming back with thunderous effect.

"It was nicer once we had Technicolor," and she fished around in an old handbag, bringing out a fragile grey rectangle of paper. "We would cut out film stars from books. We had some up on the wall."

The worn piece of paper was stamped with the words "Admit One". It was from about the right period.

"Did you ever see Merle Oberon on screen?" I asked.

"Yes, I've seen her," and she took back the ticket. "Why?"

Part IV: Oyster Bay

I

Daughter of Tasmania

"It is just where knowledge is least sure that feeling always runs highest!"

We Europeans, Julian Sorell Huxley

"I verily begin to think there is some peculiarity in the atmosphere around Van Diemen's Land, which is adverse to the transmission of truth, for somehow all or other accounts carried home partake of the same distorted or wholly imaginative character."

My Home in Tasmania, Louisa Meredith

NOT MANY PROOFS OF TASMANIA'S REMOTENESS, AND OF THE TENDENCY OF Tasmanians to deny their history, can surpass the case of Merle Oberon who overnight found herself billed as "a true daughter of Tasmania". In some quarters it is an eminence that she still enjoys. In my *Examiner* of February 19 are listed under "Today's Birthdays" Carson McCullers, Prince Andrew, Hana Mandlikova and "Tasmanian-born British actress Merle Oberon".

The story of Merle Oberon illustrates a common Tasmanian habit of concealing social or racial origins, and of emphasising some aspects of one's past to the cost of others. Before he burst with his musket through a settler's door, the bushranger Michael Howe blackened his face with charcoal, presumably to give the impression to the house's appalled occupants that he was an Aborigine. Buried next to Kemp in Albuera Street Cemetery was the "White Aborigine" William Buckley, who spent 32 years with the Wallarrange tribe in West Victoria. Kemp himself used to drink at the Labour in Vain in Campbell Street, for which perhaps he also supplied the spirits. The bar's sign was of a charlady scrubbing a black child with soap suds. This became Merle Oberon's predicament.

It takes a while to extract Merle's first 21 years from the biographies, essays, soap operas and documentaries that had accumulated like duck-fat around her. Her origins were complicated, but not, in the end, mysterious.

She was born in February 1911 in St George's Hospital, Bombay (now Mumbai), christened two months later Estelle Merle Thompson and nick-named "Queenie" following a visit by Queen Mary to India that year. She grew up in the Bombay suburb of Khetwadi. Her mother Constance was 14 years old, part Maori, part Eurasian. Her father, Arthur Thompson, an engineer from Durham, worked for the Indian railways. Three years later, he was sent as a sapper to Flanders and died of pneumonia at the Somme.

In Bombay, Constance married another Englishman and gave Merle to her grandmother to look after. Merle grew up believing that Constance was her half-sister and that her grandmother Charlotte was in fact her mother.

Charlotte took Merle to Calcutta when she was six. There they lived in Lindsay Mansions. At 16, Merle was working as a switchboard oper-ator. In the evenings, she put on a backless dress and danced at Firpo's nightclub with English stockbrokers, flirting with them in a high-pitched Anglo-Indian voice. She had an olive complexion, almond eyes, a heart-shaped face, gondola black hair, a long neck, the fluttery hands of a "temple-dancer" and the ambition of Eva Peron. Already she viewed her mixed-race origins as an impediment. To disguise her Eurasian blood, she started using "Fair and Lovely", a powder containing a potentially damaging chemical that did eventually ruin her skin. She never appeared to her best advantage in colour films.

In 1928, she set out with Charlotte for Europe on an Italian freighter. From this time on, she introduced Charlotte as her Bengali servant. In London, she worked in a flower shop next to Bucks Club and as a hostess in the Café de Paris alongside the future Lady Docker. She became the mistress of a film producer who gave her bit parts. She was not a natural actress. After one of her screen tests, Jack Warner telegraphed the producer: "If you want to sleep with women go ahead, but don't waste my money testing them."

Towards the end of 1931, the flamboyant Hungarian director Alexander Korda arrived in London and set up London Film Productions. The following April, his studio announced the signing of four starlets on a five-year contract at £20 a week, including the "exotic" Merle Oberon. She appeared wearing thick spectacles in *Wedding Rehearsal*, after Ann Todd was injured in a car crash. One reviewer remarked that she seemed "totally at a loss as to how to behave, let alone act". The French critic Marcel Ermans wrote: "If I were Korda I would get up in the night, steal the negative and quietly drop it into the Thames."

In 1933, her fortune changed when she was auditioned for the part of Anne Boleyn in *The Private Life of Henry VIII*. As the author and editor Michael Korda tells it, his uncle entered the studio with his wife Maria who took one look at Merle, dug her nails into Korda's arm and cried out, "There she is, you fool! Look at that face! It's worth a million pounds. There is your damned Anne Boleyn."

It was most probably Korda's publicity director, John Myers, who came up with her stage name as well as the story that she had been born in Tasmania. He decided that her prospects would be improved by eliminating all traces of her Indian background. Tasmania had two advantages. It was famous for having no native population, and it was too far away to check the story. The actor Maurice Bredell remembered Myers "roaring with laughter" as he made Merle memorise her upbringing in a place "so remote that most people had not the slightest idea where it was".

For the next 45 years, Merle Oberon suppressed all mention of "Queenie" Thompson of Bombay. She remembered a father she tragically had never met, a dashing English Major (rather in the mould of Kemp), who worked in a vague capacity for the government in Tasmania where he had died in a horse-riding accident (sometimes it was pneumonia) while out hunting kangaroos (sometimes it was foxes) shortly before she was born. Fortunately, she had been able to fall back on the generosity of her uncle, Major-General Sir George Bartley, and her godmother, a Lady Monteith, who ensured that she not only completed her education in Hobart but went on to finishing schools in Paris, London and Darjeeling.

In Tasmania, the story was swallowed hook, line and sinker. On December 19, 1933, the *Mercury* carried extracts from an interview that "the tiny dark-haired Merle with her glistening white teeth and oh-so-trim figure" had given to *Film Pictorial*, under the banner:

"The remarkable rise to fame of Merle Oberon, the Tasmanian-born girl who has been proclaimed one of the most promising actresses of the day."

Some months later, a black and white film appeared at the Leven Theatre in Ulverstone in which a young Tasmanian actress dressed as a queen prepared to have her head chopped off. As she knelt to receive the blow, she said: "Mine is such a *little* neck."

Merle's success in *The Private Life of Henry VIII* galvanised the *Launceston Weekly Courier* to include her in a list of the most famous Tasmanians alive. "Just 13 years ago a small girl, then seven years old, lived a typical girl's life near Hobart. Her name was Merle Thompson O'Brien." Presently, she had travelled to England and there she had adopted her stage name. "Take a small, slenderly-built figure, warm brown curly hair to match curly eyes, a creamy magnolia skin and an expressive scarlet mouth. In other words meet Merle Oberon, famous at the age of 21. And what is more important, a true daughter of Tasmania."

"In Tasmania we tell stories to reassure ourselves we have not slipped unnoticed over the rim of the world," writes the Tasmanian historian Cassandra Pybus in a clear-headed essay on Merle Oberon – whose Tasmanian origin was recorded on the Fantales wrappers that Pybus collected as a child. In the month of her interview in the *Courier*, November 1934, Merle met an as yet unknown actor who *had* been born in Tasmania. Travelling to New York on the SS *Paris*, she was appalled when a man from second class burst into her presence. It is a tantalising moment. Did he question her about Tasmania? Did he ask about the Freycinet Peninsula? Or Wineglass Bay, where his father, a professor of marine biology and discoverer of the squaladont, a mammal 26 million years old, would every Easter go camping (and once found washed up a large species of jellyfish, "a somewhat distant cousin of man himself . . . ")? Or Kempton, where as a boy he used to stay, right on the edge of Kemp's estate, and scandalise the farmers by chloroforming sheep (and once tied a prize rooster to the blade of a windmill and watched it spin)? No-one knows what passed between them, but shortly before her death she gave vent to her "total disgust" at the mention of his name. Errol Flynn, she said, she considered "utterly despicable".

Merle's inability to produce a Tasmanian birth certificate threatened to scupper her marriage to Korda in 1939. As the couple prepared to wed in Antibes, Korda had to call on his lawyer, the formidable Maître Blum, to persuade the Mayor of Antibes to conduct the ceremony without the necessary document.

That year she starred opposite Laurence Olivier in *Wuthering Heights*. The film marked the zenith of her career. Lady Korda's dependence on "Fair and Lovely" had begun to disfigure her skin with the kind of leper spots that John Updike inflicts on one of his characters, "in the same relation to one another as Australia and Tasmania". According to her biographer Charles Higham, "her entire face and neck were covered with hundreds of red, oozy pustules." Higham quotes her friend Edie Goetz, the daughter of Louis B. Meyer: "I couldn't believe what I saw. It was like the disease that sometimes attacks the exquisite white leaves of a camellia. That perfect face and now just a mass of sores!" In her mania still to be perceived as white, she built Ghalal in Acapulco, a white palace in which everything was the colour of snow. The effect intimidated her neighbour,

Rod Steiger, who remarked that the bathroom was so clean he felt unable to urinate.

Not until 13 months before her death did Merle Oberon visit her "birthplace" for the first time. She would not recover from the experience.

The idea came from Robert Wolders, her fourth husband, a Dutchman 20 years her junior. In October 1978, at the end of a trip they had made to Sydney, he pressed Merle to fly south. "I wanted to see her birthplace. I realise now that she must have suffered terribly." No sooner did she agree than she regretted her decision. "She became increasingly nervous and ill. She wept often, clearly from the strain," Wolders told Higham. "When we got to Hobart she was more and more upset." She could not explain to Wolders what the matter was. "When I asked her to come to a graveyard to look for her family, she refused." They hired a car and took a two-hour drive to Port Arthur, during which she said little. "She was so sad." But on her return she waved in a vague way at the crenellated sandstone towers of the Governor's Residence and told her husband: "That's where people say I was born."

In Hobart, they stayed at the Wrest Point Hotel, built on foundations taken from Kemp's convict quarters at Mount Vernon. The telephone started ringing as soon as she checked in – people who remembered Merle at school in Hobart, at a hotel in St Helen's on the east coast, watching her boyfriend "Skitchy" James play cricket at New Town. Declining to give interviews, she left "strict instructions that she would speak to no-one" and that she "had decided to stay silent while in Tasmania".

On Friday, October 13, she emerged to judge the Miss Tasmania Quest in the Wrest Point's Cabaret Room. In white pearl earrings and a high-collared, white sparkling dress, she awarded the title of "Miss Tasmania 1979" to the

Merle Oberon visiting Tasmania, 1978

weather-girl Sue Hickey. Three days later she attended a civil reception at the invitation of the Lord Mayor of Hobart. It was an afternoon event, played down as a cup of tea with the Lord Mayor. Neil Coulson drove her from the hotel to the Town Hall. According to Coulson, as they walked up the steps, she said to him: "It's probably a bad time to bring up the fact I wasn't born in Tasmania."

"Where were you born?"

"India."

Once inside the building she signed her name in the Lord Mayor's visitors' book, giving as her address: "Malibu & Tasmania". Soon afterwards, according to several who were present, she fainted. Her husband said: "She began her speech of acceptance, referring to her childhood, and then started to cry and I had to leave the room."

Another witness was Alderman Doone Kennedy. "I couldn't believe this was the film star," she told me. "When I went home, I said to my husband she was the kind of lady who if you passed her in the street you'd stop and ask if you could help. She was wearing a cotton frock and a cardigan and looked drugged."

Why had she fainted? The pressure of the false biography she had been living must have contributed. Her husband realised: "She would have to say to me that she had committed an untruth." One guest had overheard her fielding questions from a group who were eagerly probing into the circumstances of her upbringing in Tasmania. She had become quite agitated. "No, no, I was born on a ship that was passing through." But the situation was more complicated than simply the anxiety of watching cracks race through the foundation on which she had constructed the last four decades of her life.

Several guests who spoke to Merle had no inkling of her Indian blood nor of her childhood in Bombay. On the other hand, they seemed perfectly aware that her father was called Thompson. Stranger still, they claimed to know her mother. They knew, for instance, that Merle's mother was not English, nor was she Indian.

"She was Chinese," Doone Kennedy said.

Kennedy's father-in-law had owned the An Hor tin mine at Lottah in Tasmania's north-east where there were many Chinese workers from Guandong, among them Alfred Ernest Chintock, one of whose 13 children was Charlotte or "Lottie" Chintock. "My father-in-law told me it was common knowledge, Merle being Lottie's daughter."

It suggests an encounter as devastating as her meeting at sea with Errol Flynn. A day later Merle and Wolders left Hobart. Not long after her return to Malibu she collapsed with a myocardial infarction. The following November Tasmania's famous daughter was dead.

Merle did give one interview while in Tasmania, to Edyth Langham, a radio journalist. The recording is lost, but one Easter Sunday, I visited Edyth at her property outside Hobart airport where she bred horses and red setters.

I obeyed instructions to go slowly up a drive and halted at a low building with a notice: "Please leave your pets in the car until advised." This was the kennels. Edyth lived in an identical building on the right. She opened the door, a petite, sparky lady in her sixties. Groomed blonde hair, turquoise track suit, red lipstick. An Irish setter at her side.

We went into her drawing room, decorated with porcelain setters and casts of racehorses. A string quartet was playing and there was a bunch of lilies beneath a painting of Edyth as an intense young lady in a lilac evening gown.

I complimented her on her dog's looks and she revealed the secret. "Mutton-bird oil is wonderful for setters' coats. Give it in their food and it comes through in their coat and they just gleam."

She settled on a chaise longue, stroking her dog.

"Tell me about your interview with Merle Oberon," I said.

She had requested the interview for the reason that Merle's story was well known to her. Edyth's aunt and uncle, Con and Zel Bidencope, used to go for holidays at St Helen's and they remembered Merle as a child running in and out of their hotel and making sandcastles.

This was the story as she learned it from them: Lottie Chintock was the daughter of a Chinese tin-miner from the myrtle forests near Weldborough. As a young woman she took the bus from Weldborough to St Helen's where John Willis Thompson, who ran the bus service, also owned a hotel. Thompson gave Lottie work as a chambermaid.

"She was very beautiful and quite gracious. My uncle and aunt treated her like a treasured friend. Con used to go into the hotel and they'd say to him, 'Lottie's in the kitchen, go in and talk to her.' She was more than a retainer. She had a long affair with Thompson while his wife just stayed in a room upstairs, a recluse."

Round about 1910, Lottie became pregnant by Thompson. She travelled to Hobart to have the baby. Merle was born at 62 Montpelier Retreat in a room that became Pipkin's, the barber shop. Edyth knew a woman who swore that her grandmother, Philadelphia Flyn, had delivered her at 3 a.m. using forceps. She weighed ten pounds.

"Lottie takes the baby back. So the baby grows up in the hotel. People are aware of her in the St Helen's area. Especially a couple called O'Brien, from India, who played with her on the beach.

"St Helen's is very different now," Edyth said. "Then it was quite social. Everyone went for their holidays. It was an especial favourite with the Indian Army. According to the story — and I'm sure this is right — Thompson had this cousin O'Brien and he and his wife didn't have any children and so they adopted Merle and took her back to India. They adopted children in those days in the way you pick up dogs these days. I believe she was six."

The next time Merle returned to Tasmania, 61 years later, Edyth was waiting.

To begin with, there were to be no interviews, but Edyth telephoned Wrest Point, was put through to Merle's suite and was told, yes, Merle would like to speak to her — "although I might have been warned to keep off Tasmania". An interview was arranged for 4 p.m., but when Edyth arrived "there was suddenly a big flurry and the interview was off. No way was there going to be an interview."

Edyth left the hotel to pick up her daughter from Collegiate, where she received an urgent message: "Merle had gone to the Town Hall and where was I?"

Merle was waiting in the Lady Mayoress's room.

"She looked absolutely perfect. A beautiful blue dress, powder blue frock and coat. Her young husband was there, he was divine. I remember he discussed their age difference. He said there was no difference. 'I feel she's my age. She's so child-like.' And she *was* child-like. She wasn't cunning or manipulative. I don't like Chinese dolls, but, yes, she was very doll-like."

"What about her skin?"

"I was close. She had a magnolia complexion. It wasn't pitted. The significant thing for me was the wide cheekbones. She didn't have Indian features."

"Are you sure?"

"Listen, I've judged Miss Tasmania pageants, Woman of the Year, dog shows all over Australia. And I breed horses. Breeding is something that stands out for me: it's all to do with heredity, particularly with dogs. It's the bone structure that interests me. I look at someone to see what's behind them. It's so interesting in dogs, it comes out generations later. It's like people who have convict heritage and want to hide it. Or Aboriginal blood." And she mentioned a descendant of Kemp's, still alive, who, she told me, was always believed to have "black blood".

"It's in the mmmoouth," she said, blowing up her lips. "He has the lubra look."

No, she could tell that Merle Oberon was definitely Chinese.

Gloria, the large and cheerful woman who ran the History Room (the little museum) in St Helen's, had no doubt: Merle Oberon's father was John Willis Thompson, the taciturn former coach driver who had owned the Telegraph Hotel.

She showed me his photograph – a short Alf Garnett figure with a walrus moustache, round spectacles and a thick neck. "He was known as Gimlet or Grandfather or JWT."

"How do you know he was Merle's father?"

"Just feelings I have."

Friends of Gimlet Thompson described a chubby, weather-beaten face, a deadpan humour and a quick mind that liked to live up to a reputation for "closeness" and for never letting "his right hand know what his left was about". He was regarded in St Helen's as eccentric, wandering around with his eyes half-closed, seldom removing his hat, and hardly saying a word. On the few occasions that he did open his mouth, he spoke with excruciating slowness. He was a teetotaller, who would reply, if offered a drink, "No, thanks. But I'll have a cigar." This is almost his only recorded utterance, although there was one in particular that he liked to sing, "The Holy City". I found a postcard that he wrote in February 1909 to a friend called Flossie. "About those two boys, you want to whack hard and often. Don't ever let them be top dog or you will repent it. You need never be afraid of being too harsh so always go one more than what you think is a fair thing." It was around this time that Gimlet Thompson employed Lottie Chintock as a chambermaid.

Lottie laid out starched cloths in the dining room, polished the silver till it gleamed, and carried out trays of home-made lemonade, a marble in the top of each bottle. Among the guests whose sheets she changed were Lord and Lady Rowallen, Sir Ernest and Lady Clark, Sir Hugh and Lady Binney. She may have also scrubbed the floor of the silent movie theatre that Thompson had created in a hall attached to the hotel.

Dudley Edward Madden worked as a porter and was one of several who noticed that Thompson and Lottie were very close. When Lottie became pregnant, it was "common knowledge" who was the father.

I spoke to Thompson's great-granddaughter. She had been brought up on the story, like mutton-bird oil. How Merle was Thompson's daughter by Lottie, who had risen to become his housekeeper and who nursed

Thompson when he became ill after his wife's death. "My father worked as a porter at the hotel, and in his later years he would tell me that when JWT became older – he owned the picture theatre in the hall, but then it moved up the street – this particular night he wasn't very well, he had a cold, and the family tried to stop him going out. 'I'm going, Will, because that's my daughter in the film.'"

Thompson died in May 1934. *The Private Life of Henry VIII* had come out in England in 1933. It is possible – just – that his last sight of his daughter was of her execution.

At the hotel in St Helen's where her mother was said to have worked the name Merle Oberon drew a blank with the new manager, Jobi Watts.

"Merlot?" He had not heard the story. He led me into a bar where five men were drinking. Bearded, tattooed, doleful, these were the heirs to Lord Rowallen and Con Bidencope.

"Jumpy – he'd know," one of them said. "But you'll have to pay him. How much do you want to know?"

Jumpy was summoned by telephone from a counter splashed with beer. Meanwhile, Jobi took me up to the chambermaid's quarters above the kitchen.

In the 1980s Jobi had worked in the hotel as an apprentice and used to climb to the attic for a smoke.

"I reckon the rooms are haunted," he said, creaking ahead of me up narrow hardwood stairs that were worn in the centre. He led the way into a small bedroom with green skirting and mustard yellow panels carved from Tasmanian blackwood. The slanting window was painted over, admitting a treacly light. There was not much space for anything in here but a bed.

I lingered a moment, battling to picture Lottie in bed, the creak on the staircase, the door-handle turning. Was Merle Oberon really conceived here?

In the bar Jumpy, hair slicked back, pointed nose, a 76-year-old ex-sailor, told me what I already knew.

I bought him a beer.

Aged 13, he, too, had been a porter in the hotel. "I quite believe Merle was Tasmanian born."

"Give him another and he shagged her round the bushes," cackled a beard with a tattoo.

Late one night, while most Tasmanians slept, the ABC put out a documentary that dared to challenge Merle Oberon's status as a Tasmanian, and also showed the first photograph of Lottie I had seen, a snapshot taken in 1920 when she was 34. I had the impression of a long face beneath a dark hat, an elbow resting on a fence and a hand cupping her left ear, smiling. Standing beside her was a son, Ronnie, aged nine.

I recognised several of the people interviewed: Edyth Langham, Cassandra Pybus, Doone Kennedy. The director had spoken also to Lottie's great-nephew (who said that Lottie saw every film with Merle in it, sighing "I wish Merle was with us"); to Lottie's doctor, who remembered Merle returning to Weldborough after Lottie's death in 1951; and to an archivist in the Hobart births and records office who could not trace a single reference to Lottie having given birth to a daughter.

According to the film, in another variant of the story Lottie was forced to leave her baby girl in Hobart, where an Indian silk merchant who lived in Argyle Street opposite the fire station adopted her. She went to the Old Model school until she was seven, then to India. Other versions had her fostered out to the O'Brien family in Moonah, to a group of travelling players also called O'Brien and to a policeman in New Town called Thomson. The film showed a clip of Merle Oberon in a black and white movie, saying: "One can never be sure of anything with a past like mine."

The documentary ended in Toronto, tracking down Harry Selby. He was the son of Merle's mother Constance, who after Arthur Thompson died on the Somme had married Selby's father. Constance told Selby when he was twelve that Merle was her sister. Selby had now located Merle's birth certificate in Mumbai. This was a revelation. Giving her date of birth as February 18, 1911, it showed that Estelle Merle Thompson was the daughter of Arther [sic] Thompson and Constance Thompson, of Khetwadi. In other words, Merle was not his aunt but his half-sister. And there was nothing Tasmanian about her after all.

The unearthing of Merle's birth certificate did not deter the audience at a screening of the ABC documentary in Hobart's State Cinema.

"It didn't worry me a tiny bit," Edyth Langham told me. "I've known lots of Indian students – boys who come out here with the papers of their dead brother. They don't think twice about forging."

Bill Penfold was another who had grave doubts about the Indian birth certificate. "You can knock one up in five minutes."

"But why hasn't anyone knocked one up in Tasmania?" I asked.

"We're truthful people," he said.

Edyth Langham was determined to have the last word. After the credits had rolled, she stood and faced the audience. "I said, 'Could we have a show of hands to say whether or not we believe Merle Oberon is Tasmanian?'"

"And the result?" I asked.

"An overwhelming show of support for Merle being Tasmanian."

On the wall of an empty pub above the Weldborough myrtle forest, I was pointed out an old photograph of a broad-faced Oriental woman in a mannish pinstripe. The publican dipped his head at a corrugated iron barn across the road. I stared obligingly at the four boarded windows, the bolted door. In that shed, he claimed, Charlotte Chintock conceived her famous daughter. "Merle was definitely born here."

The pub followed a Tasmanian tradition of wrestling to be three things at once: the Irish pub, the Worst pub, and the Weldborough Hotel. I wondered if clients might have been put off by the menu outside, advertising cooked Tasmanian devils, kangaroo tits, witchetty grubs, possum pie and maggot mornay. In boom-time, I had read, "the lights were never dimmed and there were three shifts to every bed".

I drove up three dead ends looking for Weldborough's cemetery. Then I saw a wisp of smoke coming from the roof of a wooden house. A small woman with no teeth pointed the way, speaking in an American accent. Bev Warren once owned a fish and chip shop in the English town of Amesbury. Yes, she knew Lottie's son, Ronnie. He used to help out in the Weldborough Hotel. Uniquely, Ronnie would never talk about Merle Oberon. "He'd say, 'Nothing to do with me.'" As I was shortly to discover, he was probably quite right.

I walked across two fields up past blackberry bushes to a peaceful cemetery on a slope facing the myrtle ridge above Weldborough. The ridge ran north to Lottah, once site of the An Hor mine and now of a 20-acre garden where I had stood two weeks before and gazed and gazed in the direction of the gardener's finger. John Ward from Nottinghamshire was pointing at an old growth forest above the Ransom River. "See over there? I would guarantee that no-one has ever been there. Ever." He moved his hand a fraction. "And over there, the last time – 60 years ago. You don't know what's there."

A month before, in April 2003, a tin-miner's shed was discovered in these hills. Only a handful of people had been allowed to visit the site, including Gloria from the St Helen's History Room. The shed was undisturbed, she said. On the floor were some ceramic alcohol and medicine bottles, some Chinese coins and an opium tin. A frying pan with a long rusty handle was in the dirt next to the remains of a fire. "It looked like he'd gone out and never come back."

The shed was home to one of 1,500 Chinese workers who arrived here from the Victorian goldfields, after tin was discovered in 1874. Among them was Alfred Ernest Chintock, who came from Ballarat with a European wife. The locals nicknamed him "Alf", and the community of the pigtailed miners they called "Celestials". The Celestials roasted their pigs in underground ovens with granite lids. They drank Dutch gin and gambled, and on the occasion of the Chinese New Year home-made fireworks spiralled across the sky. Most were gone by 1910, some taking Tasmanian wives back to Guandong and so completing a journey begun by those escaped convicts who believed they only had to cross the Blue Mountains to reach China. Behind them they left a couple of musty joss houses and, according to some sources, the expression "fair dinkum", which local legend derives from the Cantonese word for gold, signifying something that is genuine.

At last I find the grave of Alfred Chintock's daughter. It is near the top of the slope, to the left of a row of upright ornate tombstones, mostly English names – Grose, Walker, Symons. Lottie's grave is one of nine rough concrete slabs. She shares it with her son Ronnie and a vivid wreath of green and pink ceramic flowers, their unchipped petals the only colour in the cemetery.

I am looking at Ronnie's dates when something clears for me. He was born on October 6, 1911. Seven and a half months after Merle. So maybe Merle was not born on February 18 or 19 in the same year to the same mother.

II

Tigers and Devils

"They say there are compensations for living in Van Diemen's Land – some very quaint marsupials."

Patrick White, *A Fringe of Leaves*

EVERY THIRD TASMANIAN HAS A STORY THAT CONFIRMS THE CONTINUED existence of the Tasmanian tiger or thylacine: an Alsatian-sized marsupial with chocolate stripes across its back, the stiff tail of a kangaroo and jaws that open wider than a snake's.

Ivy was no exception. On Gunn's Plains Road five years before, her nephew came within yards of a Tasmanian tiger. "He'd never seen anything like it, what he saw. 'I thought I was seeing things,' he said. Reckoned it was a young one. He took his dog next morning to see if he could track it." But her nephew's thylacine had melted away, like each and every one recorded as sighted since 1936.

In Burnie, Laurelle Shakespeare told me that she saw a thinnish-looking thylacine near a shack in the Great Lakes in January 1980. She was with her mother and the owner of the shack when the animal appeared in the middle of the day on a big ridge behind them. "It just stood there and we stood there and then it flipped around and walked off, quickly disappearing into bush. I can remember feeling scared, a kid seeing something that was not supposed to exist. I turned to Mum. 'That's a Tasmanian tiger.' She said: 'Yes, and we're not telling anyone.' Can you imagine? Three of us, seeing the same thing. There'd be people all over the place."

A neighbour of ours on Dolphin Sands was married to the keeper of the Eddystone Lighthouse and saw a Tasmanian tiger – twice – on the north-east coast, where a third of all sightings have taken place. In 1974, she was approaching the village of Gladstone when a large striped animal crossed the road not ten yards from her car.

"Do you think it was a tiger?" I ask.

She says: "I *know*."

A few months later, she saw another one – or the same animal – beside the road. She waited for an hour, but it did not reappear. This time she reported it to the local Parks and Wildlife officer, for his ears only. She told him that she would deny it if everyone descended on Eddystone. She did not want people to think her mad.

Nothing is more emblematic of Tasmania than its vanished marsupial. In the most recent study of the animal, David Owen writes: "The thylacine has about it a sufficiently powerful and ambiguous mystique that it is able comfortably to represent and embrace much that is Tasmanian." From the label on bottles of Cascade beer to the logos of Launceston city council and Tasmania's local television channel, its distinct outline tracks you at every turn. "It isn't just a symbol of Tasmania," explains the designer who adopted the image for the masthead of Tourism Tasmania. "It's a symbol of the Tasmanian Experience." Counterparts to unicorns on the royal arms, a pair of heraldic thylacines stand rampant in the state's coat of arms. The creature has even lent its name to the island's first eleven, the Tasmanian Tigers. "It is/was a sleek, cunning and aggressive carnivore – a killer," according to the former batsman David Boon, himself a local legend also known as the Keg on Legs. "If it still exists, it is . . . surrounded by mystery and extremely hard to track down. It certainly projects an appropriate image for our cricket team."

This was not, however, the first example of a team named after the thylacine. The convict workers at Mount Vernon played against workers on neighbouring estates under the name of Kemp's Tigers.

The Tasmanian Aborigines knew the thylacine as Corinna, the Brave One. The only legend about the animal to filter down from their culture is contained in a collection of stories retold by Jackson Cotton and gathered from Timler, an Aboriginal elder, near the Cotton property at Kelvedon. Palana, the little star, son of Moinee, ruler of Trowenna, mixed ashes and blood into a thick brown paste and sketched a number of parallel stripes across a hyena pup's back, "from the top of his shoulders to the butt of his rigid tail".

Abel Tasman was the first European to allude to the thylacine. On the beach at Marion Bay, his Dutch sailors came across Tasmania-shaped pug-marks in the sand – "the footing of wild beasts having claws like a tyger . . . " Most probably they were a wombat's footprints, but the name stuck.

Among the first to hear the animal's eerie nocturnal yelp, described as a hissing cough or terrier-like "yip-yip", was Midshipman François Desiré Breton of the *Naturaliste* who listened to a noise that came from the vicinity of Maria Island and in February 1802 wrote this deadpan entry in his diary: "A dog was heard barking on shore."

The first Europeans to set eyes on a thylacine were five escaped English convicts near Hobart. On May 2, 1804, according to Kemp's friend the Reverend Robert Knopwood, who interviewed them shortly afterwards, they saw "a large tiger" in the bush, "and when the tiger see the men, which were about 100 yards away from it, it went away".

One of the first Europeans to touch a Tasmanian tiger was Kemp himself, who was present when the body of a mauled female thylacine was brought into York Town. On March 30, 1805, "an animal of a truly singular and novel description" was killed by the settlement's dogs on the hill behind his quarters. The carcass was immediately examined by Colonel Paterson, who sent it in a wooden box to Joseph Banks together with the "very perfect native's head". The strange animal reminded Paterson of a hyena and also "a low wolf dog". It had a forefoot with blunt claws, large black eyes, canine teeth and 20 blackish stripes along its grey back. "It must be a brute peculiarly quick of digestion," reckoned Paterson, who found five pounds of kangaroo in its stomach. "It is the hope the breed of so destructive a creature is not very numerous as it will be a great scourge to the weaker kind of stock."

In the letters and diaries of colonists, there are references, too, to a

Tasmanian wolf, a Tasmanian hyena, a Tasmanian zebra, a Tasmanian dingo, a Tasmanian panther and a dog-faced dasyure. Not until 1824 did the Tasmanian tiger settle down as *Thylacinus cynocephalus*, a pouched dog with a dog's head.

About its habits and ecology, writes Owen, "we know pathetically little". When it was alive concentration was on shooting, clubbing or trapping it, and not on studying it. All accounts agree that it was shy, elusive and – with its fused backbone – not gainly. Unable to pounce, it had to wear down its prey. It stalked wallabies and possums and had a particular liking for Kemp's merino sheep, which it would bring to the ground with its vice-like jaws and kill by suffocation. "The tiger would tear out the jugular vein, suck the blood, then, ripping a piece of flesh from the shoulder, discard the rest," said William Cotton, who as a boy in the 1920s took part in a tiger hunt near Swansea. Other accounts describe its taste for vascular tissue: lungs, hearts, livers.

The thylacine's stiffened tail was adapted for swimming, but when walking through the bush it appeared to one trapper to be "turning in a piece like a ship". If cornered, it would rise on hind legs and hop off like a kangaroo. It ran with a stiff loping movement, although in short bursts it was capable of reaching high speeds. Nocturnal and nomadic, it moved in a circular pattern covering an average daily distance of 35 miles. A female such as the one viewed by Kemp at York Town produced three or four pups in a good year.

In *Thylacine*, Owen suggests that when Kemp arrived there were 2,000–4,000 thylacines on the island, a figure which is close to some estimates of the Aboriginal population. The "perfect native's head" and the pickled thylacine that Paterson sent back as curios to England had also this in common: beside competing for the same protein, each species would in a very short time have a bounty placed on it and be hunted near to extinction.

The clip lasts 62 seconds and was taken in the 1930s by a man who was bitten on the buttock while filming. It shows the last known Tasmanian tiger in captivity at Hobart's Beaumaris Zoo, an animal known to everyone as Benjamin. As if her species had not endured enough misconceptions, the footage shows Benjamin to have been female.

I meet Benjamin on the other side of the world, in the Natural History Museum in East Berlin. The loop of black and white film ran and ran and was a welcome flicker of life in a procession of cavernous rooms devoted to the skeletons of plesiosaurs.

Benjamin has an elongated muzzle and a striped back and is the size of a large dog with short legs. I do not know how long I stood and gazed at her pacing in her cage. Watched by a man in a floppy hat, she yawns, squats, tears flesh off a bone, looks around with an air of hopelessness and distress, and leaps now and then at the cage wire. The sequence is mute. No recording exists of Benjamin's bark, but the last curator at Beaumaris Zoo, Alison Reid, wrote that it sounded like "ah-ah-ah-ah".

The scratched fragment of film is the unique record of this perhaps extinct animal in motion. Benjamin died of pleuro-pneumonia and kidney failure on a cold night in September 1936.

"Old timers will tell you that tigers came out galore at lambing time," says a wine-grower outside Swansea, who claims that he saw a tiger near Sorell when he was twelve.

Kemp's success at promoting sheep-breeding guaranteed a steady source of food for thylacines. By 1830, some 680,000 sheep were grazing in the open pastures between Hobart and Launceston. Adam Amos complained that near Swansea: "Tigers are plentifull amongst the rocky mountains and destroy many sheep and lambs." Moulting Lagoon behind my house was the site not only of an alleged Aboriginal massacre but of a slaughter of thylacines. William Cotton lived for a time on a bend of the river nearby. He claimed that on a single day in 1900 three men and their dogs killed 17 adult thylacines and their pups that had come to feed on swans' eggs.

The original attempt to eliminate these "noxious animals" was made by the Van Diemen's Land Company as it struggled to establish sheep flocks on its huge property in the north-west. In 1830, the Company offered a bounty of five shillings for a male and seven shillings for a female. Six years later, a "tiger man" was appointed at Woolnorth, the Company's headquarters near Cape Grim, and operated as a full-time tracker on a salary of £20 (about £1,200 today). But what really signalled the beginning of the end for the thylacine was the bill proposed by Swansea's member of parliament, John Lyne.

Sometimes referred to as "Leghunter" on account of his sexual wanderings, John Lyne was the son of William Lyne who had built the Cellar and brother of Susan who was struck by an Aboriginal weapon. In 1831, he took part in Meredith's Freycinet Line against the Oyster Bay tribe. Elected to the House of Assembly for Glamorgan, he tabled a motion to extinguish "the dingo", as he called it. In a speech shot through with wild inaccuracies, Lyne claimed that "these dreadful animals may be seen in hundreds, stealthily sneaking along, seeking whom they may devour, and it is estimated that they will have swallowed up every sheep and bullock in Glamorgan." Supported by not a scrap of scientific evidence, Lyne calculated that a single thylacine could kill as many as 100 sheep a year. He assured members that the destruction of 500 thylacines would safeguard the 30,000–40,000 sheep presently lost every year on the east coast. This claim was ridiculed, but Lyne's motion was passed by a single vote, and by a majority of 12 to 11 the government agreed to pay £1 for every adult carcass presented and ten shillings for every pup's. The carcasses had to be taken to polling stations to have their ears or toes clipped off in order to prevent fraud.

The first bounty was paid on April 28, 1888, to J. Harding of Ross, the last to J. Bryant of Hamilton on June 5, 1909. In its 21-year operation, the Tasmanian Government Thylacine Bounty Scheme accounted for 2,184 skins. Popular belief is that many were sent to Europe to be fashioned into gentlemen's waistcoats, but Owen claims that "no such waistcoat is known to exist".

In 1909, the bounty scheme was stopped. A distemper epidemic had apparently drastically reduced the thylacine population and the toll of dead sheep and sightings grew less and less frequent, although in 1912 a new hotel in the north-west still advertised "Tiger-Shooting" as one of its attractions. The highest number of claims – 600 – were in the central plains. By contrast, in Swansea, where the Glamorgan Stock Protection Society paid £2 for every dead adult tiger, there were only 17 claims. One morning, William Cotton startled farmers in the main street by walking into town with a thylacine at the end of a lead. He had snared it four miles west of Swansea and tamed it like a dog. After a few days kept chained in his stable, the animal grew restless and "one night jumped over the partition between the stall, and choked itself, the chain not being long enough to let its feet touch the floor on the other side".

Benjamin's death on September 7, 1936 caused no stir at all. The day had been fine and mild, but at night it was exceptionally cold and Benjamin was exposed to freezing temperatures without access to a protected shelter. The passing of the last verified representative of its species did not merit a mention in the local press. On the day that Benjamin succumbed to pneumonia, Hobart's Theatre Royal (founded by, among others, Kemp) was enjoying a full house for the opening night of "Gaieties", a variety show that featured the tenor Domenico Caruso ("nephew of the late famous tenor Enrico"); some acrobatic tumbling from The Flying Martinetties ("whose famous Riseley Act caused a furore"); and Miss Nellie

Kelle, "the male impersonator", whose performance was so popular that he/she "had to submit to numerous recalls".

The newspapers did, though, devote plenty of space to the prize dogs on show at the Tasmanian Kennel Club in Launceston. "Interest in exhibition dogs in Tasmania has never been so marked as at present," wrote the *Mercury*'s correspondent. Not to be outdone, the *Examiner* printed the photograph of a black cocker-spaniel, Peggy of Kareem: "We are open to just criticism if we fail to look after our pets." Ironically, the correspondent "Kennel" contributed a piece under the title "New Breed for Tasmania" about the first arrival on the island of an Afghan hound. This "dignified" dog, called Umbra Singh of Kandahar, was imported to Hobart by Mrs Pedder and had arrived by car from Launceston on the day that Benjamin was discovered dead. "This was the breed favoured by Noah and taken into the Ark with him," wrote "Kennel" in a paean to Umbra's "extraordinary feet" and blue blood. "He has bluer blood in his veins than any other breed in the world and his pedigree traces back to centuries before the Christian era."

September 7 is now National Threatened Species Day.

One of the leading exporters of the Tasmanian tiger to foreign zoos was Errol Flynn's father. In October 1914, Professor Thomas Flynn visited Maria Island and proposed that a thylacine sanctuary be established there. It was finally acquired for this purpose by the Fauna (Animals & Birds Protection) Board in 1966. At the time of writing, Maria Island is still designated to become that reserve should any elusive thylacines be captured alive. But innumerable sightings since 1936 have not been followed by a live, even a dead body of the species. "The overwhelming evidence is that the thylacine is extinct," says Nick Mooney. On September 7, 1986, it was officially declared so.

It is a sombre afternoon on which I visit Mooney, one of Tasmania's most experienced Parks and Wildlife officers. A colleague has drowned, swept into the Southern Ocean from a rock off Tasmania's south-east coast where he was studying the endangered Pedra Blanca skink, a charcoal grey lizard four inches long and not found anywhere else. Mooney knows the rock well: he was stuck there once in bad weather. Running out of food, he had to frighten the gannets into regurgitating mackerel, which he then swallowed.

Mooney is a lean, energising figure who for more than 20 years has been the officer responsible for assessing thylacine evidence. In 1982, Mooney investigated "one of the best sightings on record", by another of his colleagues, Hans Naarding. The ranger had gone to sleep in the back of his car in a remote forested area near Togari in the north-west. "It was raining heavily," Naarding wrote. "At 2.00 a.m. I awoke and out of habit scanned the surrounds with a spotlight. As I swept the light-beam around, it came to rest on a large thylacine, standing side on some six to seven metres distant. My camera bag was out of immediate reach so I decided to examine the animal carefully before risking movement. It was an adult male in excellent condition with 12 black stripes on a sandy coat. Eye reflection was pale yellow. It moved only once, opening its jaw and showing its teeth. After several minutes of observation, I attempted to reach my camera bag, but in doing so I disturbed the animal and it moved away into the undergrowth." Naarding left his car and walked to where the animal had disappeared. There was a strong scent.

The sighting was kept secret for two years while Mooney searched 150 square miles. He pegged out road-killed wallabies south of Smithton. He planted automatic cameras in mud pits along the Arthur River. He made plaster of Paris casts of tracks and collected animal faeces that he subjected to high performance liquid chromatography. He was full of hope. The "wilderness" near Togari might not have been a traditional habitat for thylacines, which preferred eucalyptus forests and coastal plains, but unexpected patterns of behaviour emerged sometimes when the equilibrium of a species was disrupted by clear-felling and settlement. Naarding had seen his thylacine in March, the start of the breeding season. Perhaps it had been travelling in search of a mate. "I prefer to throw frustrations aside and be optimistic that more of us will see this mysterious and beautiful creature," Mooney wrote in 1984.

Twenty years on, Mooney is less certain that Naarding saw a thylacine. "Hans Naarding is as close as you're going to get – one of your own mates, a very reliable, extremely experienced Wild Life officer. But one could also add that he knew exactly what he should see, where, when, how."

Nothing would excite the biologist more than to discover a healthy specimen alive: "The only thing that has kept me in Tasmania is that off-chance." Mooney has no truck with scientists who seek to clone it. "'Clown it', we call it. I would argue it's quite irresponsible. It's teaching people 'extinct' is not for ever. The same technology should be applied to preventing extinction."

Mooney's experience of following up thylacine sightings over two decades has inevitably left him jaded. "With every sighting there are four options. *Did* they see one? Was it a mistake? Did they have a vision? Are they lying?"

In a place where people seldom keep secrets, a surprising number of people will promise you that if they saw a Tasmanian tiger they would not tell a soul. While Tasmania has no shortage of people who believe that they *have* seen a thylacine, fear of ridicule or a wish to prevent a media feeding frenzy encourages most of them to keep the sighting to themselves. Others have contacted Mooney and are disappointed that he has not seemed to take their claim seriously. They say he is sitting on the information.

Buck and Joan Emberg are retired university teachers. Joan is the grand-daughter of a Hamburg stowaway who jumped ship at Strahan and ended up in Queenstown managing the F.O. Henry store. Buck came to Tasmania in 1971 from North Minnesota for some adventure and to avoid conscription to Vietnam.

"We were the first who really went public," Buck says.

Late one evening in the spring of 1978, they were driving home from Launceston. It was wet, Buck says, but not raining. "I was travelling at 75 kilometres an hour when at about 11 p.m., two kilometres west of Lilydale, there in the lights stood a mother thylacine and baby thylacine right next to the road. We caught both of them full side on and knew immediately. The very big head, the stance – like a kangaroo on all fours – the stiff tail and the stripes. I braked and missed them and as I pulled in I said to Joan: 'Don't say anything until you've thought this through, but are you sure of what we just saw?' She paused for 15 seconds. 'I just saw two tigers.' 'That's what I saw,' I said. We turned around, hoping. But they had moved off."

Until that moment, Buck had accepted that the thylacine was extinct. What he encountered on the road to Lilydale changed his life. "I'm considered to be this crazy person. I won't go into a bar. I've been run off the road twice. They even used my name illegally in a website to say bad things about the Green Party."

Next day, he telephoned friends. They laughed at him. He began to interview other people known to have sighted the thylacine in the same area. Quite soon, he had gathered 30 witnesses. One was an electrician who had caught a Tasmanian tiger in his gun-sights before realising what it was. Another was a Welsh woman who had trained with the police. A third was a local photographer who came to be known as the Tiger Man.

Buck showed me three black and white photographs that the Tiger Man had taken in 1995 of an animal's footprints in the mud. They were photographed within walking distance of Buck's house.

"These are the prints of the animal," he says.

I ask if I can fetch my camera. Buck says not. The Tiger Man does not wish his photographs to be seen and has put the negatives in a safe with a lawyer. But I may draw them if I like.

As I make a quick sketch, Buck tells me that almost everyone who reported what they saw was told to shut up and has been derided by his or her community. "Especially by the government, especially by Nick Mooney."

A year after the sighting in Lilydale, Buck was out walking when he came upon a giant scat. "It was bigger than anything I'd seen. Like a thick cigar twelve inches long and not twisted like devil scat." Buck put it in a plastic bag and took it to Mooney. "He looked at it and threw it in a drawer with other scats. 'Just a devil,' Mooney told me. 'We will not believe the animal exists until we catch it with the morning's *Examiner* in its mouth.' This," Buck says, "is what we're dealing with."

I drive with Buck and Joan to the other side of Lilydale, to where they saw their thylacines. In answer to the charge that no squashed tiger has been found on any road, Buck says that there are an estimated 250,000 feral cats in Tasmania and yet how many end up as road-kill? He talks about pandas in China that were rediscovered in an area of a mere 500 square miles. "Tasmania has 26,000 square miles." In *Thylacine*, Owen writes of other "extinct" animals that have come back. He cites the examples of the coelacanth, the golden hapalemur, the noisy scrub bird, the Vietnamese rhino and the giant sable antelope of Angola. Then there are the three Tasmanian emus, believed extinct for 25 years, seen on a beach at Emu Bay in October 1911.

At last we reach the place. There is a garage workshop opposite and cars speed by. The mother and puppy had stood at the entrance to a small, steep field in which there is a green-roofed bungalow. A notice on the gate warns of a guard dog.

"Do you regret having seen a Tasmanian tiger?"

Joan answers immediately. "No."

Buck goes on thinking. "No," he says at last. "I feel treasured and privileged to have seen it. It has altered my life in that I don't give a damn about what people feel and it has strengthened my resolve."

"In the face of ridicule, I might add," says Joan, who turns out to be blind in one eye. "*You* can handle the ridicule. Most Tasmanians can't."

In February 2001, Mooney received a photograph purporting to show a furry red animal streaking through a pine forest in northern Tasmania. His life has not been the same since.

I meet him at the Epping service station on the Midlands Highway where he is engaged in tracking down a predator whom he believes poses "the greatest risk to biodiversity in Tasmania and to Tasmanian mammals since the last Ice Age".

Better than most, Mooney is in a position to understand that Tasmania is an intensely fragile place. As the scientist seconded to the "Fox-free Tasmania" programme, Mooney is behind an effort to exterminate between five and ten red foxes that may have been smuggled across Bass Strait from Victoria, where foxes – introduced by the English to keep down rabbits – have made Australia, he says, "a world leader in mammalian extinction".

Mooney knows of at least one previous attempt to introduce foxes. "In the 1890s, an English army officer imported a pair to Hobart without permission, to breed up for release. The authorities heard about it and went at once to Anglesea barracks. They shot one in the grounds. The other ran up a culvert and was cornered." The story may have reached John Myers at his office in London Film Productions, because in one version of the biography that he concocted for Merle Oberon her putative father was fox-hunting in Tasmania when he suffered his fatal fall. Certainly, Anthony Trollope felt that he looked out over a country "well adapted for running a drag". Of the road from Hobart to Launceston, he remarked that "the English traveller would imagine that there was a fox covert on each side of him". Halfway to Launceston, Trollope passed through Campbell Town, where still stands the Foxhunter's Return: a grand, three-storey convict-built inn with Victorian hunting prints above the staircase – *Bolting the fox*, *Run to catch*, *Whoop*, *A sure find* – and, hung on a hook outside the office, a hunter's pink jacket made by a tailor in England. Here at the opposite end of the earth is enacted, once a year, a ritual lacking its crucial ingredient. Contemporary photographs in the hall show the riders of the Midlands Hunt Club assembled at a meet in March. Surrounded by a pack of excited hounds, they prepare to drag a dead kangaroo through the Campbell Town bush.

In the lounge of the Foxhunter's Return, the landlady shows me two 80-year-old fox pelts draped over a pair of red velvet chairs. She bought them in a garage sale. "That's Izzy and that's Rudolf," she says. "I reckon they're the only foxes in Tasmania."

Just then an old man enters who disputes this. He says that he saw a fox a year ago, halfway from here to Ross. "It was just off the road, heading for the sandstone quarry. That colour," and he taps Izzy's fur. "I said 'Look!' to the missus. 'Look bloody there!'"

"Did you tell Parks and Wildlife?"

"I'm not that silly. They harass you." He says: "If you rang to say you'd seen a Tasmanian tiger, they'd say 'Don't be stupid.' If you rang to say you'd seen a fox, in five minutes you'd have ten men here with special dogs – and next day, 20."

Mooney is unrepentant about his response to fox sightings. He calculates that 70 species in Tasmania would come under pressure if a fox population established itself, including the eastern quoll, the bettong, the barred bandicoot and the small native kangaroo known as the pademelon. He is concerned that not enough people are taking his alarm-call seriously and that many in authority, including the Premier, do not even believe that such a threat exists. "Once we've got proof of foxes breeding, we're screwed."

He walks me through an area of bush where 60 baits impregnated with "1080" poison were buried recently, stopping occasionally to check footprints.

Of 25,000 baits laid in a $2.4 million programme (compared to a budget of $200 allocated to investigate thylacine sightings), ten have showed signs of being dug up by foxes.

"Have you caught one yet?"

"No," Mooney says, with frustration. "They'd have to be in my office for me to catch one."

His twelve-man team have found fox scat with grooming hair in it as well as a set of pug-marks on a clay pan, and at least 20 fox baits have been taken in a style characteristic of foxes. But despite 600 sightings, they have yet to produce a body. To date [June, 2004], only two corpses have presented themselves: a 14-month fox with a partly digested endemic mouse in its stomach shot by a pensioner near Longford, and one road-killed near Burnie.

Mooney says: "Once foxes get below a certain density it's very difficult to find them."

I am still puzzling it out. "Here you are, trying to get rid of an introduced animal which you are convinced exists – even though you can't find it. And yet you don't believe in the existence of a native animal, which you dearly would love to find?"

Mooney stoops to check a footprint. He admits: "The difficulty of finding foxes has made me re-question the thylacine a bit. It reminds me that we could have overlooked finding a thylacine."

The closest relative of the Tasmanian tiger is the Tasmanian devil, known by the Aborigines as Taraba, the Nasty One. In a legend recorded by Jackson

Cotton: "He would skulk around on very dark nights, silent as a ghost, attacking the very small, the very young and the very old."

When I first lived in Tasmania, I sometimes startled a pair of devils in my garden after dusk. They would pelt off in a black blur, leaving behind a hole chewed in the wire. In 2003, the wire remained unbitten. It turned out that the devil was suffering from an epidemic known as Devil Facial Tumour Disease, possibly related to the distemper that reduced the thylacine population in the first years of the twentieth century. Mooney's latest information was that about one-third of devils had succumbed to the epidemic across eastern Tasmania, but it had not yet reached the south or west of the state. Only adults developed the disease and they died within five months of showing symptoms. Diseased animals could breed, but one huge risk was foxes. "It's the best opportunity foxes will ever get for establishment."

I drive to the west coast where there is a friend of Mooney's who knows about devils.

On a farm south of Cape Grim, Geoff King ties a road-killed possum to the back of his pick-up and drags it through a scrub of boobyalla to leave a scent trail. It is 7.30 p.m. and in the evening light a young male wedge-tail eagle glides over the ti-trees on the hunt for a pademelon. "They can crush a skull, like that." King stiffens his hand into a talon.

He turns off the engine and we watch the eagle settle in the fork of a peppermint gum. The light in the sky is brilliant and intense. There is no haze or humidity and it produces in me a feeling I frequently experience in Tasmania, an absurd illusion that I can see an enormous distance, back almost to when this landscape was looked upon for the first time with human eyes.

I confess this to King. I am glad I do. He tells me that on his own property the last surviving Tasmanian Aborigines in the bush surrendered themselves to sealers in December 1842. They were a family of middle-aged parents and five sons, one of them the young William Lanne. King says laconically: "There's been a quiet noise in the landscape since 1842."

He restarts the engine and we drive on, dragging the dead possum behind us in the hope of enticing our prey.

King is surely the world's most enthusiastic "devil watcher". His fisherman's shack near the Arthur River is one of the few places where it is possible to observe Tasmanian devils feeding in the wild.

The Tasmanian devil or *Sarcophilus harrisii* is a nocturnal marsupial the size of a small bulldog and so elusive, says King, that the animal rarely appears in early records and journals. "It's unlikely the first settlers would have seen them. Devils would have announced themselves only by damage and noise." He reconstructs the scene: the glow of a campfire, the cooked wallaby remains thrown to the side, the black flash through the bush. At York Town, Colonel Paterson lamented the loss of 76 of his ducks to quolls and other animals. "Some say they have seen the *Devil*, but none as yet have been caught."

Tasmanian devils, once found on the mainland, are now restricted to Tasmania. King estimates that a population of circa 50 roams in a 12-mile radius of his property.

The shack lies a few hundred yards from the ocean. A south-westerly has blown up and the waves crash into an inlet of lethal-looking rocks. The biggest of them by far is Church Rock. It was named by Clement Lorymer who camped here with Jorgen Jorgenson in 1827. Another surveyor, Charles Sprent, left this description. "This is a wild, desolate looking coast. The sea has a hungry rattle about it as it roars on the beach. Savage rocks stick up in all directions and the surf goes flying over them. The vegetation is stunted and low . . . "

In the dying sun, King pegs out the possum carcass. A baby monitor and a lamp are attached to his pick-up's battery, and he switches them on. The light will not frighten the devils.

"Why are they called 'devils'?"

"Because of their scream."

Half an hour after sunset, I hear it on the baby monitor: a low-intensity growl growing to a banshee screech. To King, it sounds like an exhaust pipe dragging on bitumen.

"Here she comes."

If Tasmania has gained an image as a sort of Lost World/Jurassic Park, then part of the credit must be given to the artist Robert McKimson of Warner Brothers who adopted the Tasmanian devil for a character in one of his cartoons: a stylised dog on hind legs whose signature is to spin in a whirlwind and scamper here and there, devouring all in its path.

A whiskered face emerges from the tussock grass, attached to a large boxy head and a compact black body with a white streak across the chest. It belongs to a hungry female, who tears into the possum's intestine. Now and then she glances up, her nose glistening with blood.

"Let her get committed to the carcass," whispers King.

A 10-kilogram Tasmanian devil has the jaw strength of a dog four times its size, which explains why this scavenger approaches all it meets with an open mouth. According to King, devils can eat 40% of their body weight at one sitting. "They fill up like you've never felt on Christmas Day."

I ask what is apparently the most commonly asked question. "Do they eat everything?"

"Everything," nods King. "Big bones, offal, fur."

Just occasionally the lower jaw of a pademelon is left intact. Otherwise devil scat has been found to contain echidna quills, bottle tops, cigarette ends. Strong acids in their stomach as well as a bone-dissolving enzyme help to break down this hotchpotch.

Another screech. Suddenly, the animal freezes. We have not made a sound, but she can hear up to distance of a mile and smell up to five. Her ears give a nervous twitch.

The Tasmanian devil has no natural predator. And yet within the cast of living memory it competed for protein with its larger marsupial cousin. I read in the *Mercury* of June 21, 2002, that a Tasmanian tiger was spotted north of King's shack, not far from where William Lanne grew up. "The tiger was no further than five metres away," reported the witness who saw it for ten seconds. "It just stopped and stared."

I ask King: "Do *you* think Tasmanian tigers still exist?"

He considers the black shape still frozen in the lamplight and says carefully: "If the Tasmanian tiger exists, it's in the mind of the Tasmanian devil who doesn't know that the thylacine is extinct."

The potter moves slowly through his small bright drawing room overlooking Hobart. Yes, he saw Benjamin alive. Edward Carr Shaw, a cousin of George Bernard Shaw and great-grandson of the magistrate at Swansea, was a pupil at Hutchins School in 1930. "We used to walk down to Beaumaris Zoo at weekends," he says. "The tiger was in a little cage half the size of this room. It used to wander backwards and forwards, backwards and forwards. It was the last one."

It was in the quixotic hope of finding a thylacine in the wild that the state's best-known public figure came to Tasmania. In 1972, Bob Brown, a policeman's son from New South Wales, accepted a six-month locum post as a GP in Launceston. On the ferry, as he arrived, he looked out and saw the Western Tiers and headed straight for them. His reaction to the crags and lakes and the pencil-pine forests is typical of the attachment felt by most of the 8,700 bush-walkers who hike the Overland Trail each year.

Next day, he sent a postcard to his parents in Coffs Harbour. "I am home," he wrote.

With two others, Brown started the Tasmanian Tiger Research Centre and for eight months spent his weekends in "chook sheds" in north-east

Tasmania, monitoring a network of wired boxes. Each box was fitted with
a live chicken and a camera bought from an RAAF disposal store, a little
Kodak flash camera with a fishing-line trip. "We had stacks of pictures:
devils, wombats, wallabies, everything you could think of – except the
tiger." He also checked out 200 tiger sightings dating back to 1936. "I
accounted for all but four." Most were dogs.

Brown had hoped to emulate the medical doctor in New Zealand who
in 1948 went walking in the Murchison Mountains and heard calls and
rediscovered a family of takahe, a bird similar to a turkey. But with each
passing weekend he grew more sceptical. He had spent his formative years
in Bathurst, where he had come across the Black Panther of Emmaville,
presumed to be a giant marsupial cat. Sir Edward Hallstrom had offered
£1,000 for anyone who caught it. A man claiming to have observed it
some weeks earlier led Brown to a patch of grass where the panther lay
partially concealed. "I went slowly along the fence with a pair of small
binoculars, and it got up, grunted a number of times and ran off. I got
the shock of my life." The panther was a wild pig.

He says: "I wanted to believe – though the pig had planted doubts.
There is nothing in life I wanted to be more wrong about than the
thylacine."

One summer night Brown was driving home when, a mile from his
house in Launceston, at the end of Vermont Street, he saw – five yards
away – a large animal trotting: a kangaroo tail, buff-coloured and with four
large stripes across its backside. "And guess what? It was a greyhound. A
mutant greyhound. But it brought home to me that a thylacine was even
less likely to find than a mutant greyhound."

Brown never has found the tiger, but on a two-week rafting trip down
the Franklin River he discovered his vocation. He saw platypus, marvellous gorges, astonishing side caverns, rapids thundering, Huon pine – some
of them thousands of years old – the occasional eagle floating overhead,
"and nobody".

And then as he came round the bend into the majestic Gordon, there
they were: jackhammers, helicopters, barges. In 1972, Tasmania's Hydro-
Electric Commission had submerged Lake Pedder and its halo of pinkish
sand. Now the Commission was preparing covertly to flood the Franklin,
one of the last wild rivers in the world but regarded by the Liberal Premier
Robin Gray as "a ditch, leech-ridden, unattractive to the majority of
people". Early convicts like Robert Greenhill and Alexander Pearce had a
similar perception of the rainforest, and it had reduced them to cannibals:
to Brown, the Franklin was an invigorating paradise, and he felt that he

had been placed on earth to protect it from the fate suffered by the thylacine.

Brown translated his love affair with the Franklin into a campaign of public awareness that gathered up behind him the passions of other people wedded to the place. For the novelist James McQueen, the Franklin was not just a river. "For me it is the epitome of all the lost forests, all the submerged lakes, all the tamed rivers, all the extinguished species. It is threatened by the same mindless beast that has eaten our past, is eating our present, and threatens to eat our future: that civil beast of mean ambitions and broken promises and hedged bets and tawdry profits." Brown's success in saving the river led to many people hearing of Tasmania and made tangible the word "wilderness". Today, 39% of the island (1.74 million hectares) is a World Heritage Area, and Brown is a federal senator for the Greens, a party that in Tasmania in the 2002 general election polled 18% – the largest Green vote, according to Brown, recorded in any general election anywhere in the world.

In his office, which overlooks the Derwent River, Brown describes Tasmania as "this special little crucible". But his crucible is not as protected as he would like. He shows me a photograph of himself standing at the base of a huge charred eucalyptus, dubbed El Grande by the press. He tells the tree's story. At 439 cubic metres, this 300-year-old *Eucalypt regnans* in the Styx Forest, 50 miles west of Hobart, was the largest tree in Australia. And yet not long ago Forestry Tasmania accidentally burned it in a regeneration programme.

Brown takes the scorched eucalyptus as the symbol of a culture that risks devouring itself. Thirty years on, he has shifted his ire from Hydro-Electric to Forestry Tasmania, whose logging of old growth forests he sees as the sure destruction of Tasmania's habitat, just as Nick Mooney sees the fox.

Everyone in Tasmania has tales of being caught behind a logging truck. On my way to speak to Brown, I have passed 23 trucks – each loaded with between a dozen and 20 trees, and one or two emblazoned with "Doze a Greenie" stickers.

"This year," says Brown, "150,000 trucks will take 30 tons of logs every morning, every noon and every night to the woodchip mills for paper which will be used by Japan and Korea and end up in the rubbish dumps of the northern hemisphere."

For Brown, old-growth logging is Tasmania's modern "stain". In a vote taken in 2001, 67% of the island's population supported his call to stop it. They included the novelist Richard Flanagan: "Without an end to clear-felling, our old-growth forests will share the fate of the Tasmanian tiger: a lost object of awe, one more symbol of our feckless ignorance and stupidity." Brown says: "We're destroying the biggest carbon bank in the southern hemisphere with these grand trees, and with them the best hedge against global warming. If, in a rich and democratic society like Tasmania, we can't turn the log-trucks back and get this place to be a centre of natural beauty for a world that is being rapidly depleted, who can? How can we ask Brazil, Cameroon, Korea? If we can do it here, then we can then bring optimism to people working under much more difficult circumstances."

It has taken 30 years, but Brown senses that he is winning his argument that Tasmania's worldwide fame and fortune is its wilderness. In 1982, while leading a blockade to prevent the flooding of the Franklin, he was arrested south of Strahan, not far from Sarah Island, and spent three weeks in a cell. "Today, I wear a smile when I think of Strahan," he tells me, saying goodbye outside his office. "One hundred and forty thousand people a year coming to see that wilderness, those rivers."

III

Oyster Bay

"Old man, I've one particular spot in mind not far from here: a coral reef and white sand, real white sand that you could build castles with, and behind are green slopes as smooth as real turf and God-made natural hazards – a perfect spot for a golf-course . . ."

Graham Greene, *The Comedians*

ONE MORNING AFTER A STORM I TOOK MAX ONTO NINE MILE BEACH TO PICK up shells.

A Pacific gull watched us, neck tucked into chest, and a steady line of breakers threw up brogues of bull-kelp polished to a military shine.

The south-easterly had rolled Jimmy's ancient cowrie onto the shore in front of our house. Already in the three years that we had lived here the sea had washed up a whale, a six-foot sun fish and a giant squid. Plus various skeletons that we could not put a definition to. The French explorer Nicolas Baudin was conscious that his countrymen back home "will have difficulty in believing that the sea can contain living animals with a form as strange and extraordinary as those we have met". At Lisdillon further along the bay, Sarah Mitchell found a strange sea-creature which she sent to the Hobart museum. The sea-mouse – the first to be discovered – was named after her: *Sarahi mitchelli*. No wind had ever exposed the decapitated body of one of Michael Howe's banditti, George (Bumpy) Jones, who on August 3, 1817 was shot in the head (reward: 80 guineas) and buried in the sand where he fell after the sergeant followed his footprints to their end.

Max points at a solitary black swan in the bay. I wish it would turn around and stop heading into the wind. "When you see a swan in the water like that," a friend who lives on Kelvedon beach told me, "it probably means that someone has shot the female. They're monogamous. They get fretful after seeing their mate die. He'll just exhaust himself now and you'll find him on the beach tomorrow."

My son and I had once found a dying black swan. It must have been heading for Moulting Lagoon, but was beyond fear or care when we picked it up out of the water. We laid it on the wet sand. Its orange eye looked at us unblinking and then at the crows on a gum tree that had assembled to peck it out once we were gone. The story of the black swan was the most beautiful of the legends that Tapte, chief of the lagoon people, passed on to Timler before his death in 1820. He told of how Mitaweena the whale became stranded in the shallows behind our house and how, as his heavy body crushed down, he blew spurts of black mud into the air from his blowhole. "In his last struggles the muddy jets flew higher and higher until reaching the rarer atmosphere, they turned into great black birds wheeling and trumpeting above the body of their dying creator. They were as black as the mud from Mitaweena's grave and their eyes and beaks were blood red from the bursting lungs of the great whale. Their wings were tipped by the clouds as they soared high above his last resting place in a sad salute of farewell. And this was the coming of Pickerdas the black swan."

Off this selfsame beach in 1942 in March a Japanese submarine launched its own strange bird.

"This area was not too beautiful," complained Admiral Tatsuo Takudo. "There were high cliffs of orange-coloured rock and no trees." Two hours before dawn on March 1, his gigantic submarine surfaced in Oyster Bay on a voyage to reconnoitre the ports of Sydney, Melbourne and Hobart. Under a bomber's moon, his crew assembled a collapsible float-plane while the 2,900 ton submarine drifted, engines turning, alert for any sign of life from Swansea. The pilot who strapped himself into the cockpit was Warrant Flying Officer Nobua Fujita, who claimed to be the first man to drop bombs from a plane on the United States. Fujita took off south and when he reached Hobart he pushed back the canopy to get a clear view of the Derwent. He noted the glow of a furnace, the barn-like shape of Mount Wellington, a white concrete road and five cargo ships at anchor. Then with the slipstream tugging at his helmet, he flew back to Oyster Bay, landing as the sun rose. A ship had been detected on the horizon and his plane was speedily dismantled, but the wind had started to come up, and the tips of one of the wings smashed against a derrick, snapping the plywood ribs.

If one believed the *Mercury*, an aircraft even stranger than Fujita's passed above our house on a clear afternoon in March 2003. I got in touch with the witness who reported it, Bruce Sullivan, and he confirmed that he had been fishing with his girlfriend on Coswell beach, south of Swansea, when a flash startled him. "What we saw was nothing more than a silver ball-shaped object keeping the same height and speed 500 metres above the sea." This "thing" crossed the bay, travelling south to north, and then evaporated into the air over Nine Mile Beach. "It was travelling fast in a straight line, no sound or lights, clear as the nose on your face." Then, Bruce said, it reappeared quite close to where our house was, "moved right and left, up and down, and disappeared". A few locals had made jibes, but "the UFO people" took it seriously. "They came with a form to fill out and it was printed in the newspaper."

"Could it have been a raft of mutton-birds?" I asked.

My friend Michael who lived on Kelvedon beach liked to watch the young mutton-birds gather in a dense elliptical flock before they flew to the Bering Straits. "They look like a swarm of fish," he told me, "except just above the water." I suggested to Bruce that the sight of so many chicks trying out their wings might have had the shape of a flying saucer, but Bruce had worked on crayfish boats around King and Flinders. "It wasn't a raft of mutton-birds, no way."

On calm days Nine Mile Beach is one of the cleanest beaches in the world: no dead birds, no cans, no plastic bags, no tar, no people. Just the three peaks known as the Hazards leading into Mount Freycinet and the sea stretching for 1,200 miles to Antarctica.

In 1642, Tasman marked down the ten-mile spit of land as three islands. It was in trying to prove him wrong 160 years later that Nicolas Baudin lost the race to map the south coast of Australia. On March 6, 1802, he lowered a small boat containing Charles-Pierre Boullanger, his short-sighted hydrographer (he could only take his bearings "with his nose on the ground", Baudin complained). That night a briny northerly carried Boullanger away and Baudin spent a crucial two months scouring for him although an English brig had picked him up three days later. The delay very probably cost the French Tasmania. Instead, it was Captain Ebor Bunker on the *Albion,* on his way to set up the first European settlement in the Derwent, who sailed into Oyster Bay in early September 1803. He was so excited by the number of sperm whales in the water that he interrupted his important mission to capture three. His expertise with the harpoon gave rise to the whaler's cry: "Lay me on, Captain Bunker! I'm hell on a long dart!"

Bunker, sadly, left no description of Oyster Bay, but this is how the view from the beach struck one of Baudin's crew: "two chains of lofty mountains

of parallel direction embracing the whole shore and giving it the appearance of a beautiful valley invaded by waves". Jorgen Jorgenson, pausing to
take in the prospect from what is now the Lake Leake highway, gave his less
than level-headed opinion that after travelling the world as he had, and after
seeing its many splendid sights, this was a view "impossible for the most
luxuriant imagination to conceive more lovely within the whole circle of
the creation". F.J. Cockburn remarked in June 1855: "The scene was inde-
scribably beautiful . . . A glorious broad yellow beach runs round the top of
the bay to the Schoutens and from this beach the view is magnificent. On
your right you see the long line of the mainland for many miles, fringed
with trees, houses and fields, behind which the hills rise; looking down the
bay you see the cliffs and peaks of Maria Island rising darkly from the sea,
and to the left of Maria Island you can look straight away to the wide ocean,
with nothing to intercept the sight but a solitary white and distant rock,
called by the French voyagers the Isle of Seals . . . I could not have had five
pleasanter days anywhere."

And we were now in our third year on the beach.

On the Beach. I must have remembered Nevil Shute's novel when, in 1999,
at the end of our trek in the Central Highlands I saw a house for sale on
a shelf of coastal dunes. It was a single-storey building made from Canadian
cedar and glass, and through the glass I could see a rock.

I was 42. But nothing in Europe or South America or Africa had prepared
me for the vision of the Freycinet Peninsula on that March morning, or
the dense colour of its granite: smoky and compact like a watercolour
pigment. I knew that I was gazing at the most beautiful place I had seen
on earth, a conviction that all subsequent experience has served to deepen.

We knocked at the door. Helen, a middle-aged woman in a lavender
sarong, told us she had built the house with her husband, a retired radio
executive who was now ill and needed to be nearer to a hospital. She
was an artist and photographer – the house was hung with her vast red
moodscapes – and as she led us on an impromptu tour of the room, she
chattered about "destiny" and "serendipitous unions".

Inside the house, the glass seemed to intensify the sunlight. Strangely
suspended by the light, I followed Helen into "the solarium" and "the
veranda café" and then through clumps of boobyalla to the deserted beach
and a small clearing in the spinifex where, she said, she liked to sunbathe
naked. There was a fenced-off garden below the house, planted with apple
and peach trees, and a tin shed where I pictured myself at a desk. Less
than an hour later, we were bidding her an emotional farewell.

We had no family connections, no friends, no reason to linger, but I could not stop thinking of the view from the window out to the peninsula. By the time we arrived at our bed and breakfast that evening on the road to Hobart, we were seriously considering the possibility of the house – and Tasmania – becoming a destination as well as an escape.

There was a message at the convict-built bed and breakfast from Helen. She just wanted to say that she saw herself in us and how rare it was to feel such a connection to strangers and that there were no accidents in life. Oh, and incidentally, did we like the house?

We went home to England and began immediately to plot our return. I phoned Helen and proposed that we take a six-month lease. Whether impressed by our karmic connection or by a want of other offers, she agreed. At the end of six months we would make a decision to buy or not.

In the last fortnight of our lease, my father flew to Tasmania with the express purpose of persuading us not to sink our savings into a beach house at the end of the world. On the morning after his arrival, I came upon him standing barefoot on the strand. His eyes were nailed to the horizon and I could have sworn that there were tears in them.

"I. Have. Never. Been. Anywhere. More. Beautiful."

We telephoned Helen. We would buy the house.

For drama nothing touched the little thumbnail of porcelain which Max found on Nine Mile Beach that morning. We were walking along, a pair of hooded plovers tripping ahead of us and Max tracking their tiny convict arrowheads in the sand – when he spotted something. Not a shell, but a fragment of blue and white china worn to soapy smoothness.

He turned it over, uncertain what to do with it.

The willow-pattern had spilled from a shipwreck – but which one? In our local History Room at Swansea, I discovered that Kemp's son-in-law Lieutenant Wharton Thomas Young had drowned here in July 1837. Already married two years to Kemp's daughter Amy (described in his obituary as "a most amiable and accomplished lady"), Young was rowing across the bay when he "foolishly interfered with the cockswain". The boat filled with water – and righted herself. Young, an excellent swimmer, was clambering into her when "a second sea washed him out again and he was not seen afterwards". Days later his body rolled onto the beach. "The melancholy bereavement is much felt by Mr Kemp and his family and more particularly by the young widow who has been thus suddenly deprived of a husband by whom she was most fondly regarded."

Wharton was not Kemp's only son-in-law to drown. In 1854, Samuel

Barrow, a magistrate married to his daughter Margaret Louisa, and known as The Christ Killer by convicts on Norfolk Island, was stepping ashore in Port Philip Bay when an ex-convict recognised him – and pushed Barrow into the rough sea. Published in 1850, *Medical Hints for Emigrants* commented: "Accidents of this kind are very common in all the colonies."

In November of the same year, the *Resolution*, a 49-ton smack, 45 feet long, sank off Waterloo Point. Everyone told me that the fragment of willow-pattern most likely had seeped from her cargo.

The story of the *Resolution* was known to Thomas Arnold, who rode along this shoreline a few months before she sailed from Hobart.

In March 1850, Arnold had proposed to Kemp's granddaughter, Julia. He had never been happier. She had written to him: "I am afraid it is useless attempting to keep our secret. It is being generally believed that we are engaged." Arnold had replied: "So it is well known, well, be it so; we are neither of us, I hope, ashamed of what we have done."

In Swansea, Arnold inspected the local school. Among those hoping to enrol their children in November that year was Thomas Large, a Somerset brewer who was in the process of setting up a brewery at Schouten House. Come spring, Large intended to charter a boat and fetch his family from Hobart. Arnold entered the names of Large's children, mounted his horse Harry and, impatient to return to Julia, set off home. And yet the view from the cliffs was so arresting that at one point he had to rein in Harry to gaze at Maria Island. "The blue boundless ocean was before me, stirred here and there into white horses glittering in the sun by a fresh breeze."

But that breeze could be lethal, and when it blew from the south-east it turned into Tasmania's nastiest wind. Not a gusty wind, but a consistent strong wind that stayed five days and was ugly and rainy and washed boats off their anchorages.

Early in November 1850, Large, his wife Mary and their six children, ranging in ages from twelve to two, left Hobart on the *Resolution*. The cutter had already capsized in the Tamar six years before, causing the death of one passenger. She now ran into a thunderous south-easterly.

The storm was felt throughout the whole island. Lightning killed a boy on a horse, toppled chimneys and "struck with the electric fluid" a girl sewing a shirt. But nothing matched the viciousness of its impact on Swansea.

On the night of Sunday, November 3, the *Resolution* arrived off Waterloo Point and by 11 p.m. had managed to drop anchor. As day broke, Quested, the ship's owner, told Large to prepare his family to disembark. His wife and children assembled on deck, dressed and ready for the sailors to carry them ashore. A crewman measured the water's depth with an oar: only three feet. But with the heavy sea and the wind blowing they decided to wait another hour. The wind blew harder, the rough surf making the children ill. A second anchor was lowered to prevent the ship dragging. Finally, Mrs Large said: "The children are untidy. Wait until morning."

They lay, fully clothed, in their bunks listening to the wind howl and the ship straining at her chains. At 12.50 a.m., Large got up to check that his children were all right. He had returned to bed when he heard the rudder grating on the bottom – then a roar. Water was gushing into the ship. He yelled to Quested, but getting no answer ran up on deck where a sailor told him the vessel had sprung a leak in the stern and there was no pump that could save her. Minutes later one of the anchor chains snapped and the *Resolution* ran onto the shore.

Thomas Large bustled Mary, their children and his servant John Drinkwater up to the bow and wrapped them with blankets, but the vessel was tilting to one side and the sea washing over the decks with such force "that the blankets were swept away and we were obliged to hold the children. It was then breaking daylight."

Large remembered with bitterness to the end of his life how none of the four sailors made any attempt to lash any of his children to the ship, nor offer to piggyback them ashore – even though the beach was only 50 yards away. "Each person was trying to save himself in confusion and danger."

All this time the wind was increasing and the sea "coming more over". One sailor swam to the beach with a rope but failed to find anything to which he could tie it. Two sailors launched a dinghy that smashed against the hull. They continued swimming until their legs touched sand. The owner's behaviour was the most shocking. He had retreated to the bow. "Mr Quested though called upon both by myself and wife to assist in holding the children he did not offer to do so. After sitting there for some time he left the vessel and I believe swam to the shore."

Soon all the crew had abandoned ship except the cook, "who could hardly keep himself up", and Joseph Stanley, the old captain of the *Resolution*, who thrust his foot against the windlass "and after much persuasion did lay hold of one of the children".

Large and his wife took care of the two youngest. His servant Drinkwater looked after the remaining three. Drinkwater told the inquest: "I held the three children in my arms as long as I could and as long as they were alive . . . I had the eldest boy, the eldest girl and I don't know which of the other children it was I had."

But the storm was greater than ever. Large remembered: "The vessel all this time kept turning on her side more and more and the sea washing right over us, the children then became very weak and we kept hold of them as long as we could with one hand being obliged to hold on ourselves with the other, until the sea washed them away from the different persons who had hold of them."

Drinkwater said: "I saw the old man they call the sailing master of the vessel with one child in his arms. It died in his arms alongside of me. I also saw the mother of the children with a child in her arms. I saw Mr Quested the master of the vessel in the bowsprit of the vessel, he had not a child in his arms." He believed: "The children perished by the sea breaking upon them and I am sure they were dead before I parted with them . . . I then found it necessary to use all my strength to hold on myself."

Stanley agreed that "the fury of the sea" had caused the death of the little girl he was trying to protect. "She perished in my arms and I held her for ten minutes after she was dead."

Next to him, Large also had one of his children expire in his arms. "The one I had was quite lifeless some time before it was washed away."

He looked through the wind and spray. A crowd had assembled on the beach. Desperate, he thought that if he could swim ashore he would be able to get hold of a boat to save his wife. "I jumped into the water."

Four days later, Joseph Stanley recalled the events of that morning at the inquest in the Swansea Hotel: "I have been nearly 50 years at sea and I never experienced worse weather for the time it lasted nor saw a vessel and people in a more dangerous position." Among those who watched helpless from the shoreline was Swansea's magistrate Edward Carr Shaw, an uncle of the playwright George Bernard Shaw.* He became so distressed at the sight of the family clinging to the wreck that he shouted: "A free pardon to any one who would take a line out." Responding to a promise that Shaw had no authority to make, a ticket-of-leave man plunged into the sea – and was washed back three times. Meanwhile, Captain Lyons had fetched a four-oared whaleboat on a cart and he ordered six convicts to row out and rescue Mrs Large, who now had been hanging on to the rigging for twelve hours. The boat was only a short way out when the breakers swamped it. The men refused to go a second time. As Shaw's grandson told it: "The captain then went in the bush and got a big stick called a waddie and told the men to man the boat again and the first one

---

* GBS said of him that Edward was his favourite uncle as he never met him.

that refused he would knock his brains out, so they made another start, and reached the wreck and rescued the mother."

Mrs Large was carried by cart to George Meredith's house, Cambria. She travelled beside her unconscious husband. When Large came to, he said: "My poor children."

The next day Drinkwater found bobbing in the waves the body of one of the boys he had held on deck. The corpse was "much mutilated", according to the doctor who examined it, but from their appearance the wounds had been inflicted "after life had become extinct" and were caused by the body "being jammed between parts of the wreck or driven against any hard substance". One by one the other bodies turned up on Nine Mile Beach, all except one.

They were laid out for Large to identify in the Swansea Hotel. "I have seen the dead bodies of five of my children lying in the adjoining room to this in which I now am and I have recognised them, their names are as follows, Elizabeth Large, my eldest daughter [12], Edmund James Large, my eldest son [10], Hannah Large, my second daughter [6], George Large, my third son [4] and Frances Mary Large my youngest child [2]. My second son William's body [8] I have not seen, I believe it has not yet been found."

After recovering at Meredith's house, he and his wife left Swansea. A memorial in the north-west corner of the graveyard overlooks the bay in which their children drowned. Painted white and covered with seashells, it has this inscription:

> *Weep not for us but be content*
> *We was not yours but only lent*
> *Wipe of [sic] those tears and weep no more*
> *We are not lost but gone before*
> *We was not yours but Christ's alone*
> *He loved us best and called us home.*

But the story did not end there. More than six decades later, in April 1918, an old lady walked into the cemetery, looking for the memorial. Clara Travers had waited all her life to visit the beach where her siblings had drowned. She had been born to Thomas and Mary Large in November 1851, one year after the shipwreck.

Clara wrote a diary of her visit:

"We soon found it. You could read all that was on it quite plainly. Tried to find someone to paint the stone next day but could not get anyone anywhere, then went along jetty and watched breakers coming in, it was a grand sight . . . An old couple pointed out where it happened and said it was visible at very low tides."

The grave was covered with grass and gorse bushes. Clara asked permission from the rector to tidy it up. He lent her a spade and her husband William cleaned the rubbish off and righted the headstone. "While he was doing that I went to the beach which is close by and gathered some shells and put them on the grave in the form of an anchor and pruned the hedges, it looked very nice when done."

"April 11 in afternoon. Went to see Mr Shaw. Only three when it happened, but could remember his grandfather talking about it." Shaw told them about the boat that had rescued her mother. "I don't know how father was saved but he was a splendid swimmer. They had been going to [Swansea] to open a brewery and they lost everything they had. Five of the children's bodies were washed on shore but one was never found . . . Returned to tea after spending a very sad day."

"April 13. Sat on beach till dinner time."

"April 14. Had dinner then went on the Nine Mile Beach to see if we could find the wreck but could see no signs of it. Walked about 5 miles there."

I expect she was told the stories. The woman who vowed always to keep a lighted candle in the window of Schouten House so that the children could find their way home. The servant girl who had woken, 40 years later, to see an angel with a golden candlestick standing at her bed. The wan light that sometimes appeared in the window "that even the gales of winter cannot extinguish". But Clara left Swansea before she could hear the most tantalising story, about her missing brother William – the eight-year-old whose body was never recovered.

I found it handwritten on a scrap of paper dated February 2, 1946. A memory recorded at Lisdillon by Sarah Mitchell, about her brother Edwin, who lived at Mayfield. "About 1920 a man came to him with a pack on his back and told him he was the boy that was saved in the sailor's arms, said he was going to see his brothers' and sisters' graves."

All that remains of the *Resolution* is a rusty anchor and the occasional scrap of brass or china plate that a storm tosses up.

I ask Max if he wants to keep his piece of blue and white willow-pattern, but he would rather play ducks and drakes. I send it skimming out, towards where the Freycinet Peninsula ends in a full stop in the Tasman

Sea. It bounces on the water – once, twice, a third time – and sinks back to its proper place among the rest of Large's possessions.

We walk back along our footprints that the sea has not washed away and not for the first time do I have the feeling that I am following the tracks of a strange backward-walking creature.

IV

Doubles

"How small the cosmos (a kangaroo's pouch wouldn't hold it)."
Vladimir Nabokov, *Speak, Memory*

Hello Chatwin Groopies. Can anyone help me with the Chatwin family tree? My grandfather was Alfred Chatwin, born in Eng. around 1836–38. Joined a ship's crew and sailed to Australia as a young man, and jumped ship in Tasmania. Any info. Thank You, Lindsay.

Message on the Internet

I

THE OLD MAN WAS ALSO CALLED MAX. HE WAS 77, HAD THE SAME WIDE forehead and piercing eyes as his namesake, and was six foot tall. But a midget compared to his brothers. "Our family are *big*," he said.

"What else can you tell me about them?" I asked.

"My father was a good sample of a Chatwin: he could turn his hand to anything, mend boots, cut firewood, make fences. He'd love to be out in the bush. Another thing Chatwins seem to like were bees. Quite a few were bee-keepers. My father had 70 hives."

"Anything else?"

He laughed: "Most of them lost their hair early in life. But you should speak to my wife. She's written a book about them."

When I first came to Tasmania I had just finished writing a long biography, seven years' work on one man, the writer and traveller Bruce Chatwin, and I was burned out. One of the attractions of Tasmania was that Chatwin, who specialised in the remote, had never been there. The island would be *terra incognita*, unevoked by his writing or my research into his life. Tasmania's freshness – its wind and its light – might empty me of the biographer's condition: that dull abstraction brought on by many months in the shade of old documents.

That something is 200 years old does not make it interesting. My time in the archives had taught me the frustration of going through the letters of the dead. We want the dead to reveal to us what they did not reveal in life, some confessional strain they had kept hidden from the world. More often than not what we exhume are the random husks of their everyday lives: barely legible wishes for good health, hellos, how are you's, thank you's, numbing résumés of the day got through – and scattered among them faded receipts and photos without dates or names.

I was, at that period, sick of a life already lived. I hoped never to read another old letter again. I had planned to stay a week.

But in coming to Tasmania to get as far away as I could from where I knew – and in particular from Chatwin – I found a house and a story that was my own. Perhaps it was inevitable that I should also discover, five miles from North Motton, in the village of Kindred, so called because everyone was related, an entire hamlet of Chatwins.

I could not arrest my need to make patterns whatever banalities it turned up, and I contacted the head of the family. Max Chatwin was one of 37 Chatwins listed in the directory for north-west Tasmania. He told me that they descended from his grandfather Alfred, a prophet-bearded, manic-eyed Yorkshireman who ran away to sea when he was 14 and jumped ship in

Victoria to join the Gold Rush. Not making his fortune, Alfred drifted across Bass Strait in 1857 and married a 19-year-old Norfolk girl, Elizabeth Pearmain, who drove a horse and buggy and was "handy with the whip". In 1862, they bought a farm in Swamp Road above Kindred where Alfred built a cottage with his own hands. They had 11 children and 114 grandchildren and were buried side by side in a white marble grave in Kindred, right next to the Lehmans.

Alfred's messianic face looked out from the cover of the thick book self-published by Max's wife. Entitled *Chatwin: 6 generations in Tasmania,* it was prefaced with a quote from Edmund Burke:

People will not look forward to posterity, who never look backward to their ancestors.

I knew as soon as I opened it that I would find Kemps. With the discovery that Myrtle Ilma Chatwin had married William Lott Clifford Kemp in 1903 I resolved – then and there – to stop rootling about in the family tree.

2

Among his family in England, Kemp was popularly reputed to have reached the age of 112. He lived, in fact, to 95, but his declining years were uneventful. Perhaps it is that after Potter washed his hands of him a certain fire had gone out of Kemp. Once Tasmania achieved self-government he found no further project to challenge his energies.

"It is impossible to epitomise this cranky, intolerant, courageous man, half-buccaneer, half-patriot, half-capitalist – the arithmetic seems appropriate." So Murray Kemp, one of his descendants, tried to assess a personality that was prone to bursting out of its seams. The level-headed George Boyes was aware of just how much Kemp's character had left its mark on Tasmania, to such an extent that colony and colonist at times appeared inseparable. In February 1845, Boyes encountered Kemp's son George. "He spoke of the state of Society here – apparently without being aware of the part some members of his family have been said to play in the proceedings."

Kemp saw himself as the Father of Tasmania, but Boyes considered him "a great Ass". One of the few anecdotes about Kemp as an old man was told by his seven-year-old granddaughter Louise.

"Lou?"

"Yes, Granddad, what is it?"

"Lou, Lou, come buckle my shoe."

"Oh, oh, grandfather."

Later.

"Lou?"

"Yes, Granddad?"

"Lou, Lou, come buckle my shoe."

Repeated several times.

"Lou!"

"I am not coming!"

"What a pity. I had a golden sovereign waiting to give to you but as you did not come you will not get it."

This sounded characteristic Kemp behaviour, but then I discovered that in his last days – as an invalid being pushed around Hobart – he was known as "Dollar Kemp", after his habit of dispensing coins to alarmed passers-by from his wheelchair.

Kemp died on October 28, 1868. He was buried in the Albuera Street Cemetery opposite The Bertrams, his town house in Hobart, and just down from where Bridie O'Reilly's bottle shop now is. In 1936, he was still within living memory, remembered by a man who called him "a Jewish type". In the late 1940s, the cemetery was concreted over and a primary school built in its place. I asked a teacher where his body was likely to be and she took me out into the playground and pointed at the base of a basketball hoop. "He's underneath us."

A class of ten-year-olds finished playing hopscotch over his bones and filed out beneath a large sign that Potter might have nailed above the courtyard for Kemp to contemplate:

Think . . . is it fair?

Is it safe?

Does it show respect?

Despite his 18 children, he has now no descendants called Kemp in Tasmania. Today, his first house in Hobart is occupied by Madame Korner's beauty college and a hearing-aid retailer. His gravestone has disappeared. Almost all that is left of him are some letters in a yellow plastic bag.

In the early 1930s, about the time that Merle Oberon was shedding her Indian skin and becoming a pure white Tasmanian, Kemp's great-great-grandson – Aldous Huxley's brother – was seeking to demonstrate that "there was no such thing as a 'pure race' anywhere in the world".

Julian Sorell Huxley planned *We Europeans* as a scientific spoke in Hitler's wheel and to expose the German leader's nonsensical rantings about "the dangers of contaminating the purity of the so-called Aryan race". Hitler's concepts of race were based on self-interest and wish-fulfilment, and they were dangerously wrong. (The word "Arya" was Sanskrit anyway, and used to distinguish the speakers of certain Indian languages.) In his counterblast to *Mein Kampf*, Huxley attacked the Nazis for their "vast pseudo-science of 'racial biology'", which had turned the Jews into a colonial people within Europe.

All humans were of mixed descent, Huxley wrote, and all great nations "melting pots of race", the results of the amalgamations of many tribes and of many waves of immigration. "Man's incurable and increasing propensity to wander over the face of the globe had effected a thorough mixing between the hypothetical primary sub-species long before the dawn of the historic period." Not even the Tasmanian Aborigines could be said to have been pure. "Even in its state of maximum isolation, such a group will certainly have contained many genes derived from other similar groups."

Huxley was particularly scathing about family trees cherished by genealogists like Ivy, in which a family was traced back to a single founder and their spouse. These trees had little to do with biological heredity: "They are social not genetic documents." The whole point was that "our ancestry will diverge as well as converge as we trace it back."

I do not doubt that if I had come to another place – shall we say Idaho? – I would have found exciting cousin upon cousin. The clearances that devastated Scotland, the famines and unemployment that devastated Ireland and Wales, gave life to New Zealand and Patagonia. Icelanders made their way to Brazil and Lake Winnipeg. New York and Buenos Aires and Sydney were ceaselessly reinvigorated by new arrivals from across the ocean, by Lebanese, Italians, Germans, Greeks, escaping potato blight, volcanic eruptions, the English. Or yielding to the mutton-bird instinct that Chatwin had understood – in his case it was an arctic tern – and that Huxley had characterised as: "Man's incurable and increasing propensity to wander over the face of the globe."

By coming to Tasmania, I had repeated the pattern of two hitherto undreamed-of relatives and the discovery pleased me in a profound and mysterious way. However tenuous, they linked me to this place. They reminded me that life was not a string of arbitrary events. That there were, if you like, no accidents.

3

I drove up a cul-de-sac and parked outside a red brick bungalow next to a church. I could tell by the front garden which was their house. Maud's White Ladies bloomed in pots along one wall, and the beds were bursting with tall phlox, tulips and daffodils. I was looking at *Wishing-Well Lane*.

I rang the two-tone organ bell and watched Ivy's shape grow towards me through a frosted glass door that had a stork engraved on it. I had missed by only a few moments a visit from one of her neighbours. The woman had popped in to say that Ivy's garden put them all to shame. "She had a husband she had to get back to. I told her, 'We don't have that problem.'"

Ivy unfastened the chain. As soon as I stepped inside, I recognised the ceramic plates, the dolls, the photographs of Petre Hordern and Boode.

She showed me over the house. It was spacious, with rooms leading off one another and three doors into the garden.

"What do you like most about it?"

"The chains," she smiled. "They make us feel secure."

The move from North Motton to Ulverstone had been painless. Eleven cousins had welcomed them with doughnuts and cakes, and Heather, her twin, had lent the sisters a mattress so that they would not have to sleep on the floor.

We went into the kitchen where Heather was talking to Maud, and Ivy introduced us.

A train went by, shaking the windows. Ivy pulled a face. She had been here six months, but after living in the country nearly 80 years she was still adjusting to town noises. She noticed that an ambulance nearly always drove by when she was having her tea in the afternoon. "So that must be a stressful time."

"Car doors banging, that's the worst thing," Maud said.

"What else is different?" I asked.

"You got a few more people looking at you," Ivy said. "Maudy won't go out in front to do the garden. She keeps to the back with her vegetables. You should see them. They're that big, her pumpkins."

In their first fortnight, Ivy and Maud had left their property only twice – to buy groceries. Since neither sister drove, Ivy had telephoned Mr Jones and he had taken them in his taxi to the supermarket two streets away. "We wouldn't get far without taxis! You meet a lot of people and you hear things."

"Really?"

"Mr Jones said to us: 'You ought to go somewhere.' We said, 'We don't dare – in case we like it.'"

They had been back twice to Boode. Ivy evidently disapproved of certain changes that her nephew was making, being especially taken aback by the gnomes. "It's *not* a gnome garden!"

But a surprise awaited her in Ulverstone. Ivy had employed Greg Lehman's first cousin Dean to landscape their new garden. One afternoon Dean was clearing the front patio when his excavator unearthed a small brightly coloured figure. "He's only a little bloke," Ivy said. "I sat him up on the cement. I've heard that if you take a gnome from where he's living, it's no good."

"Do you miss North Motton?"

"No, there's too much going on. That is the past, isn't it? You've got to look forward. This is our home now and that's what we're trying to do, getting it to suit us."

There was a roar outside and then two chimes. Ivy pulled a face.

"That'll be Nevin," I said.

He had brought spare leathers and a helmet, and I changed into them while Ivy, excited, got out her chart and magnifying glass.

"They're our cousins!" she said.

"Who are?"

"His brother's wife and us."

"Of course, they are," I said, and tried on the helmet.

Heather had a gift for me: a jar with a purple jelly inside.

"Bet you've never eaten this before."

"What is it?"

"Laurel jam." Their mother had taught her how to make it out of the berries, a recipe handed down from grandmother Hordern. "Some people don't like it and some people love it."

The jar reminded me of what I had forgotten, and I went to collect it from the car. For the journey here, I had wrapped it in damp newspaper, as I had seen Ivy do.

"What do you think?" I asked. "Could you strike a cutting?"

Ivy studied the stem that I had snapped from the laurel tree at Stoke Rivers. I thought – from her expression – that she was going to say it was impossible or that I had damaged it beyond hope. She said: "I'll grow it for you if you like, but we don't want that big thing here."

"Ready?" asked Nevin.

Minutes later, from behind a rampart of phlox, the three sisters watched

Nevin start up his motorbike. Ivy's face was a mixture of fascination alternating with terror, and I knew that she was thinking of her unfortunate schoolfriend Margaret Viney.

"Ever been on a motorbike?" I asked.

"No, don't think I have."

"Me neither," I said, kissing her goodbye. "But you should listen to Mr Jones. You should come to the east coast and see us."

"Too far for us, I reckon."

"Anyway, I think you're very lucky to live in Tasmania."

She grinned. "Supposed to be special isn't it? We won't tell them what it is, what it's like, because too many will want to come."

"Just lean into the corners," said Nevin.

4

I had spent the night before in a bed and breakfast outside Wynyard where there was a locally published history of Tasmania which began: "For Europeans, it represents the literal end of the world: if you travel any further you are on your way home again." On his arrival in 1849, Thomas Arnold had written to his mother: "I look upon Hobart Town as one step on the road to England." So far, my journey in Tasmania resembled the trajectory of the flat, crescent-shaped hardwood that my grandmother had given me as a boy in Oxford, which if hurled as far as possible into the air actually comes back and lands in your hand.

The three sisters waved.

Nervous at first, I held on to the grab bars as Nevin thundered out of the cul-de-sac and up Ulverstone main street, onto the Devonport highway. I felt every bump on the road, but was also a part of the road. My attention was fixed with greatest concentration on the two wing-mirrors. On a motorbike, I swiftly realised, you live by the mirror, in which the white roadmarks appear to be ripping into the sky like a trail of artillery flak, chasing you. I was conscious of the road in other ways. Gravel hitting the visor; butterflies; the smells of paddocks and cows and damp earth. And the cameraderie of other bikers. Whenever we passed one, they raised a gloved hand or nodded. It did not matter where you came from, who you were, where you were going. On your "hoon".

As soon as we reached the highway, Nevin opened up. The whoosh of the air rushing over my helmet mimicked the sound of a wind tunnel. It was exhilarating, as if Nevin was giving me a passage back into the present and I was hurtling forward 200 years.

So we roared past Squeaky Crossing, over the Rubicon, past Glengarry Protestant church to Exeter and Beaconsfield. The reflections of the sky and trees converged into the back of his blue helmet, and I was as far away from meandering around with old documents as I could possibly be. And as we passed Kemp's Parade at the Port Dalrymple Yacht Club on Beauty Point and headed towards York Town, I looked forward to abdicating my role as keeper of the ledger. What this other N. Shakespeare did with what I was about to tell him was out of my hands.

Acknowledgements

I am indebted to the following for reading the work in progress and giving suggestions and corrections: Paul Edwards, Damon Hawker, Michael Roe, Dan Sprod. I would like to thank the staff of the Tasmaniana Library and the Archives Office of Tasmania, Hobart, and in particular Gillian Winter and Tony Marshall.

For permission to quote from the Thomas Arnold papers, I am grateful to the Master and Fellows of Balliol College, Oxford and to Mrs Janet Davies. The poem "Off the Map" is quoted by kind permission of the Shoestring Press. The verse from "Blue Eyes Crying in the Rain" recorded by Willie Nelson, words and music by Fred Rose is quoted by permission of Campbell Connelly & Company Ltd., © Copyright 1945 Milene Music Incorporated, USA. All rights reserved. International Copyright Secured. I am grateful to David Higham Associates for permission to quote from both Graham Greene's *Monsignor Quixote*, Jonathan Cape, 1982; and *The Comedians*, Jonathan Cape, 1976. To The Random House Group Ltd. and to Barbara Mobbs Literary Agency for permission to quote from Patrick White's *A Fringe of Leaves*, Jonathan Cape, 1976. To the Estate of Vladimir Nabokov to quote from *Speak, Memory: An Autobiography Revisited*. All rights reserved. To The Random House Group for permission to quote from Günther Grass' *The Tin Drum*, Martin Secker & Warburg, 1975. To the Carmen Balcells Agency for permission to quote from Gabriel García Marquez's *Living to Tell the Tale*, Jonathan Cape, 2003. I have made every effort to trace copyright holders. I greatly regret any omissions, but these will be rectified in any future edition.

I would also like to thank Judy Anderson, Murray Bail, Rebecca Chambers, Pat Cleveland, James Cox, John and Jo Fenn-Smith, Bill Howroyd, Gillian Johnson, Gillian Kemp, Tom Keneally, Matthew Kneale, Christopher MacLehose, Caroline Michel, Delia Nicholls, Margaret-Ann Oldmeadow, Chris Pearce, Cassandra Pybus, Anne and Trevor Rood, Rachael Rose, Michael Stutchbury and Becky Toyne.

Part of the Kemp material has already appeared in different form in *Granta* 74, 2001.

Sources

Abbreviations used in Sources section:

J.R.A.H.S.	Journal of the Royal Australia Historical Society
T.H.R.A	Tasmanian Historical Research Association
T.L.S.	Times Literary Supplement

Part I. Father of Tasmania

Based on conversations with Anna Agnarsdottir, Murray Bail, Peter Chapman, Kaia Davey, Richard Davey, John Dent, Zelda Dick, Peter Donaldson, Tim Dwyer, Paul Edwards, John and Jo Fenn-Smith, Patricia Greenhill, Damon Hawker, Pete Hay, Judy Humphries, Murray Kemp, Tom Keneally, George Masterman, Margaret-Ann Oldmeadow, Barrie Paterson, Ian Pearce, Bill Penfold, Pat Quilty, Henry Reynolds, Andrew Sant, Dan Sprod, Robert Tiley.

Unpublished sources: John Shakespeare, Adrian Potter, Penelope Eaton-Hart, Murray Kemp, Herbert de Hamel, Balliol College, Guildhall, Tasmaniana Library.

Newspapers: *Bent's News, Britannia, Colonial Times, The Historian: Journal of the West Tamar Historical Society, Hobart Mercury, Hobart Town Courier, Hobart Town Gazette, Launceston Examiner, Sydney Gazette, Tasmanian Times, True Colonist.*

Books and articles: *The Historical Records of New South Wales*, ed. F.M. Bladen, Sydney, Library Committee of the Commonwealth Parliament, 1921; the *Australian Dictionary of National Biography*; the records of the Tasmanian Historical Research Association; *The History of Tasmania,* by John West, Launceston, 1852; *A History of Tasmania*, by Lloyd Robson, Vol. I, Oxford, 1983, Vol. II, 1990; *A Short History of Tasmania*, by Lloyd Robson, updated by Michael Roe, Oxford, 1997; *The Fatal Shore*, by Robert Hughes, Harvill, 1987; *Step Across this Line*, by Salman Rushdie, Vintage, 2003; *In Sunshine or in Shadow*, by Martin Flanagan, Picador, 2002; *Australia and New Zealand*, by Anthony Trollope, Chapman & Hall, 1873; *More Tramps Abroad*, by Mark Twain, Chatto & Windus, 1897; *On the Beach*, by Nevil Shute, William Heinemann, 1957; "Darwin in Hobart, 1836", by Michael Roe, *Island 16*; "Garden of Antarctic Delights", by Pat Quilty, *Australian Garden History*, Vol. 11, No. 1, 1999; "Tasmania and Antarctic: a Long Association", by Pat Quilty, *Australian Gemmologist*, 19, 1996; *An Autobiography*, by Agatha Christie, Berkley, 1991; *The Journal of Mrs. Fenton: A Narrative of Her Life in India, the Isle of France & Tasmania During the Years 1826–1830*, by Bessie Fenton, Edward Arnold, 1901; *The Diaries and Letters of G.T.W.B. Boyes, Volume 1, 1820–1832*, ed. Peter Chapman, Oxford, 1985; *Down Home: Revisiting Tasmania*, by Peter Conrad, Chatto & Windus, 1988; *Vandiemonian Essays*, by Pete Hay, Walleah Press, 2002; *The Islanders*, by Andrew Sant, Shoestring Press, 2002; *Beer, Blood and Water*, by Bernard Lloyd, Hobart, 1998; *Journal of A Voyage from New South Wales to England*, by Elizabeth Kent, *Athenaeum*, July 1808; *A Voyage to Terra Australis*, by Matthew Flinders, ed. Tim Flannery, Text, Melbourne, 2001; *George Bass*, by Keith Macrae Brown, Oxford, 1952; *Geographic and Descriptive Delineations of the Island of Van Diemen's Land*, by Charles Jeffreys, London, J.M. Richardson, 1820; *Godwin's Emigrant Guide to Van Diemen's Land, more properly called Tasmania*, London, 1823; *An account of the colony of Van Diemen's Land, principally designed for the use of emigrants*, by Edward Curr, London, 1824; *Medical Hints for Emigrants*, R. Druitt, London, 1850; *Bennelong, First Notable Aborigine*, by John Kenny, J.R.A.H.S, 1973; *The journal of a voyage from Calcutta to Van Diemen's Land: comprising a description of that colony during a six months' residence*, by A. Prinsep, London, 1833; *Sydney Cove 1789–90*, by John Cobley, Angus & Robertson, 1963; *A colonial regiment: new sources relating to the New South Wales Corps, 1789–1810*, by P. Statham, Canberra, 1992; *Memoirs of Joseph Holt*, London, 1838; *John Macarthur*, by M.H. Ellis, Sydney, 1955; *Rum Rebellion*, by H.V. Evatt, Sydney, Angus & Robertson, 1937; *Terre Napoléon*, by Ernest Scott, Methuen, 1910; *The French Reconnaissance: Baudin in Australia 1801–1803*, by Frank Horner, Melbourne, 1987; *Voyage de découvertes aux Terres Australes, Historique, Vol. 1*, by François Péron, Paris, 1807; *Australian Navigators: Picking up shells and catching* *butterflies in an age of revolution*, by Robert Tiley, Kangaroo Press, 2002; *The Explorers*, ed. Tim Flannery, Text, 1998; *The New South Wales Freemason*, July 1956; *Europeans in Australia*, by Alan Atkinson, Oxford, 1997; "Remarks on Settlement of Port Dalrymple", by John Oxley, in *Historical Records of Australia, Series III, Vol. I*; *The Story of Port Dalrymple*, by L.S. Bethell, Hobart, 1957; *The Life of Vice-Admiral William Bligh*, by George Mackaness, Angus & Robertson, 1951; *Report of the Commissioner of Enquiry on the Judicial Establishments of New South Wales and Van Diemen's Land*, by J.T. Bigge, London, 1823; *Obliged to Submit: Wives & Mistresses of colonial governors*, by Alison Alexander, Montpelier, 1999; *Knopwood: A Biography*, by Geoffrey Stephens, Hobart, 1990; *The diary of the Reverend Robert Knopwood 1803–1838*, ed. Mary Nicholls, T.H.R.A., 1977; *The Hermit in Van Diemen's Land*, by Henry Savery, ed. Cecil Hadgraft and Margriet Roe, Queensland, 1964; *Captain Anthony Fenn Kemp*, by Murray C. Kemp and Thérèse B. Kemp, J.R.A.H.S., 51, March 1965; *Of Yesteryear and Nowadays*, by P.B. Edwards, Edwards, 1994; *Van Diemen's Land; or Settlers and Natives*, by William Thomas Moncrieff, John Dicks, 1830; *Michael Howe, the Last and Worst Bushranger of Van Diemen's Land*, by T.E. Wells, Platypus, Hobart, 1966; *The First; the Worst? Michael Howe and associated bushrangers*, by R.F. Minchin, Hobart, 2001; *A Bloodthirsty banditti of wretches: informations on oath relating to Michael Howe and others between 1814 and 1818*, Adelaide, Sullivan's Cove, 1985; *Mike Howe, the bushranger of Van Diemen's Land*, by James Bonwick, London, 1873; *Observations upon secondary punishments*, by Sir George Arthur, Hobart, 1833; *The Sarah Island Conspiracies: being an account of twelve voyages to Macquarie Harbour & Sarah Island, 1822–1838*, by Richard Innes Davey, Strahan, 2002; *Gould's Book of Fish*, by Richard Flanagan, Picador, 2003; *English Passengers*, by Matthew Kneale, Hamish Hamilton, 2002; *The Great Shame*, by Thomas Keneally, Chatto & Windus, 1998; *Representing Convicts*, edited by I. Duffield & J. Bradley, London, 1997; *Convicts and Colonies*, by A.G.L. Shaw, Melbourne, 1973; *Nine Years in Van Diemen's Land*, by James Syme, Dundee, 1848; *Alexander Pearce of Macquarie Harbour: Convict-Bushranger-Cannibal*, by Dan Sprod, Cat and Fiddle, 1977; *Hell's Gates*, by Paul Collins, Hobart, 2002; *The Usurper: Jorgen Jorgenson and his turbulent life in Iceland and Van Diemen's Land, 1780–1841*, by Dan Sprod, Blubber Head, 2001; *Jorgen Jorgenson and the Aborigines of Van Diemen's Land*, by N.J.B. Plomley, Blubber Head, 1991; *The Convict King, being the life and adventures of Jorgen Jorgenson*, retold by James Francis Hogan, Hobart, 1891; *Loitering in a tent: Jorgenson in the High Country*, by John Mitchell, Hobart, 1995; *Journal of a Tour in Iceland in the Summer of 1809*, by William Jackson Hooker, John Murray, 1813; *Great Britain and Iceland 1800–1820*, by Anna Agnarsdottir, PHD thesis, LSE, 1989; *A shred of autobiography*, by Jorgen Jorgenson, Adelaide, Sullivan's Cove, 1981; *The convict proba-*

tion system in Van Diemen's Land, 1839–1954, by Ian Brand, Blubber Head, 1990; *Highway in Van Diemen's Land*, by G. Hawley Standcombe, Sydney, National Trust of Australia, 1968; *Edward Markham's voyage to Van Diemen's Land 1833*, by Edward Markham, Launceston, 1952; *A Fringe of Leaves*, by Patrick White, Viking, 1976; *Point Counter Point*, by Aldous Huxley, Chatto & Windus, 1928; *Wainewright, the Poisoner*, by Andrew Motion, Faber, 2000; *New Zealand Letters of Thomas Arnold the Younger*, ed. James Bertram, Oxford, 1966; *A Victorian Wanderer: The Life of Thomas Arnold the Younger*, by Bernard Bergonzi, Oxford, 2003; *Thomas Arnold the Younger in Van Diemen's Land*, by P.A. Howell, Hobart, 1964; *Passages in a Wandering Life*, by Thomas Arnold, London, 1900; *The Life of Mrs Humphry Ward*, Janet Trevelyan, London, 1923; *A Writer's Recollections*, by Mrs Humphry Ward, London 1918; *Mrs Humphry Ward: Eminent Victorian, Pre-eminent Edwardian*, by John Sutherland, Oxford, 1990.

Part II: Black Lines

Based on conversations with Ruth Amos, Patsy Cameron, Peter Chapman, John Clark, Clem, Bernice Condie, John Cusick, Tom and Cynthia Dunbabin, Ilewka, Greg Lehman, James and Lyndsay Luddington, Mary Mactier, Furley Mansell, George Masterman, David Montgomery, Margaret-Ann Oldmeadow, Henry Reynolds, Frances Rhodes, Anne Rood, Andrew Sant, Toly Sawenko, Julie Spotswood, Edith Stansfield, Emily Stoddart, Daniel Thomas, Liz Turner, Edna Webb, Dusty Willcox.

Unpublished source material: Swansea History Room.

Books and articles: "Some recollections of the Tasman Memorial Controversy, 1922–24", by John Reynolds, T.H.R.A., vol. 13, 1966; "Tasman and a Dutch Discovery", by Peter Chapman, *Australian Natural History*, vol. 20, 2; *The Voyages of Able Janszoon Tasman*, by Andrew Sharp, Clarendon Press, Oxford, 1968; "Imagining Australia: a case of fact being as strange as fiction", by Murray Bail, T.L.S, 1978; *Some account of the wars, extirpation, habits & c., of the native tribes of Tasmania*, by James Erskine Calder, Henn & Co, 1875; *Tasmanian Aborigines and their descendants*, Bill Mollison and Coral Everitt, Mollison, 1978; *Pride against prejudice*, by Ida West, Canberra, 1984; *Friendly Mission: The Tasmanian Journals and Papers of George Augustus Robinson 1829–1834*, ed. N.J.B. Plomley, T.H.R.A., 1966; *Weep in Silence, A History of the Flinders Island Journal of George Augustus Robinson 1835–1839*, ed. N.J.B. Plomley, Blubber Head, 1987; *The Last of the Tasmanians; or the Black War of Van Diemen's Land*, by James Bonwick, London, 1870; *The Aborigines of Tasmania*, by H. Ling Roth,

Halifax, 1899; *After the Dreaming*, by W.E.H. Stanner, 1968 Boyer Lecturers, Australian Broadcasting Commission, Sydney, 1969; *Community of Thieves*, by Cassandra Pybus, Minerva, Melbourne, 1992; *Black Robinson: Protector of Aborigines*, by Vivian Rae-Ellis, Melbourne, 1988; *Trucanini: Queen or Traitor*, by Vivian Rae-Ellis, Aboriginal Studies Press, Canberra, 1981; *The Aboriginal Tasmanians*, by Lyndall Ryan, Queensland, 1996; *Fate of a Free People*, by Henry Reynolds, Penguin, 1995; *The Fabrication of Aboriginal History, Volume I, Van Diemen's Land 1803–1847*, by Keith Windschuttle, Macleay, 2003; *Whitewash: On Keith Windschuttle's Fabrication of Aboriginal History*, ed. Robert Manne, Black Inc., 2003; "Better to be Mistaken than to Deceive": the Fabrication of Aboriginal History and the Van Diemonian Record, by James Boyce in *Island 96*; *The Freycinet Line, 1831: Tasmanian History and the Freycinet Peninsula*, by Emily Stoddart, Freycinet Experience Pty Ltd, 2003; *The Aboriginal people of Tasmania*, by Julia Clark, Tasmanian Museum and Art Gallery, Hobart, 1983; *The East Coasters: the early pioneering history of the east coast of Tasmania*, by Lois Nyman, Regal Publications, 1990; *Pioneers of the East Coast from 1642*, by Karl von Steiglitz, Launceston, 1955; *The Memoirs of Field-Marshal Montgomery*, Collins, 1958; *H.H. Montgomery – the Mutton Bird Bishop*, by Geoffrey Stephens, Hobart, 1985; *Living to Tell the Tale*, Gabriel García Márquez, Cape, 2003.

Part III: Elysium

Based on conversations with Madge Brett, Jill Cainey, Paul Edwards, Bernard Eisele, Mick Evans, Greg Lehman, Wendy Newton, Vivien Van Dam, Laurie Porter, Bob and Molly Shepheard, Petre Tamlyn, Imogen Vignoles, Randall Wheaton. Some of the names have been changed.

Unpublished source material: Imogen Vignoles, Ivy.

Newspapers and journals: *The Advocate, Launceston Advertiser, The Northern Standard, North-West Post, Tasmanian Tramp.*

Books and articles: *Round the World Cruise Holiday*, by S.P.B. Mais and Gillian Mais, Alvin Redman, 1965; *We Wander in the West*, by S.P.B. Mais, Ward Lock, 1950; *Lorna's Author: Letters by R.D. Blackmore to his sister*, by David Blackmore, Blackmore Books, 2003; *R.D. Blackmore, author of Lorna Doone*, by Waldo Hilary Dunn, Robert Hale, 1956; *A home in the colonies: Edward Braddon's Letters to India from North-West Tasmania 1878*, T.H.R.A., 1980; *Bushlife in Tasmania*, by James Fenton, Regal, Launceston, 1970; *My Home in Tasmania*, by Louisa Meredith, Sullivan's Cove, 1979; *Louisa-Anne Meredith: a tigress in* *exile*, by Vivian Rae-Ellis, Blubber Head, 1979; *Ulverstone, An Outline of its history*, by Bruce Ellis, Latrobe, 1988; *Pioneers of Tasmania's West Coast*, by C.J. Binks, Blubber Head, 1988; *King of the Wilderness: the life of Deny King*, by Christobel Mattingley, Text, 2001; *Trampled Wilderness: the history of southwest Tasmania*, by Ralph Gowlland, C.L. Richmond, 1977; "The Castra Scheme" by Geoffrey Stilwell, in *Tasmanian Insights, essays in honour of Geoffrey Thomas Stilwell*, State Library of Tasmania, 1992; *Letter to the Officers of H.M. Indian Services, Civil and Military*, by Lt Col. Andrew Crawford, Hobart, 1865; *Under the Southern Cross*, by H. Cornish, London, 1880; "A Home in the Colonies", by S. Bennett, T.H.R.A. vol. 27, no. 4, 1980; "From Raj to Rustic", by P. Mercer, T.H.R.A. vol. 25, no. 3, 1978; *The Unexpected*, by Frank Penn-Smith, Cape, 1933; *A Divided Society: Tasmania during World War I*, by Marilyn Lake, Melbourne, 1975; *Chrissie Venn: "Suffer Little Children"*, by L. & N. Smith, Ulverstone Press, 1999; *On the Black Hill*, by Bruce Chatwin, Cape, 1981.

Part IV: Oyster Bay

Daughter of Tasmania

Based on conversations with Gloria Andrews, Ian Jack, Lynn Johnson, Doone Kennedy, Edyth Langham, Peter Lawrence, Bill Penfold, Cassandra Pybus, John Ward, Bev Warren.

Unpublished source material: St Helen's History Room.

Newspaper: *Launceston Weekly Courier.*

Books and articles: *Princess Merle: The Romantic Life of Merle Oberon*, by Charles Higham and Roy Mosely, Putnam, 1983; *Queenie*, by Michael Korda, Warner, 1986; *Till Apples Grow on an Orange Tree*, by Cassandra Pybus, Queensland, 1998; "Errol Flynn", by Bob Casey in *40 degrees south, 27*; *Errol Flynn, The Tasmanian Story*, by Don Norman, Hobart, 1981.
TV: "The Trouble with Merle", ABC documentary, August 27, 2002, written and directed by Maree Delofski, producer David Noakes.

Tigers and Devils

Based on conversations with Bill Bleathman, Buck and Joan Emberg, Geoff King, Marlene Levings, Menna Jones, Nick Mooney, David Owen, Laurelle Shakespeare.

Books and articles: *Touch the morning: Tasmanian Native legends*, by Jackson Cotton, Hobart, OBM Pty Ltd, 1979; *Tasmanian Tiger: A lesson to be learned*, by Eric Guiler and Philippe Godard, Abrolhos Publishing, Perth, 1998; *Thylacine: the tragic tale of the Tasmanian tiger*, by David Owen, Allen & Unwin, 2003; "Tasmanian Tiger Sighting", by Nick Mooney, Australian Natural History, 1984; "Dining with the Devil", by M.E. Jones, Australian Natural History, 1994; *Valley of the Giants, a guide to Tasmania's Styx River Forests*, by Bob Brown, Brown, 2001; *Groundswell: the Rise of the Greens*, by Amanda Lohrey, *Quarterly Essay*, issue 8, 2002.

Oyster Bay

Based on conversations with Helen and Malcolm Boyd, Bill Matthewson, Michael Stutchbury, Bruce Sullivan, Rueben Wells.

Unpublished source material: Balliol College; Swansea History Room.

Books and articles: *A General Collection of the best and Most Interesting Voyages and Travels in all parts of the world 1808–1814*, by John Pinkerton, London, 1817; *Letters from the Southern Hemisphere*, by F.J. Cockburn, London, 1856; *My memoirs laced with East Coast tales of Van Diemen's Land*, by Edward C. Shaw, Shaw, 2000; *Journal of Charles O'Hara Booth*, ed. Dora Heard, T.H.R.A., 1981; the story of the Japanese submarine is printed in *Battle Surface: Japan's Submarine War Against Australia, 1942–44*, by David Jenkins, Random House, 1992.

Doubles

Based on conversations with Max Chatwin, Michael Mackenzie, Nevin Shakespeare.
Books: *Chatwin: 6 generations in Tasmania*, researched and compiled by Daisy Chatwin, Barbara Pendrey and Vince Scarcella, privately printed 2001; *Memories*, by Julian Huxley, George Allen & Unwin, 1970; *We Europeans*, by Julian Huxley, Cape, 1935; *Tasmania*, by Peter Collenette, D. & L. Book distributors, 1990.

List of Illustrations

Map of Tasmania (Professor Pat Quilty, University of Tasmania)

Anthony Fenn Kemp on enamel (Courtesy of Professor Murray Kemp)

Alexander Pearce: Sketch by Thomas Bock (State Library New South Wales)

Ross Bridge (Courtesy of Matthew Kneale)

Tom Arnold: Daguerreotype made shortly before his departure to New Zealand in 1847 (Dove Cottage, The Wordsworth Trust)

Julia Sorell: A watercolour by Thomas Wainewright, c.1847 (Collection: Tasmanian Museum and Art Gallery)

Mount Vernon (Courtesy of Barrie Paterson)

Necklace (author's photograph of Gillian's necklace)

Tongerlongerter, chief of the Oyster Bay Tribe in 1831: Reproduction of pencil on paper sketch by Thomas Bock c.1832 (Queen Victoria Museum and Art Gallery. Launceston)

Mr Robinson on his conciliation mission (Etching from Mr Duterreau's great picture)

The Jetty at Wybalenna (Courtesy of Matthew Kneale)

Colonel Andrew Crawford taken by J.W. Beattie (Allport Library and Museum of Fine Arts)

Cape Grim Baseline Air Pollution Station (Davis Whillas, CSIRO Atmospheric Research, Cape Grim)

Merle Oberon on her visit to Tasmania in 1978 (Newspix. Tony Palmer historical)

Tasmanian tiger: Thylacine. A juvenile male at Hobart Zoo, taken by Ben Sheppard in 1928. The animal died the day after it was photographed (Collection: Tasmanian Museum and Art Gallery)

Alfred Chatwin and Elizabeth Chatwin (Daisy Chatwin's Collection, Sprent, Tasmania)

Index